Just Leisure

Things That We Believe In

Keri Schwab

Daniel Dustin

editors

SAGAMORE
PUBLISHING

©2013 Sagamore Publishing LLC
All rights reserved.
Publishers: Joseph J. Bannon, Peter L. Bannon
Director of Sales and Marketing: William A. Anderson
Director of Development and Production: Susan M. Davis

ISBN print edition: 978-1-57167-753-2
ISBN ebook: 978-1-57167-754-9
Library of Congress Catalog Card Number: 2013935129

Printed in the United States.

Sagamore Publishing LLC
1807 N Federal Dr.
Urbana, IL 61801
www.sagamorepub.com

To Karla Henderson

for her pioneering work in women's leisure

The Möbius Strip

A Möbius Strip is a one-sided surface created by placing a single twist in a strip of paper and connecting the ends. The strip appears to have two sides, but really has no discernible front or back, beginning or end. If you were to draw a line starting on one side and try to go all the way around that same side, you would end up with a line around the entire strip without ever crossing an edge. You might think of social and environmental justice similarly. In the long run, they may be part and parcel of the same thing.

Contents

Part One—Questioning Injustice

Part Two—Naming Injustice

Part Three—Teaching Justice

Part Four—Doing Justice

Acknowledgments

We would like to thank Sagamore Publishing's Joe and Peter Bannon for their unwavering support of this work and Susan Davis for managing the production process so meticulously. We are also indebted to delegates to the "1st International Symposium on Speaking Up and Speaking Out: Working for Social and Environmental Justice through Parks, Recreation, Tourism, and Leisure" held on the campus of the University of Utah, May 17-19, 2012. Their keen interest in social and environmental justice energized the three-day conversation and provided much of the grist for what follows. A special thank you to Rhonda Larson and Lee Stetson as well for embellishing the symposium's theme with their artistry. Finally, we would like to thank the book's contributors, many of whom spent the better part of a year refining their thinking for presentation and publication.

Preface

This book is the product of a three-day symposium held on the campus of the University of Utah, May 17-19, 2012. The symposium was a follow-up to *Speaking Up and Speaking Out: Working for Social and Environmental Justice through Parks, Recreation, and Leisure*, edited by the University of Utah's Karen Paisley and Daniel Dustin and published by Sagamore Publishing, LLC in 2011. Capitalizing on the momentum of that book, Joe Bannon, publisher and CEO of Sagamore, suggested holding a symposium to further the conversation to see if an interest in social and environmental justice in the context of the work we do in parks, recreation, tourism, and leisure could be sustained.

We took Dr. Bannon up on his suggestion and organized the "1st International Symposium on Speaking Up and Speaking Out: Working for Social and Environmental Justice through Parks, Recreation, Tourism, and Leisure." We circulated a call for papers and selected 19 for presentation.

The symposium attracted 75 delegates from the United States, Canada, and Australia. All of the presentations were plenary, which meant that everyone in attendance had a chance to hear what everyone else had to say. This made for a spirited give and take on a wide range of social and environmental justice themes. It also motivated us to share the essence of what transpired in book form.

Just Leisure captures much of the symposium's content. In addition to the 19 invited chapters, we have divided the book into four sections with syntheses at the end of each section. The syntheses were written by delegates who were moved sufficiently by what they heard at the symposium to comment on some aspect of it.

When we put the symposium together, our intent was to try to get beyond the ideas of social and environmental justice in a way that combines them into one larger comprehensive notion of justice. The Möbius Strip represents that aspiration. We fell short of that goal. What we learned instead is that social and environmental justice, at least in the short term, are often at odds with one another. In our enthusiasm for securing one kind of justice, we often compromise the other. We do not know if this is a temporal problem. Perhaps we are still correct in thinking that social and environmental justice will come to be seen as opposite sides of the same coin in the long run.

Our hope for this book is that it causes you to stop and ponder long-held assumptions and beliefs and that it challenges your world view. Social and environmental injustices do not always announce themselves. They often lay hidden beneath the surface of what otherwise appears to be a civilized world. In the absence of people speaking up and speaking out about such injustices, we risk being lulled into moral and spiritual complacency. This is as true of parks, recreation, tourism, and leisure as it is of any other human service profession. With this thought in mind, we encourage you to read this book with discerning eyes and take its lessons to heart.

Keri and Dan

"Justice is what love looks like in public."

—**Cornel West**

Foreword

"We're seekers of truth, keepers of faith, makers of peace, wisdom of ages..."

—Ysaye M. Barnwell

I have been asked to speak on behalf of Black folks, women, Black women, the LGBT community, lesbians of color, and the mythically homogeneous Black church's stance on homosexuality. My assumption is that these requests were well-intended, from individuals who sincerely want to understand the perspective of someone they view as different. The fact that I have not been asked to speak on behalf of the middle class, Christians, or the temporarily able-bodied, would suggest I am viewed first and foremost as someone who is a member of traditionally oppressed groups in the United States (U.S.) rather than as someone who also has privilege.

All of us are complex beings made up of multiple social identities that intersect in numerous ways with our personality traits. We live, work, and play in a variety of settings. Everything is interconnected. The choices we make regarding fuel efficient automobiles, city planning, and energy policies impact the environment. What we do in one part of the world impacts people living in other parts. When we speak out against bullying, yet deny equal rights and equal pay, we send mixed messages about who is valued in society. The relatively inexpensive food prices in the U.S. rely on unfair labor and ineffectual immigration policies. The air we breathe has passed over oceans, mountains, farmlands, remote villages, and waste sites into the cities we inhabit. All of these issues are intricately interconnected, and it is a condition of privilege that creates false boundaries between issues of identity and social and environmental justice.

While it is important to see the connections between issues, it is helpful at times for me to view issues more discretely when I am trying to deepen my own understanding of the broad interdisciplinary nature of social and environmental justice. If nothing else, our machinations to parse people's identities, control variables, and isolate justice issues are great entertainment for the gods. Moreover, we need to be aware that too often activists in both areas have built silos for specific issues and engaged in what some have called "Oppression Olympics," futilely trying to establish a hierarchy of oppressions with each other and other justice movements, such as animal rights activists, child welfare activists, etc.

Issues of social and environmental justice are intimately intertwined with one another. We are who we are wherever we are. Often our privilege determines the quality of our environments. I grew up in a rural suburban area in central Ohio, where having a car was essential because my parents commuted 10 to 15 miles to their workplaces in Columbus. Thanks to my continuing class privilege and a reliable car, I, too, have ready access to fresh produce and other healthy foods, a wide selection of healthcare providers, and green space far removed from environmentally toxic locations. I understand that every day we breathe in contaminated air, and people who live in areas with traffic congestion, refineries, bus stations, docks, mills, and landfills, are being harmed to a greater extent than those of us who live at a comfortable distance from congested highways or large scale agribusinesses in homes free of lead paint and asbestos.

Research shows that low-income communities and communities of color often do not have access to the benefits our transportation system can provide, yet they bear the burdens of that system. For example, many low-income neighborhoods have little or no efficient, reliable public transportation to get them to jobs and essential goods and services. But these communities are often situated near bus depots, highways, and truck routes, where pollution levels are high—and not coincidentally, asthma rates are high as well.

When Keri and Dan asked me to write the foreword for *Just Leisure*, I did not hesitate to accept. I have known Dan for more than 20 years and have a great deal of respect for his persistence and openness as a learner, and his unwillingness to rest in what is comfortable. This book grew out of the "1st International Symposium on Speaking Up and Speaking Out: Working for Social and Environmental Justice through Parks, Recreation, Tourism, and Leisure," held in Salt Lake City in 2012, which was a wonderful combination of thought-provoking sessions by well-known scholars and practitioners, as well as undergraduate and graduate students. As someone who left leisure studies and moved into social justice education in the mid-1990s, attending this symposium was akin to leaving home one day and returning later to find it beautifully remodeled.

This book has particular cultural significance and relevance in today's world. There is growing awareness of the intertwined nature of justice issues, and combined with the proliferation of social networking, it is possible to view the aftermath of natural disasters within minutes of their occurrence and witness the disproportionate impact on poor communities around the world. Some of the issues addressed in *Just Leisure* are particular to the U.S., while many are relevant to a broader global context. Thirty years after the first Earth Day and numerous oil spills and the contamination of ground water in many communities, there continues to be proposals for new drilling sites and pipelines, and the expansion of hydrofracking. More than 40 years after the Stonewell riots, federal civil rights for lesbians, gays, and their families are still considered "special rights." Nearly 60 years after *Brown vs. Board of Education* our K-12 schools are more segregated today than they were in 1960s. And almost 95 years after the passage of the 19th Amendment to the U.S. Constitution, gender bias continues to create huge barriers for many, especially poor women, women of color, and immigrant women.

Fortunately, this book brings together a wide range of respected scholars in the field of parks, recreation, and tourism who are passionate about issues of social and environmental justice in one insightful publication. If you are someone who is generally interested in justice issues but are cautious about discussing them in mixed company, this book will not disappoint. *Just Leisure* will spur your curiosity and bring you to your learning edge—the place that I know I have come to when I am a little anxious and uncomfortable, and can either pull back into my comfort zone and stay with the familiar or lean into my discomfort, suspend my disbelief, and open myself to the possibility of learning something new.

Just Leisure is for anyone who wants to deepen his or her understanding of social and environmental justice in the context of leisure. It is for the white woman who primarily works against sexism, and who wants to expand her understanding of how race and class intersect with gender. It is for the antiracist educator who wants to learn how working to reduce negative impacts on the physical environment is inextricably linked to living conditions in poor communities and communities of color. It is for the heterosexual man who works for disability rights and wants to develop greater awareness of the pervasive nature of heterosexual privilege and how to increase civil rights for LGBT people. And it is for the environmentalist who wants to deepen her or his knowledge of the bias inherent in the dominant view of wilderness.

Whether you come to this work through your concern for the environment or through your desire for greater social equity among people, we all come to justice work because we recognize the need for it, and believe we can make a difference. We are colleagues connected through our shared interests and persistence on multiple fronts. Like a pebble dropped into a body of water causing ripples radiating outward, let our actions for greater social and environmental justice touch the lives of others, pointing to a future where justice, as Cornel West so eloquently put it, will be "what love looks like in public."

Sharon J. Washington, Ph.D.
National Writing Project, Executive Director
July 2012

PART ONE

Questioning Injustice

"Should all children have legitimate opportunities to realize their potential? If yes, are children lacking those opportunities part of my family? If yes, what am I going to do about it?"

—Tom Goodale

1

What Will Become of Our 20 Grandchildren?

Tom Goodale
George Mason University

This year is the golden anniversary of two warning shots fired across the bow of the American Titanic steaming toward disaster: Carson's *Silent Spring* and Harrington's *The Other America*. Both addressed problems largely invisible until then; both had a profound and positive impact on America.

By 1970 *Silent Spring* spawned the National Environmental Policy Act and the Environmental Protection Agency (EPA). Today the EPA is under attack—from the left for not doing enough, from the right for doing anything at all. Meanwhile, the environment deteriorates in alarming ways: species extinction,[1] global warming, severe weather events, and not only "peak oil" but also peak water and food and much more.[2]

Like *Silent Spring*, *The Other America* was largely invisible. Disproportionately Black, the poor were found in remote rural communities and congested urban enclaves. Coupled with a Civil Rights movement well underway, Harrington's book helped launch a flurry of activity in the 1960s summarized as "The Great Society" and the "War on Poverty."[3] As important as Civil Rights are, poverty fighting initiatives may be more important. Paraphrasing Dr. Martin Luther King, it does not matter if you can eat in any restaurant you want if you cannot afford a hamburger.

Our Grandchildren's Future

I share Dr. King's view and thus will focus on economic or distributive justice, but with the caveat that justice is justice whatever adjectives bring focus to our discipline or career field. In addition, as teachers, scholars, and service providers, we are duty bound to advocate for justice for those we serve. But that is not enough. We can succeed as careerists but fail as citizens. Furthermore, we cannot speak of justice without speaking of government. After all, the government is not some alien "them." The government is us (Remember Pogo? "We have met the enemy and it is us."), and we cannot speak about government without speaking of economic or distributive justice because much of government is about protecting property, allocating resources, and providing insurance against numerous forms of harm.

Although social and environmental justice often involve some form of oppression, the focus of this introductory chapter is not on the oppressed but on the ignored. In pursuing justice, we should give priority to those among us who are the most vulnerable and the least culpable. The focus here is on children, especially poor children. In this chapter, justice means every child has a good opportunity to realize her or his potential. Anything short of that is injustice. Clearly, to focus on children and grandchildren means to focus on the future.

We ignore poor children probably because too many of us know too little about being poor in America. In our culture, time and effort are required to determine what is verifiably true. We do not separate facts, evidence, and logic from opinions and non sequiturs. Popular media, especially electronic formats, often entertain, simplify, and misinform. The alternative to being un- or misinformed is that we do not care, that our ignorance is willful, which of course we deny.

That problem is compounded by millions of voters living in a mythological America. We are not God's chosen people; based on Jesus's teaching, our being (mainly) Christians is even questionable. Because we strive mightily to avoid taxes, we are not patriotic. We are not a generous people.[4] Growth is not going to feed us. Technology is not going to rescue us. America is no longer the land of opportunity. Education is not the answer to unemployment. Our justice system might not be just if you are a person of color, or poor, or female, or. … "American exceptionalism" is mostly negative.

Evidence that we will do better in the future than in the past is not compelling. Today our college programs are "embarrassingly white."[5] Forty-one years ago, at a Park and Recreation Educator's workshop, a resolution was introduced to increase the number of Black and other minority students in our park and recreation master's and doctorate degree programs. The resolution was adopted by a vote of 25 to 17, reminding me of a card, the front of which reads, "Your office mates decided to send you this get well card." Inside it reads, "The vote was 11 to 8."

A Nation in Disarray

In global terms, five institutions exist that should advance justice for children, the government primary among them. The others are the private (market) sector, community, family, and not-for-profit charities.[6] Even with all these efforts combined, we are failing our children and will continue to do so without significant and wrenching change.

Today we have a safety net in shreds, in part due to a president with a booming economy and government surpluses seeking to end welfare as we know it. Welfare legislation, enacted in 1996, was titled The Personal Responsibility and Work Opportunity Act. A more Orwellian title would be hard to conceive.[7] Consequently, those for whom welfare is a true lifeline have suffered dramatically. For example, more than 2 million people now experience severe poverty, defined as not more than $2 per person per day, $56 per week, $2,912 per year, for a family of four. At the other end of the spectrum, between 2009 and 2010, our national income grew by $288 billion; 37% went to the top 0.01%, whose average income of $23.8 million rose an additional $5.12 million, or 21%. The average increase for the bottom 99% was $80.80.[8] There are far too much similar data into which to delve, but as others have noted before me, mining such data fills us with equal measures of outrage and sorrow. This also dispels "the land of opportunity" myth, as Gini coefficients (a measure of mobility between income classes) indicate that as of 2008–2009, the United States ranked 26th of 34 countries. After accounting for taxes and transfers, the numbers are worse; the United States ranked 31st of 34, and gaps between ranks were wider.[9]

Sixteen million of our children live in poverty today—more than the population of 14 states combined. But the children do not have 28 senators representing them. In fact, those whose incomes place them in the lower one third of households appear to have no representation or, apparently, no influence over their members of Congress.[10]

The poverty rate for children (aged 18 and younger) is for Whites 12%, Blacks 38%, Hispanics 35%, and Asians 14%.[11] The poverty line for a family of four is $22,350, an amount so low many states have expanded eligibility for benefits to 150% and even 200% of the poverty line.

Some economists argue "low income" should be defined as 200% of the poverty line, $44,700 per year for a family of four. That now includes 50% of America's households, thus well over 50% of our children.[12]

Shifting from United States data to international comparisons, among the 33 most developed nations, 32 have universal health care.[13] The United States is the unconscionable exception. Among 31 nations ranked by the Organisation for Economic Development and Cooperation (OEDC), the United States ranks 27th in Social Justice. The top ranked countries were Iceland, Norway, Denmark, Sweden, and Finland.[14] Because we find these countries at or near the top on measures of well-being, the names are not repeated below.

In a United Nations research report, *Child Well-Being in Rich Countries*,[15] the United States ranks 20th of 21 countries. In a Save the Children report titled *State of the World's Mothers, 2011*, the United States ranks 31st of 43 "More Developed Nations."[16]

"Why doesn't the United States do better in the rankings?" the authors asked.
1. The United States ranks 40th on maternal mortality.
2. The United States ranks 41st on under age 5 mortality.
3. The United States ranks 38th on preschool enrollment.
4. The United States has the least generous maternity leave policy.
5. The United States lags behind regarding political status of women.[17]

"Why is Norway number one?" It is at or near the top on all indices, including
1. the highest ratio of female-to-male income,
2. the highest prevalence of contraceptive use,
3. the lowest under age 5 mortality rate, and
4. one of the most generous family leave policies.

Which country is dead last? Afghanistan. Why? The status of women. That is not an oversimplification. Such contrasts beg discussion of the status of women in the United States, but we must pass on that; just chant "We're #31." The war against women is real, violent, and destructive. It is also a war against children.

Public and Private Downfalls

We must also pass on wealthy people complaining about class warfare.[18] Chesterton explained away the apparent irony; his last sentence explains much of what has been happening to federal and state governments for the past 30 years:

> The poor have been rebels but never anarchists; they have more interest than anyone else in there being some decent government, the poor man really has a stake in the country. The rich man hasn't, he can go away to New Guinea in a yacht. The poor have sometimes objected to being governed badly; the rich have always objected to being governed at all.[19]

As heiress Leona Helmsley said, "We don't pay taxes. Only the little people pay taxes." Though she went to jail for flaunting it, she was right. The Internal Revenue Service (IRS) is losing an estimated $410 to $500 billion per year in fraudulent tax reporting. Little of that fraud is committed by people whose income is from salaries and wages. Those with W-2s are the little people.

Much of the fraud comes from Schedule C or S Corporations, mainly from treating all manner of personal benefits as business expenses. But fraud is not the biggest drain on government revenue. "Tax expenditures" include revenue lost through tax concessions such as mortgage interest deductions and subsidies to giant, extremely profitable corporations. Beyond subsidies, billions are lost each year through loopholes. G.E. made $5 billion last year and paid no taxes. Apple made $34.2 billion last year, paid $3.3 billion in taxes worldwide, and has $31 billion parked in Ireland.

In addition, regulatory capture, a large chunk of the billion-dollar lobbying business, ensures that an enterprise for which regulations may be forthcoming is minimally affected by the regulations. That is why banks "too big to fail" are now bigger than ever and why no one complicit in a massively corrupt and illegal financial meltdown is in jail—or even in court.

The government is paralyzed and broke. The private sector, or the market, does an excellent job with most goods and services but fails at three that are critical for poor people: food, shelter, and health care. Furthermore, nefarious behavior of corporations and their chief executives is not uncommon. Tyco's CEO threw a $2 million birthday party for his wife and charged it off as a shareholder meeting. Enron had 881 subsidiaries before it collapsed, 692 in the Cayman Islands, the rest elsewhere in the Caribbean.[20] Now, mortgage fraud occurs on a massive scale; derivatives are dealt behind closed doors, and securities known to be worthless are hyped. Thus, in 2009, Harvard MBA students pledged to behave ethically, embarrassed that B in MBA had come to stand for Boot Camp for the war of everyone against everyone.[21]

To Whom Can We Turn?

If the government has been brought to a standstill by polemicists and has been starved by tax cuts, wars without budgets, unfunded benefits, and a weakened IRS, and if the pursuit of profit makes the private sector amoral, to whom or what can we turn to seek justice for the most vulnerable and least culpable among us? The family? The village? Charitable organizations?

Some say it takes a village to raise a child. Some of us were raised in such villages. But the villages we have in mind are increasingly scarce. Everyone knows about *Bowling Alone* and bemoans the lack of social capital. Now millions live in virtual communities, everyone in their smart phone bubbles, oblivious to the actual community around them.[22]

Actual capital is also increasingly scarce at the village (i.e., local government) level. The thousands of government jobs lost from the recession and compromised efforts at recovery impact municipalities and school districts, fire departments and police departments, libraries and parks, and special districts of various kinds. In short, the village is beleaguered; preschool and other services for children are among the cuts made routinely. Furthermore, funds transferred from federal and state agencies to fund local services, for children with disabilities for example, are shrinking and were never adequate to begin with. Local workers trying to coordinate these programs regard them as Band-Aids designed to cover up but not remedy problems. Underfunding programs makes them ineffective, hastening a downward spiral.

When families fail, children wind up in public welfare agencies and the courts, many landing in foster care. Nearly half a million children were in foster care in 2012 nationwide; detailed data on foster care are sketchy given inherent difficulties such as confidentiality protections. If Massachusetts data are representative, most children will be released back to parents, relatives, guardians, or other agencies. About 8% will be adopted by foster parents. About 15% are *emancipated*, an ironic term used to describe those who "age out" of foster care. Most face daunting challenges with precious few resources other than their own wits. Additional thousands of children are homeless but still living with a parent or relative. Massachusetts also reports more than 6,000 high school students who are homeless, parentless, and not in foster care.[23]

There are obvious truths about it taking a family to raise a child but, like villages, the conjugal family of mom, dad, and kids is a shrinking minority household type. Today, only 30%

of all children live in such households. The divorce rate is 50%, only 49% of women over 18 are married and living with a spouse, and 56% of births to women under 30 are to unwed mothers. Social pathologies among children without fathers are by large multiples more numerous than average; for example, they are 9 times more likely to drop out of high school.[24] The United States ranks 54th of 184 nations on premature births; its rate is above the global average.[25] Again, most children live in low-income or below poverty line households. To what other source can parents turn for support?

Among major categories of charitable organizations, such as education, health and medicine, environment, and culture, religious institutions receive the largest share of charitable giving, about 35% of the total.[26] In addition to maintaining the faith, the church provides a source, a sense, and a site for belonging, especially for the elderly. But most church spending goes to maintain the institution. Despite its aspirations, only a small sliver of church revenues goes to caring for the poor. There are exceptions, of course, but even vaunted Catholic Charities receives about 70% of its revenue from governments and most of the rest from foundations.[27] Because categories of charitable giving are broad, one can only estimate how much of the $291 billion total giving in 2010 went to help those in need of food, shelter, or emergency health services. It appears to be about 12% of total giving, or about $35 billion.[28] Although a considerable sum, it is only 12% of what we give to "charity."

In brief, all institutions combined do not meet, much less reduce, current needs, and needs continue to grow. Gerrymandered congressional districts result in even greater polarization in Washington, D.C., and in state legislatures, and political polarization is highly correlated with income disparity.[29] Huge sums are spent on elections, making candidates beholden not to voters but to sponsors. Huge sums remain offshore, to be repatriated only if granted tax concessions costing billions in lost revenue. Huge sums are lost to fraud, tax expenditures, and waste, often due to half-hearted or compromised efforts. Besides being trillions of dollars in debt to others, the United States has a backlog of trillions more in infrastructure alone and in extremely costly new challenges such as severe weather events and an obesity epidemic.

What Will Become of Our Grandchildren?

We all have at least 20. Or do you not consider them family? These 20 children are poor. These 20 children are poor, very young, and multiracial. A few have a disability, way too premature to label. Some speak no English. That is the average Head Start class. We have about 53,000 grandchildren. We should have many thousands more.

Our scale of justice is already badly tilted against our children. Now we know it is badly tilted against their future as well. Highly respected, independent economists have clearly demonstrated this. Saez from the University of California-Berkeley and Piketty from the Paris School of Economics have produced a series of studies demonstrating the greater a nation's economic disparity, the poorer its economy is going forward.[30] The chair of the President's Council of Economic Advisors reported data clearly indicating the higher the Gini coefficient, the lower the intergenerational mobility. The United States and United Kingdom were nearly tied for last on this measure. The greatest intergenerational mobility is found in Sweden, Norway, Denmark, and Finland.[31]

In their seminal book, *The Spirit Level: Why Greater Equality Makes Nations Stronger*, British epidemiologists Wilkinson and Pickett analyzed a huge volume of health and economic data. They concluded the health status of any nation—all of a nation's people, not just the poor—was influenced by the degree to which income was distributed equally or disparately, healthier nations being those with higher degrees of equality.[32]

More recently, Acemoglu and Robinson concluded in *Why Nations Fail: The Origins of Power, Prosperity and Poverty* that a nation must be orderly if it is to prosper, but it must also have inclusive institutions, especially economic and political, if it is to be sustained.[33] In other words, prosperity must be widely shared and government truly democratic. If not, the institutions are captured by a wealthy, powerful elite. "If the very rich can use the political system to slow or stop the ascent of the rest, the United States could become a hereditary plutocracy under the trappings of liberal democracy."[34] Might the rich seek to slow or stop the ascent of the rest? Perhaps. A summary of seven studies conducted by researchers at the University of California-Berkeley and at the University of Toronto is captured in the title "Higher Social Class Predicts Increased Unethical Behavior."[35] Are the rich targets or sponsors of the voter suppression activity already legislated in about 20 states and under consideration in a dozen more?

A few corporations spent over $400 million lobbying from 2009 through 2011, mostly to block the EPA, the Affordable Health Care Act, and the Consumer Financial Protection Bureau. In March 2012, HR 347, the Federal Restricted Buildings and Grounds Improvement Act, was passed. It restricts protests on or near federal buildings and grounds. We often see police power used to suppress demonstrations. Lieutenant John Pike, for example, used military strength pepper spray 3 or 4 ft from the faces of University of California-Davis protesters. Paranoid? No, attentive.

Our Jobs Large and Small

Those most familiar with the work of Saez, Piketty, Acemoglu, Robinson, and other scholars find them not particularly optimistic. The election and the "Tax Armageddon" looming at the end of 2012 have put Americans and the global village even more on edge. Things could be very different before very long. Surely the concentration of wealth and power in fewer hands must and will be addressed somehow.

If it is not, many believe we will need a nonviolent political movement at least on the scale of the Civil Rights movement a half century ago. A worst-case scenario is a revolution accompanied by more violence than in the 1950–1970 period. A pie-in-the-sky alternative for restoration of justice is found in Edelman's "The Next Century of Our Constitution: Rethinking Our Duty to the Poor."[36] Substantive due process coupled with equal protection should ensure that every American child has a legitimate opportunity to realize his or her potential.

Fortunately, there is much potentially fertile soil between those extremes. Prior to getting in harness, we must ask ourselves three questions: Should all children have legitimate opportunities to realize their potential? If yes, are children lacking those opportunities part of my family? If yes, what am I going to do about it? We need to start by ridding ourselves and everyone we can reach of the mythological America and find, at bottom, who we really are. That requires the most complete and objective information we can gather about our situation and prospects, nationally and locally. From students and professors, we should expect no less.

The best alternative might be to speak up and speak out about social and environmental justice and economic or distributive justice, too. Then we must add actions to our words and children to our worlds. Speaking up and speaking out means advocating where it does the most good, not so much in the woods as in city halls and state capitols, at aldermen and women's and supervisors' meetings, in court houses, in hearing rooms, at public comment sessions, and in the print and electronic media. Should not advocates for justice be on a first-name basis with local and state officials and delegates in Washington, D.C.? Lobbyists are.

Thus we become better models of the behaviors we espouse. We should take our expertise, interests, energy, colleagues, and students into the community; adopt a school where most of the children are eligible for free or reduced price meals; teach sustainability or compare rivers to arteries or teach whatever children can get enthused about (outdoors maybe, but in classrooms as well); meet with the area director of Head Start (take colleagues and students along); volunteer as a classroom assistant 1 day a week for a semester or a year; or volunteer to give a science or geography lesson in a few Head Start classes 1 day a week, but we should not skip the Head Start class—the kids will miss us, and we better not let them down.

Can we instill in our students the sense that they can make a difference and offer curricula and schedules in such a way that making a difference becomes central to their preparation? Poor children need thousands of advocates, as smart as highly paid lobbyists, with inexperience offset by committed faculty, a never give up attitude, and history and justice, on their side. We can do this.

Discussion Questions

1. The United States prides itself in being a leader in world affairs. Tom paints a different picture of the country when it comes to quality of life. Do you agree or disagree with this assessment? Please explain your thinking.

2. Tom thinks we could stand to learn a thing or two from other countries. If you agree, give an example of something you think we could benefit from knowing about another country. If you disagree, why do you think we have nothing to learn from other countries?

3. If the United States does not lead in quality of life measures, what does it lead in? What, if anything, should other countries look up to in the United States?

4. Tom believes each generation has an obligation to leave the next generation a solid foundation upon which to build its future. He also thinks we are not doing a particularly good job of it. Do you agree or disagree? Please explain your response.

5. How does this chapter relate to social and environmental justice? What is Tom calling for? What is he asking of us? More specifically:

   a) Having thought through the issues raised in this chapter, what are three things you could do to address them in your community?
   b) Do you know your local, state, and national elected officials? What issues are they working on right now? How can you get involved in helping resolve those issues?
   c) Tom's concerns are directed toward children. As park, recreation, and tourism professionals, we often work with children. In what ways do we have the opportunity to improve the quality of their lives through the work we do?

2

At Whose Expense?

How Our Commitment to Conservation Has Propagated Social Injustice

Diane Samdahl
University of Georgia

A quick look at the history of leisure studies reveals deep roots in the environmental movement. After all, our heritage lies with the establishment of national parks and the protection of outdoor areas in the face of encroaching urbanization. Those historic roots also reveal a long-standing concern for people, especially children, whose access to the outdoors was constrained by urban development. The growth of urban parks and the development of programs such as summer camps attest to our belief that everyone should have access to the outdoors. Taken together, those are the foundational roots—in parks and in recreation—that shaped the early years of leisure studies.

Throughout the 20th century, our field took an activist stance on many issues relating to parks and recreation. We portrayed ourselves as stewards of the environment, lobbying strongly for passage of the Wilderness Act and promoting environmental education in our outdoor programs. We also were influential in promoting the Americans With Disabilities Act, creating adaptive recreation programs and accessible parks designed to meet the needs of all citizens. Thus, it is not surprising that we view ourselves as environmentally and socially responsible. We have been urged to embrace environmental and social justice as two sides of the same coin, reflecting the core values that drive our profession.

But do they really? Although we are comfortable being self-congratulatory about our accomplishments, we do not have to look far for instances that challenge our claim to environmental and social justice. In many of our communities, city parks are located in some neighborhoods more readily than in others; likewise, funding for some recreation programs has been safeguarded and other programs are vulnerable to cuts. The inequitable distribution of parks and programs clearly shows recreation management is more complicated than simply providing access and resources; each managerial decision impacts different segments of the community differently.

Today, concern is increasing that our historic activism has been unknowingly biased in ways that reflect the lifestyles and worldviews of the majority. Are race and class biases embedded in our protection of the environment? Do age, gender, or ethnic biases shape the nature of recreation programming? No longer is simply documenting our actions enough; in the contemporary world, we must reflect more critically on the central question, "Who benefits and who does not?"

In this chapter, I propose that the form of environmentalism embraced by the park, recreation, and tourism profession has been inherently biased toward a White, middle-class, American view of the environment. Even more troubling, I claim that our commitment to the environment has blinded us to the negative impact our actions have had on other segments of society. Has our commitment to environmental protection been a source of social injustice?

The Cultural Creation of Nature

A critique of race and class bias in the environmental movement dates back at least 25 years. In 1990, three Black environmentalists wrote and sent a letter to several major environmental groups including the Sierra Club and the Wilderness Society. In that letter, they expressed concern that "racism and whiteness of the environmental movement are our Achilles heel."[1] Almost immediately, a similar letter was sent from a group of Native American and Latino leaders requesting environmental groups to stop fund-raising in minority communities until a significant proportion of the organizations' membership was non-White. This accusation of White bias came as a surprise to members of those environmental groups, many of whom viewed themselves as activists working to protect minority communities and Native American values. This issue was clearly larger than a simple matter of membership. Minorities wanted increased representation because they were critical of the "White" philosophy that was driving the environmental movement.

But how can environmentalism be a White value? Is not the environment simply out there, absorbing our pollution and needing our protection? Well, not exactly. In a widely read and controversial essay titled "The Trouble With Wilderness," Cronon[2] laid out a compelling argument that the contemporary view of wilderness (indeed, of nature more broadly) stems from the romanticism of the 19th century matched with nostalgia for a way of life that was being replaced by modernity. Romanticism and modernity, of course, pertained to the culture of European Americans who were settling the land at that time. Cronon said of this era, "Wild country became not just a place of religious redemption but of national renewal, the quint-essential location for experiencing what it meant to be American."[3]

In developing his point, Cronon pointed to the enormous country estates that emerged toward the end of the 1800s, built by the Rockefellers, Vanderbilts, and other prosperous families of the Gilded Age. Those estates, he claimed, established a uniquely American vision of nature with wide vistas, mountains, and clean grassy meadows that bordered well-kept forests. Of course, this imagery was not inherently natural, but rather required extensive landscaping that shaped lakes, meadows, and forests into desired patterns. Our own field traces its heritage back to Olmsted and other landscapers who created those designs and thereby crafted an enduring cultural ideal of what nature should look like. Olmsted brought this imagery into urban areas as well through his designs for Central Park and metropolitan "natural" spaces.

Nature, as it was constructed and shaped during this era, was deeply imbued with symbolism relating to Christianity. DeLuca and Demo[4] examined this in the photography of Carleton Watkins and the writings of John Muir, both of whom were influential in shaping the early wilderness movement. Through photographs and essays, those early proponents of wilderness compared America's mountains not to the comparable exotic geography of Africa or South America, but to the sacred cathedrals of Europe, instilling a sense of religious splendor in what had originally been a frightening, godforsaken landscape. DeLuca and Demo claimed that creating wilderness in this fashion "offered cultural legitimacy to a nation seeking a heritage that could compete with the cathedrals and castles of Europe."[5]

Before wilderness was infused with spiritual meaning, unsettled lands had been perceived as savage places that needed to be brought under man's—and God's—dominion. Indeed, the wilderness (the *Wild* West) was often the site of brutality where savage "Indians" threatened to block the "colonizing imperative of manifest destiny."[6] But the romantic era was underway throughout Europe and the United States, resulting in a significant reframing of nature into something that was majestic and sublime. Describing this transformation, Cronon stated, "Sublime landscapes were those rare places on earth where one had more chance than elsewhere to glimpse the face of God."[7] In the United States, that missive was channeled into the creation of national parks.

This image of wilderness was constructed to be the antithesis of civilization; its appeal was as God's creation—Eden—untouched by man. Because of this, wilderness could have no permanent inhabitants, adding further justification to the ongoing removal of Native Americans. Not coincidentally, the beginning of the environmental movement corresponds with a massive relocation of Native Americans to lands that held no economic or symbolic value to intruding European Americans.

DeLuca and Demo argued the removal of Native Americans was not enough. Because wilderness was to be protected from all forms of modernization, it could not have farmers or loggers or anyone else whose presence was tied to productive labor. Wilderness was to exist devoid of human influence.

So this is where we might ask, "Who was benefiting and who was not benefiting from this view of wilderness as separate from civilization?" Obviously, the wealthy elite not only shaped and fostered this image of nature, but also were the only ones who could visit these sites as tourists unfettered by the need to labor. From its inception, wilderness was never intended for Native Americans, African Americans, or lower class blue collar Whites whose livelihood was tied to farming, mining, and other forms of industry. Wilderness became a museum set aside for reveling in the pleasures of nature. In fact, shortly after winning the long battle to preserve Yosemite, Muir proclaimed, "A large first-class hotel is very much needed."[8] Clearly, wilderness emerged at the end of the 19th century firmly entrenched in a classist notion of work and wealth.

Nothing is inherently natural about nature. Our concept of wilderness, and of nature more broadly, intentionally imbues the "natural" environment with an older, grander, more spiritual essence than human civilization; it is shaped by an intentional binary that separates it from our social world. If we view the environment and the social as two sides of the same coin, as stated at the beginning of this chapter, we must also acknowledge that this coin has currency only within our own limited worldview.

So there is danger, I believe, in framing discussions about social and environmental justice as if they are independent of one another because that prevents us from seeing how one often impinges upon the other. This, perhaps, was the point behind the protest letters that Blacks, Native Americans, and Latino leaders wrote to the environmental organizations in 1990. In essence, they were highlighting the contested nature of nature.

The Contested Nature of Nature

A good example of the contested meanings of nature is the adversarial relationship between the National Park Service (NPS) and Native Americans. This conflict is more than a historical artifact stemming from Indian removal; it is an ongoing dispute that even today erupts into hostilities and lawsuits. A typical instance is the recent battle between park visitors to Devils Tower and members of several nearby Plains tribes.[9] Devils Tower became the first national monument in the United States in 1906, described by President Theodore Roosevelt as "an extraordinary example of the effect of erosion . . . and an object of historic and great scientific interest."[10] The declaration that preserved Devils Tower made no reference that it had been a sacred site for local tribes since before Europeans migrated to America.

For obvious reasons, Devils Tower is a mecca for recreational rock climbers. By the mid-1990s, up to 6,000 people per year climbed the tower, and park management expressed concern about physical damage from pitons and the unintentional erosion of rock and vegetation; in addition, climbers were disturbing nesting sites for birds. At about the same time, leaders of the Dakota, Nakota, and Lakota nations wrote a resolution declaring the importance of Devils Tower as a sacred cultural place for their people. In submitting this to the NPS, they requested their religious traditions be respected. The resulting Climbing Management Plan, released in 1995 and updated in 2006, established stringent rules intended to reduce the physical impact of climbing and to protect the nesting sites of birds; it also contained a *voluntary* restriction on climbing during the month of June when native tribes hold many sacred rituals. The absolute ban on actions that degrade the rock are in stark contrast to the voluntary restraint on actions that degrade native culture. This is a telling example of the clash between environmental protection and social justice. Who benefits and who does not? The answer is obvious.

The situation at Devils Tower is more than a skirmish between conflicting users; it stems from incompatible views of the environment. In Native American culture, the physical environment is infused with intense spiritual meaning; it is not separate from Native Americans but rather deeply intertwined into their daily living. Native Americans find it difficult to understand the Anglo idea of a wilderness that should not be inhabited or of nature that exists separate from civilization. When Native Americans are dispossessed of their land, they are also dispossessed of their culture. According to Spence,[11] "[T]his impasse reflects the powerful cultural values that remain embedded in two very different conceptions of the same landscape."

A recent book by Dowie[12] made a similar claim on a much broader scale, asserting the conservation movement has become the major cause of population displacement worldwide. Not surprisingly, the displaced victims are almost always indigenous people. Dowie pointed to agencies such as the Nature Conservancy, which he called the "conservation aristocracy," that sweep into third world places with an overzealous enthusiasm for nature. Armed with good intentions and multimillion-dollar budgets, agency missionaries attempt to protect the land from people who, for centuries, have lived in harmony with their environment. Dowie indicted the conservation aristocracy for promoting its American concept of wilderness and the ensuing belief that nature can be protected only by moving people out. Dowie framed this problem as a conflict between science-based conservation and rights-based conservation, a framework that also describes the fight at Devils Tower.

Science, in fact, is our strongest tool for hegemonic policing of Western ideology. We resort to science for proof without understanding that science itself is a product of our culture. Our contemporary view of nature, developed during the romantic era of the 19th century, rests solidly upon a large and growing body of research developed during the positivist era of the 20th century. The answers our science provides are not always adequate for people who live within a different worldview. I believe our inability to see the constructed nature of nature and our related inability to understand the entanglement between the natural environment and the social environment lie at the heart of many forms of social injustice.

At the Expense of Social Justice

For more than a century, our fierce defense of nature has blinded us to the social impacts of our actions. One clear example of this can be seen in the American desire to preserve the Amazon rainforest. Most Americans, from scientists to ecotourists, embrace a belief that the Amazon is a complex, irreplaceable arena of biodiversity that has significant impact upon global ecology. Destruction of the Amazon habitat has potentially massive consequences. Without disputing the science supporting those claims, I want us to acknowledge that the Americans working to save the Amazon live in an abhorrently consumptive society built upon centuries of environmental abuse. When we deny indigenous people within the Amazon a similar right to convert their natural resources into economic profit and modernization—and the global power associated with those changes—we impose a clear double standard in which Americans are win–win: We already have the social, political, and economic benefits gained at the expense of our own environment, and we indulge our concept of conservation by preventing others from doing the same. Indigenous people within the Amazon are not blind to this hypocrisy.

My intent is not to open debate about the biological importance of places such as the Amazon, but rather to explore how our decisions about the environment—even seemingly easy decisions such as saving the rainforest—are inherently entangled in questions of social justice. The environmental and the social coexist in a messy imbroglio, impacting one another more deeply than we suspect.

Clearly, our commitment to conservation has instigated social injustice. Dowie's discussion of global displacement due to conservation and the above example of the Amazon rainforest illustrates how a blind adherence to Western views of nature can erode the cultural integrity of indigenous people. But our loyalty to nature has had social consequences close to home.

We can see this first in the U.S. Forest Service (FS) and the NPS, both of whom are federally empowered to conserve and manage our national resources. Although these great agencies have accomplished significant tasks, they both have had to confront a White, class-based bias in their missions. User studies document these areas do not effectively serve low-income or minority citizens. In the 1990s, the FS took steps to ameliorate this problem by establishing an outreach program for urban forestry. The NPS has had more visible cultural biases, evident in the Anglo-centric naming and the historic meaning of many of its sites. It too has taken steps to redress this concern. The Custer Battlefield, for example, was renamed Little Bighorn Battlefield to acknowledge both sides of that battle. This bias is equally pronounced at the state and local level in terms of the selection, location, and naming of parks and historic markers.

Our blinding allegiance to conservation has had a more damaging impact on cultural heritage communities that reside in those forgotten regions that we now want to protect. We can clearly see this in the barrier islands off the coast of Florida, Georgia, and the Carolinas. I have written before about the historic African American resort called American Beach,[13] a small oceanfront development established by and for African Americans during the repressive segregation of Jim Crow. For over 30 years, American Beach had regional and national prominence as one of the few places where Blacks could vacation on the Atlantic coastline. The motto of American Beach was, "Rest and relaxation without humiliation." In an unforeseen consequence of the Civil Rights Act of 1964, places such as American Beach were abandoned in favor of locales that had previously been off limits to Blacks. Today, American Beach is a scraggly, impoverished community with a few proud, determined residents who are fighting for historic preservation.

American Beach is located on Amelia Island off the coast of northern Florida. Like other barrier islands in this region, Amelia Island has received millions of dollars from state and federal funds for stabilizing and preserving wetlands, sand dunes, and nesting sites for sea turtles. In the 1980s, these islands were "discovered" by developers who converted them into high-end tourist resorts and upscale gated communities—Hilton Head is perhaps the most well known of such sites. These resorts have eradicated thousands of acres of live oaks and natural dunes, replacing them with luxurious, manicured grounds with exotic vegetation that is water and labor intensive. Ironically, by implementing management practices that protect the remaining dunes, these resorts have received acclaim as being environmentally friendly; one resort was even designated as an Audubon Cooperative Sanctuary for its efforts to protect migrating birds. In the background, lost in all the attention directed at environmental stewardship, residents of the impoverished American Beach have struggled for someone to hear their plea about the historic significance of their land.

In some respects, the situation with American Beach parallels that of Devils Tower, highlighting ways we acknowledge an obligation to protect nature, yet are oblivious to the need for cultural preservation for marginalized groups. A similar but more egregious threat faces the Gullah-Geechee culture on the islands just north of American Beach. Whereas American Beach is a small piece of land with symbolic importance, the Gullah-Geechee is a uniquely rich culture that developed in isolation from mainstream America, but now faces the threat of extinction.

Gullah-Geechee communities date back to the early 1700s when slaves were brought to the United States to work the rice paddies of coastal Carolina. These slaves had been intentionally kidnapped from certain regions in northern Africa where local tribes had longtime expertise with rice production. Because there was little traffic to or through the islands off the Carolina coast, this group of slaves remained in relative isolation. Even after the Civil War, ex-slaves remained on the islands and their White plantation owners moved inland. The ensuing isolation lasted another 100 years until highway bridges were built from the mainland in the late 20th century. That long span of isolation allowed the Gullah-Geechee to retain language and cultural traditions that clearly reflect their African roots. Today, an estimated quarter million people speak the Gullah language or were raised with Geechee traditions.[14]

Like the future of American Beach, the future of the Gullah-Geechee is threatened by the intrusion of upscale development including golf resorts. But unlike American Beach, the Gullah-Geechee is an entire culture with its own language, religion, culinary, and artistic traditions, not just a piece of land with symbolic meaning. Though many Gullah communities are learning to market themselves to tourists, the loss of land and the influx of visitors mean that their traditional culture is quickly disappearing. The Gullah-Geechee culture is a victim of beach tourism, overlooked and ignored during the extensive (and expensive) development of upscale golf resorts that proudly showcase themselves as stewards of the environment.

Concluding Thoughts

Our cultural understanding of nature, especially our belief that nature exists independent of human culture, has allowed us to pursue a conservation agenda that blinds us to companion issues of social importance. I strongly believe that our allegiance to the environment has made us complicit in many forms of social injustice. It is time to ask whose cultural heritage has been overlooked in our focused attention on nature.

DeLuca and Demo raised a similar critique, noting the environmental movement never joined forces with other grassroots movements that arose during the same time. The 20th century saw protests related to the labor movement, the farmer's movement, the civil rights movement, the feminist movement, and other social concerns. When these protests overlapped historically, they often joined forces. However, the environmental movement has always stood alone. As DeLuca and Demo noted,

During its first 100 years, the environmental movement has been concerned with preserving pristine places. This narrow, class- and race-based perspective. . . [has isolated] the movement from labor and civil rights concerns and render[s] it vulnerable to charges of elitism.[15]

Is it possible, as they suggest, that the environmental movement never joined forces with the labor movement or civil rights movement because the environment embraces inherently class-based priorities? Is it possible, like Cronon and Spence and Dowie proposed, that our elitist concept of nature was intentionally designed to exclude people whose cultures and livelihoods derive a different understanding of nature? If the schism is indeed this deep, the environmental movement might be inherently incompatible with the more democratic goals of social justice. It is time to reexamine that two-sided coin that serves as the central currency of our field.

Discussion Questions

1. Diane challenges us to acknowledge our privileges and biases in thinking about how we look after the natural world. What are some of these privileges and biases? How do they express themselves in the definitions we create and the actions we take?

2. Diane suggests that a concern for environmental justice can lead to social injustice. Give examples from your own experience that illustrate her point.

3. Does this mean social and environmental justice will always be at odds with one another, or is there hope for bringing them together somehow? Please explain your reasoning.

4. When we talk about social and environmental justice, there is a tendency to equate social justice with people and environmental justice with nature. In effect, this may separate people from nature and put people at odds with nature. Do you see people as being separate from nature? Please elaborate.

5. Do you think matters of social and environmental justice are opposite sides of the same coin, or do you think they are different from one another? Can you really have one without the other? What might be gained by thinking about social and environmental justice as part and parcel of the same thing?

3

Beyond the Right to Inclusion

The Intersection of Social and Environmental Justice for Individuals With Disabilities in Leisure

Mary Ann Devine
Kent State University

Jennifer Piatt
Indiana University

Social justice is present when the rights of all citizens are fulfilled, equal opportunities to engage in life are experienced, and the dispensing of fair and equitable goods is distributed to everyone.[1,2] Yet the case has generally been that not all members of society, especially individuals with disabilities, are provided with equitable access to life's opportunities. Unequal power, oppression, unearned privilege,[3] and imbalanced life experiences make social and environmental justice elusive. Nevertheless, individuals with disabilities have the right to participate in the same activities guaranteed to others, without their disability being in the forefront. We should remember that as citizens of the United States, each of us has the right to life, liberty, and the pursuit of happiness in all aspects of life, including leisure pursuits.

Every human has the civil right to engage in the pursuit of happiness, but this right cannot be achieved if social oppression and exclusion are present. Rights cannot be practiced if opportunity does not exist. In particular, the pursuit of leisure has been neglected for underrepresented populations within society for years, including individuals with disabilities. Yet the provision of leisure opportunities as important components of the human experience is a moral obligation of society.[4] Although this moral obligation has yet to be lived up to, the pursuit of social and environmental justice for individuals with disabilities has been a concern for years. As far back as 1982, the National Therapeutic Recreation Society has stated, "All human beings, including those individuals with disabilities, illness, or limiting conditions have a right to, and need for, leisure involvement as a necessary aspect of the human experience."[5] This means that every human being, regardless of race, ability, or disabling condition should have the opportunity to choose to participate in a wide range of leisure activities.[6] When these "normalized" leisure experiences are not provided, individuals with disabilities may not engage in everything society provides to others, thereby they are deprived of their basic human rights.[7]

Leisure, taken for granted as a natural occurring life experience for the general population, is not as easily accessible for individuals with disabilities. Many of us practicing in the leisure industry assume if an individual wants to participate in a healthy, positive leisure lifestyle, constraints to leisure can be negotiated and overcome. From this perspective, access to leisure becomes the responsibility of the individual rather than the leisure professional. Additionally, leisure professionals are often taught to believe that if the individual wants to engage in a particular activity, he or she will find a way to make it happen. This individualistic perspective places the responsibility on the individual to negotiate barriers so the leisure experience may occur. Yet unequal opportunities, inaccessibility to programs, and uninformed staff are only a few of the overarching obstacles created by the leisure service profession itself that inhibit participation and are beyond the control of the individual with a disability. Often unaware of the consequences of their actions, leisure service providers thus create constraints to participation rather than eliminate them. In so doing, their actions burden people with disabilities rather than promote autonomy and independent functioning.[8]

Justice in a leisure context means equity of opportunity (i.e., power) for individuals with disabilities to be and do what they value.[9] This includes the elimination of barriers and constraints to leisure whenever possible. If constraints to leisure remain present for individuals with disabilities, social oppression works against the principles of social justice. More specifically, structural, interpersonal, and intrapersonal constraints can promote inequities for individuals with disabilities.[10, 11] Inequities experienced in a leisure context can affect environmental and social justice in other life contexts as well. For instance, many industries, including leisure services, collaborate to decrease sedentary lifestyles and promote active living within their communities. If leisure service providers do not address constraints for people with disabilities to pursue active living as well, they not only exclude individuals with disabilities but also send a message to other potential collaborators (i.e., policy makers, local businesses) that inclusion of this segment of our communities is not important. Exclusion of this kind is a subtle way of disempowering individuals with disabilities on multiple levels.

Segregation of services also makes constraints more pronounced. Lack of transportation, communities with limited resources, unsupportive social networks, and environments lacking universal design make promoting social and environmental justice more difficult. Facing these obstacles, the individual with a disability may have difficulty accessing transportation to and from leisure activities, developing friendships and relationships, and engaging in community life. Indeed, learned helplessness, self-fulfilling prophecies, and negative self-beliefs have been identified in the literature[12, 13] as common barriers and constraints to individuals with disabilities. When leisure service providers are not cognizant of how the development of inaccessible programs can reinforce oppression rather than eliminate it, social and environmental injustices continue to manifest themselves.

Social Justice and Individuals With Disabilities

Tenets of a "right to leisure" have to do with inalienable rights as U.S. citizens—in essence, freedom and equality. Social justice is founded on the same tenets of respect, dignity, and equal opportunity. This also encompasses the right to fair treatment and a share of the benefits of society based on the foundations of human rights and equality of all people.[14] Scholars have examined social justice relative to numerous marginalized groups including women, people of color, and those living in poverty. As a result of these inquiries, individuals with disabilities have been able to use those experiences, strategies, and perspectives to enhance their struggle toward achieving social justice as well.

Defining social justice for people with disabilities can be complicated because of varying religious, political, and cultural views of disability. However, Smart[15] offered these parameters relating to social justice and individuals with disabilities: (a) everyone receives equal treatment, (b) everyone receives what he or she earns, and (c) everyone receives what he or she needs. These parameters should guarantee the opportunity for valuable and valid life experiences.[16]

Receiving equal treatment refers to the ways in which people without disabilities not only have access to resources but also are recipients of similar outcomes or benefits. This tenet of social justice for people with disabilities insists that the equity of the outcomes experienced by those without disabilities be available to those with disabilities as well.[17] Social justice relative to receiving what one earns stems from the vocational counseling field. According to Smart,[18] receiving what one earns brings to light the shortsightedness of attributing the absence of one's success only to inferior aptitude, desire, or ability. Smart asserted that the perceptions of a lack of success of people with disabilities in the United States have much to do with stereotyping, prejudice, and discrimination. Receiving what one earns relative to social justice requires shifting the paradigm to view abilities or contributions more broadly. Merit then relates to a broad interpretation of the contributions of people with disabilities and to viewing these contributions as virtuous. This brings into question the ways in which leisure has socially constructed the contributions people with disabilities can bring to a leisure experience and considers whether leisure has socially constructed how much people with disabilities can potentially gain from a leisure experience. Last, individuals with disabilities should receive rights and opportunities to aid in meeting their needs. This parameter of social justice for individuals with disabilities is founded on systemic changes such as the passage of the Americans With Disabilities Act (ADA), which recognizes that biological and functional realities of disability necessitate accommodations. The social justice notion of equal outcome is predicated on all people getting what they need. In other words, all people should have their economic and social needs met at the same rates and standards, but with different accommodations.[19]

Additionally, achieving social justice for people with disabilities must include a discussion of the overemphasis of the expectation that people with disabilities conform to able-bodied society. The principle and spirit of inclusion is that everyone makes changes, shares power, and acknowledges difference. According to Nussbaum,[20] to focus on social justice and individuals with disabilities, we must consider situations in which these individuals are hampered in various ways by the structure of their society. This is most evident in the medical model of disability where the problem of disability is treated as an abnormality. The medical model aims to transform people with disabilities to be more like people without disabilities.[21] Within this model, treatment is centered on curing the individual, with the goal of eliminating the abnormality. It clearly positions people with disabilities in a socially disadvantageous position as their point of comparison is always the person without the disability. The medical model clearly differs from the social model of disability, which positions disability as a social construct. Within the social construct, disability results in discrimination, prejudice, and stigma.[22] Both models account for ways in which society has hampered individuals with disabilities and lead us to ask, "What does society owe people with disabilities?"

Health care reform, public health policy shift, and the introduction of the World Health Organization (WHO) International Classification on Functioning, Disability, and Health (ICF) have started to redefine how disability is described and classified within the health care industry. This has been accomplished by focusing more on what the individual can do, rather than by categorizing each individual only on the medical diagnosis of the disability. This recent shift in thinking may ultimately have a significant role in social justice for individuals with disabilities. Defining health through the traditional medical model where the individual has life restrictions due to an illness, medical condition, or disabling condition focuses only on the disability and not on how other factors contribute to the individual's overall health. The medical model conceptualized disability as a problem to be solved, thus disadvantaging people with disabilities in general.[23, 24] The ICF model takes an entirely different view of the disability by not only looking at the medical diagnosis of the condition, but also examining "...individual, societal, and environmental factors that influence health."[25] Because society's definition of health and wellness directly impacts leisure engagement,[26] this shift in defining disability through the ICF may lend itself to promoting social and environmental justice. For example, the ICF is broken down into two parts: (1) functioning and disability and (2) environmental and personal factors. The first part (functioning and disability) explains body functions and structures that physicians typically use to diagnose a condition. The second part (environmental and personal factors) directly relates to the structure of one's environment including the built environment, support structures, and social/community structure. Within this part of the ICF, various components beyond the medical diagnosis of the illness or disabling condition are taken into account. This includes, but is not limited to, natural environments, man-made changes to the environment, support and relationships, attitudes, transportation, and civic engagement.[27] This new definition of health and wellness may ultimately change how we view, define, and perceive disability, thereby promoting social and environmental justice for all humans.

Many complexities exist within the disability movement and its struggle for social justice. These range from demands for equitable economic distribution to access to political systems for policy changes. However, what most studies have in common is the aim of people with disabilities to have access to services within systems that is equal to those who do not have disabilities.[28] In other words, social justice for individuals with disabilities is not about rights but about opportunity. These opportunities should offer valuable and valid ways for people with disabilities to access political, social, economic, and educational systems. Nevel,[29] for example, asserted that individuals with Down syndrome not only have the right to the same access to support services and networks as those without disabilities, but also should have the opportunity to seek everything to which they are rightfully entitled. She goes on to recommend that social justice for those with Down syndrome includes a fight for policy changes that expand community-based options enlightened by values of caring, compassion, and dignity. Tollefsen[30] contended that a society indifferent to people with disabilities is an unjust society. He claimed concern for social justice goes beyond the critical examination of the hurdles society places on people with disability and questioned what further steps must be taken to create more inclusive societies and environments. What society owes people with disabilities is not only recognition of rights but also valuable and valid opportunities to engage fully in society. Tollefsen[31] used the notion of independence as an example of what society owes its citizens with disabilities. He argued no person is truly independent. We each need something from one another. Thus, the goal of independence for everyone, but particularly for people with disabilities, is flawed. Instead, the goal of society should be interdependence and self-determination for all citizens. In this regard, social justice alone cannot pave the way for interdependence of citizens. Social justice must be coupled with environmental justice for a fully inclusive society to exist.

Environmental Justice

Cutter[32] defined environmental justice as environmental rights for all people regardless of race, gender, economic power, or life span. She based this assumption on the 1992 United Nations declaration that environmental risks are "unevenly distributed within and between societies."[33] Although most scholars of environmental justice accept this definition as the basis for this movement, the dominant discourse centers on fair treatment and meaningful involvement of people in environmental policy formation and implementation.[34] According to Abel and Stephan,[35] although multiple frames of reference exist from which to view environmental injustices, the dominant dialogue centers on political, social, and economic contexts. The question we pose for this discussion is, "How does environmental justice resonate for people with disabilities?"

Environmental justice has predominantly focused on the inequity of exposure to environmental hazards for people who are poor, those living in urban areas, or people of color. For instance, Mohai and Bryant[36] examined race and income levels as they relate to exposure to hazardous waste facilities. They concluded race was a greater predictor of proximity to hazardous facilities than income. Charles and Thomas[37] argued the struggle for environmental justice is to recognize that, along with others, people with disabilities are part of that movement. Recently studies have been conducted that go beyond historically marginalized groups and exposure to environmental hazards to broaden the discussion to include additional groups of people as well as other ways environmental justice can be explored.

Lucas[38] examined the lack of access to public transportation for poor people, people living in rural areas, and people with disabilities as an issue relevant to environmental justice. She characterized this issue as environmental exclusion, pushing the boundaries of environmental justice beyond the environmental hazard focus. Specifically, Lucas[39] noted that a lack of community planning for access to public transportation is relevant to environmental justice and results in hazardous environments. From this perspective, hazardous environments constitute environments in which people cannot fully realize their capabilities because of a lack of equity in resources. People are excluded from opportunities their communities have to offer because of a lack of resources; thus, they cannot participate fully in community life. This lack of access to resources inhibits full engagement in society for individuals with different accessibility needs than the norm. Lucas contended poor access to transportation as a form of environmental injustice can be linked to social injustice issues such as limited employment and leisure opportunities.

Rose[40] characterized environmental justice as an ecological notion. In doing so, he questioned the privilege of having access to natural areas such as national parks by virtue of not only socioeconomic means but also desire, options, and an absence of constraints. He challenged readers to consider the compatibility (or lack thereof) of social and environmental justice in that policies to protect the environment can constrain access to natural areas—a social injustice. Rose's notion of access to public space helps frame the case for environmental justice in leisure contexts, specifically, people having the privilege of freely moving from place to place without physical barriers or constraints. Leisure spaces are essential to environmental justice for individuals with disabilities in providing them the opportunity to experience natural environments as the rest of society does.[41] Thus, those who are privileged have access to environmental resources, and people with disabilities are often not in that group.

Leisure and environmental justice can also be viewed through a social construction lens. Social construction theory contends that the meaning of behavior, language, and objects is constructed in specific contexts.[42] Additionally, meanings can change from context to context such as the meaning of a wheelchair. A wheelchair can take on the meaning of a burden or an obstacle in an inaccessible environment or be a means to independence in an accessible environment. Relative to leisure, environmental justice implies a physically and programmatically accessible context. Specifically, it means a context designed for all to have an optimal experience. For instance, environmental justice for an individual with autism can include staff who are knowledgeable about autism and who are able to respond to the individual's specific characteristics related to autism. It can also be a leisure environment that is designed in recognition of someone's autistic sensitivities and offers options such as a quiet space to calm down. In this example, the focus is on environmental justice rather than the person's autistic characteristics. Some disabilities, such as deafness, are contextual as well. For example, Charles[43] noted, "There are some people in the deaf community who do not consider deafness as a disability" because they view disability as a product of society. In a society of deaf people, deafness is not a disability. Thus, we question the role environmental (context) justice plays in reinforcing disability or ableism. Would environmental justice entail acknowledging the privilege of those who have the opportunity to access natural environments?

The ability of people who use wheelchairs to navigate in public spaces is based on whether their community has taken them into consideration when developing public spaces. Charles and Thomas[44] noted community engagement is often lacking for the deaf community, and this lack of engagement is an environmental justice issue. They offered an example of a lack of consideration of deaf people as participants in community development issues. All too often, society does not consider people with disabilities and access to public spaces, and according to Nussbaum,[45] this is a matter of environmental justice. Even if a person has unlimited resources (e.g., financial, human) and could pay and arrange for access, it would not constitute environmental justice. The root of the matter is that access to public spaces, or inclusion in public discourse, is a public task that requires planning, discussions, and use of resources so all members of the public can access space. How can we guarantee that people with disabilities are included in these conversations and planning decisions?

Critique of Social and Environmental Literature Relative to People With Disabilities

Although social justice scholars have conducted inquiries and raised philosophical questions relative to the women's movement, inequality of access to resources (i.e., transportation, community events) by people from low socioeconomic groups, and the plight of people of color, little research has been conducted relative to individuals with disabilities. The environmental justice literature, in particular, has contributed little to understanding how that movement specifically relates to or impacts people with disabilities. The research that has addressed people with disabilities has been focused mainly on philosophical positions related to political and economic issues. The introduction of the ICF model by the WHO attempts to shift the paradigm from perceiving individuals with disabilities as sick and in continual need of medical attention to broadening the definition of health to include individual, societal, and environmental factors, thus introducing the notion of a healthy active person who happens to have a disability. Despite this global movement to change the perceptions, stereotypes, and stigmas surrounding people with disabilities, the health care industry, in particular, has not embraced this notion of a healthy person with a disability.

Loewen and Pollard[46] advocated for the reframing of disability from a medical view to a social view to facilitate social justice. Tollefsen[47] argued the intersection of social and environmental justice occurs in promoting interdependence, which in turn raises several questions: How do leisure environments contribute to the promotion of interdependence? Why do we push to achieve independence rather than cooperative engagement? Do we acknowledge the privilege of ableism relative to the natural environment when working for environmental justice? Nussbaum stated, "Citizens enjoy fully and equally only when they are capable of exercising a range of capabilities."[48] In other words, passive engagement in society diminishes the rights and capabilities of people with disabilities. The question we must ask ourselves is, "Are leisure professionals including individuals with disabilities in discussions of social and environmental justice?"

Intersection of Social and Environmental Justice's Relevance for Inclusive Leisure

Kivel[49] challenged leisure service professionals and scholars to engage in social and environmental justice matters by posing the question asked by Dr. David Gray: What does society need done and how can we do it? This question is thought provoking when considering social and environmental justice relative to people with disabilities; it challenges us not only to think about the issues but also to attempt to resolve the fundamental problems of opportunity these members of our society face. Foreman and Arthur-Kelly[50] identified social and environmental justice, along with legislation, as the principles of inclusion. Clearly opportunities and access to leisure are not equal between people with and without disabilities. The intent of the inclusion movement that began in the mid-1990s was to promote social and environmental justice for those in our society with disabilities. This intent has not been fully realized, which may be due in part to framing inclusion in a legal context (i.e., ADA) rather than in a moral context molded around social and environmental justice.

The ADA recently celebrated its 20th anniversary. The leisure field has experienced many changes in service provision, building construction, and development of natural areas to comply with the ADA. An outgrowth of compliance with the ADA in the leisure field has been the inclusion movement, where people with and without disabilities engage together in leisure as peers. This has also been the dominant paradigm within which the field of leisure has responded to social and environmental justice for people with disabilities. This movement has resulted in an increase in awareness and opportunity for people with disabilities to have their leisure needs met, but has not given rise to the paradigm shift needed to meet the principles of social and environmental justice. Specifically, in spite of this movement 20 years in the making, the leisure profession has been slow and often resistant to include people with disabilities in leisure alongside their peers without disabilities.[51] We contend that inclusion of people with disabilities in leisure contexts must reflect an intersection of social and environmental justice because disability is not only biological and functional, necessitating accommodations, but also political in the form of legal mandates, civil rights, and policies regulating access to environments. Furthermore, social and environmental justice in the field of leisure requires a shift in the current paradigm of meeting the ADA mandates to embrace inclusion as a civil right to pursue opportunities available to people with disabilities in all leisure environments.

In examining environmental justice, Rose[52] posed the question, "Who has access to public spaces, including natural environments, and how do they access it?" One conclusion he drew was that understanding our relationship with the natural world from a leisure perspective means reconciling the principles of social and environmental justice. In other words, how we understand our interactions with natural spaces and the relationship people have with nature can aid in better understanding the role of leisure as an intersection of social and environmental justice. The same question can be addressed to individuals with disabilities: How and in what ways do people with disabilities interact with and relate to built and natural environments? What role can environmental justice play in that interaction? According to Loewen and Pollard,[53] universal design is the most effective method to achieve environmental justice in communities. Would the same principle apply to leisure contexts? Should every leisure environment be designed using the principles of universal design so all have access to them? Should certain environments (e.g., climbing walls, skate parks, backcountry trails) be exempt from universal design, thus contradicting environmental justice for individuals with physically limiting disabilities? Or is this where social and environmental justice intersect? Leisure professionals must strive for a fairer distribution of power and resources, for greater valued and valid opportunities, access to services, and benefits for people with disabilities. Tollefsen[54] argued that clearing barriers for people with disabilities requires elimination of an array of hostile attitudes toward these members of society. The ADA serves as a formal statement of public policy regarding social and environmental justice for people with disabilities in the United States. Although the ADA can mandate physical and service-related access, the law cannot mandate positive attitudes. As we contend, civil rights policies have only formulated the beginning discussions. Opportunity needs to be present, not just talked about, for rights to be expressed.

Loewen and Pollard[55] contended a paradigm shift from social welfare to social justice for people with disabilities is needed to achieve and realize the spirit and intent of social justice. Their position and the concepts of social and environmental justice appear to offer new and appropriate frameworks for examining the inclusion of people with disabilities in leisure contexts by analyzing the fundamental tenets of these frameworks through the lens of Gray's question, "What does society need done and how can we do it?" Inclusion of individuals with disabilities in leisure contexts is a right they deserve. However, opportunity appears to be a barrier. We frame opportunity using the arguments Nussbaum[56] and Tollefsen[57] posed to suggest that people with disabilities have valuable and valid opportunities, opportunities that reflect a recognition of their rights, and opportunities that are framed in the construct of interdependence. This leads us to ask, "What do we need to do to increase opportunities? How do we accomplish this paradigm shift?"

The leisure and inclusive leisure literature has focused mainly on the more pragmatic aspects of services for people with disabilities, often coming up short with findings that explain why professionals or individuals with disabilities have not fully embraced the inclusion movement. The social justice literature has paved the way to examine leisure contexts from the perspective of opportunity. Specifically, having the (civil) right to access to leisure is not enough; one must also have opportunity. Tollefsen[58] and Nussbaum[59] contended that only active and interdependent engagement in society will lead to social justice for individuals with disabilities. Leisure inquiries can be conducted with this framework with an emphasis on valuable and valid opportunities, recognition of rights, and the promotion of interdependence. In this regard, Silva and Howe[60] argued the issue is not whether to offer separate or inclusive services for people with disabilities, but rather to focus on meeting the interests of the person. At the center of addressing the interests of the person should be the tenets of social and environmental justice, specifically, opportunities for individuals to be and do what they value. Thus, we suggest one way to shift the paradigm in the leisure literature and practice relative to people with disabilities is to focus not on the mode or pragmatic aspects of service delivery, but rather on the needs and interests of the person.

The intersection of social and environmental justice in leisure services may be informed using the capability approach. This approach provides a framework for examining theoretical underpinnings, assumptions, and past practices relative to inclusion in several ways. One is by evaluating our perception and meaning of function. According to the capability approach, functioning includes the range of life experiences an individual values for well-being.[61] These experiences include, but are not limited to, fundamental values such as safety and health, typical values such as gainful employment or sustained personal relationships, and extraordinary values such as completing a triathlon, playing a complicated piece of music, or contributing to one's community. The other component of the capability approach is the notion of capabilities. Robeyns[62] described this as a genuine opportunity for people to engage in and be a part of activities they value. Capability recognizes that for people with disabilities to be capable of living a fulfilling life, opportunities must be accessible and available so they can achieve the things they value.[63] Applying this approach provides the opportunity to better understand the social justice notion of receiving what one earns. As previously discussed, this component of social justice raises the awareness of attributing the absence of one's success or capability only to inferior aptitude, desire, or ability. Like capability, receiving what one earns is also intimately linked to opportunity. The underpinnings of social and environmental justice are equity, opportunity, and access.

Early in this chapter we discussed the idea that the individualized approach to addressing leisure constraints not only places the responsibility on people with disabilities to "fix" their barrier problems, but also may perpetuate a lack of inclusion of people with disabilities in other segments of community life. Although the individualistic approach is effective for addressing a person's illness, condition, or specific modification, it is not effective for addressing barriers related to social or environmental justice.[64] Placing the responsibility of addressing social or environmental justice on individuals with disabilities only negates the role communities and society play in creating inequities. This includes the leisure professional manifesting the notion of separate and not equal. The purpose of promoting the collective responsibility in addressing social and environmental justice in leisure is to foster dignity and well-being of all community members.[65] Leadership relative to social and environmental justice investigates and poses solutions for issues that generate and reproduce social inequities.[66] Applying these leadership and justice principles to the field of leisure requires the profession to take responsibility in addressing inequities of social and environmental justice in all leisure contexts. This can include training professionals to recognize and address social and environmental justice; adopting a philosophy of inclusion that places the responsibility of access to leisure with all, not just individuals with disabilities; respecting the individuality of each person; and approaching such accommodations with respect.[67]

Because people with disabilities make up the largest minority group in the United States,[68] leisure scholars need to examine inclusive leisure as one of many critical issues attendant to social and environmental justice. Our moral obligation is to include all individuals, regardless of race, gender, or ability level, in the social and environmental justice discourse. We challenge the profession to pay particular attention to the following questions:

- What has the park, recreation, and tourism profession done to promote social and environmental justice for persons with disabilities?

- Why is there a dearth of leisure scholarship focusing on social and environmental justice for people with disabilities?

- How can we better articulate, both theoretically and empirically, a rationale that supports the importance of leisure for the expansion of human capability and opportunity?

- What role, if any, should park, recreation, and tourism professionals play in making social and environmental justice a reality for every citizen across the planet?

- What particular changes should park, recreation, and tourism professionals make in professional practice that will contribute to social and environmental justice for people with disabilities?

Disability can be biological, physiological, social, or cultural. For people to participate fully in society, they should have the opportunity to exercise their repertoire of capabilities.[69] The park, recreation, and tourism profession cannot move toward social and environmental justice for all until it has successfully addressed these questions.

Discussion Questions

1. In *America as a Civilization*, historian Max Lerner suggested the most telling characteristic of American culture is its concern for *accessibility*. How do you think Mary Ann and Jennifer would react to Lerner's claim?

2. Do you think access to leisure opportunities should be viewed as a fundamental right for all citizens, regardless of ability level? Please elaborate.

3. Discuss the differences between the medical model's view of people with disabilities and the social model's view. What are implications for the way in which we think about and work with people with disabilities?

4. Discuss the rights of people with disabilities to be fully engaged in all aspects of life in the context of social and environmental justice. Do you see particular conflicts between the goals of social and environmental justice when it comes to making leisure opportunities accessible to all? Please elaborate.

5. Historically, moving people toward independent functioning has been viewed as a main goal of therapeutic recreation service. How does this goal fit with the idea that we are interdependent beings rather than independent beings? What are the implications for the goals of therapeutic recreation service?

4

Meeting at the Crossroads

*Progress for Multiracial People or Delicate Balance
Amid Old Divides?*

Nina Roberts
San Francisco State University

Human nature is at least as complex as its outside environment. When it comes to understanding multiracial and multiethnic identity, the gnawing question is, "Who are we, really?" Making sense of this should come with consideration of all forms of social and environmental justice, as one affects the other depending on how deep our understanding goes. How can we understand, accept, and respect our environment if we have not started that process within ourselves and our own colorful species?

The 2000 census spurred a fundamental change in how race is measured in America.[1] Ten years later, the 2010 census gave us more insight, and useful comparisons became possible. The 2010 census and other statistical documents[2,3] tell us that one in seven marriages is interracial and that a growing number of American families engage in cross-cultural adoptions. Blacks are three times more likely to marry Whites today than they were in 1980.[4] Our families are changing and the United States population is evolving into a cornucopia of diversity. Conventional wisdom concerning recreational opportunities and park/forest visitation is morphing into something entirely different. Old adages and expectations are a thing of the past. Yet, as is the case with all new and growing social changes, the multiracial and multiethnic experience in relation to parks, recreation, and tourism is a phenomenon we still do not know much about, and research in this area is sparse. The numbers cannot be ignored. Workplaces, social environments, and public spaces are now places where cultural and racial divides become narrower as people coexist and mingle to share in both human and nonhuman creations. Nonetheless, "racial boundaries are not going to disappear any time soon."[5]

Parks are spaces where environmental and social justice concerns meet at the crossroads and become one under the same sky. What will the new dynamics of interaction be like among a growing diversity of visitors? What will be the future experience of a multicultural workplace? Are we truly ready to break bread, sing, work, play, and study alongside others who no longer fit neatly into one box on government forms? To what truths must we be committed to build healthy multiracial, multiethnic, economically, and socially diverse communities?

Park, recreation, and tourism scholars have explored race relations and cultural diversity since the Outdoor Recreation Resources Review Commission work of the early 1960s.[6,7,8] However, there is a dearth of literature on multiracial populations. Scholars have looked at race relations through interracial interactions and contact,[9,10] yet this is only one perspective.

Other research has examined interracial couples.[11] However, even this line of inquiry does not acknowledge that biracial/multiracial children must become more visible if we are to embrace a culture of inclusion. Hibbler and Shinew[12] have written about enhancing multiracial families' leisure experiences, and community engagement across cultures has been on the rise, yet organizations continue to struggle with comprehending how to break down barriers that obstruct multiracial families' leisure experiences.[13]

In *"What Are You, Anyway?"* one of the key points Roberts conveyed about her personal and professional multiracial experience is that the social pressure to assimilate into dominant cultural ways of being is still intense.[14] Not "rocking the boat" is easy when we know we should for fear of being criticized, scorned, lectured, or even ostracized. So, Roberts posed two questions: How do we break the cycle and challenge the system, and how do we respect difference, challenge oppression and the status quo, and still be heard? This is an increasingly important topic for our scholarship, teaching, and service. As Root avowed, "Multiracial people blur the boundaries between races ... and [our] existence challenges the rigidity of racial lines ... Oppression always fragments people, as energy and attention are diverted from the experience of wholeness."[15] When we refuse to fragment ourselves or others, we become less fearful and learn to approach differences with respect. This respect gives us courage. We are not mixed up. We are simply mixed race.

Facing the Facts

Between the years 2000 and 2010, over 57% of the 27.3 million increase in the U.S. population was attributed to a rise in the Hispanic population, followed by Asians of various ethnic backgrounds, mostly due to "higher levels of immigration."[16] In the 2000 census, Whites made up 69% of the population, Latinos and African Americans 13%, and Asian Americans 4%.[17] By 2010, 50.5 million of the U.S. population was Hispanic. Although the White population is still considered the largest in the United States, it is also experiencing growth at the slowest rate. The same could be said of the Black population, which is trumped only by Whites when it comes to slow growth. The multiracial group is hard to classify, but "people reporting more than one race was another fast-growing population and made up large portions of the American Indian and Alaska Native population and Native Hawaiian and Other Pacific Islander population."[18] The South and West of the United States are home to the largest number of minorities.

Johnson[19] reiterated a 2007 U.S. Census Bureau statement that in the next half century, "the number of Latinos and Asian Americans in the United States will triple, while the White, non-Latino population will increase a mere 7%." In the coming decades, "White non-Latinos will make up only 50% of the population, with Latinos accounting for 24%, African Americans 15%, and Asian Americans 8%."[20] The increase in the Asian population in the United States between 2000 and 2050 is expected to rise over 200%, the Latino population will grow by 188%, and the African American population will grow by almost 75%. Whites, according to the 2010 census, will exhibit only a slight increase compared to other races. For the purposes of race classification, the U.S. Census Bureau considered the following to fall under "Some Other Race": multiracial, mixed, interracial, or a Hispanic or Latino group (e.g., Mexican, Puerto Rican, Cuban, or Spanish).[21] Over 9 million people reported themselves as belonging to more than one race in 2010, compared with 6.8 million in 2000. This means the proportion of people identifying themselves as belonging to two or more races has increased by approximately one third. Although the recorded number is not huge, it does make up 2.9% of the population and reflects a fast-growing portion of the population. What does that mean for our nation? How will leadership shift and resources be distributed differently?

In 2010, White and Black had the largest number of multiple-race combinations recorded. The most significant four groups in this context are White and Black (1.8 million), White and Some Other Race (1.7 million), White and Asian (1.6 million), and White and American Indian and Alaska Native (1.4 million).[22] This total number makes up just less than three quarters of the multiple-race population in this census. Moreover, 92% of people who self-identify as belonging to more than one race reported exactly two races, 8% reported three races, and less than 1% identified themselves as belonging to four or more races. In the case of Hispanics, the majority of multiple-race combinations included White, but "Some Other Race" also featured broadly in the individual reports. The general outcome of the 2010 census was that many counties across the United States experienced significant to substantial growth in their minority populations from 2000 to 2010.

Nearly 15% of all new marriages were between interracial couples in 2008, doubling from 1980.[23] Price[24] also stated 41% of all interracial marriages were between Hispanics and Whites. Ironically, suggestions have been made that by 2050 the United States will be "Whiter" as many of these couples' children (e.g., Hispanic–White and Asian–White) will probably identify as White.[25] Nevertheless, one thing is certain. What we are experiencing now is a break from the past as taboos fade and forbidding behaviors and attitudes slowly change. Some still oppose racial mixing, but the majority, especially young people aged 18 to 32, have expressed approval.[26] Yet some prejudices remain. For instance, a 2009 Pew Research survey found that "acceptance of out-marriage to Whites (81%) is somewhat higher than is acceptance of out-marriage to Asians (75%), Hispanics (73%) or Blacks (66%)." The survey also showed that "Black respondents are somewhat more accepting of all forms of intermarriage than are White or Hispanic respondents."[27] Gaps exist in acceptance patterns, which have narrowed in the last 10 years; yet, since 2001, "Whites have grown somewhat more accepting of interracial marriage and Blacks somewhat less."[28] As Kennedy noted, "Malignant racial biases can and do reside in interracial liaisons. But against the tragic backdrop of American history, the flowering of multiracial intimacy is a profoundly moving and encouraging development."[29]

Biracial and Multiracial Identity Development: Fluid or Constant?

As a multiracial woman, I cannot separate my identities one from another. I do not stop being any one of my identities because it is convenient for someone else. It is essential for professionals in parks, recreation, and tourism to think about the different ways our identities interact with one another if we are to do a better job of serving mixed-race people in our programs.

Multiracial population has acquired several definitions in scholarly research, and these multiple indicators stem from how people identify themselves, how they are identified by others, how their ancestors were identified, and combinations of these criteria.[30, 31, 32, 33, 34, 35, 36, 37, 38] This shift in perception has produced divergent estimates in racial classification schemes, which have the potential of hindering true understanding of the growing multiracial population. Similarly, this creates fluidity, which tampers with our understanding of single-race populations.[39] Harris and Sim,[40] for example, found race is not merely a social construct but also fluid. When statistics depend largely on self-reports, inconsistencies arise. Results have shown that to comprehend racial fluidity patterns, the following two factors are crucial: (1) Patterns of racial classification have been tangibly and vastly influenced by kaleidoscopic racial regimes. For instance, in the current age, diversity is seen as a value to be touted, and the validity of multiracial identity is stressed.[41, 42, 43] Our self-perception, in addition to how others perceive us, has an impact on race and multiraciality viewpoints. Thus, sometimes there is a mismatch between the race of a parent and that of a child, depending on the circumstances and the individual's mind-set. When questioned alone, a youth might be more forthcoming about race than when parents are present. In the case of census race data, more often than not the completed form "reflects the beliefs of the household member who completes the census form."[44] (2) Patterns of racial classification are varied because "multiracial groups comprise socially distinct mono-racial groups."[45] The most sizable but least committed multiracial group turned out to be White–American Indian youth in Harris and Sim's[46] study. This identity is often expressed by Whites who have little ancestral, phonotypical, or cultural connection to American Indians, but who nevertheless wish to appeal to popular norms of multiculturalism by presenting a diverse portrait of themselves.[47, 48, 49, 50] In the case of White–Black youth, the one-drop rule on racial self-identification prevails, and for White–Asian youth, racial identification is optional and strong social rules are lacking.

Cases exist where multiracial people—"particularly those who are part black—shun a 'multi' label in favor of identifying as a single race."[51] Certain estimates have shown that "two-thirds of those who checked the single box of 'black' on the census form are actually mixed, including President Barack Obama, who identified himself as black in the 2010 census, even though his mother was white."[52] Harris and Sim[53] recognized the need for further study on race fluidity, particularly on how this is affected by factors such as age, time period, and environment. Their general assumption is that the stronger the attention given to multiraciality, the more flexible and fluid racial identity will be among all cohorts, especially in the case of adolescents, because identities are generally less stable within this age group,[54, 55] adulthood affords greater stability, and older generations grew up in stricter racial environments and regimes.

Yet, the 2010 census clearly shows that Harris and Sim[56] are correct only to a certain extent because the rate of individual identification with multiple racial groups has increased. In a growing number of cases, the person who filled out the 2010 census form in the multiracial household was clearly of a less restrictive mind-set. This perhaps, more than anything else, sheds light on how the census captures race like the snap of a picture. It gives a representation of things at one point in time, with certain people, within a certain situation, context, and purpose.[57] The available data on race may not match the ideal data, and if more precise racial measurement tools are not used, racial diversity in the United States will continue to be misunderstood.

How Do We Ensure Justice for Multicultural Families?

The psychological and sociological problems multiracial individuals face, more than anything else, are due to race relations in America and how "society's preoccupation with race" affects their state of being.[58] This in turn affects the leisure patterns of interracial couples. The literature has demonstrated, for example, that people of different cultures and races also have different leisure patterns.[59] Hibbler and Shinew's study focused mainly on distinctions between African and European Americans. They concluded that despite the headway made in research relating to leisure patterns of different races, little has been done to explore what they refer to as the "other," namely, the leisure patterns of multiracial families and biracial/multiracial individuals.

In their study, Hibbler and Shinew learned many multiracial families experience a feeling of isolation when it comes to work, family, and leisure. In the latter context, they have had negative experiences of discrimination and racism that impacted their perception of and desire to engage in outdoor recreation. The authors recognized the need for multiracial families to engage in positive leisure activities that fulfill their distinct needs, as well as other basic expectations and needs they share with all other individuals and families. With the rise in multiracial families, there is no doubt that parks and other outdoor recreation areas will be increasingly frequented by a blend of cultures whose needs must be met.

Leisure activities are important because they enhance the quality of life and life satisfaction.[60] From past studies, we know leisure experiences provide interracial couples with a sense of joy, satisfaction, and happiness. These feelings are expressed as "companionship, integration, rest and relaxation, family relationships, etc."[61] Leisure activities are chosen by people to sustain or improve their lives, but an interesting question to consider is, "Do interracial couples and multiracial families have to adjust their attitudes and behavior to fit into a particular Black or White model of leisure behavior?" Stated differently, how do leisure choices for interracial couples or multiracial families imply or bring about a racial identity shift? Perhaps the harshest product of an interracial relationship is the social isolation that often results from negative societal reactions to the relationship.[62] Park, recreation, and tourism professionals have their work cut out for them when it comes to a discussion of how best to address the needs of interracial couples and multiracial families in a satisfactory way.

Leisure participation among ethnic minority groups continues to be discussed in a growing body of literature touching on experiences of people of color in parks. A main goal over the last several decades has been to understand the constraints and barriers that some underrepresented minorities experience when they visit outdoor recreational areas.[63, 64, 65, 66, 67] Federal agencies such as the National Park Service and national nonprofit organizations including the National Parks and Conservation Association are forthcoming in the implementation of programs aimed at encouraging minority use of parks, as well as environmental advocacy and stewardship. At the same time, studies have also shed light on the subtle racism that is to blame for feelings of isolation and exclusion in parks.[68, 69] One way to counter this is to encourage more aggressive hiring of a new generation of outdoor leaders and park managers with biracial and multiracial backgrounds. This would require extensive organization and preparation and would entail a shift in agency culture and general way of thinking vis-à-vis the community. By hiring a diverse workforce and encouraging full participation of employees, the organization would be affected in positive and worthy ways.[70] If the demographic changes are recognized but not reflected in the workforce, an organization cannot question poor feedback and performance prompted by its lack of commitment to diversity. Such commitment, in fact, can be instrumental[71] to the nurturing of a socially and environmentally just world.[72]

The way to achieve success in the future is to transcend the limitations of tradition. Organizations and individuals must find new ways to tap into shared beliefs and to create better working, living, and recreational environments. It is certainly possible and desirable to engage more diverse communities in initiating these changes. Moreover, park, recreation, and tourism professionals should be called upon to implement these measures with enthusiasm and determination so that access, opportunities, and information are provided to all, thereby creating a more sustainable future for all.[73]

As our nation grows more diverse, the need to reach out to all segments of society becomes more pronounced.[74] However, the first item on the agenda is for leisure professionals to establish trust and good communication with the communities they wish to serve.[75] The conservation of resources must be strongly connected to recreational programs devised and offered to diverse constituents. Effective and adaptable communication that is culturally relevant is crucial,[76, 77] and relationship building is imperative.[78] The community should always be involved, and the citizenry must understand resources are at their disposal. How can people come to a cross-cultural understanding if there is no attempt made at building rapport? How can differences be celebrated and respected if the community does not express its expectations? Awareness on all fronts lends itself to transparency in intentions, and then those intentions become a real commitment, which ultimately solidifies trust. This is how progress is made over time.

Recommendations for Continued Progress

Hibbler and Shinew[79] provided several practical recommendations for creating connections with biracial and multiracial families and facilitating their leisure activities in parks and outdoor recreational areas. These include the following:

1. Implement a diversity management system at the agency policy level, which fosters respect of individual and group differences and values equality of people and cultures. With a top-down approach such as this, park attendees will be guaranteed a comfortable recreational experience. Several institutions can assist in the creation of a diversity management system, including relevant university faculty who may be involved. This said, one element here cannot be discounted: the safety of interracial couples and their families. Park administrators, through such a diversity management system, need to ensure no physical or emotional harm or threats are experienced.

2. Develop new and improved programs that cater to the needs of a wider range of multiracial families and biracial individuals. Although our views have expanded in recent years in relation to single-parent and same-race blended families, a feeling of exclusion in some environments still exists when it comes to less traditional families, such as same-sex couples and families, and multiracial families. One of the expressed needs of multiracial families is "improved family relationships and cultural understanding."[80] Marketing efforts should include a broader definition of a family. Moreover, the depiction of multiracial families on printed materials such as brochures could foster feelings of inclusion. Multiracial families want to understand themselves and learn about all aspects of their heritage, as well as have others view them with an open mind and heart. Innovative marketing strategies, more competent staff, and culture-centric educational programs, as well as further involvement of local leaders in the community would enable better access to this shared resource and allow community members to preserve national treasures.[81, 82] When people know they are valued and accepted within a holistic and inclusionary model created for their benefit, their comfort level is heightened when visiting parks and participating in other leisure experiences, and they feel encouraged to champion the protection of shared green spaces.

3. Practitioners should employ current theory in their work, and a line of communication should be open between practitioners and academicians. If both are aware of the others' needs and knowledge, and if information is shared in an accurate and timely manner, this would enhance policy formation and ensure that more effective services will be delivered to the evolving multiracial population of America. Harris and Sim characterized the challenge:

    …Analysts must think critically about what they mean by race, design surveys that more precisely measure race, and be aware of the implications of mismatches between available and ideal racial data. Failing to do so will ensure that as the racial diversity of the United States grows, so too will our inability to understand that diversity.[83]

To carry out these recommendations successfully, park managers and policy makers must open their minds and look beyond stereotypes. Cultural competency is not just an academic notion. To be culturally competent is a way of life. In talking about the national parks, Gwaltney said,

Cultural competence represents the willingness and ability of the national park system to value the importance of culture in the delivery of services to all segments of the population. It is the use of a systems perspective which values differences and is responsive to diversity at all levels of an organization (i.e., policy, governance, administrative, workforce, provider, and consumer/client).[84]

Cultural competence is about constant improvement and learning. According to Gorski,[85] a culturally competent person rejects deficit ideology and understands the problems many minorities face in disenfranchised communities are a symptom of contrary educational and social conditions. Such a person would spread his wealth of knowledge by teaching about sensitive multicultural issues, including racism, sexism, poverty, and heterosexism. There are dangers in being clueless or ignorant. The reality is harsh; although social policies and institutional practices remain in place for the benefit of only a few, and although resources, power, and wealth are disproportionately channeled, there will never be true equality.[86]

Conclusion

It is stunning to think that as much as one third of the U.S. population is composed of racial and ethnic minorities. Biracial people have existed for centuries, yet they have largely been rendered invisible until the 20th century. Increases in interracial marriages mean that more multiracial families are being created, and these families may have unique leisure needs.[87] It is also widely understood that access to parks and open space affords a type of leisure that can be extremely beneficial to individuals on many levels.[88] Yet, barriers to participation for multiracial people continue to exist in the form of social isolation, inadequate facilities, and subtle discrimination. Managers must consider these groups in the planning process and encourage research that provides a deeper understanding of outdoor recreation patterns and preferences of mixed-race people.[89] This knowledge is crucial for both enhancing the mechanisms of social and environmental justice and encouraging the citizenry to be good stewards of the natural world.

All people, regardless of race, should have the right to experience the benefits afforded by green spaces, and protecting this right is the responsibility of park, recreation, and tourism professionals.[90] The more inclusive we are, the bigger the contribution we will make to achieve social and environmental justice through the work we do.[91] The way to make things better is through the continuing education of the citizenry we serve. As long as labels such as *underrepresented* or *underserved* are in existence, social and environmental justice remain elusive ideals.

Discussion Questions

1. Nina discusses how rapidly changing demographics can alter the kinds of leisure activities citizens may be interested in pursuing. What examples can you give of new or different leisure activities that relate to demographic changes?

2. Nina also points out how rapidly changing demographics can lead to personal and social stressors for those in interracial marriages, blended families, and other nontraditional domestic arrangements. How might these transitions present challenges to traditional leisure programming? How would you address them?

3. If social and environmental injustices imply power differentials between the dominant culture and new and emerging cultures, what might be the social and environmental justice implications for a future when today's minorities become tomorrow's majorities?

4. When it comes to checking boxes on government forms, how do you see yourself? Do you fit into one box, or do you have trouble fitting into any of the boxes? How does this kind of categorization feel to you?

5. In general, do you see the increasingly diverse social, cultural, racial, and ethnic diversity of the U.S. citizenry as a good or bad thing? What particular challenges or opportunities do you envision regarding achieving social and environmental justice in an increasingly diverse society?

5

Ecofeminism(s) and Just Leisure in the 21st Century

Karla Henderson
North Carolina State University

I have considered myself a feminist ever since I was told as an 8-year-old that girls could not play Little League baseball. However, I did not realize that a feminist critique could be made of leisure until after I completed my PhD in 1979. In my first year as a faculty member at the University of Wisconsin-Madison, a group of graduate students approached me about teaching a seminar on "women and leisure." I told them I did not know of any literature within the leisure field that addressed women specifically. They told me this dearth of thinking was precisely the problem. Several of these young women were aware of the growing body of research in women's studies and suggested that we could explore the leisure literature alongside women's studies perspectives. That approach had never occurred to me, but I was willing to develop the seminar. As they say, the rest is history. That seminar put me on a path toward exploring leisure, women, gender, and feminism for the next 35 years.

The initial seminar experience exposed me to many ways of thinking about feminism and to women I did not know existed. I had identified myself as a liberal feminist with a focus on equal rights for women. However, I quickly learned feminism had many dimensions beyond liberalism. For example, Firestone articulated man's domination of women was the most fundamental form of oppression and pervaded all aspects of life.[1] Daly called for a world based on a model supplanting patriarchy.[2] I found the discussions fascinating.

I also learned about ecofeminism. Unlike other forms of feminism, ecofeminists emphasized how the domination of women and the domination of nature were integrally connected. Although studying the outdoors was not my area of academic expertise, I had always found the outdoors to be central to my personal leisure pursuits. Therefore, I was intrigued by examining the parallels between "how an understanding of human liberation (feminism) and concern for the interdependence and relationships between human and nonhumans (ecology) can provide a personal philosophy...."[3] In some of my writing, I tried to make connections between ecofeminism and professional practice,[4,5] but I found ecofeminism was most useful as an intriguing and interesting foundational philosophy. Because the applications of ecofeminism for social change seemed somewhat limited and because feminism was expanding its scope, I looked for other ways to link leisure and recreation with ethical and fair behavior.

My thinking moved toward recognizing gender was not the only form of social oppression and to addressing the variety of oppression I understood. I wrote about *just recreation* and *just leisure.*[6,7] *Just leisure* emphasized moving beyond equality (i.e., sameness) to connoting equity (i.e., fairness) and doing what is right. This idea focused on both social and environmental justice from varying perspectives but did not necessarily integrate them.

When the call for proposals came for the 1st International Symposium on Speaking Up and Speaking Out: Working for Social and Environmental Justice Through Parks, Recreation, Tourism, and Leisure, I wanted to be a part of this critical discussion. When considering "spaces and places integral to instituting a more just world" as offered in the call for papers, I immediately thought of discussions of ecofeminism as a means for exploring the integration of social and environmental justice. As I had not delved into literature about ecofeminism for several years, I was eager to see what new ways of thinking had developed and how that thinking might relate to aspects of justice and leisure. I also had concerns that sometimes women become lost in discussing all types of oppression, and I wanted to keep women in the discussion. Therefore, the initial focus of this chapter was to examine in greater depth how scholars focused on *just leisure* might consider dimensions of ecofeminism, which seemed to me to clearly link social and environmental justice. After attending the symposium and hearing the discussions, I revised the chapter to offer personal perspectives and reflections on broader aspects of justice, which emerged for me at the symposium.

Ecofeminism Described

Ecofeminism and ecofeminist ideas have contributed to social and environmental thinking. Ecofeminism is one of a number of ecophilosophies that describes beliefs about the environment, and, some radical ecophilosophers would even add, the survival of humans on the planet. A discussion of ecofeminism can make the connections between humans and nature visible in relation to an area such as leisure.[8] An ecophilosophy that incorporates ecofeminism also can be one way to evoke critical theory about leisure and recreation and the impacts on social and physical environments.

Ecofeminism represents philosophical, theoretical, critical, spiritual, and practical efforts to address the interrelated dominations of women and nature.[9] The primary discourse is the premise that the oppression/domination of women is connected to/with the oppression/domination of the earth.[10, 11, 12] More recently, ecofeminism perspectives have been based on linking objects of oppression to an analysis of the structure and functioning of oppression itself.[13, 14] For example, women, people of color, people living in poverty, and aspects of nature are linked to systems of oppression (i.e., sexism, racism, classism, and speciesism or environmental destruction). Although by its earliest definitions ecofeminism connected women and nature, the philosophy has come to represent the intersectionality of gender, race, class, and nature. Ecofeminists today would suggest this intersectionality must be theorized.

Ecofeminism grew from a concern that feminism was inadequate in describing solutions to ecological problems[15, 16] and that environmentalists hardly ever acknowledged women and feminism in their discussions.[17] Buckingham suggested some change, although not much has occurred in discussions about gender inequality and environmental sustainability since the term *ecofeminism* was originally introduced in the mid-1970s.[18] For example, the World Bank today considers women in its agenda not out of political correctness or kindness but because evidence suggests when women and men are relatively equal, economies tend to grow with consideration given to environmental sustainability.

The value of ecofeminist beliefs is that they go beyond liberal feminist issues of equality toward integrity and dignity related to human and environmental concerns. No one form of ecofeminism exists, but all views share a common commitment to making visible the ways that patriarchy dominates women/disadvantaged groups and nature. Patriarchy is a way of thinking related to dualisms, for example, opposites such as male or female and nature or culture. It emphasizes the superior male qualities of reason and analysis (i.e., women are treated as inferior to men, nature is treated as inferior to culture).[19] Patriarchy also has roots in the possession of women, animals, and land, which are symbolically and socially linked.[20] However, not all eco-feminists agree men are not the enemy. Most men also are the victims of dualism and patriar-chal thinking, which has implications for the quality of life of all species.

Ecofeminists embody their beliefs by developing practices aimed at ending the exploitation of women and of nature. Vance argued the rationalist policy of controlling nature is the same one used to control women (and others). She contended wilderness protection is a patriarchal way of thinking and is part of the overall scheme of domination.[21] From another perspective, Marris claimed humans have taken over the earth and cannot undo this situation. Therefore, running it consciously and effectively means admitting and embracing the role.[22] The question Marris did not address and Vance also raised relates to who has the power to manage the earth and what is the best way to manage it. Ecofeminists would suggest as long as patriarchy is the dominant system, management practices must be carefully scrutinized.

Ecofeminists propose all acts should focus on respect for and the diversity of human beings and the life enhancement of natural environments. Some ecofeminists embody their beliefs through spirituality that unites women and the earth with the underlying belief that women have more connection to the earth than men. Many religions emphasize how humans should have dominion over nature, whereas ecofeminist spirituality emphasizes the interdependency of life. Some ecofeminists also argue practices such as veganism are a necessary component of ecofeminist ethics.

Regardless of whether ecofeminisms are viewed from philosophical, political, and/or spiri-tual perspectives, they can help us understand what people do, why they do it, and ways that ideas about ecofeminism might contribute overall to ending the oppression of people within nature. These philosophies can provide a means for academic multidisciplinary refocusing of how something such as leisure must be aligned with ecological, political, and social movements to promote and facilitate justice.[23]

Just Leisure

The meanings of justice, social justice, environmental justice, economic justice, and eco-justice, as well as attributes of distributive and procedural justice, were discussed at the sym-posium. Relationships among these terms were also discussed. Whether these words require differentiation may not be important in my way of thinking. All seem to hold justice as the basis for action. Furthermore, although not all presentations at the symposium focused on parks, recreation, tourism, and leisure, the people who came together for the most part held up these application areas as important. I believe, regardless of the adjective used, justice is the focus. Furthermore, I believe leisure and recreation have the potential to contribute to justice, but without intentional effort they can also contribute to injustice. Rather than overanalyze whether social and environmental justice are two sides of the same coin or whether they are so interde-pendent that they cannot be separated, I chose to focus on the idea of just leisure.

Just leisure or just recreation has roots in the notion of justice.[24, 25] My definition of justice refers to fairness and doing what is right. Social justice includes a vision of society where the distribution of resources is equitable and all members are physically and psychologically safe and secure. In such a society, individuals are both self-determining and interdependent. So-cial justice involves a sense of social responsibility toward and with others and for society as a whole.[26] Social justice implies opportunities and behaviors where people believe they make a difference in the world. Social justice, like ecofeminism, focuses on the disparity of power that exists historically and must be transformed to ensure fairness.

Just leisure also has implications for environmental justice related to social disparities that occur in spaces and places. Taylor, Floyd, Whitt-Glover, and Brooks described how the first wave of the environmental justice movement focused on the fair treatment and meaningful involvement of people relative to environmental laws, regulations, and policies.[27] Taylor et al. suggested the second wave of environmental justice is dedicated to urban design, public health, and access to and quality of opportunities such as outdoor recreation. This wave relates to how social and environmental justice must be considered together and also the ways ecofeminism might relate to just leisure. Environmental justice is directly tied to social justice.

Recreation management and programming are usually considered deliberate acts designed to bring about positive outcomes for individuals and communities. If equity is to occur, recreation opportunities and leisure experiences should be intentionally framed within social philosophy and environmental ethics. Matters cannot be left to fate.[28] Just leisure can be demonstrated by commitments to the protection, growth, health, and well-being of people as well as of natural and physical environments, just as ecofeminism also espouses. Radical approaches such as ecofeminism allow individuals and communities to go from interests to choices, from paternalism to self-determination, and from invisibility to visibility.[29]

Just leisure as well as ecofeminist perspectives cannot occur without acknowledging the power of privilege and diversity among people. Just leisure requires gender, race, class, and ability inclusivity rather than neutrality as important parts of any environmental or outdoor consciousness.[30] Arguing that no differences among people (i.e., gender, race, class) exist denies actual differences in power and resources among groups such as men, women, humans, and species that cannot speak for themselves.[31] Affirming the similarity between groups (e.g., men and women) may inadvertently universalize or validate norms of the dominant social group. These norms often have not addressed diverse interests, experiences, and perspectives related to leisure activities and environmental protection.

The goals of just leisure and ecofeminism are similar. The changing discourse about ecofeminisms has the potential to move these ideas closer together. As useful as ecofeminism has been for thinkers in past decades to identify global feminist and environmental issues, it is not without critiques.

Critiques of Ecofeminism

I have had skepticism for a number of years about the applications of ecofeminism, and this doubt largely explains why my thinking moved toward discussions of just leisure in recent years. As noted earlier, part of my interest in writing a chapter about ecofeminism was to delve back into the literature to see if my uncertainty had been addressed in the 21st century. Identifying the criticisms of ecofeminism has been constructive to me in elaborating the relationship to just leisure as well as in describing some of the applications, or lack thereof, of this ecophilosophy. Critiques of ecofeminism have largely centered on concerns about idealism, essentialism, and scapegoating of men.

A common critique of ecofeminism has been that it is too idealistic and mystical. I argue, however, that idealism is not negative as it provides a basis for articulating desirable goals. An earlier critique of ecofeminism was that classism, racism, and colonialism also had led to environmental destruction and not just sexism. However, more recent interpretations of ecofeminisms indicate the need to address intersectionality.[32, 33] Though my colleagues and I provided applications of ecofeminism in earlier writings,[34, 35, 36] I found that idealism continues to make concrete applications difficult. Critics also question the proposition that a nonsexist society would imply an ecologically benign society. As noted earlier, just adding women to the mix and continuing business as usual in the same unjust way will not result in a just society.

The major critique about ecofeminism has related to its essentialism. Essentialism suggests, in this case, all women have the same nature and differences between women and men are biological and distinct.[37] The premise of ecofeminism has typically been the dualities suggested in the subject–object and male–female propositions put forth by ecofeminists.[38] Essentialism also suggests women and girls are inherently and naturally closer to the earth. One example often used is that the menstrual cycles of women coincide with the moon suggesting closeness of body and natural rhythms just because an individual is female. Not all women, however, experience closeness to nature. Furthermore, a reinforcement of the idea that biology is destiny has been debunked. Normative femininity also may be disempowering for women because it defines particular stereotypical behaviors.[39] Seager confronted the assumptions regarding the "earth as mother."[40] The earth as mother as a sacred and honored female life force is a powerful icon. However, according to Seager, "The complex, emotion-laden, conflict-laden, quasi-sexualized, quasi-dependent mother relationship … is not an effective metaphor for environmental action."[41] If the earth is mother, then people might be regarded as children with less responsibility for being accountable. It is not women's role to clean up after what others, mostly men, have done. MacGregor also argued the aspects of care associated with women may obscure their political potential.[42] For example, motherhood associated with caring is important, but it is not enough to create social change. Furthermore, as governments have abdicated responsibilities for public good (e.g., health care, air pollution), responsibilities have been downloaded to individuals and families, which results in women becoming more responsible for caring roles without any political power. Women cannot change society alone.

A related critique is that ecofeminists sometimes are criticized for scapegoating men. Ecofeminisms are targeted at injustices created by patriarchy. Men have made up the patriarchy, but many men are just as powerless as women. Men share characteristics of race, income, and ability just as women do. Although some men may be complicit in injustices against women and nature, many men are also disenfranchised. Many men lead humble lives and do not necessarily have more power than women.[43] Nevertheless, institutional power creates a form of cultural masculinity that privileges many men, but not all. Therefore, men must be partners with women in addressing these social and environmental (in)justice issues. Patriarchy is the problem, not all individual men. Allowing women to have more equality in policy making without having men also take on a role of caring will not address the basic pattern of patriarchal exploitation or help to promote just leisure.[44]

Reflecting on Just Leisure

After examining the limited literature about ecofeminism, I continue to be somewhat disappointed in not having better road maps for using ecofeminism to address social change. The application of ecofeminism specifically to recreation-related fields (i.e., parks, recreation, tourism, sport, and leisure) has received little attention. However, the premises of social, environmental, and economic justice have not been absent even if ecofeminism or just leisure has not been widely discussed.

Before offering ways to incorporate ecofeminism further, I will reflect on my personal perspective regarding justice. My thoughts center on historical perspectives, the role of recreation and leisure, and the dearth of applications. Many of the discussions during the symposium and in this book are not new to the field of parks, recreation, tourism, and leisure. The implications of justice have been evident since I began my exploration of leisure and recreation in the mid-1970s. Different words have often been used, but I believe the notion of justice has been omnipresent. For example, the first introductory text to leisure I read was by Jim Murphy.[45] I was inspired by his argument that parks and recreation had to have a social consciousness related to civil rights. Although I know I am biased, the work that my colleagues and I have done over the years related to women's leisure has had at its roots a foundation of justice.[46, 47] Furthermore, in 1991, the Society of Park and Recreation Educators Teaching Institute focused on "Teaching for Social Responsibility." Even though the terminology of social and environmental justice has come into our field as the 21st century has unfolded, the idea has been central to much of our teaching for decades. I would contend this topic is not new, but unfortunately the problems have not been solved.

The idea that justice is not new to the field raises another concern related to the role of parks and recreation. Academics as well as practitioners have not articulated how social and environmental justice is a core concern. I strongly believe parks, recreation, tourism, and leisure services have a central role to play in promoting justice. Professional practices are not inherently just, but the potential for doing good through recreation and leisure must be consistently examined. Though social and environmental justice are not the purview of recreation-related fields only, I question how our efforts can make a difference unless we have a target for social change such as leisure or recreation services. I believe recreation and leisure are important, and as academics exploring these topics, we must not abdicate our responsibility to elevate the potential of leisure and recreation.

Identifying problems is a relatively easy first step. By nature, researchers and academics are good at identifying problems. Solving them is another matter. A frustration I have with the field currently is the lack of practical recommendations. Identifying solutions requires more effort. If academics do not move toward social action, 40 years from now those who follow after us will continue to believe that justice, or whatever term is used then, is a new idea. Maybe the role of academics is primarily to analyze problems, but I believe we should also be part of solutions, whether providing a body of knowledge as a foundation for action or working in partnership with colleagues in other disciplines and human services to use information to create social change. Not every academic needs to be a community activist, but perhaps we should be academic activists with thoughts always centering on the possible applications of our work. These thoughts about roles in addressing just leisure led me to think about the value of ecofeminisms in addressing social change.

Incorporating Ecofeminisms

My discomfort with ecofeminism many years ago related to reflections concerning application. A philosophy such as ecofeminism was useful in articulating problems and dilemmas but was weak in addressing tangible solutions. Although ecofeminist perspectives have moved to some extent beyond the essentialism of womanhood, broader frameworks such as just leisure seem to be more fruitful. Nevertheless, the challenge to anyone concerned with social and environmental action is to identify potential applications. Ecofeminisms can provide opportunities to link social and environmental justice, use language, identify injustices associated with recreation management, and identify opportunities for women and men as well as other groups to work together. I hope the suggestions that follow will offer potential for moving the field and society closer to justice:

1. Using ecofeminist perspectives to create social change through just leisure provides one way to link human and environmental worlds. Social justice must be connected to the environment as all social life is dependent on the environment. Assessing leisure and recreation from the standpoint of what they mean to women and nature, as well as questioning power relationships, is a means for establishing respect for ourselves, for others, and for living and nonliving entities that have no voice.[48] These applications might relate to recreation activities undertaken as well as to the management of natural areas for leisure purposes.

2. Ecofeminism can give recreation professionals a way to examine language. For example, phrases such as *rape the land, tame nature,* and *reap nature's bounty* may imply an unconscious disrespect for women. The term *Mother Nature* and the pronoun *she* may connote that ecological sustainability is only the responsibility of women who, socially, may have little power. Ecofeminists see how important language is to the way problems are identified as well as to how they are addressed.

3. Humberstone suggested using ecofeminism to examine philosophies and ideologies embedded in organizations that make any leisure in the outdoors a possibility.[49] As a recreation resource, human recreation needs should be considered in light of the sustainability of the natural world.[50] For example, perhaps some sports (e.g., golf or downhill skiing) should be acknowledged as potentially creating ecological destruction and managed to prevent those consequences.

4. The influence of organizational policies on women and nature is needed beyond integrating women into business as usual. Buckingham[51] emphasized that more than simply adding women will be needed for a just society. Women, along with men, can fundamentally reorient the mainstream to focus on quality of life issues and not on economic growth alone. Structures in recreation organizations could be changed to move away from a hegemonic hierarchical system. Applying ecofeminism in recreation-related organizations could result in shared power as well as in finding power within rather than power over people and nature.

5. Vance applied a compelling argument from an ecofeminist perspective regarding wilderness management.[52] The notion of wilderness suggests that only a privileged few get to experience it. Furthermore, other forms of the outdoors aside from wilderness are presumed inferior. She argued further, similar to Marris,[53] that hypocrisy exists in idealizing wilderness as pure nature. A wilderness experience requires a leave no trace ethic, yet humans enter with all their high-tech gear. They appear physically alien to wilderness but have the notion that human (i.e., primarily patriarchal) ingenuity can overcome all challenges. Marris argued wilderness should not include the absence of humans, but that it should include a healthy, complete, functioning ecosystem that includes humans, both women and men. Furthermore, wilderness is governed by a bureaucracy of backcountry rangers, biologists, hydrologists, fire management, and recreation planners. According to Vance, ecofeminists may agree that managing for solitude and isolation, physical challenge, opportunities for unmediated contact with spirituality, re-creation of pioneer experiences, and appreciation for aesthetics of nature is important. But these values appear to come from patriarchal views of the world. In many ways, they suggest that male experiences should be the standard for all activities and that females are invisible. For example, the appeal to physical challenge and risk is for people for whom mobility is a given and who do not face danger as always at hand (e.g., living in crime-infested neighborhoods). Ultimately, Vance concluded the focus on wilderness distracts people from bigger issues of domination that intrude in all things whether between humans and non-humans or among humans related to any type of environment. Managers might also want to consider this ecofeminist critique and assess its implications so they do not continue to reproduce inequality.

6. The potential for ecofeminism lies with how men must also be instrumental in addressing the nature and culture nexus. Working together is essential. Women's characteristics can be

metaphorically and socially imposed, but the value of ecofeminism may lie in how men see that they have as much potential as women to adopt a deeper environmental awareness and a concern for human dignity and integrity. Women need more power in decision making, but men must also share in the caring roles typically associated with women. Ecofeminism demands a critique of nature and culture and suggests traditional female qualities such as being cooperative, nurturing, supportive, nonviolent, and sensual are necessary for an environmentally aware society. These qualities should be available to everyone and not just women.

Summary

People interpret ecofeminism in different ways. However, the basic premise is that the domination of women and the domination of nature are integrally connected and interdependent. The natural and built environments where people work, live, and play remain gendered. Therefore, ecofeminism can contribute to discussions about just leisure for everyone. Ecofeminists would argue that social and environmental justices are not opposite sides of the same coin, but are interdependent on the face of all justice efforts and are necessary for just leisure. Discussions and debates must occur at practical and theoretical levels to synthesize ecological approaches and to be sensitive to a plurality of voices, identities, and practices.[54]   ·

Ecofeminism represents a movement for social change arising from the struggles of people to sustain themselves, their families, and their communities in the face of environmental degradation. The idea is not just to change who holds power but to transform the structure of power as typically wielded by patriarchy. An analysis based on ecofeminisms and just leisure may help to change attitudes, raise consciousness, and promote societal and organizational change.

Discussion Questions

1. As Karla points out, in a patriarchal society, ecofeminists think a parallel exists between the domination of women and the domination of nature. Do you agree with this line of thought? Why or why not? What is the evidence?

2. Much of what Karla has to say is about power and oppression and the need to critically examine who holds power and who is oppressed by it. Based on your experience, who holds power in our society and who is oppressed by it? Can this power differential be changed for the better? How?

3. What insight(s) might ecofeminist thinking offer us in connecting social and environmental justice?

4. What does Karla mean by "just leisure"? Does leisure have a special role to play in modeling social and environmental justice? Please elaborate.

5. What does Karla have to say about males in this chapter? What, in particular, is their responsibility regarding social and environmental justice from an ecofeminist perspective?

SYNTHESIS

Living With Our Imperfections

A Personal Reflection on Justice, Accountability, and Social Change

Jada Lindblom
University of Utah

Early on a Friday morning in mid-May, I joined a conference room full of professors and graduate students who had gathered to delve into the tricky territory of justice. The night before, we had listened to an inspiring opening address and enjoyed a meet and greet—some familiar faces, many new—over strong Salt Lake City microbrews. (Yes, they really do exist.) By Friday, most introductions had been made, and now was the time to commit not only our minds but also our future intentions to confronting the realities of injustices that exist within parks, recreation, tourism, and leisure.

Justice as a concept and as a societal goal can be overwhelming. "If you don't believe in justice, what do you believe in?" was a question that came my way about a year ago while shooting sporting clays (a large stride outside of my comfort zone), from the southern drawl of a charismatic, cowboyish, and very successful personal injury lawyer. I was stumped. Justice is the ultimate concern; its power over people is infinite and undeniable. Its applications are limitless as well. Parks, recreation, tourism, and leisure, although often associated with seemingly carefree adjectives such as *enjoyable*, *healthy*, and *relaxing*, are no exceptions to this rule. Professionals and academics in these fields have all seen how well-intentioned programs, activities, and pursuits are liable to the damage of social and environmental injustices. This is why we had all gathered at the University of Utah for 3 days of deep discussion and analysis.

My interest in this topic is twofold. As a master's student of Parks, Recreation, and Tourism, I constantly draw upon my undergraduate major in Environmental Studies and past work experience as an environmental educator and outdoor guide to examine the implications of our actions and practices in tourism and outdoor recreation management. These days, I also wear a different hat outside of the classroom, as I am also the Director of Membership and Public Relations for the Utah Association for Justice. This is a Salt Lake City-based nonprofit organization with the mission of preserving justice and accountability. Our membership, made up mostly of trial attorneys, works collectively to defend the often overlooked Seventh Amendment to the U.S. Constitution, the right to trial by jury. Through legislative advocacy and legal education, the organization strives to ensure public access to the civil justice system. Yes, our members can be seen on billboards and television commercials, and the legal profession is sometimes described as ambulance chasing, but the attorneys also represent individuals who face David-versus-Goliath tasks of taking on large corporations, insurance companies, hospitals, and government agencies after facing a wide range of life-altering injustices.

My occupation may seem a far cry from my current educational pursuit, but I am often surprised how these areas interconnect. If the television program *Law and Order* were to take place in Utah, it would feature hair-raising and heart-wrenching plotlines that reflect the state's ever-present ties to outdoor recreation and nature-based tourism. In Utah, despite our generally peaceful existence, dramatic mountain scenery often meets its match in the drama of human tragedy. One episode might tell of a family suing the U.S. Forest Service over their son's untimely death by a ravaging campground bear. The next week's show might regale viewers with the hard-earned victory of an expert Utah skier-come-plaintiff, who, having survived massive internal injuries and a monthlong coma, at last receives a $1 million reparation for a ski resort injury that occurred on an idyllic Wasatch powder day. Primetime television would have no need to draw from fiction in this state. Land managers and outdoor recreation practitioners might even be able to learn a thing or two.

The brand of justice that I work with on a 9-to-5 basis is about accountability and trying to correct past mistakes. It focuses on bringing closure and a sense of betterment, if possible, to those harmed by the wrongdoing of others. This is certainly a theme brought up during our symposium, primarily in terms of the displacement of people from their land and resources, particularly indigenous people and low-income residents. However, as our symposium reached full speed, an overarching theme extended further than this. Issues regarding social and environmental justice in the 21st century are not just about righting wrongs, but about ensuring equal access to opportunities. Our societies have laid thick, seemingly impenetrable foundations of inequality and widespread lack of opportunity. This is seen through income disparity, racism, sexism, and educational shortcomings, among other concerns.

My work with the Utah Association for Justice has shown me examples of access to the outdoors or participation in recreational opportunities gone awry. During our symposium, however, this was a secondary concern—a next stage in a course of action that might almost seem frivolous to address as it skirts the big picture. Here, the issue was not access gone wrong, but rather oppression and imbalance, which prevents access in the first place.

In the areas of parks, recreation, tourism, and leisure, access can mean many things. Perhaps it implies an ability to visit or inhabit a certain place and use its resources, or it might refer to participation in physical activities, or maybe it's more about having a forum to speak up for one's group in community or governmental affairs. The formal presentations continually returned to this theme of uneven access and lack of opportunity. Many of our presenters seemed to struggle to reach their specific points about parks, recreation, tourism, and leisure in their allotted 30 min because so much information about injustice in a more general societal sense was needed to paint a contextual backdrop.

The morning presentations, featuring a wealth of slides with broad information including demographic statistics, scholarly definitions, and quotes from citizens facing subordination, illustrated case after case of deeply rooted injustices in the United States and abroad. Collectively, speakers reiterated the question at the heart of the symposium: How can we be just in parks, recreation, tourism, and leisure when we live in an unjust world?

Only hours into this first morning, we all nodded in agreement that we had far more questions to pose than answers to give. But this did not discourage lively discussion during our synthesis section. After the first five presenters, ideas were offered to take steps in positive directions with aims of leveling the playing field, a well-worn metaphor that is apropos to parks, recreation, and leisure.

Indeed, injustices are widespread in our world and certainly evident in many areas of our expertise. But our group discussion offered reminders of hope and promise. At the very least, we have the power to ensure that in our spheres of influence we can advocate methodologies of justice and do our part to see that justice, in fact, does prevail.

We recognize that to move forward we must identify the issues that most plague our practices and studies. In the presentations and discussions, certain concerns became increasingly familiar. We repeatedly returned to the problem of Whiteness in our field. White people (or, in best lingual practice, people who are White) occupy higher education, occupy national park trails and visitor centers, and occupy fireside sofas at ski resort lodges. I too am often blind to my bleachy surroundings, as they have typically been my norm. I grew up in a northeastern state where beach vacationing French Canadians in snug swimsuits were the closest thing we had to diversity. I now work for a mostly White organization, attend a mostly White graduate program, and live in a mostly White neighborhood.

But I might go out on a limb to question how much of our problem of underrepresentation in academe is a problem of Whiteness and how much of it is a problem of academe itself. Higher education often seems disconnected from racial minority groups. But an even larger problem might exist: academe's detachment from the world in general. How can higher education better demonstrate its relevance? How can academicians write so that someone with only a general education degree, or less, will take interest? How can our proposals for action find practical applications in businesses, organizations, and communities? This is a focal question for me at this time of writing, as I try to hone in on a final graduate project that I feel can rival the academic oomph of my peers who have opted for the thesis route. What I may miss in statistical crunching, I hope to make up for in real-life connections of both scholarly and non-scholarly nature.

As pioneers of thought, professors and graduate students have an important duty to model best behavior of cultural sensitivity and open-mindedness. But I do hold a concern that our constant lingual fine-tuning and fostering of self-critical insecurities (i.e., "I'm White, middle class, and my parents still love each other after 40 years. What could I possibly know?") may also cause damage. We may be intimidating ourselves away from taking necessary personal risks with our work. We may fear, as I do now, misstepping with our words and appearing insensitive or ignorant. Simultaneously, our criticisms and insecurities may create a greater divide with those not involved with higher education, as we reach out mainly to each other rather than the citizenry beyond the university. We may become isolated by our positions in higher education and be reduced to the function of mere critic. We may end up on the sidelines as others follow the paths of activity and risk. They may not always get it right, but they can and often do.

In this way, scholars may not be all that different from lawyers. They can serve as the crucial link between everyday people from all walks of life and what should be happening for these people in their lives, when things may in reality be askew. They can ask daring questions that others may shy away from and then step forward in a quest to initiate change. Some battles will be riskier than others, and making champions of underdogs may at times seem futile. But with success comes precedent for future standards of ethics and fairness. Institutions of higher learning, much like the civil justice system, not only uphold justice but also create it.

If colleges and universities can serve as pillars of social change, perhaps we need to accept that they are imperfect pillars, yet still perfectly functional. They are pillars made of adobe, not marble, and they are made of some of the best resources available, strong enough to weather storms, but in need of patching now and then. So let us continue to build not only pillars but also welcoming doorways and connecting pathways. Together, as humans, we define the parameters of justice; injustices should not define our abilities as people.

PART TWO

Naming Injustice

"There is no justice if there is not a space in which that justice can occur."

—Don Mitchell

6

Our Town's a Drag

Drag Queens and Queer Space in Athens, Georgia

Joshua Barnett
Indiana University

Corey Johnson
University of Georgia

I'm sitting across the coffee table in my living room from two of Athens' older drag queens, or at least that is how other, younger performers have described them to me. They are out of drag today, both sporting blue jeans and T-shirts, but they ask that I call them by their drag names for the interview. We're all nibbling on the Gouda and crackers I have spread out, mostly enthralled in conversation about the unfortunate history of gay bars in our hometown. It is sad, really, we collectively decide. There are moments of laughter and others of common despair. All of a sudden, Phaedra raises her voice and vehemently recalls a time when she had to defend "the one place in town that we could come and be ourselves. And I absolutely refused to let straight people come in and take that from us." Her face red, there was no doubt that Phaedra was willing to fight for the little gay bar where she used to perform. And suddenly I was aware of the important niche that gay spaces fulfill for gay people.[1]

Athens, Georgia, home to the University of Georgia and a thriving music and party scene, serves as an interesting site for a study about drag queens. The town, teeming with performers and troupes, plays host to one of the biggest and most well-known drag balls in the country, the annual Boybutante Ball.[2] Since the late 1990s, there has been at least one gay bar in Athens' downtown business district, but the last one closed in 2009. Even without a gay bar in the city, the drag scene has thrived with regular performances in downtown nightclubs, in bars on the outskirts, and at university events. Some weeks, drag enthusiasts can delight in more than two or three separate shows at different bars with different performers.

The queer[3] community exists and flourishes in many areas of Athens without an institutionalized space where queer individuals congregate. In fact, various individuals and organizations in Athens have created temporary queer spaces, some for simply social reasons[4] and others for political or charity work. One monthly event, a queer "takeover" of a downtown bar initiated by four gay men including the first author, attracts hundreds on a regular basis,[5] and local drag shows routinely draw large crowds. Yet the drag queens we introduce in this chapter identify the lack of any designated queer space as a serious barrier to a healthy queer community. Indeed, as we discuss later, our participants think gay bars are not only desirable but also necessary elements for the maintenance and creation of community in small towns where queer people have few outlets to come together.

The purpose of this qualitative inquiry was to explore how drag queens, queer leisure spaces, and notions of community function in a small college town. We illuminate ways our participants negotiate nuances of heteronormativity and capitalism in their efforts to maintain and create queer spaces. Before we examine the drag queens' roles in this negotiation, we provide background on previous work related to drag queens, leisure spaces, and community. We then describe the context of our work and our methods for undertaking the investigation. Finally, we highlight performers' voices and share their stories about designated queer leisure spaces as part of a larger queer community.

Drag Queens, Leisure Space, and Community

To say that queer people are intricately involved in particular leisure spaces is neither new nor revelatory. Indeed, it has been said many times in many ways.[6, 7, 8, 9, 10, 11, 12] Drag queens have long been part of leisure contexts, at least since their resistance at the Stonewall Riots in 1969.[13, 14] Their role within queer communities is oftentimes a mixture of entertainer and gender-queer activist.[15, 16] Often at the center of queer leisure spaces, drag queens appear at gay bars, pride parades, and other community events to perform, interact with guests, and speak on behalf of particular causes. As we have written elsewhere, drag performers oftentimes view gay bars as both community centers and places of employment and thus work hard to preserve them.[17] Some drag queens have even taken to the digital stage, engaging in what Fox described as "q-podding,"[18] a mixture of drag queen chatter and podcast.

Beyond the idea of a greater queer community, notions of queer leisure spaces have also emerged.[19, 20] Space is a complicated idea still being explored by scholars across a variety of disciplines, but in general it refers to the "physical manifestation of … community."[21] Physical areas, then, are at the core of queer spaces. However, queer spaces are separate from queer-friendly spaces insofar as they are designed by and for queer people. That is not to say that queer-friendly businesses and the like are unwanted additions to a growing repertoire of amenable institutions, but rather to note the distinction between those spaces and explicitly queer spaces.

Queer space is not always constant (i.e., in the same location), as is the current case in Athens. Sometimes heteronormative spaces are queered, or made queer by the presence of queer bodies doing queer things.[22, 23, 24] Gay kiss-ins in public malls, die-ins on the steps of the U.S. Capitol, and queer people taking over straight bars[25] exemplify how spaces have been queered. In Athens, queering takes place when local organizations host "Drag Brunches" at restaurants or hold drag shows at traditionally straight bars downtown. Thus, nearly any space can become queer temporarily, but explicit, permanent leisure spaces (e.g., a gay bar) are what many queer people ultimately desire both for a sense of safety and for the opportunities they afford to meet and bond with others, to form social groups, and to participate in leisure activities and social events with other queer people.

Drag queens have also become accustomed to performing both in and out of one of the most visible queer leisure spaces, gay bars.[26] Gay bars are also the best spaces to find groups of queer people together, and these spaces are usually populated by gay men.[27] Indeed, the most commonly studied leisure settings for queer people have been bars and dance clubs that offer an after-dark home.[28, 29] Scholarly attention has been given to them primarily because, as Johnson argued, "gay bars offer a place where patrons can find and/or build community."[30] Bars are an ideal gathering space for queer people in heteronormative cultures. They are often dark, are open mostly in the evenings when one can shield one's appearance, and are often separated spatially from the straighter (and thus more dangerous) parts of town. For instance, Athens' two previous gay bars were located on the margins of the downtown business district, effectively out of sight of the more frequented straight bars and restaurants. Thus, gay bars are particularly well-suited places for gay community to occur, especially because their patrons are often in need of an out-of-view place to congregate. Bars and dance clubs are also often the singular space within a larger community where queer people can meet and engage intimately with one another with minimal fear of being attacked by homophobes. Halferty put it simply:

> And although, today, one is able to find a diverse array of establishments providing goods and services to queer communities, the bar, in particular, represents an important and sexually charged site around which socially and politically effective gay, lesbian and trans communities have been spatially organized, recognized and experienced by queers themselves and by the broader community.[31]

Halferty pointed out that gay bars are important not only to how queer people relate to and perceive one another, but also to how the broader community thinks about and interacts with them.[32]

Whatever the space, Bennett and West argued,[33] drag queens can be vital in social and political battles, lending their voices to various causes. Thus, some drag performers go beyond mere entertainment and breach political and social boundaries. Moreover, drag queens are active participants in the social (and physical) construction of their communities.[34] For them, community is the sum of all institutions and sociopolitical actors that make up the populace. Community is not limited by environmental conditions, but rather by social ones; in other words, many (sometimes competing) communities can exist in one area. Bars are often central to queer communities, but they are also just one part of a matrix of spaces and events where queer people simultaneously meet, talk, flirt, and forge relationships.

Across the United States, other queer leisure spaces, such as circuit parties, bathhouses, and gay male resorts, remain popular. Parks, bookstores, and cafés often serve as queer spaces too. They are frequently owned, managed, and patronized almost exclusively by queer people. Sometimes streets and sidewalks serve as the drag performer's stage, especially during pride events or political rallies and marches. Universities, colleges, and secondary schools are increasingly adding safe spaces where queer youth can come together safely; some companies and organizations are doing the same. In some towns, particularly more urbanized environments, queer consciousness-raising and support groups are in place (e.g., Families, and Friends of Gays and Lesbians), and some of these groups have their own physical space or have access to other buildings or conference rooms. Faith-based queer leisure spaces are also being formed in some areas. Indeed, Paris and Anderson[35] noted, an entire neighborhood in Washington, D.C., is being reformulated according to the religious institutions that occupy its street blocks on which the growing, largely queer population has come to rely. More specifically, there are churches that cater to queer individuals as well as churches that welcome queer individuals into their congregations, even though queer people are not their primary clientele. Consequently, different people desire different leisure spaces for different needs. Christians might desire a fellowship to perform Christianity, just as queer people might desire queer space so they can more effectively express their identity. Yet a multitude of queer spaces exist, and queer people can and do choose among them; not all queer people feel comfortable or happy in all queer spaces. The diversity is as rich as it is among the general population. So, how do drag queens contribute to queer communities in leisure space? And what do drag queens do if no designated queer leisure space exists in a community?

How We Approached Our Work

To understand how drag queens, leisure space, and notions of community function in the small college town of Athens, we chose to follow a general interpretive qualitative approach.

According to Glesne,[36] qualitative tools are used to understand social phenomena by gaining access to multiple perspectives of individuals and interpreting how participants construct and make meaning of the world around them. "The researcher[s] becomes the main research instrument as he or she observes, asks questions, and interacts with research participants."[37] During data collection and formal methods of analysis, researchers look for patterns and write descriptive accounts of what is found. In our work, qualitative research methods provided a way of describing in detail and in depth how drag queens in this southeastern college town negotiated the lack of a designated queer space, specifically a gay bar.

We interviewed five drag queens from the metropolitan Athens area.[38] Drag queens who had been performing for any length of time in Athens were encouraged to participate, but we were particularly interested in comparing the narratives of the city's newer (performing in Athens for only a year or two) and older (performing in Athens for several years) drag queens. We made our first contact with the participants by sending a message via Facebook to local drag queens who met our criteria. Our affiliation with a local nonprofit organization that raises funds for HIV/AIDS services by hosting drag shows and other assorted entertainment events increased our access to participants. In addition, our regular attendance at local drag shows resulted in casual friendships with many local performers. All participants defined themselves as biological males who frequently dress and perform as women for economic and entertainment purposes.

The participants verbally responded to a number of open-ended interview questions crafted to elicit information about their histories as drag performers and their feelings toward the notion of community vis-à-vis their drag persona and performances. Each interview lasted about an hour and a half and took place in the first author's living room, which was chosen because it was private and convenient for the performers. Following each interview, the first author documented the thematic patterns he heard in the interviews. Once general thematic patterns were identified, passages from each interview were transcribed and organized for further analysis.[39, 40] Once themes were identified and confirmed, a queer theoretical lens was used to interpret and theoretically complicate the data. Our themes were subsequently shared with the drag queens to build trustworthiness related to our findings. What follows are two patterns we found most relevant to these questions: How do drag queens maintain queer leisure space, and what do drag queens do without a gay bar?

Queens With and Without a Palace

Queer theory suggests that within particular spaces and throughout one's life, identity will move and shift in different ways. "Movements in queer spaces are not ... progressive or linear. They are jagged, backward, upside down, discontinuous,"[41] which is certainly what materialized in our discussion with the queens and the material reality of living in this small southern college town, which supports a strong queer community, but has no gay bar.

However, if anything was readily apparent, it was that the drag queens we talked to desired a permanent queer space where they could perform and where queer people could socialize with one another. Most pointedly, and not all that surprisingly, they desired a gay bar. Lacking a local gay bar, these drag queens found themselves in a peculiar position—entertainers without their own stage on which to perform, socialites without a bar to call their own—queens without a palace. First, these drag queens engaged in activities they believed functioned to maintain a gay bar when it existed (1994–2009) and to create a new gay bar when it did not (2009–2012). Using the knowledge gained from their interviews, we detail two important patterns, paying special attention to the ways in which these drag queens negotiated the nuances of heteronormativity, performativity, and capitalism as they discussed their lives in Athens.

Maintaining Queer Leisure Space

When Athens' original gay bar, Boneshakers, was still open, Phaedra and Fernandina—two of the older queens we interviewed—were regular performers in the downtown space. Because they used the bar to generate some of their income and because they appreciated the community it harbored, both performers recalled times when they were willing to fight to maintain it as a safe gay space. These moments ranged from speaking out against people they felt were intruders to engaging in physical altercations with others. In these instances, the drag queens exerted agency to maintain the spaces as queer spaces. Phaedra, billed as the "red-headed bitch of Athens," recalled one such instance:

> The bitchiness really came out of necessity after Boneshakers opened, um, because, when Boneshakers first opened, the sorority girls always thought it was a cute thing to bring their boyfriends and not tell them where they were going until they got there. And it really pissed me off. And I believe this to this day, that was the one place, at that time in Athens, that gay, lesbian, bisexual, transgender, intersex, queer, whatever the label that you put on yourself, that was the one place in town that we could come and be ourselves. And I absolutely refused to let straight people come in and take that from us. And just like a strong woman gets labeled a bitch, since I'm portraying a woman, then I became labeled a bitch. And I was like, if you want a bitch, then I can give you a bitch. Um, and that's basically where that came from, was out of necessity, out of standing up and going, "You know what, fuck you, you're not coming in here." I've had to be escorted out of the bar. I've been in fights. But I was like you're not coming in here and running over me.

In this moment, Phaedra exercised a degree of agency by defining herself as a "bitchy woman," by characterizing the leisure space as a safe haven for queer people, and by vocalizing her (and probably other bar goers') ill sentiments toward the "sorority girls" and their "boyfriends" who became frequent visitors to the bar on show nights.

Insofar as Phaedra adopted her title, "bitch of Athens," she realized and performed an identity that was empowering for her as a marginalized individual. Being the bitch also provided Phaedra with the agency needed to make direct comments that could potentially anger unsuspecting audience members, and this privileged identity made it possible to do so without obligating Phaedra to apologize or engage in theoretical conversations about the decisions she made and exerted. Simply put, being the bitch meant Phaedra was freer to say and do what best suited her, her friends and colleagues, and the safer spaces she inhabited as a drag queen.

Phaedra exercised this agency most explicitly by defining Boneshakers as "the one place in town that we could come and be ourselves." Dominant groups often possess the power to define the groups to which they belong,[42] and by subverting this notion of definitional power, Phaedra actively reworked the politics of this gay bar. The power to define who belongs, and thus who does not belong, in any given space, especially marginalized ones, is a way of asserting one's authority to give new meanings and uses to a leisure space. Defining Boneshakers as a safe haven for some—a group Phaedra also defined as "gay, lesbian, bisexual, transgender, intersex, queer, whatever the label that you put on yourself"—Phaedra meant that some people were unwelcome and unwanted in that space. Specifically, Phaedra felt the sorority girls and their boyfriends threatened the safety of the space for those who needed it most. For this reason, she actively worked to define them as undesirable in the bar. In this case, it seems the space itself, a designated queer space, made agency and definitional power more accessible for Phaedra. Perhaps because in this particular gay space Phaedra was surrounded by others like her (at least in terms of nonnormative sexual orientation and gender identity), and because that group of people constituted the majority, Phaedra had a safe and believable enviroment in which to act out to protect the space. In other words, the particularities of Boneshakers enabled and encouraged Phaedra to be more agentive and to exercise this agency to protect the space, but it also highlights how particular places produce the possibility for certain people to wield more power and authority than others.

A final way that Phaedra acted to maintain Boneshakers as a queer space was by vocalizing her ill sentiments toward some of the straight bar patrons. After making it clear that Boneshakers was "the one place" where people like her could come, Phaedra confronted some straight patrons directly. "Fuck you, you're not coming in here," she said on one occasion in an effort to deter local straight students from coming in, presumably to gawk at the men in dresses. Phaedra's identity as the "bitch of Athens" is apparent in her relations with these straight audience members; her confrontational style clearly shows some patrons are unwelcome. Thus, queer spaces sometimes reverse precisely who is an agent of power and who is able to comment on "straights" with little or no negative consequence. The power shifts from the heterosexual to the queer as a result of the space. Phaedra later commented that she "had to be escorted out of the bar. I've been in fights. But I was like, 'you're not coming in here and running over me.'" By vocalizing and acting out the ill sentiments that she, and likely other marginalized bar goers, felt toward some straight patrons, Phaedra was able to moderate who was and was not a part of Boneshakers, even if she had to fight for it.

A Need for Queer Leisure Space

When a designated gay bar no longer existed in Athens, the drag queens we interviewed said they then began to temporarily queer a variety of straight spaces and to indirectly lay the foundation for a new gay bar, underscoring their dire need for and desirability of a permanent queer space. These efforts have been particularly salient in the years following the 2009 closure of the town's gay bar, but have also been ongoing since Boneshakers shut its doors in 2005. Without a designated gay bar, local drag troupes have turned to queer-friendly or queer-owned spaces downtown or on the outskirts to host regular performances, and local organizations frequently queer spaces (restaurants, bars, theaters) for fund-raisers or social events. Despite this, our participants mutually agreed a gay bar would make Athens a better place for queer people to live and is an absolute necessity if queer people are to thrive.

Although no gay bars have opened since 2009, the drag queens we talked to are driven by what they perceive to be the opportunity to revive what has recently been "killed" off. Indeed, Elizabeth, the youngest of the drag queens we interviewed, suggested the closing of Blur (the most recent gay bar in town) "killed all the gay bars and *everything* in Athens" (emphasis ours). The "everything" of which Elizabeth speaks is troubling for the queer community in Athens. It appears as though the queer community had all of its assets in one centralized space: the lone gay bar. Without it, the queer community is cast as dwindling in size, presence, and power (whether true or not). It makes sense, then, that queer people would advocate for the opening of desinated queer spaces in their town if they were central to individuals and communities alike.

Another queen, Fernandina, suggested that for those who see the gay bar as the only place where they can truly be themselves, slipping back into what she calls "living the straight life" is easy. Fernandina felt the lack of a designated queer space greatly damages the queer community. In fact, when offering her definition of the queer community, Fernandina noted the community used to "be the venue when we had a venue ... but it's not even that now." Fernandina thus conceptualized community in Athens as the gay bar (and vice versa) and made clear when those spaces close down, the entire community suffers and perhaps perishes as a result. It is easy to see, then, why drag queens are so insistent on creating some semblance of a queer space that might mirror the gay bars of days gone by. Their struggle is one to re-create the basis of their assemblage: walls and stages, bars and dance floors, back rooms and patios. Fernandina put it bluntly: "If we had a gay bar in Athens, and specifically just a gay bar, and, you know, we could do our shows there, I think things would be a lot different now."

Not only did the drag queens desire a queer space to call their own, but they also seemed to prefer that it be "as gay as possible." The queens expressed an interest in the space being occupied mostly, if not exclusively, by the queer community. For instance, Phaedra commented:

> I sincerely believe if we had a venue that was gay all the time, that was run by gay people, um, that the sense of community would come back. Where the sense of community for me started leaving was when Boneshakers was sold to a straight man. And everything went downhill after that.

Thus, for Phaedra and her drag colleagues, it was important that efforts to create queer spaces were done in such a way that they would create designated queer spaces, not just temporary versions that would soon revert back to everyday uses that might preclude queer people.

Butler's[43] theorization of performativity highlighted not only how subjectivity is constituted within space, but also specifically how we become queer beings within it. This discursive process of becoming challenges humanist notions of stable, all-knowing identities and recognizes the constant renegotiations of self that take place within power relations around leisure space. For Butler, individuals cannot view themselves as actors simply choosing to perform, but rather must understand they are subjects constituted by the performances expected of them in the space. Specifically, Butler viewed gendered (and sexual) subjectivity as a social construction, and rather than an actor choosing to perform a subjectivity or a "doer behind the deed," Butler's subject did not preexist the deed but instead was only recognized as a subject because of doing the deed.

In Phaedra's case, without the stable gay bar, where the subject of drag queen has been produced, has been reproduced, and is awaiting her as a subjective performer, the performance of that subjectivity becomes diminished, and therefore the feeling of being a drag queen, or even a queer person in that space, means Phaedra is less able to be herself. Her words provide evidence that queer spaces produce queer people's queer subjective positions and ultimately result in specific kinds of queer performances. Simply put, queer people both produce and are produced by the queer spaces they occupy or do not occupy. Without a place designated as queer, the queer subjectivity suffers in the (re)production of that subjectivity, highlighting the instability of any identity—drag queen or queer.

In addition, when considering the sociopolitics of space, the physical landscape, location, social practices, human interactions, and the economic system in which it functions have to be considered because they intersect to produce that particular leisure space. We were particularly interested in Phaedra's comment when she expressed interest in such a space being run by gay people and noted the queer community in Athens was lost when Boneshakers was sold to a straight man. In this way, Phaedra suggested that a truly helpful space would be created, organized, and maintained by and for other queer people and that only in this way can a particular space support and enhance the community it serves.

Despite Phaedra's insistence that a future gay bar be owned, run, and inhabited by gays and lesbians, the drag queens' current and ongoing efforts have focused on temporarily queering straight bars for their drag shows. Not only did the drag queens seem to view this as a necessary part of creating temporary spaces for queer people to come together, but also some of them engaged in these practices as strategic components of a larger plan to lay the foundation for another gay bar.

This act of queering straight space is what Butler[44] called "performative politics," a performance not expected or accepted in a particular discursive space, a performance that has the potential to disrupt the normalizing forces of the heteronormative discourse if it is recognized as legitimate and taken up in positive ways by others in the discursive space. This is a theoretically interesting way to consider what is happening in Athens as exhibited by Elizabeth, who described her efforts to make clear the positive benefits drag shows can offer to the community:

> If they can see [us perform] and say, "Wow, Athens does have their drag scene back, and this is something that they can look forward to," then they're gonna keep coming. And the more we build that up, then I think the more that other club promoters and club owners are gonna see we need to turn this into a gay bar, or we need to have a drag show here, or something to promote their business.

In this instance, Elizabeth identified drag shows as a possible catalyst for the creation of a new gay bar or the conversion of a current straight bar into a gay bar. By demonstrating that drag shows draw large crowds in Athens and by highlighting the profitability of these shows, Elizabeth suggested drag queens might be able to influence the landscape of the local bar scene. Thus, as Elizabeth and her colleagues perform, they are not only performing for their audiences but also for the owners and managers of these spaces, whom they hope they can convince of the legitimacy and profitability of drag.

To reach their desired end—a home venue explicitly oriented toward a queer clientele—drag queens in Athens must work through the heteronormative, capitalistic system and prove drag is a profitable business opportunity, with the hope that eventually the bar owners and promoters will see that a designated queer club is appropriate.

However, so far this has been an unsuccessful way to go about securing queer space in the community. In fact, the current economic climate, capitalism in particular, has rendered gay spaces in Athens largely invisible and seemingly unviable. Straight bar owners have opened and closed gay bars for upwards of 20 years because they have been unable to maintain any semblance of profitability. Yet here, the only organized efforts at regaining those types of public gay space are being launched by drag queens aimed at the current bar owners and club promoters who likely are analogous to the previous owners of Athens' gay bars. For working-class drag queens that have trouble breaking even on any given performance, opening a new gay bar appears to be the only viable and accessible option, but not one they can exercise complete agency over.

These efforts to lay the foundation for another gay bar are interesting because they function within and alongside heteronormative capitalist practices that position drag queens, and perhaps the entire queer scene, as commodities from which bar owners can profit. In performing for straight bar owners and hoping they might see the profitability of drag shows and thus create new gay bars, the drag queens rely on a system that has failed them time and time again. However, our participants continue to engage in performative politics in queer-friendly straight bars and hope they might persuade someone to create the queer space they so desperately desire for drag/queer performativity.

Conclusion

We were not surprised that our work, like the work of Aitchison,[45] Johnson and Samdahl,[46] Johnson,[47] or Lewis and Johnson,[48] illustrated that gay bars can serve a pivotal role for queer people. Even today, amid major progress in social acceptance of queer people and equal rights being afforded them, major obstacles of harassment, marginalization, and discrimination still exist even in the progressive college town of Athens, Georgia. Consequently, many queer people desire leisure spaces, separate from heteronormative spaces, even as queer people are mainstreamed into heteronormative life.[49]

Despite political debates over which is better, radical abandonment of heterosexual privileged traditions, or the mainstreaming acceptance of queer people into previous traditions (i.e., gay marriage, gays in the military), our drag queens articulated they wanted spaces owned, managed, and frequented by other queer people. Our participants described how their leisure involvement (and sometimes economic sustenance) was tied to a particular sort of leisure space that allowed them to establish and maintain a particular social identity—that of a drag queen and a queer person.[50, 51, 52] From their words, we can see how important the role of place and the sociopolitical space is for providing positive and empowering subject positions for them as queens and queers in the Athens community. For these drag queens, gay bars were places to assert agency, to acquire power, to provide shelter to others, and, most important, to be defended from heteronormative practices.

After gay bars disappeared from Athens, the drag queens saw it as their duty to begin the struggle to create a new gay bar. We think this is a result of a deficit in performativity.[53] With no gay bar to (re)produce their subjectivity, they felt a loss—a loss of community and a loss of identity. How could they be drag queens without a space to reproduce their drag? One way our drag queens sought to fill this void in performativity was by engaging in performative politics by queering straight space/bars, that is, taking their subjective drag-selves and disrupting the heteronormative discursive practices of straight bars. In doing so, they were also trying to convince a small business community that drag might be profitable. This latter point illustrates how, in a capitalistic society, we often seek to commodify the body to create such space. However, commodification of the body is a form of labor, not leisure. The labor in this case is performing in drag, seeking legitimization from straight people, and performing in a straight bar to show that drag is profitable. If this is the case, our participants are certainly working girls, which is why we believe "our town's a drag!"

Discussion Questions

1. The United States prides itself in championing minority rights. Based on this chapter, what rights of the gay community are being compromised in Athens, Georgia, and by whom?

2. Do you see this as a social justice issue? If so, please define the social injustice being done in Athens. If you do not see this as a social justice issue, please explain why not.

3. Power seems to be at the center of this conflict. Based on Joshua and Corey's description, how might the dominant culture in Athens oppress the gay community? How have the drag queens developed their own power structure to combat such oppression?

4. Joshua and Corey imply that capitalism has worked against securing the rights of the gay community in Athens. Do you agree or disagree with their assessment? Please explain your thinking.

5. Is environmental justice part of this story? If yes, in what way? If no, why not?

7

Contesting Homelessness

Public Nature, Political Ecology,
and Socioenvironmental Justice

Jeff Rose
University of Utah

"I'm not fucking homeless!" Wayne shouted at me as we walked quickly along the concrete paths just past the creek on our way downtown. It was a cold December morning in Salt Lake City, and I had just asked him if he minded taking part in a more formalized interview with me at some point because I wanted to understand his experiences of living in what I understood to be "public nature," in a place he understood as "the Hillside." He continued, his voice dropping and slowing, but remaining clear and forceful, "I don't know if you think you're some smart sociologist or something, but I'm not talking to anyone about being homeless, because I wouldn't know nothing about that. I'm not homeless."

My ethnographic experiences on the Hillside, along the surrounding urban–wildland margins of Salt Lake City, help me to better understand public and private space and the ways in which people relate to the nonhuman world around us. Understanding the relationships between public and private space and between nature and society form the foundational questions for this chapter, and I use the experiences of the Hillside residents as an avenue of insight into these questions. This work explicitly attempts to not only describe and analyze the experiences of living on the Hillside, but also do so in a manner that contributes to the rights, dignity, and respect that each of us deserves.

For the last year and a half, I have engaged directly with a community of individuals, who, lacking adequate housing elsewhere, assumed residence in a municipal park and the open spaces nearby. These Hillside residences are neither fully public nor fully private. The residents live in spaces that are understood to be public, but they are often unwelcome in those spaces, and they do not have formal private space to which to retreat. Similarly, they live much of their lives in what many people would understand as nature, yet they are neither fully in nature nor fully within society. They live, work, and play in between public and private and in between nature and society. Discursively, public and private and nature and society are dualistically constructed, creating a bifurcated and problematic either-or conundrum. Practically, however, public and private and nature and society often operate along a dialectical spectrum, where these constructs operate conditionally relative to the perspective of the individual and also relative to other settings.

Through action, discourse, and existence, the Hillside residents acutely dismantle the socially constructed inaccuracies of dominant public–private and nature–society bifurcations.

Their presence in the park calls into question mainstream narratives of park and open space normativity, where human presence in parks—places that are generally considered both public and nature—should be temporary. Undoubtedly much can be learned from this work in terms of understanding homelessness, but my study was explicitly not about homelessness. It was about a community of individuals who, for a variety of reasons, have either chosen or been forced to live and exist in what is commonly understood as public nature. By most understandings, the Hillside residents are homeless, but from their own perspectives, they are not homeless. Understanding these individuals from their own perspective requires a justice-oriented epistemology, such as the critical and poststructural perspectives found within political ecology.[1, 2, 3, 4]

Political Ecology in the City

Political ecology examines relationships between social, political, and economic factors and ecological conditions and changes, integrating ecological and social sciences with political economy. Political ecology provides integrated and relational approaches that untangle the interconnected economic, political, social, and ecological processes. Political ecology presupposes these factors, when woven together, form highly uneven and deeply unjust material and discursive settings.[5] Furthermore, generating environmental knowledge for the promotion of social justice is an explicit goal of political ecology.[6] An explicitly ecological perspective is helpful for examining complex urban environments in particular, due to its incorporation of different actors in understanding a particular situation. Similarly, political ecology incorporates a critical stance that "builds on and enacts a relational approach in which all bodies are participants in constituting the world."[7] Political ecologists are united in their framing of human and nonhuman surrounding communities as contingent constructions that emerge from continuous interaction.[8, 9] Echoing Marx's claim that the social cannot be extracted from any political or material situation, Harvey emphasized, "All sociopolitical projects are ecological projects and vice versa."[10] Political ecology also has the potential to enhance democratic content of socioenvironmental constructions by identifying strategies through which a more equitable distribution of social power and a more inclusive mode of discursive environmental production can be achieved.[11]

Parks are but one urban ecological agent that contributes to the tensions between public and private and between nature and society. Urban locations, such as the public park and surrounding spaces with which I engaged, are "dense networks of interwoven sociospatial processes that are simultaneously local and global, human and physical, cultural and organic."[12] The metabolic processes that support urban life of all sorts, therefore, combine environmental and social processes, understanding that these processes are infinitely interconnected.[13, 14] Stereotypical constructions often situate parks as places for recreation and social gatherings. However, under larger auspices of neoliberal political and economic adjustments of the past three decades, parks are increasingly regulated by municipalities and police, requiring a reconsideration of parks in light of social and environmental justice concerns.[15] For individuals such as the Hillside residents, parks are not only spaces for recreation and social processes; they are more intimately a part of the socioenvironmental fabric of the urban environment, a space which is the site for meeting their most basic needs, including resting, sleeping, urinating and defecating, and storing possessions. Perhaps unintentionally, but ironically, such park management and regulation may be the greatest threat to each of these individual's maintenance of self. But the delicate and essential political ecology of the parks within the fabric of the urban experience bears further exploration.

Imagine, for example, standing on a busy street corner in a major U.S. city, and consider the socioenvironmental metabolic relations that coalesce in this place that are simultaneously local and global. Smells, colors, tastes, customs, bodies, and discourses from all over the world glide by, displayed, practiced, performed, consumed, narrated, visualized, transfixed, and transformed. People, clothes, spices, foods, materials, and international cultures whirl past. Local taco cart vendors on the street corners compete against national fast-food chains in a nearby mall food court. The physical landscape is dominated by towering buildings including several bank buildings, as well as new condominiums, legal firms, and perhaps a large religious building. Tourists snap photographs, and employees of multinational financial firms who have never lived outside the city begin their evening commutes to their waiting suburban dwellings. Lighting for the nearby buildings is fed by energy emanating from coal- or gas-fired electricity generators. Cars burning fuels from distant oil deposits pump carbon into the atmosphere, affecting people, wildlife, forests, climates, and geopolitical conditions around the planet. "The city is not just a built environment consisting of buildings and streets and subways and parks and waste systems and communications cables but also a living dynamic of cultural practices, intellectual circuits, affective networks, and social institutions."[16] Not far from this specific street corner are the unbuilt open spaces comprising city, county, state, and federal lands, including national forests and not too distant wilderness areas. The social, political, and ecological complexity of this seemingly common scene is nearly overwhelming.

The intermingling of material, social, and symbolic actions, events, and processes produces particular socioenvironmental settings that weld public space, private space, nature, and society in a deeply heterogeneous, conflicting, and sometimes disturbing whole.[17] The socioecological footprint of this local urban place is also definitively global. The urban processes of a city harbor social and ecological processes that are embedded in dense, multilayered networks and discourses of local, regional, national, and global connections. I conducted my research on the edge of such a dynamic urban setting, in an area abutting the less fettered nature of nearby open spaces. In Salt Lake City, where I currently live, this place is called the Hillside, a home for individuals who are living in a complex interplay of urban–wildland, of public–private, and of nature–society.

Socioecological changes, which are unavoidable in such a complex dynamic, result in the continuous production of new "natures," or new social, physical, and environmental conditions, that affect what we know nature to be.[18] These processes occur in specific realms of power in which social actors strive to defend and create their own natures in various combinations of contexts of class, ethnic, racial, and/or gender conflicts and power struggles.[19]

Throughout these ongoing processes, capitalistic commodity relations veil multiple socioecological processes of domination, subordination, and exploitation that feed various capitalist urbanization processes. According to Harvey's[20] logic, urbanization, then, might be at the heart of contemporary global economic and environmental crises of capitalism.[21, 22, 23] These processes turn urban spaces into a kaleidoscope of metabolic socioenvironmental processes that stretch from the immediate place to the most remote yet still interconnected corners of the globe. The commodification of nature that serves as the fundamental foundation of Western market-based societies not only obscures the social relations of power in the political economic system, but also permits the disconnection of the perpetual flows of transformed and commodified nature from its foundation, which is the transformation of nature. In other words, by excessively commodifying nature, capitalism disconnects us from the ecological roots that sustain us. The environment of the city, both social and physical, then, is the result of a series of historical processes of the urbanization of nature itself.

Bifurcations of public and private and of nature and society bring to the fore questions of social and environmental justice. In my research, for example, as the Hillside residents' place within these two sets of dichotomies remained constantly in question, Salt Lake City's socioenvironmental landscape also became an explicit question of justice. In this context, social justice can be understood as work toward a world of equity, dignity, and basic rights through demo-cratically organized social spaces.[24] Environmental justice is work that addresses questions of "inequality, fairness, and rights with respect to environmental conditions and decision-making processes."[25] Embedded within this construction of environmental justice, the concepts of rec-ognition and participation emerge as key ingredients in the decision-making process.[26]

Although social and environmental justice cannot be fully divorced (as discussed below), separate elements of the Hillside residents' experiences speak directly to injustices in specifically urban settings:

> Evicted from private spaces … homeless people occupy public spaces, but the con-sequent presence in the urban landscape is fiercely contested. Their visibility is con-sistently erased by institutional efforts to move them elsewhere—to shelters, out of buildings and parks, to poor neighborhoods, out of the city, to other marginal spaces. Evicted people are also erased by the desperate personal campaigns of the housed to see no homeless, even as they step over bodies in the street. This ongoing erasure from the public gaze is reinforced by media stereotypes that either blame the victim and thereby justify their studied invisibility or else drown them in such lugubrious sentimentality that they are rendered helpless puppets, the pathetic other, excused from active civic responsibility and denied personhood.[27]

No justice exists if a space does not exist in which that justice can occur.[28] Supporting this spatial component of justice, Foucault claimed, "To decipher discourse through the use of spatial, stra-tegic metaphors enables one to grasp precisely the points at which discourses are transformed in, through, and on the basis of relations of power."[29] This critical perspective on the powers embedded in sociospatial relations is as old as critical theory itself. In the *Grundrisse*, Marx[30] detected in capitalism a tendency toward "the annihilation of space by time," a construct that has been taken up since then in terms of people's relationships with each other and their collec-tive relationships with the spaces they inhabit on a daily basis, fully incorporating their relation-ships with the unbuilt world around them, for example, nature.[31] All of these contestations have particular ramifications in the production of social and environmental justice.

What is public space and what is private space? What is nature and what is society? These perplexing and complicated questions have inspired philosophical, academic, and practical thought for centuries. Unfortunately, there are no easy answers. However, a particular com-munity, local in its daily processes and global in its manifestation of political and economic processes, sits at the overlapping and often competing nexuses of the liminal spaces between public and private, between nature and society. This community does not offer solutions to public and private and nature and society as much as it offers additional layers of complexity to the equation. The Hillside residents' physical geography places them along Salt Lake Valley's ur-ban–wildland interface, as their immediate proximity to both urban density and wildland open space is undeniable. This subculture actively complicates what is commonly understood as pub-lic space and private space. Simultaneously, the Hillside community adds complexity to what we commonly understand to be "nature" and, therefore, what we understand to be "not nature."

Homelessness and Public Space

Public space is always a negotiation,[32] it is always contested, and it is always a contention.[33] Individuals facing homelessness, almost by definition, lack consistent access to private spaces, spaces that are often taken for granted. Although these individuals live, work, play, and reside in public spaces, they are nearly ubiquitously marginalized in large and small cities, in rich and poor nations, preventing them from fully participating as democratically engaged citizens. "Although homeless people are nearly always in public, they are rarely counted as part of the public."[34] The issue of homelessness and its often controversial intersection with public space is not a new issue for researchers,[35, 36, 37, 38, 39, 40, 41, 42, 43] but remains underresearched and undertheorized in parks, recreation, and leisure studies.

Criminalization of homelessness is a problem for those interested in justice. Individuals facing poverty and homelessness have been increasingly criminalized through the greater regulation of space.[44] Regulated space often legally denies access to individuals facing homelessness, creating one of the most basic yet most prevalent injustices in contemporary society. Simultaneously, those seeking justice for individuals facing homelessness tend not to reference dignity and respect for all individuals, but to reduce the argument to a minimalist discourse about rights. These most basic rights are often restricted to the material conditions of daily experiences, including basic human functions such as the rights to urinate in alleys, to sit on sidewalks, to beg, or to sleep on sidewalks or in public parks.[45][46] Fulfilling these basic functions hardly represents dignity and respect. Mitchell,[47] in a series of essays concerning the justice of public space for individuals facing homelessness in Berkeley's People's Park, explained that rights are conferred to individuals not based upon basic constitutionality, citizenship, or even some inalienable human quality granted in the U.S. Constitution or elsewhere, but based upon the ownership or possession of property, a point supported by Hardt and Negri.[48] Property, in effect, is what separates the haves from the have nots, in terms of material wealth, social status, political representation, and the possibility of fully democratic engagement. Through this perspective, housing, or consistent access to private space, is therefore a precondition for individual and social justice. As homeless individuals lack this level of ownership or access to private property, they therefore lack agency in access to a variety of democratic participation structures.[49] Mitchell[50] contended that because of the lack of privateness, public spaces, such as parks, require reclamation as sites for struggles for justice.

Public space regulation is important for the rights of all people, but particularly for individuals facing homelessness. The regulation of public space is at the forefront of homeless individuals' rights to exist,[51] prompting its need to be questioned and further problematized. Mitchell considered it necessary to turn the spaces of the city into sites for demanding justice:

> Rights to public space . . . have only been expanded when they have been forcefully demanded, quite often by people breaking the existing laws and thereby showing those laws—about picketing as much as about sleeping—to be oppressive, in their geography if not in their actual wording.[52]

Such resistances are often met with thorough countermovements that are supported by contemporary capitalism. Through neoliberal ideology, contemporarily, private not-in-my-backyard (NIMBY) ideas are extrapolated into popular discourse and then into legalized dictum,[53, 54] creating a situation where individuals facing homelessness—those most in need of public spaces—suffer through their exclusion from public spaces.

Those lacking access to private space are often referenced as being homeless, and defining homelessness in any way is fraught with problems as well.[55] Many people who access different social services might be without access to living spaces that they own or rent, but in studies that quantify homelessness, these individuals may not appear to researchers as being any different from individuals who have access to private living quarters each day. "Difficulties with enumerating the homeless population accurately have plagued efforts to describe homelessness effectively."[56] Furthermore, many people who spend nights on streets and in shelters might not self-identify as homeless for a variety of reasons. Many definitions of homelessness exclude a time factor, indicating that a person who spends one night without access to private property might be "homeless" demographically. The question of who is homeless and how they are quantified ultimately leads researchers, social workers, and politicians to a similar syllogistic problem. Understanding the scope of homelessness depends, to some degree, on understanding how many people are involved. To quantify homelessness, a useful and reasonable definition is required. Definitions of an individual facing homelessness are difficult to construct, and they are riddled with problems. Without sufficient working definitions, then, counting and quantifying homelessness is an extremely difficult and problematic task.

Despite these seemingly persistent vagaries, homelessness is often considered either a pathological condition at worst or a state of victimization at best.[57, 58] Ellickson[59] questioned whether the order of public space should be disconnected from issues of homelessness, ultimately leading to the question of whether homelessness is a condition imposed by society or a behavior controlled by an individual. At one extreme of this dichotomy is the conservative construction of urban street people as an unclassifiable and uncontrollable mix of individuals who are sick, desperately poor, and/or mentally ill, combined with possible drug and alcohol addicts, runaway youth, and prostitutes.[60, 61] At the other end of this spectrum is the more politically liberal view of homelessness as primarily a social and political structural phenomenon interconnected with various complex sociopolitical and socioeconomic conditions such as unemployment rates, housing markets, mental health clinic overcrowding, gentrification, and inadequate treatment options for substance addictions.[62, 63, 64, 65] Consonant with both of these views and the various spectral positions in between held by media, businesses, law enforcement, city officials, and sometimes even social workers and sociologists is a view of abjection, pathology, and/or victimization.[66, 67] The politics of compassion and the politics of those interested in ridding public spaces of individuals facing homelessness are problematically and fundamentally linked in their assumption that individuals facing homelessness are something less than citizens,[68] a troubling analysis for both sides of this intellectual, political, ideological, and practical debate. Also consonant with both views, and without argument from the political right or left, is that homelessness is a problem in need of a solution.

More often than not, individuals facing homelessness are studied as a sociological problem, and the dynamics of power on the part of these individuals are not studied.[69] In this sense, portraying individuals who face homelessness either as defective units to be repaired or removed or as unwitting victims of local sociopolitical circumstance results in stripping individuals facing homelessness of agency, autonomy, and, potentially, rights.[70, 71] Denying individuals who face homelessness their capacity to exercise choice and construct their identities is to deny them status as full human agents. Furthermore, dominant portrayals of homelessness often overlook various actualities of homeless life, where people are not simply passive victims or irrational subjects, but make active and intentional choices in areas basic to survival such as food, shelter, and hygiene and in numerous encounters and confrontations with authorities, merchants, and passersby.[72] "Far from being dupes—impassive in their stigmatization—the homeless constantly and consciously negotiate these meanings, attempting to transform their relationship to those around them."[73] This was certainly the case for the residents of the Hillside, and from a certain perspective, the Hillside residents were most in need of a politics of justice that is lacking from all of our lives, but to the greatest detriment of those living on the Hillside.

Socioenvironmental Justice

The often false separation of social and environmental justice has been widely critiqued as narrowly focused, ecologically impossible, and antithetical toward a progressive and productive envisioning of sociopolitical and socioenvironmental relations.[74, 75, 76] Social justice cannot exist without environmental justice and vice versa, and the historical overlap between such groups has been significant.

Perspectives from political ecology help intellectually align social justice and environmental justice movements. Explicitly environmental justice movements are often closely aligned with groups that are more focused on explicitly social justice issues, but an important reconceptualization of nature is helpful in this alignment process. Stereotypically, environmental justice groups have focused on an objectified notion of the natural world, and social justice groups have implied that many of their causes lack any connection to the surrounding nonhuman entities and systems in which they live, work, and play. These different perspectives of nature are both problematic and subtle, yet significant shifts would better align social justice and environmental justice narratives.

Without denying the materiality of forests, streams, fields, mountains, and furry megafauna that populate most mainstream notions of nature, it is helpful to acknowledge "...all claims about nature are discursively mediated. Knowledge and language are the tools we use to make sense of a natural world that is both different from us and yet which we are a part of."[77] Nature, or the environment, exists in a concrete manner, but there is not a "prediscursive metalanguage for us to use to describe that reality."[78] From this perspective, nature is a highly subjective effect of power (through discourse), and neither nature nor society is a separate or stable category of being. Rather, nature (and also society) is only the discursive meanings we place upon it. We cannot come to know nature without acknowledging and critiquing the very real social, political, economic, and ecological histories that inform our popular contemporary notions of what nature means to each of us individually, as well as to our collective societies. Coming to understand the multiple, unstable definitions of the nonhuman world would enable social justice movements to recognize the densely embedded notion of nature in all we do and simultaneously enable environmental justice movements to focus on more subjective notions of nature as being a reflection of ourselves as much as an objective entity to weigh, count, and measure.[79] Beyond academic semantics of the names of various justice movements, environmental justice groups' "... redefinition of environment has enabled them to forge links with groups concerned with race, class, and rural issues."[80] Redefining and expanding nature is a central component for justice movements of all sorts to proceed.[81]

The instability of the socially constructed categorizations of nature and society is at the heart of attempts to separate social and environmental justice movements. A more helpful theoretical and practical implementation of a single justice movement—perhaps named "justice" or "socioenvironmental justice"[82, 83, 84] —is more ontologically coherent for moving such movements forward. Such justice movements, when organized not at the poles of the nature–society spectrum but at the nature–society nexus or overlap, have the greatest promise for social and ecological stability, rights, and democratic organization at local and global levels.[85]   Harvey[86] further pointed to the futility of separating social and environmental justice, illustrating that, through a Marxist perspective, a politics of class would easily subsume any specific politics of race, gender, or any environmental-specific cause. From this perspective, social and environmental justice concerns cannot be addressed until the most pressing problem is addressed: the oppressive and highly unjust dominion of capitalism. Regardless of one's epistemological disposition—be it Marxist, poststructuralist, feminist, critical race, Freirean, or otherwise—any critical perspective can clearly acknowledge that justice-focused movement or reenvisioning of our social, political, and ecological world cannot address any single descriptor or avenue for justice without tangentially or significantly altering all others.

In parks, recreation, tourism, and leisure studies, social and environmental justice—if addressed at all—are focused on either people (social justice) or place (environmental justice). Combining these concerns has manifested in advocating for issues of access to particular leisure space, a position that might not engage with social and environmental justice. This perspective tends to be anthropocentric because environmental justice can often be framed as simply enabling greater access to a space, a resource, or some other common good. This anthropocentric perspective is ideologically vexing. Personally, much of my social justice grounding comes from Karl Marx, who was as stringent a humanist as there ever has been. My environmental perspectives are largely derived from a strange mix of Aldo Leopold's interconnectedness, Henry David Thoreau's romanticism, Edward Abbey's radicalism, and Vandana Shiva's advocacy of people and places. These four folks and Marx would not have mixed well at a dinner table. The place where all might align probably has to do with an ethic of respect and dignity. Perhaps this is the core of the justice movement. It becomes incumbent, then, to train our minds to locate the places where respect and dignity are lacking most pressingly. Maybe that site for advocacy occurs in greater wheelchair access in a national park, maybe it occurs in protecting a mountain stream's substrate material, or maybe it occurs in the locating of a new coal mine. It still feels a bit anthropocentric, but maybe it's a softer, humbler anthropocentrism.

The Hillside

For the individuals living on the Hillside—those individuals facing homelessness in their everyday practices of living in public space and of living in nature—lack of respect and dignity exist as material and epistemological tensions that characterize faulty separations of social and environmental justice. Wayne's pronouncement that he is "not fucking homeless!" is a basic articulation that he and other individuals living on the Hillside actively contest mainstream constructions of public space and of nature. Wayne continued to clarify that he is not without private space, even if his private space is found on what most people consider to be public land. He lives in what many people would consider to be nature, although Wayne's experience, after living on the Hillside for 8 years, did not seem any different to him than someone living on the 15th floor of the plush, new City Creek Condominiums in downtown Salt Lake City. His life and his experience were a direct contestation of the binaried and simplistic constructions of public and private and of nature and society, and he demanded his subjectivity not be reduced to something so relatively banal as mere homelessness.

The Hillside residents' daily experiences illustrate the false dichotomies of public–private, nature–society, and urban–wildland, among others. The residents mostly reside in tents, on land that is nominally public. Simultaneously, they have appropriated much of this public space as their own, effectively, although not legally, privatizing it. They have many of the possessions of outdoor recreationists: camping stoves, dome tents, and synthetic sleeping bags. Although this space is a short walking distance to downtown Salt Lake City, the Utah State Capitol building, and the University of Utah, it is also seemingly well beyond the confines of the city's urban core. A daily commute into the city provides access to formal and informal day labor and social services provided by government, nonprofit, and religious agencies. The space is also directly adjacent to two of Salt Lake Valley's numerous superfund sites, as well as multiple industries focused solely on resource extraction and production. The Hillside, depending on one's perspective, is both pristine and horrendously impacted; it is an example of conservation and of exploitation. The Hillside is a place where social justice and environmental justice concerns align in a visceral manner, indicating these two avenues for progress should recognize their significant inseparability. Environmental analysis and policy should be reframed toward addressing the problems of socially vulnerable people,[87] such as those living in the tenuous margins of the Hillside.

The needs of the Hillside residents are many, and fortunately, avenues of support exist for them. Charitable food is plentiful in Salt Lake City, and social service agencies focus on various aspects of basic life maintenance. Health care clinics, sparse and underfunded, provide modest outreach to some of the Hillside residents. Various justice-oriented movements exist and have had implications for the individuals living on the Hillside. Specific attention was recently brought to the plight of individuals facing homelessness with the Occupy Salt Lake City protests of the fall of 2011. Local Utah environmental movements regularly focus upon ski resort expansion in the Wasatch, stopping nuclear plants or resource extraction along the Colorado River Watershed, or wilderness preservation in the southern canyonland areas of the state. Social justice movements and environmental justice movements, as they are currently constituted and implemented, do little if anything to address the specific needs of the individuals living on the Hillside.

Attempts to ordain or prophesy from above the direction of justice movements is fraught with epistemological and practical perils,[88] and simplistic solutions to complex problems are not readily available. Furthermore, offering solutions tends to present problems with discursive closure, and solutions are filled with their own problematic power dynamics that are in need of further critique.[89] With such caveats firmly in place, I will attempt to do just that. Although the Hillside residents could benefit from a singularly focused movement on, say, health care or toxic emission regulation, any single such benefit omits large portions of their everyday life experiences that are in dire need of support. Cleansing superfund sites does nothing to address Hillside residents' need for stable employment, just as local agencies' provision of clean socks fails to take account of the spatial encroachment pressures coming from nearby resource extraction industries. A socioenvironmental justice movement, or a movement focused on a more comprehensive notion of justice, might recognize and address these interconnected and complex webs of oppression and material difficulties that people, such as those living on the Hillside, face on a daily basis. Furthermore, such a movement would acknowledge there cannot be healthy people without a healthy and productive set of living and nonliving ecological entities surrounding them. What might such a movement look like? It would be driven from within,[90] would be anticapitalist in its formulation,[91] and would advance notions of nature that do not objectify, romanticize, or disintegrate humans from the construct.[92]

Discussion Questions

1. Jeff defines social justice as "work toward a world of equity, dignity, and basic rights through democratically organized social spaces" and environmental justice as "work that addresses questions of 'inequality, fairness, and rights with respect to environmental conditions and decision-making processes.'" Do these definitions work for you? Why or why not? What other definitions might you propose?

2. What does Jeff mean when he says "homeless" people are denied both public and private space? How can this be?

3. What does Jeff mean by public–private and nature–society bifurcations? Why does he see them as oversimplifications of reality? What is he driving at here?

4. What are the power issues in this chapter? Who has the power? Who doesn't? What are the ramifications?

5. Jeff offers up "socioenvironmental justice" as a way to think about a more comprehensive form of justice. What assumptions underlie this idea? How might it be operationalized?

8

John Dewey's Moral Philosophy as a Route to Social and Environmental Justice Through Youth Development Theory

Daniel Theriault
Texas A&M University

Rudy Dunlap
Middle Tennessee State University

One of the first questions Dan (the first author) asks colleagues is, "Why leisure studies?" Almost without exception, he has found that they respond with vivid, sometimes heart-wrenching tales that illustrate the significance of leisure in their lives. Leisure studies, then, was a natural choice, a means to understand and extend those powerful experiences to others. His story began on the summer of his 16th birthday when his mother drop-kicked him into the world of employment with an interview at a local summer camp. Dan quickly learned that summer camp was so much more than a place where young people had fun; it was a place where they could acquire the skills and support needed to become healthier and happier. The pay was awful, but he was hooked. In the 10 years since, first as a summer camp counselor, then as a director, and throughout his graduate studies, Dan explored how recreation can help youth become successful adults, a process often referred to as youth development.

Despite this passion, leisure studies scholars have generally failed to translate research into recommendations that can improve the everyday lives of the constituencies served. Indeed, depending on how the research–practice relationship is constructed,[1] many leisure scholars have not viewed immediate application as a significant aspect of their work.[2] In this chapter, however, we proceed under the assumption that illuminating research–practice linkages is central to the identity of the leisure studies field[3] and explore ways theories can create rather than sever connections to everyday life. We focus on one theory in particular, Youth Development (YD) theory, which is a set of propositions about how youth might become successful adults.[4, 5] YD theory states that if youth possess certain individual characteristics and environmental supports, they are more likely to complete tasks, such as obtaining a job, that are characteristic of becoming an adult. The underlying assumption is that all youth have the same basic needs, regardless of gender, sexual orientation, race, social context, religion, nationality, and so forth.[6]

In our chapter, we take issue with YD theory's claims to universality. In particular, we contend that certain aspects of YD theory are irrelevant or even harmful to some youth who identify as lesbian, gay, bisexual, transgendered, and queer/questioning (LGBTQ). We employ LGBTQ throughout our chapter, along with queer and nondominant sexualities, to refer to all youth who do not identify as heterosexual. Our position is that in the absence of a theory that faithfully describes the experience of being LGBTQ, resources such as academic courses and leisure programs that could be used to improve the everyday lives of queer youth are wasted. As such, we offer recommendations to close the gap between YD theory and the everyday lives of LGBTQ young people based on John Dewey's moral philosophy.[7]

What Is Youth Development?

YD theory emerged out of the child study movement of the late 1800s and early 1900s. Although societies have always been concerned with ways to ensure their survival by preparing children for the future,[8] the Progressive Era was a period of intense social upheaval, reform, and uncertainty brought about by industrialization and urbanization, among other factors. Scientists, especially sociologists and psychologists, examined ways to ameliorate the effects of these forces and to introduce greater stability into society.[9] The work of scholars such as G. Stanley Hall, Joseph Lee, and James Baldwin was driven by three key research priorities of the era: (a) describe the milestones of development, (b) explain the processes underlying development, and (c) identify environmental factors that cause deviation from the norm.[10] Collectively, these studies created what was considered to be a normal child as the basis for comparisons, which, though a fiction, exerted huge influence in classification and judgment of children of the era.[11] For example, developmental theories were used to guide the design of team activities in leisure settings. Leaders of the early recreation movement, such as Joseph Lee, believed youth exercised innate capacities needed for survival in the modern world during properly structured play.[12] Recreation during the Progressive Era was also motivated by a desire to prevent and cure delinquency. For instance, Addams[13] argued that recreation may be an attractive alternative to delinquent behavior, an idea that still resonates today. Each of these motives for recreation, survival skills (e.g., teamwork), and delinquency prevention, contributed to the more general aim of most reforms to create a sense of stability in a chaotic world.[14]

Key legacies from Progressive Era developmental thought include the idea of a hierarchical, age-graded progression through childhood and the quest for universal indicators and processes of development. These ideas are mirrored in modern YD theory, which describes how young people might become successful adults. If we begin at the end, the goal of YD is for youth to fulfill a set of basic needs[15,16] such as completion of school, involvement in a long-term monogamous relationship, and community contribution.[17,18,19] Others describe these needs as developmental tasks, which Arnett[20] categorized as follows: (a) role transitions such as marriage, (b) independence such as moving out of a parent's house, (c) interdependence such as forming a long-term love relationship, (d) norm compliance such as avoiding illegal drugs, (e) biological transitions such as having sex, (f) chronological transitions such as reaching age 21, and (g) family capacities such as supporting family. Accomplishing these tasks is thought to be evidence that a young person is successful and that they have transitioned out of adolescence into adulthood.

YD theorists reason that community and individual resources—sometimes called assets—can help young people achieve the aforementioned goals.[21] The Search Institute's 40 Assets Model is an example of such resources. The *40 Assets Model* is composed of 20 external and 20 internal assets. External assets are features of environments or resources given to youth such as feeling safe in the community and being involved in religious institutions. Internal assets are individual qualities such as honesty and sense of purpose.[22] Several studies have shown the more assets youth have, the less likely they are to engage in risky behaviors (e.g., alcohol or tobacco use) and the more likely they are to achieve thriving indicators (e.g., school success, delaying gratification).[23,24] To summarize, the more assets an individual has, the more likely one will achieve her or his developmental needs, which in turn signals progression out of adolescence into adulthood.

Shortcomings of Youth Development Theory

Generations of scholars have criticized YD theory. Of particular significance for this chapter is the deployment of a universal youth subject by YD scholars. As mentioned, proponents of conventional YD theory assume that success and assets are the same for all youth and that these developmental formulations are inherently beneficial and alternative conceptualizations of development are inaccurate or simply unimportant.[25, 26, 27, 28] This approach presents social context as unimportant or, at best, of secondary importance to the process of growing up.[29] Emerging constructionist and postmodern perspectives on development suggest interactions with social context create not only the problems of development but also the resources available for addressing those challenges.[30, 31] As such, the utility and the justness of a universal youth subject is questionable.

If context is irrelevant, then forces of oppression that shape the everyday lives of LGBTQ youth are equally insignificant to developmental processes within YD theory.[32] However, the everyday experience of many LGBTQ young people is much different than this ideal. For example, compulsory heterosexuality refers to a network of forces that rewards heterosexuality and punishes other sexual identities.[33] In many contexts including schools, families, the workplace, leisure programs, and communities, youth are presented with the message that heterosexuality is normal and that fitting in and being normal require one to be heterosexual.[34] As a result, many LGBTQ youth are denied traditional sources of social support,[35] which in turn challenges their ability to learn about their identity and roles as citizens.[36] Work in leisure contexts has demonstrated that LGBTQ youth respond to these prejudices by avoiding activities altogether or by only participating with other individuals that identify as LGBTQ.[37, 38] Many youth have responded to compulsory heterosexuality by forming their own spaces where they can explore their identities and engage in activism such as online communities and high school gay–straight alliances.[39] If leisure research is to function as an instrument of development in the name of justice, compulsory heterosexuality must become the focus of scholarly and professional scrutiny.

Similarly, leisure scholars and practitioners need to think about why these assets and goals of development were selected instead of others and the consequences of our selections for diverse populations. Although there is little research on this topic, evidence suggests that assets and markers of success within YD theory may actually be detrimental to some LGBTQ youth. Marriage is often described as an important development marker in conventional YD theory,[40, 41, 42] despite LGBTQ marriages being illegal in many U.S. states. On the one hand, this denies queer couples the benefits of marriage and amounts to a legalized constraint against successful development. On the other, Warner[43] argued marriage never enjoyed a broad base of support in the LGBTQ community and violated a central idea of the queer movement that heterosexual norms should not be used to judge the queer community. In either case, the use of marriage as a developmental standard without considering what it means to individuals who identify as LGBTQ may create psychological and social dissonance.

Other researchers[44] describe community contribution as a marker of successful adulthood. However, many LGBTQ youth face harassment and physical violence in their communities for not conforming to "normal heterosexual" standards of behavior such as attraction to the opposite gender.[45] Attempts at community contributions by LGBTQ youth may result in stress, depression, and isolation and decrease youths' desire to be civically engaged.[46] Youth who are not active in their communities may be demonized for seeking safety and connection outside of their communities. Finally, involvement in a religious institution is considered a developmental asset[47] even though religious arguments are frequently engaged to criticize unmarried, nonprocreative sex (i.e., LGBTQ sex) and queer identities more generally.[48] As some religious institutions are not supportive of the LGBTQ lifestyle, religious involvement may lead queer youth to question their identity and withdraw from social institutions.

Important issues for many queer youth, such as the process of coming out, are absent from the youth developmental paradigm. The coming out process refers to publicly acknowledging sexuality. Coming out has been explored in queer theory,[49] but these discussions have yet to affect mainstream YD theory. Valentine and Skelton[50] described coming out as a marker of success for LGBTQ youth, but it is often a difficult process characterized by a lack of information and fear of losing family and friends. As such, coming out also indicates a need for safe spaces where youth can learn about their sexuality and develop support networks.[51] Although safe spaces for identity exploration are often included on lists of environmental assets,[52] contexts for coming out necessitate specific educational content and design features that differ from conventional formulations. For instance, studies have shown sex education programs, which occur in some leisure programs, including the program discussed later in this chapter, may ignore homosexuality or reinforce heterosexuality as normal through positioning sex as being exclusively reproductive and best saved for marriage.[53] Other research has indicated that when LGBTQ sexuality is discussed, it is engaged in relation to a negative topic such as acquiring HIV/AIDS.[54]

The central point is that YD theory is disconnected from the everyday lives of LGBTQ youth. On the one hand, this perspective focuses the attention of researchers on the youth themselves at the expense of the broader communities and societies in which in they live. On the other, the values underlying YD theory are important beyond their application. In overlooking the significance of context and values, YD theory furthers an idealized vision of maturation that may be irrelevant, harmful, or exclusionary to many LGBTQ youth. Given the continued influence of YD theory on youth policy and organized leisure programs, it is vital to discuss ways that YD theory, research, and practice might become more relevant to the experience of being LGBTQ. This brings us to John Dewey's moral philosophy.

John Dewey's Moral Philosophy

John Dewey's philosophy arose in response to problematic divisions within education, aesthetics, politics, and philosophy.[55] In each field, theorizing isolated its subject matter from the everyday experience of individuals. Curricula were designed around abstract notions of an educated person, art was resigned to museums, democracy was reduced to principles, and philosophy was reduced to speculation. This state of affairs created a disparity between theory and practice. For instance, youth were taught facts that had no relevance to the challenges they faced on a daily basis. Art was viewed as the pursuit of the educated or cultured and irrelevant to the life of the common person. Philosophy without a foundation in experience offered the public no practical guidance for problems encountered in everyday life. The challenge, as Dewey understood it, was to make these institutions continuous with experience so that each could become an instrument of social reform in everyday life.[56]

Dewey crafted his moral philosophy in response to the gap between moral theories and moral practice. He suggested this disconnect might be because philosophers were developing moral theories without reference to actual situations. For example, many ethical arguments used hypothetical subjects who acted on the basis of what a rational, objective, or detached observer might do under ideal conditions. Other ethical theories offered a universal rule or rules of moral life that were purportedly deduced from human nature or divine authority. Dewey argued such theoretical standpoints erected artificial barriers between theory and morally problematic situations as experienced in daily life.[57] Stated differently, the issue was that criteria to judge right versus wrong behavior were being developed without reference to a single concrete case from the experience of actual individuals. Engagement within an actual situation might suggest that multiple ethical theories have something useful to offer the problem at hand, that current perspectives should be modified, or that new frameworks are needed. As such, the potential of moral frameworks developed from the theoretical standpoint to address practical problems is, at best, attenuated. If moral theory was to become an instrument to improve the quality of our everyday lives, the barrier between moral theory and moral practice must be dismantled—the starting point for moral theory must be as it is experienced in daily life.[58]

Dewey's[59] approach to moral theory reversed the theoretical standpoint. Rather than using general rules to investigate everyday situations, he believed theories should be developed through engagement with everyday experience, what he called the engaged standpoint. This means that inquiry must begin in experience,[60] which is the dynamic flow of situations that constitute our practical lives.[61] The problems of science should emerge from concrete situations rather than literature reviews, debate, or speculation because otherwise risks impose an artificial problem on the population under study. Of course, he was not recommending that we attempt to disregard all prior knowledge before beginning a project, only that we treat it as provisional. Even our best theories and concepts are only mock-ups of the world they purport to represent and may require revision to be relevant to the problem at hand.[62] What, then, are the implications of these elements of Dewey's theory—beginning inquiry in experience and treating prior knowledge as provisional—for conventional YD theory and practice?

Implications for Research

As described, the starting point for YD theory and subsequent inquiry is an abstract and presumably universalized youth subject. This starting point is fraught with assumptions about what constitutes success and what youth need to be successful outside of the experiences of actual youth. In the case of young people who identify as LGBTQ, the result is scholars have prescribed a vision of development that excludes important ideas such as coming out and have recommended developmental tasks that may be harmful to many nonheterosexual young people. Dewey[63] offered a useful alternative to development with his formulation of growth. If inquiry should begin in experience, then the problems of development are best studied as encountered in everyday situations by actual people. In other words, growth meant for Dewey that the theory and practice of becoming a successful person are one.

Dewey[64] suggested we encounter problems in the course of everyday life that require resolution. The habits to overcome many of these problems have already been acquired through past experience. Dan, for example, has found through trial and error that pleasure reading in a coffee shop is an efficient means to relieve stress. However, sometimes previously accumulated habits are not sufficient to the problem at hand, and in these instances, new habits or perhaps enhanced old habits are needed. Graduate school for Dan was a gradual process of learning how to learn, how to be receptive to new ideas, and how to interrogate them in light of past understanding. Learning how to learn would be evidence of growth, which Dewey interpreted as the ability to resolve, overcome, and recover from non-linear based problems.[65] Thinking about development as growth suggests the supposed goals of development emerge in the course of everyday experience. Learning how to learn only became significant for Dan because of Rudy's repeated insistence that he fully engage with ideas before dismissing or criticizing past work. Without these interactions, Dan would have likely held on to his "judge a book by its cover" mentality, unless of course, a similar situation arose that required him to rethink that approach.

Similarly, thinking about development as growth also suggests assets only become useful in the course of experience. The resources that aided Dan's problem of learning how to learn were only those within that situation. For example, Rudy provided feedback on manuscripts and provocative questions in classroom discussion that helped Dan learn. Rudy also recommended other resources, such as the writing of Dewey that helped Dan navigate through the problem at hand. Rudy's and Dewey's writings were assets in this situation but might act as roadblocks to solving other problems. For example, when faced with a stressful situation, Dan reaches for books written in an easy to digest, engaging style. For Dan, however, Dewey's writing is anything but easy to digest and engaging. Indeed, problematic situations may require reaching beyond assets immediately available to us to create new relationships, such as attending a writing workshop. The central point is that assets only become useful (or act as roadblocks) in specific problematic situations.

This is in no way meant to suggest that YD theory should be discarded or even that it is universally harmful to LGBTQ youth. Many people, including nondominant sexualities, experience marriage as the utmost expression of love for one another, and community contribution has been a central aspect of the queer movement for generations. For many people, regardless of sexual identity, nothing is wrong with these goals or other elements of YD theory. The problem arises when those who do not achieve these goals are deemed to be at risk or deficient in relation to those that do.[66, 67] This is problematic for at least two reasons. First, it may demonize youth for inequitable social relationships. A youth may desire to become civically engaged but not act upon it because they experience bullying or harassment for failing to conform to heterosexual standards of behavior. Describing this young person as unsuccessful may not only be inaccurate but also leave the root cause of the problem (compulsory heterosexuality) unchallenged. Second, some youth may not experience marriage as a goal of development, viewing it instead as an ideal foisted upon them by high profile court cases. Asserting these unmarried individuals are then less likely to become healthy, happy, contributing members of society does not follow.

Following Dewey, we recommend reversing the starting point of inquiry to address these challenges. YD theory defines young people in terms of "inherent biological and psychological processes" that are taken to be "the starting point of analysis of young people."[68] Wyn and White acknowledged, "The social world is an influence on these fundamental processes, but is seen as very much a secondary consideration."[69] Thus, the starting point for inquiry is a set of propositions on how youth might become successful adults. In contrast, we suggest development may better be conceived through Dewey's[70] formulation of growth; that is, the goals of development are defined by the problems encountered in the course of daily life. The assets or resources relevant to solving the challenges are similar to those present within the problematic situation at hand. More generally, the starting point for Deweyan inquiry is with an actual young person immersed in the struggle of attempting to become a successful adult rather than a set of propositions.[71] Beginning inquiry in experience may highlight the power imbalances obscured in past research and avoid imposing irrelevant or harmful developmental goals.

Implications for Practice

Dewey[72] argued the theory-to-practice gap not only was a problem of science but also impacted everyday life. In aesthetics, viewing art as an element of high culture disconnected it from the life of common people, denying them the enjoyment and inspiration it might provide. Dewey[73] suggested theorizing and designing institutions around art as it is experienced may solve the translation difficulties between theory and practice. Again, this proposition was a reflection of the general point that inquiry, in this case relating to the design of museums, should begin in experience.

We conclude our chapter by applying Dewey's thinking to the design and implementation of an organized leisure program serving LGBTQ youth (hereafter referred to as "the program") as a practical illustration of his wisdom. The program has served more than 300 LGBTQ youths per year in the Midwestern United States for over 20 years. The program predominantly serves young people aged 12 to 19, but services for 20- to 23-year-olds are also offered. Programming is oriented around the general goals of identity affirmation and creating a safe community of queer young people. Although services are primarily directed at the youth themselves, community change is also a goal as seen through the program's youth-led activism program and outreach efforts. Such activities are offered each week, and youth are free to participate at a level of engagement that suits them. In terms of structure, activities run the gamut from highly structured sex education lessons to unstructured time for hanging out. However, staff members are encouraged to work in partnership with youth in contrast to more adult-directed services. For example, staff policies recommend, (a) be a friend, not a parent, and (b) avoid giving advice unless it is asked for. Youth are also encouraged to propose and carry out programming ideas.

The program is not explicitly oriented toward Dewey's ideas, but a number of practices employed by program staff are consistent with his thought, including the alignment of preexisting curricular goals with the everyday experiences of participants.[74] A number of specific actions facilitate working toward this goal. First, program staff members offer an array of regular programs and yearly events rooted in participant experiences. The range of programs is not only a large number of activities, but also a variety of intended outcomes consisting of individual and community benefits and of programs tailored to a variety of specific identities. For example, the program offers a drop-in center that is structured as a safe space for youth to simply hang out and escape the pressures and hostility of other environments in their lives. Other programs are more targeted, such as discussion groups where youth can learn about identities and build community. The activism component of the program gives youth the chance to educate community leaders and other youth about social justice issues and to combat oppression in schools. Yearly events, such as an alternative prom, offer a night for young adults to hold hands with whomever they want in a supportive environment.

Second, and perhaps more important, the list of program offerings is always under construction. Youth and staff often approach the director with ideas for activities, and the director is consistently supportive of such proposals. One staff member, for example, came up with an idea for an HIV testing component of the program. She was given the go-ahead and wrote a grant for the program, which was funded, and continues to this day. On another occasion, Dan interrupted a conversation where a youth leader was pitching a queer sex education program to the director. Prior research has shown that queer sex is often ignored and demonized in traditional sex education programs.[75] Therefore, such an activity might be particularly beneficial for LGBTQ participants. The challenge for the director was balancing a supportive attitude with the resources required to follow through on the idea. Such ideas often require grant support, and participants often require assistance to develop their grant-writing skills. Following through and providing this support is critical because doing otherwise risks an attitude of tokenism and disempowering youth.

Third, staffers at all experience levels are trained and encouraged to treat their past knowledge as provisional. For instance, volunteers are asked during training why they chose to work with the program. A variety of answers are offered, but many are rooted in a desire to use their past experiences to help young people. After this exercise, volunteers are asked to read a handout written by a youth that reads, "We know you have lots of experience and advice to give and we do want to know you. However, every life is different and your remedy may not cure our ills." Similarly, the director often tells a story during volunteer training about continually forgetting the preferred gender pronouns of a particular youth. We are conditioned to use pronouns that reflect the physical appearance of an individual (e.g., this person looks male so I will use masculine pronouns), but this assumption may not align with the gender identity of the person with whom we are interacting. The lesson is that we need to avoid making assumptions about youth and work with them to create a safe environment. Taken together, these three strategies allow program staff to become more responsive to the everyday experiences of youth.

Conclusion

For Dewey, justice is ultimately a matter of identifying and then working to resolve problems as they occur in everyday life. Research has the potential to contribute to just relationships and environments, but the perspective employed must be sensitive enough to account for difference.[76] YD theory may be poorly suited for describing how many LGBTQ transition to adulthood. Dewey's engaged standpoint may be better suited for capturing the potentially unique assets and markers of success that describe the experience of being a sexual minority. By studying development as it is experienced, scholars may be able to reconstruct theories to fit the realities of living as a member of a nondominant sexuality. The implications of Dewey's engaged standpoint extend into YD practice as well. Aligning preexisting curricular goals with the everyday experiences of participants may be an important step toward closing theory-to-practice disparities in leisure services for youth.

Discussion Questions

1. Daniel and Rudy question the common scientific practice of applying a general abstract theory to explain a highly individualized subject matter. Discuss what the authors have to say as it relates to the application of YD theory to LGBTQ youth.

2. What would John Dewey's criticism of typical scientific practices likely be if he were alive today? What advice would he give us about how to approach science differently?

3. Who defines what it means to be a successful adult or a normal member of society? Who has the power? Do you think this power is applied equitably and fairly in our society? Would you want to change definitions if you could? How so?

4. How do you feel about considering worldviews and lifestyles different from your own? Are you open to their consideration? Do you welcome alternative perspectives, or do you find them threatening? Why do you feel or think this way?

5. How do you feel about social norms in general? Do you think we need to have widespread agreement about how to behave and what is socially acceptable to ensure a safe and stable society, or do you think it is perfectly fine to welcome divergent lifestyles and behaviors? What, in essence, do we really need in the way of rules to live by?

9

Facebook's Status in the Lives of Generation Y

Exploring Power Structures in an Online Leisure Space

Callie Spencer
Jeremy Jostad
University of Utah

We were sitting at the kitchen table, beers in hand, brainstorming the beginning ideas of a paper. As I opened my laptop to take notes, I first performed the ritual of checking Facebook. As Facebook's timeline feature was just being introduced, there was a flurry of comments about it on my homepage. I read the following status update aloud to Jeremy:

Y'all, don't hate on timeline. Facebook is the last truly free space on Earth! The last place where everyone can be themselves without anyone having power over them. We should all be thankful that we can come here and express ourselves!

This status update, belonging to a 20-year-old friend, led us into a discussion of power and space in virtual social environments, specifically for our generation, Generation Y. We went to Mark Zuckerberg's Facebook page to look for his goals in creating the ubiquitous social network. He stated, "I am trying to make the world a more open place by helping people to connect and share."[1] We wondered if Facebook truly made "the world a more open place" for Generation Y or if power structures of the offline world were still present.

Contrary to Zuckerberg and the opinions of the author of the above status update, others assert that the space of Facebook is far from free. For example, Eben Moglen, founder of the Software Freedom Law Center, stated:

Mr. Zuckerberg has attained an unenviable record. He has done more harm to the human race than anybody else his age. Why? Because he harnessed Friday night, that is, "everybody needs to get laid." He turned it into a structure for degenerating the integrity of human personality, and he has, to a remarkable extent, succeeded, with a very poor deal. Namely, "I will give you free Web hosting and some PHP doodads, and you get spying for free all the time." And, it works. That's the sad part. It works. Facebook is "the web" with, "I keep all the logs, how do you feel about that?" It's a terrarium for what it feels like to live in a panopticon build-out of web-parts.... It shouldn't be allowed.[2]

With these contrasting messages in mind, the goal of this chapter is to investigate Generation Y's experiences within the space of Facebook. Does Facebook offer youth an emancipatory experience, their own space in which to explore identities and connect with friends (as Zuckerberg and my friend contend), or is it experienced as an oppressive space (as Moglen contends)? How do Generation Y Facebook users experience this virtual space?

⁑ As leisure scholars, we believe what happens in our leisure time and spaces should be thought of as a necessary piece of making this world a more just place to live. In our digital age, it is imperative to make sure not only our physical leisure environments but also our online leisure environments are just. Although online leisure spaces have rarely been a topic of focus within the leisure literature,[3] leisure scholars are uniquely positioned to study online leisure spaces and to advance a specialized body of knowledge to create a more just online leisure space.

We focus on the largest online social media site, Facebook. With over 900 million users speaking 70 different languages, Facebook is a leisure space for an enormous number of people worldwide.[4] To gain insight into user experiences within Facebook, we performed a qualitative inquiry involving a close reading of responses to questions we posed as wall posts on a Facebook community page.

We begin by introducing our theoretical (critical theory) and conceptual (cultural studies) frameworks. According to Giroux, the coupling of cultural studies with critical theory does much more than "simply provide a lens for resituating the construction of youth within a shifting and radically altered social, technological, and economic landscape: it also provides elements for rethinking the relationship between culture and power, knowledge and authority, learning and experience."[5] First, we explain the way in which we employ critical theory as a framework for exploring experiences of power within the space of Facebook. Second, we detail the way in which we view Facebook through a cultural studies lens, specifically explicating our definition of *culture* and our use of the metaphor *cultural toolbox*. We then conclude with a discussion of what we found.

Critical Theory

Critical theory emerged from the philosophies of The Institute for Social Research in Germany, influenced by Kant, Hegel, and Marx. The institute, commonly referred to as the Frankfurt School, was developed in response to social unrest in Europe following World War I. From this coalescing think tank of intellectuals, critical theory surfaced as a form of social and cultural critique. Critical theory was typically thought of as a radical social theory or a form of cultural criticism, and critical theorists believed their actions were in response to the social conditions and changes of the time.[6] The foundational premise of critical theory is that reason can be used to functionally change society and produce transformational reform in the world.[7] Hegel proposed the idea that self-reflection, an attainment of higher levels of consciousness, should be coupled with action, which would provide the connection between theory and practice.[8] These ideas gave way to a new discourse of thinking and action that focused on making improvements to the social structure of the world and to the ways individuals construct collective consciousness.

The relationships of power, knowledge, and discourse are fundamental concepts investigated through an ethical lens.[9] Critical theory assumes a critique in which a systematic hegemony is governed by institutions in power that are socially and historically positioned.[10] Systematic hegemony can therefore be understood as a power structure that is innate to society, leaving little or no agency for individuals. Kinchloe and McClaren suggested:

Certain groups in any society are privileged over others and, although the reasons for this privileging may vary widely, the oppression that characterizes contemporary societies is most forcefully reproduced when subordinates accept their social status as natural, necessary, or inevitable.[11]

Following its emergence after World War I, critical theory is now being implemented to answer questions concerning mass media and society. Critical theory's approach to studying the influence of mass media over society calls "not only for an understanding of the working of the media, but also for a grasp of the media's control over segments of cultural consumption."[12] The idea of culture as mass produced and sold as a commodity to individuals was introduced in the writings of Adorno and Horkheimer.[13] They argued culture was a product of capitalistic forces that created fictitious needs that could be bundled together and sold as a commodity, not only putting an "identity stamp" on those who purchased them, but also eliminating the needs of creativity and freedom.[14] As culture is a key element for these critical theorists, we now offer a discussion of the conceptualization of "culture" and the specific culture on which we focus.

Cultural Studies

Defining Culture

To justify using cultural studies as a conceptual lens, it is important to begin by defining the term *culture*. Geertz[15] devoted an entire book to the concept; he argued culture is public and acted, with ideological and materialist elements. He claimed, "Culture is public because meaning is. You can't wink (or burlesque one) without knowing what counts as winking or how, physically, to contract your eyelids." Swidler, following Geertz, defined culture as "the publically available symbolic forms through which people experience and express meaning ... including beliefs, ritual practices, art forms, and ceremonies, as well as informal cultural practices such as language, gossip, stories, and rituals of daily life."[16] In this chapter, we use Swidler's definition of culture because we view Facebook as both a "publically available symbolic form" for meaning expression and a ritual practice of daily life.

The Cultural Toolkit

After establishing her definition of the term *culture*, Swidler, summarizing Hannerz, described a metaphor of culture as a toolbox "from which actors select differing pieces for constructing lines of action."[17] It is important, then, to discover what tools are in that toolbox and also to unveil the tools that the specific cultural toolbox is lacking but should contain.

Cultural studies provide us with a lens to explore how young people use the visual images and messages provided by the mass media to articulate their personal identity and developmental understanding of their role within the social system.[18] This conceptual lens can help us understand the use of Facebook by Generation Y as a cultural system set in place by the mass media and capitalistic entities that seek to produce identity stamps, which intend to hold the existing structures in place:

Capitalist industrial societies are societies divided unequally in terms of, for example, ethnicity, gender, generation, sexuality, and social class. Cultural studies argues that popular culture is one of the principle sites where these divisions are established and contested; that is, popular culture is an arena of struggle and negotiation between the interests of dominant groups and the interests of subordinate groups.[19]

We contend the subordinate group is Generation Y.

Generation Y

"This is my world",[20] replied Niki Tapscott to her father, author Don Tapscott, when asked why she spent so much time on the Internet. Niki viewed the Internet as a place of freedom away from the watchful eye of her father, or any other adults, where she could be herself with her friends.[21] At 26-years-old, Niki is a member of Generation Y. Also known as the Net Generation, Millennials, or the Me Generation, Generation Y consists of people who were born between January 1977 and December 1997.[22]

In *The Dumbest Generation*, Bauerlein argued that Generation Y, who he termed "Twixters," are caught in the rat race of the culture of overachievement, and the result has produced a disconnected, shallow, and ultimately stupid generation. "For the Twixters, mature identity is entirely a social matter developed with and through their friends. The intellectual and artistic products of the past aren't stepping-stones for growing up. They are the fading materials of meaningless schooling."[23] We disagree. If anything, Generation Y is the most oppressed generation. Older generations, including Bauerlein's, have forced adolescents into online realms of communication by not providing adequate public places in which students can participate equally in society.

How We Approached Our Work

In our inquiry, we explored the cultural toolbox of Generation Y in the context of Facebook, guided by two overarching questions: What is the user's experience of the space of Facebook? What sorts of power inequalities operate in this space? We created a Facebook account and entered six questions as status updates. We then invited 70 students in our classes who used Facebook to comment. The questions were as follows:

1. How and why do you use Facebook? What are the benefits and drawbacks of using Facebook to accomplish your goals?
2. How does your Facebook page represent who you are? In what ways do you express yourself on your profile page and why?
3. Does Facebook provide you any freedoms that other forums of socialization do not? If so, what are they?
4. How do you deal with issues of privacy on Facebook? How do these choices affect your social interactions?
5. Some people believe that in any social interaction there is always one party that holds the power or control, creating inequalities. Others firmly disagree. Is Facebook a place where inequalities exist because of power and control? Or, is it a place of complete equality? Explain. Who is in control?
6. What sucks about Facebook? What is awesome about Facebook?

Students were able to log on to the site and answer the questions with typed responses from March 11 to April 1, 2011. During this 3-week period, the site was accessible 24 hours a day, 7 days a week. A total of 32 responses were provided for question one, 31 for question two, 27 for question three, 29 for question four, 27 for question five, and 29 for question six. We then analyzed the 175 responses and boiled them down into three main themes: (1) lived experiences of a new communication space, (2) lived experiences of power, and (3) lived experiences of relationship. For the purposes of this chapter, we focus on the first and second themes because we believe them to be most relevant to the topic of social and environmental justice.

Discussing What We Found

This section is presented in two columns. As you look at the page, one column ent the text of our study results. The other column is a verbatim e-mail exchange betv   ан Dustin (coeditor of this book) and Callie Spencer and Jeremy Jostad (authors of this chapter). Just as a Facebook page is set up with information streaming in several columns, the user having to choose when, what, and how to read, we suggest you also have a similar multitasking interaction with this page, reflecting specifically upon how information is presented in physical as well as online spaces and what sort of issues surrounding power this might produce. Through the transparency of the e-mail conversation in which we discuss issues arising from concepts presented in this chapter, we invite you to join us in thinking through what social and environmental justice might look like in online spaces. Our goal is not to provide answers (which tends toward closure), but to spark further conversation about power in online spaces.

The goal of our inquiry was to explore our students' lived experiences on Facebook, with the aim of critically examining aspects of this space that offer freedom and aspects that perpetuate power hierarchies. First, we discuss the students' lived experiences on Facebook, comparing their experiences to a metaphor in the leisure literature used to describe virtual places: Oldenburg's concept of third place.[24, 25] Then we employ Foucault's idea of the Panopticon to explore students' experiences of power within the space.

Lived Experiences of a New Communication Space

Oldenburg presented the concept of third place as neither home nor work, but places such as coffee shops, bars, and parks "where community is most alive and people are most themselves."[26] Oldenburg posited that in these places people truly build community; these places enable certain freedoms for experiences and relationships that are not available in either first (home) or second (work) places. Between the time he wrote his first book on third places in 1989 and the publication of his book on third places in 2001, the Internet became a prevalent force of socialization. Although Oldenburg[27] did not consider Internet spaces to be third places, and went so far as to blame the Internet for the demise of American community, many scholars have used his third place concept to describe Internet "spaces,"[28, 29, 30] and we do so as well. Oldenburg outlined 10 characteristics of third places:

1. They exist on neutral ground.
2. They are social levelers.
3. They are accessible.
4. They emphasize localized communities.
5. Conversation is the primary activity.
6. They have a low profile.
7. They are open in the off-hours.
8. They have a regular clientele.
9. The mood is playful.
10. They are a home away from home.[31]

From: Daniel Dustin
To: Callie; Jeremy
Subject: Chapter

Callie and Jeremy,

A couple of things. First, your chapter implies social justice (injustice) issues without making them too explicit. That's okay. It's far enough along in the book that Keri and I will challenge readers to tease out the social justice issues for themselves via discussion questions. It's also the case that I'm not quite sure what your chapter has to do with environmental justice per se. Something for you to chew on.

I confess I'm more interested in the subject now that I've read your paper. It smacks of Big Brother, 1984, Animal Farm, and all those other swell "science fiction" novels out of my youth—especially when you talk about "The Gaze" and "The Panopticon." Interesting stuff. I'm still trying to figure out whether I really buy into the idea that my generation (Or is it the generation after mine?) has forced this onto your generation by depriving you of legitimate third places.

Dan

❖ ❖ ❖

For Oldenburg, these characteristics are essential for third places because they allow for freeing ways of communication and relationships that form the basis for community formation and maintenance. Soukup offered a critique and literature review of the use of this model in describing what he terms "computer-mediated communication (CMC) contexts."[32] "In general, CMC contexts such as third places emphasize conversation, humor and play, are on neutral ground, provide a home away from home and involve regular members."[33] However, characteristics number 2, 3, and 4 created major problems for Soukup when overlaying the third place concept onto CMC contexts. Therefore, he concluded the concept of third space has limited utility in CMC settings and is a potentially dangerous borrowed term.

In opposition to Soukup's evaluation, students in this study experienced Facebook as an openly accessible social leveler. Students commented on the ability for anyone to create a Facebook account and then post updates, comments, messages, photographs, videos, and more on their own wall as well as the walls of their friends. "I think that Facebook is pretty equal in the sense that anybody can post and they can post as many times as they want" (Jessica). Students also mentioned the public library as a place for free (monetarily speaking) access to Facebook. In 2006, when Soukup published his article, he listed several statistics (that he retrieved in 2002) on global Internet use that suggested that CMCs were overwhelmingly accessible to only rich, White Americans. However, a look at the Facebook statistics page tells a different story, a story more in line with the students' experience of Facebook as openly accessible. Facebook has more than 900 million active users, 70% of whom are outside of the United States; Facebook is translated into 70 different languages; and 190 different countries use Facebook for business marketing.[34]

The experience of Facebook as a social leveler was multifaceted. Students noted elements of free speech, decreased censorship, and freedom of choice as indicators of equality. Oldenburg defined social levelers as nonhierarchical places that propagate "the abolition of all differences of position or rank."[35] Speaking directly to his experience of Facebook as a social leveler, Billy stated, "Facebook levels the playing field." For Douglas, free speech, whether uplifting or harmful, is a key to viewing Facebook as a social leveler. "It is a place of complete equality. Granted, I feel some people may voice opinions inappropriately, but that's why I say for me it is a place of equality." In places such as school and work, limits are placed on what can be said because of tangible and intangible consequences. As a social leveler, Facebook is experienced by Stevie as a place without the censorship of other non-virtual places:

I believe Facebook is the closest thing to free speech that is accessible to anyone and everyone. Most of the time there is some sort of censorship looming about that prevents you from saying and doing what you want. Facebook may have something of the sort

---

From: Callie Spencer
To: Daniel; Jeremy
Subject: Justice in Online Environments

Hi Dan,

I am glad we have sparked your interest! ☺ We agree that Facebook does bring up Big Brother, 1984, and Animal Farm. Jeremy and I had a chat about your comments, and here are our thoughts:

You noted that you were not sure what our chapter had to do with environmental justice. This is problematic, as part of the point of our chapter is the argument that, as PRT folks, we need to broaden our definition of "environment" to include online as well as physical environments.

Specifically, we state:

"As leisure scholars, we believe that what happens in our leisure time and spaces should be thought of as a necessary piece of making this world a more just place to live. In our current historical setting, the "digital age," it is imperative to work to make sure not only our physical leisure environments are just, but also our online leisure environments. Although online leisure spaces have rarely been a topic of focus within the leisure literature,[3] leisure scholars are uniquely positioned to study online leisure spaces and advance a specialized body of knowledge to create a more just online leisure space."

Thanks again for your time and effort in editing our chapter.

Many Thanks,
Callie and Jeremy

for lewd behavior, but that's a far cry from the other outlets I've seen. (Stevie)

Freedom of choice was a concept that appeared frequently in relation to Facebook as a leveler. The students overwhelmingly expressed the idea that Facebook was a place of equality because each individual had a choice of what to post, with whom to interact, and when to interact:

I don't think one party has power over another on Facebook because you can choose who to interact with and what information to share. Each individual is in control of how they use Facebook, with the exception of following the guidelines set forth by the creators and administrators of the company. But you agree to follow those rules when you sign up for it, so it's still all up to you. (Nancy)

I think Facebook is on the equal side. There is nothing you are forced to do, share, say, etc. Relationships in general will always have inequalities, but Facebook does not enhance it any further. (Harriet)

Soukup would agree with Harriet, as she noted the universal existence of inequalities. Soukup's main critique of Oldenburg was just that; he argued that no place, including third places, is a completely accessible or pure leveler. Harriet would agree with him, but adds that Facebook neither accentuates nor perpetuates inequalities.

In the end, however, the students' experiences of Facebook revealed a flaw hindering its classification as a third space. On several occasions, the students indicated there was a blurry line between Facebook, home, and work. For Oldenburg, a third space must be a place that is completely separate from work and home. "The *raison d'etre* of the third place rests upon its differences from the other settings of daily life and can best be understood by comparison with them."[36] Bruce responded that the downfall of Facebook was "overactive parents and bosses checking content on Facebook." Not only does this portray a power hierarchy, but also it is an indicator of work and family life from first and second spaces invading, thus invalidating, Facebook as a third space. Another student told a story about peers who, as a requirement for a job search, made sure the companies to whom they applied allowed "Facebooking" during work hours. Finally, Lucy indicated that Facebook use was rampant during class time. "I also can't believe how many college students I've seen on Facebook on their laptops in the middle of class. How can that possibly be improving their education?" School can be considered a second place, as it is a place of work for students. Therefore, using Facebook while

From: Dan Dustin
To: Callie; Jeremy
Subject: Clarification

Callie and Jeremy,

I'm not saying that "online" is not part of the environment. I can see cyberspace as part of the environment. What I was asking you was, what is the environmental justice question you address? I think the chapter is clearly about social justice (misuse of power over people). Is the connection that the environment (online) is being abused? Do we have an obligation to treat that cyberspace a certain way for its own benefit? I dunno. You tell me. Another way of thinking about this is that I think the chapter is very people centered; that's all. And I'm not criticizing you for that. It is simply an observation. It is something for me and you two to think about.

Dan

❖ ❖ ❖

From: Callie Spencer
To: Daniel; Jeremy
Subject: Ah ha and Anthropocentric?

Hi Dan,

Ah ha! Thank you for your clarification. I can now see what you meant. Very interesting question.....hmmmm. I will really have to think through this one..... My immediate reaction to the anthropocentric nature of the chapter and the notion of environmental justice is a sort of critical engagement, or poststructural critique of the term "environmental justice" focusing specifically on the choice of the word "justice" as a part of this term. If we trace the term justice to Plato, it tells us that justice has to do with man reaching his own harmony, happiness, or ideal state; if we trace it to Aristotle, justice and polis, or in class may be considered a violation of separation of third places from other settings of daily life.

Before Facebook went viral, the hot social networking site was a site called MySpace, very aptly named as it was meant to be a place where teens could connect with one another away from the watchful eyes of their parents, a space they could call their own. Facebook began as a social networking site exclusively for university students and required a university e-mail address to open an account. Similar to MySpace, it was a space created for students by students. As both MySpace and Facebook became cultural phenomena for Generation Y, scholars began to ask questions aimed at understanding the phenomena: Why do teens and young adults feel the need to create virtual spaces to call their own? What is happening to third places? What is happening to parks and schoolyards and coffee shops frequented by Generation X's youth?

One answer, presented by boyd, is the creation of an age-segregated society:

> Idealists viewed high school as a place where youth could mature both intellectually and socially, but age segregation meant that young people were being socialized into a society that did not include adults.... Collectively, four critical forces—society, market, law, and architecture—have constructed an age-segregated teen culture that is deeply consumerist but lacks meaningful agency.... What emerged with the Internet was a radical shift in architecture; it decentralized publics.[37]

Today Facebook does not require university attendance as a prerequisite for membership. It is open to anyone with an e-mail address. As Bruce, a student, articulated, the downfall of Facebook is the watchful eyes of parents and bosses, who now have access to membership on the social network. With parents and bosses on Facebook, the question becomes, "Who is in power in this space?"

Lived Experiences of Power

The gaze. Foucault[38, 39] presented two conceptions of the idea of "the gaze": the medical gaze and the introspective gaze. The latter is the idea of the gaze as an enactment of power and is most often associated with Foucault's use of the Panopticon as a metaphor for the structure of modern participatory surveillance. This idea will be applied to Facebook in the next section. This section will focus on the former, Foucault's conceptualization of the gaze in a medical setting as the "medical gaze." In this conceptualization, the doctor looks upon the patient in a dehumanizing way, separating the body from the person or soul that inhabits the body.[40]

Certain aspects of Facebook allow for a similar doctor–patient relationship, dehumanizing the person on whom the gaze falls. A

public, are intertwined; if we go Aquinas, justice is divine command to man from God... Although these are all the dead white dudes, we can see that justice and human are inseparable. The mere idea of justice is anthropocentric.

Can we enact an "environmental justice" that is truly biocentric? Is this even something we want as our goal?

Thanks for the things to think about. I really think this is an interesting question concerning "justice" and "online environments."

Have a great evening!

Callie

❖ ❖ ❖

From: Daniel Dustin
To: Callie; Jeremy
Subject: Intrinsic Value

Callie,

Yes, a very big problem is, how can we human beings be anything but anthropocentric no matter what we might say or do? How can we escape ourselves or speak outside of ourselves? We can't really.

But my question concerns whether the environment beyond humans has, or ought to have, a right to some sort of justice based on its own terms. It is most common that we think of the environment in instrumental terms. It has value to the extent it serves human purposes. The philosopher Alfred North Whitehead acknowledged such instrumental value, but added that the environment ought to have intrinsic value or value in and of itself. Its instrumental value is of a secondary, not a primary, nature.

universal way in which the students reported using Facebook was to browse a friend's page to gaze upon pictures, comments, and updates, stealing a glimpse into that person's activity. Allison explained, "I love knowing what is going on in my friends' lives without actually having to talk to them all the time. Let's just say it satisfies my curiosity and desire to be nosy." The students documented that they spent time daily scanning through other people's profiles, reading wall comments, and looking through pictures. "The benefits are that it is easy to see what somebody is up to through their news feeds, wall posts, and also pictures that they post" (Susie).

However, with this benefit comes drawbacks: addiction and stalking. Students complained that it was too easy to get wrapped up in checking profile after profile, thus "wasting time." "Facebook is the greatest procrastination enabler" (Bruce). The students described Facebook as similar to a drug addiction; when the student sat down in front of a computer, an immediate and insatiable drive to check Facebook to keep "up to date" with news followed. Four students described a negative aspect of spending time looking at other people's profiles as profile stalking or being a "creeper." Several scholars have researched the phenomena and very real dangers of cyberstalking, cyberbullying, and predatory behaviors of adults on youth in cyber spaces.[41, 42, 43] However, our students are referring to a different sort of negative Internet behavior, a more passive form, albeit not any less serious of an offense than the intrusions identified in the aforementioned research. The students are intruding upon one another's privacy, taking a piece of another person, in the form of information, without having to interact at all with that person. "Facebook allows you to be a creeper because you can look through peoples' profiles and such and see what is going on in their lives without having to talk to them" (Johnny). The creeping on each other's profiles these students were doing was akin to the medical gaze to which Foucault referred. In this specific user experience of Facebook, the power lies in the hands of the person who is "being a creeper" and objectifying, thus dehumanizing the person through whose profile they are digging. Creeping to glean information about a person at the very least demonstrates a decline in the level of interpersonal connection with and at the worst objectifies the human behind the profile.

Art critic Susan Sontag, in her classic critical piece *On Photography*, brought to light the dehumanizing and damaging aspects of the photographer's gaze.[44] Using strong metaphors, she challenged readers to reconsider the position of power the photographer holds over subjects on which he or she gazes, the aspects of soul stolen from the subject, and the repercussions of the act of photography in perpetuating and encouraging certain action. "The camera doesn't rape, or even possess, though it may

Do cows
extent the
milk or rec
have some
and is there
to which the   as well?
Therein lies the rub.

Happy thinking.
DD

❖ ❖ ❖

From: Jeremy Jostad
To: Dan; Callie
Subject: Justice and Nature

Hi there. I cannot let the two of you have all the fun.

I find it interesting that you both are critiquing "environment" and "justice" separately. Is this appropriate? Can we separate the parts from the whole and expect them to be the same as when they stand side by side? Does the term "justice" change due to its modifier? This is difficult for me to answer because I am not sure the two justices are the same. One places anthropocentric ideals into an anthropocentric world, whereas the other places it into a biocentric world.

Therefore, I don't see how they can be treated the same.

Your question about environment is a valid one, Dan, but historically when we think of environment, our predisposition is that of the natural one. However, the environment Callie and I are talking about is not natural (at least not in the biological sense). And this is where I find the problem very interesting. Does the context of the environment require a different conceptualization of justice? If you see environmental justice as action or non-action toward an environment which allows it to possess value for its own sake, can we place these same ideals on a non-natural environment?

..me, intrude, trespass, distort, exploit, and, at the farthest reach
metaphor, assassinate all activities that, unlike the sexual push and
shove, can be conducted from a distance, and with some detachment."[45] Although the difference between the photographer's gaze and
the Facebook surfer's gaze is that the objects of the gaze on Facebook
have created their profile, performing as they wish for the gazers, the
"creepy" gaze still exists as reported by the participants. The action
of stalking one another's profiles is analogous to Sontag's interpretation of the camera. Facebook allows these students to gaze upon one
another in a way in which the gazer is detached from the subject of
the gaze. In the case of Facebook, this detachment happens not only
physically but also temporally. As opposed to photography and the
camera, the subject of the virtual gaze need not be present. The students' adjective "creepy" makes sense when considering this distant
and unknown surveillance.

Facebook: A Modern Panopticon?

The second way in which Foucault conceived the idea of the gaze
is in relation to power and the metaphor of the Panopticon.[46] The metaphor of the Panopticon refers to an architectural design for a prison
in which power and control are revolutionized. A circular tower is
built as the central point inside a prison. The walls of the prison wrap
around the tower in such a way that every prisoner can be seen by the
guard inside the Panopticon tower at all times. In this design, "inspec-
tion functions ceaselessly. The gaze is alert everywhere."[47] The ever-
present gaze produces a prison in which prisoners discipline themselves:

> The efficiency of power, its constraining force has, in a sense,
> passed over to the other side—to the side of its surface of applica-
> tion. He who is subjected to a field of visibility, and who knows
> it, assumes responsibility for the constraints of power; he makes
> them play spontaneously upon himself; he inscribes in himself the
> power relation in which he simultaneously plays both roles; he
> becomes the principle of his own subjection.[48]

Foucault contended the metaphor of the Panopticon can be applied to more than prisons. It can be applied to describe the instruments of hierarchical power intervention inscribed in a variety of settings: "The Panopticon, on the other hand, must be understood as a
generalizable model of functioning; a way of defining power relations
in terms of the everyday life of men."[49] We use the Panopticon metaphor to examine the instruments of power operating on Facebook and
to critique who holds the power. Who is in the tower and who is the
prisoner? Addressing the latter question, a student, Aaron, explained
that the power is in the hands of the individual user of Facebook. He
stated four reasons for his belief:

I am not so sure; however, if
we can, then my argument is
that Facebook is not being
used for its intended purpose.
It was created to serve a
particular function, just like
the natural environment,
and has since been trans-
formed into a mechanism
for human consumption and
monetary gain, again, just
like the natural environment.
Therefore, if we want to
make it a just environment,
the intrinsic value, which I
see as its originating purpose,
should be what exists in this
environment.

Not sure this clears anything
up or just makes it messier.
Just my thoughts. Thanks for
your insights, Dan and Callie.

Jeremy

❖ ❖ ❖

From: Daniel
To: Jeremy; Callie
Subject: Non-Natural

Jeremy,

Regarding natural/non-nat-
ural. How can anything be
"non-natural." Buckminster
Fuller (of geodesic dome
fame) said anything humans
do is permitted by nature. I
would say cyberspace is part
of nature. Why do you think
it isn't?

DD

❖ ❖ ❖

From: Callie Spencer
To: Daniel; Jeremy
Subject: Social Construct-
edness of 'Nature'

Hi Dan,

First, I think that the
language choice that Jeremy
made, "non-natural" vs. "un-

a) You decide if you want to use it or not,

b) you can cancel your membership or account at any time without any type of penalty and you can subsequently re-activate at any time,

c) nobody is forcing you to see or read things you don't want to, and

d) you can be as private as you'd like on the site.

The overwhelming majority of the students would agree with Aaron's eloquent statement of ownership and control of individual privacy on Facebook. Therefore, we use his four points to structure our critique of the potential of Facebook to act as a modern Panopticon.

a)   You decide if you want to use it or not

Is participation truly optional? boyd contended it is not; she pointed to age segregation and a rampant culture of fear as culprits forcing Generation Y online if they want any practice interacting with one another in public:

> The power that adults hold over youth explains more than just complications in identity performance; it is the root of why teenagers are on MySpace in the first place....Given the overwhelming culture of fear and the cultural disdain for latchkey practices, it is likely that teens are spending more time in programs than on their own....While the home has been considered a private sphere where individuals can regulate their own behavior, this is an adult-centric narrative. For many teens, home is a highly regulated space with rules and norms that are strictly controlled by adults.[50]

Public interaction, for boyd, is the key to growth and figuring out how to interact in society:

> Restrictions on access to public life make it difficult for young people to be socialized into society at large. While social interaction can and does take place in private environments, the challenges of doing so in public life are part of what help youth grow.[51]

Oldenburg[52] blamed the decentralization of communities, a result of mass suburbanization, for the loss of physical third places or "great good places" for youth to congregate among adults. Over-scheduled youth with parents who worry and respond by segregating youth are also to blame for the phenomenon he calls "shutting out youth."

natural," is a very interesting statement. When I think through these two words, I see "non-natural" as being something that is "artificial," or "man-made" (I am thinking cubic zirconia, cyberspace, etc.) When I think of "unnatural," I think of something that once was natural and has now been altered in some way (usually has a negative connotation).

Now, if we go back to the idea of cyberspace and cubic zirconia as things that are non-natural, we can immediately trace, say, some physical element in either of those two items back to nature (cyberspace is run by servers which are made of wires, which are comprised of metals, which are "natural"). We could also make the argument that humans came up with the idea for fake diamonds, or cubic zirconia, and humans are natural, therefore cubic zirconia are in some way natural.

However, if we look at the idea of "natural" as a socially constructed term, we run into some issues. "Natural" to whom? For whom? For example, the corset created a "natural" look mirroring how women were supposed to look, how nature had designed them to look in the early 1900s. We would not, I hope, think that that sort of hourglass figure is "natural" today or mirrors anything that seems to be guided by "nature." My great great grandmother would not see soymilk as a "natural" product, but my current office mates do. For Christopher Columbus, the fact that the "Indians" were not wearing clothes was "unnatural." Hmmm.....

Let's think through some social constructions, and how even the idea of "natural" reveals a level of power in the "namer" in who gets to determine what is of nature, who gets to "speak for" nature,

If Oldenburg and boyd are right, what other options are provided to youth for interacting publically, making mistakes, and learning how to be a successfully functioning member of society? Christopher noted, "So many people are on it and it makes it so tempting to join in." Several students cited having Facebook-only relationships with some people. "It is an easy way to quickly chat and catch up, while not being time consuming or inconvenient. With some people, the only time I ever communicate with them is on Facebook" (Julie). The students noted that because either they or their friends had moved, they needed Facebook to keep up with one another as a result of the distance. Generation Y is more mobile than any previous generation. If this is the case, how can anyone expect traditional communities to form in Oldenburg's "great good places?" For a mobile, overscheduled generation raised under yet segregated by the watchful eye of older generations, is participation in Facebook truly optional?

b) You can cancel your membership or account at any time without any type of penalty and you can subsequently reactivate at any time

To discuss this statement, we refer you to statements 1 and 2 from Facebook's Statement of Rights (2011):[53]

1. For content that is covered by intellectual property rights, like photos and videos ("IP content"), you specifically give us the following permission, subject to your privacy and application settings: you grant us a non-exclusive, transferable, sub-licensable, royalty-free, worldwide license to use any IP content that you post on or in connection with Facebook ("IP License"). This IP License ends when you delete your IP content or your account unless your content has been shared with others, and they have not deleted it.
2. When you delete IP content, it is deleted in a manner similar to emptying the recycle bin on a computer. However, you understand that removed content may persist in backup copies for a reasonable period of time (but will not be available to others).

In relation to deleting content, this statement poses two problems for the user, thus shifting power from the user into the hands of friends and the owners of Facebook. First, Facebook owns anything that anyone puts on Facebook: Power is in the hands of Facebook. Second, if a person wishes to delete his or her profile completely, taking all power and ownership of any personal content away from Facebook, they would have to track down every photo, song, and comment they had ever shared with a friend and then ask that friend to delete that trace of evidence. At this point, power is completely in the hands of the friend on whose wall the information is located. Finally, what is "a

and who gets to decide what is "natural." Think of issues of gay marriage..... Many religious groups would argue that marriage of two people of the same sex is "unnatural." My question is, for whom? Whoever is defining what is "natural" is the privileged group. Is the institution of marriage "natural?" Does, as you say, "nature permit it"?

Also, I wonder if we think of nature as "permitting," are we reifying "nature," giving "nature" power? Does "nature" permit oil spills? Clearcutting? Oppressive language? Murder?
Thanks for a great conversation!
Callie

❖ ❖ ❖

From: Jeremy
To: Callie; Dan
Subject: Jeff's Chapter

Hi Dan and Callie,

I just read a draft of Jeff's chapter for this book, and I found one quote particularly helpful for this discussion.

Thought I would share...

"Socioecological changes, which are unavoidable in such a complex dynamic, result in the continuous production of new "natures," or new social, physical, and environmental conditions, those things that affect what we know nature to be. All of these processes occur in specific realms of power in which social actors strive to defend and create their own natures in various combinations of contexts of class, ethnic, racialized, and/ or gender conflicts and power struggles."

reasonable period of time" for which all of the content of the user's profile will remain on the server as a backup copy? Albrechtslund[54] foresaw a major problem for Generation Y with content remaining accessible for decades beyond its deletion. "When youngsters lead a life in mediated publics, the fear is that their adolescent thoughts, musings and immature actions might become a millstone around their neck, since the information will be embarrassingly accessible later on."[55] Deleting a Facebook membership does not come without penalty; it comes instead with the penalty of relinquishing personal power and putting oneself at the mercy of friends and the owners of Facebook.

> Based on Jeff's quote, and our previous email conversations, I can see us all as "social actors," creating our own natures. Thus, all of our arguments lend credence to understanding and conceptualizing online spaces through a discussion of environmental justice.
>
> Thoughts?
>
> -Jeremy

c) Nobody is forcing you to see or read things you don't want to

The idea of "force" is key in this statement, as well as in Foucault's Panopticon metaphor. In the Panopticon structure, the prisoners are not physically forced into compliance, as happened in dungeons with balls and chains and guards wielding weapons. Instead, prisoners act as their own control, always aware of the gaze of the guard in the central tower. "Hence, the major effect of the Panopticon: to induce in the inmate a state of conscious and permanent visibility that assures the automatic functioning of power."[56] On Facebook, participants are aware of constant surveillance, and thus they limit their content or practice self-censorship, allowing power to operate automatically:

> I'm really freaked out about the whole Potential-Employer-Stalking-and-Disapproving epidemic, so I have all the privacy settings, and even censor some things I say if the content is … illegal. Or something. It's kind of a bummer when you want your friend in Chicago to see pictures of the awesome party last weekend but are too scared to post them. (Tim)

Tim's fears are an example of the automatic functioning of the power of boss over potential employee. This case is an example of an invisible Panopticon-esque force (potential bosses) "forcing" the Facebook user to act in a way that is conforming instead of empowering.

"There are many people who spend a lot of time posting and replying to posts. Some so much that I have deleted them because I was tired of seeing their opinions splattered all over my 'news' page" (Bob). When Facebook first introduced the NewsFeed feature, there was a huge wave of angry backlash.[57] The NewsFeed is the first page a user sees when they log on to Facebook. It is a continuous stream of friends' activities, complete with time and date. Status updates, new pictures, and friends who have commented on other's walls are just a few of the things that appear on the NewsFeed. There is no way around this. Facebook essentially forces the user to access this feed first, before going on to profile pages. Randy echoed Bob's sentiments as he explained, "Status updates in your news feed that you do not care at all about certainly suck." For Bob and Randy, an overactive Facebook user can become a nuisance, as the News-Feed will continuously be filled with that person's activities. Furthermore, Facebook places ads on the side of each person's profile page. Eliza commented that having to look at these ads is a negative aspect of the Facebook experience: "I would have to say the worst part about Facebook is all of the random ads on the side." Between the NewsFeed design and the ads, there are several aspects of Facebook the user is "forced" to view.

Finally, our last critique of this concept of force has to do with unpaid labor. The advent of the Panopticon saved prisons significant amounts of money, as fewer paid guards were needed. The prisoners were basically doing unpaid labor through self-monitoring. Similarly, Cohen noted Facebook's structure makes economic sense as its members are "forced" to work without pay, doing all of the marketing for Facebook through word of mouth:

> On Facebook, almost all member activity can be conceived of as immaterial labour that benefits the company. A major task upon which Facebook is based is "adding" friends, which is the act of linking to other people's profiles and forms the basic design of the site. The work of adding friends is also Facebook's main growth strategy.[58]

A second way in which Facebook requires participants to work for free is through giving Facebook personal data that is then accessed by third parties who pay premium prices to learn valuable aggregate marketing information.

d) You can be as private as you'd like on the site

Most of the students agree with Aaron, stating they believe they have complete control over the privacy of all information they put on Facebook. Agreeing with and expanding upon Aaron's claim, Susan eloquently summarized the opinion of the majority of students who responded to our questions:

> My page reflects a lot of who I am from my status updates as well as tons of pictures of what I am doing on a consistent basis. Everything I share is stuff I don't mind making public. Any private matter is never posted or discussed on Facebook. My profile is private and only friends can see information about me.

The students reported going into their privacy settings and setting them to maximum privacy, shutting out everyone aside from confirmed friends from access to personal information. In this way, the students believe they control who is watching them (i.e., who the guards in the tower are). Ellerbrok highlighted four ways in which surveillance happens on Facebook: users are visible to one another, visible to marketers, visible to regulatory agencies, and, finally, users are susceptible to 'functional creep,' or the open-ended potential for the data to be used in a number of unforeseen ways down the line. [59] The privacy on which students focused is the first of Ellerbrok's four types of visibility: user-to-user visibility. For this type of visibility, privacy settings are a relatively viable and valid way of protecting oneself. However, the second of Ellerbrok's surveillance methods, the visibility of Facebook users to marketers, is another matter entirely.

Have does Facebook makes so much money without charging a fee to its users? The answer is in the free labor that users provide in the way of personal information that Facebook then sells to outside companies:

> Marketing visibility is enabled by one of two processes: by capitalising on members' profile information, sharing this information with third party groups; and also by collecting information about the user and their activities *outside* of the Facebook website. The latter is accomplished by installing cookies and other tracking technology on Facebook members' computers, or via website integration. These technologies are used to collect information about the individual's purchase patterns, the other websites they may visit, and miscellaneous data.[60]

Facebook's Privacy Policy directly states they keep track of user activities:

> We keep track of some of the actions you take on Facebook, such as adding connections (including joining a group or adding a friend), creating a photo album, sending a gift, poking another user, indicating you "like" a post, attending an event, or connecting with an application. In some cases you are also taking an action when you provide information or content to us. For example, if you share a video, in addition to storing the actual content you uploaded, we might log the fact that you shared it.[61]

Note the language; "we *might* [emphasis added] log the fact that you shared it." Eerily Panopticon-esque, the knowledge that the user is being watched and action "might" be taken can perpetuate power hierarchies automatically.

> Not only is surveillance the method by which Facebook aggregates user information for third-party use and specifically targets demographics for marketing purposes, but surveillance is the main strategy by which the company retains members and keeps them returning to the site….it is the unpaid labour of producer-consumers that facilitates this surveillance.[62]

Conclusion

"Everything I share is stuff I don't mind making public," Susan stated. We wonder if she wouldn't mind sharing with marketers and law enforcement as outlined in Ellerbrok's four levels of visibility? Is Moglen right? Is Facebook what it feels like to live in a "panopticon build-out of web-parts"? Can you really be as private as you like on Facebook? We think not. The creators of Facebook and the marketing companies act as the guards in the tower. They are at the top of the hierarchy holding power over the individual. Where is the justice in that?

Discussion Questions

Note: For a discussion of questions, thoughts, and ideas on power structures in online leisure environments, we created a Facebook page to engage students, professors, and anyone else who might want to join the conversation:
www.facebook.com/SpeakingUpAndSpeakingOutPowerAndOnlineEnvironments
or scan this QR code with your
smartphone to link to the same page:

You will also find the following questions posted as status updates on that page:

1. Facebook is a space in which justice may or may not occur. Based on Callie and Jeremy's account, do you think Facebook is a force for justice? Please defend your point of view.

2. In *The Transparent Society*, David Brin suggested that advancing technologies such as Facebook will force us to choose between privacy and freedom. Do you agree with this forced choice? What choice would you make and why?

3. Do you have a Facebook account? If so, does reading this chapter change your thinking about the potential costs and benefits of sharing aspects of your life online?

4. Please comment on "the gaze" and "the Panopticon" as Callie and Jeremy employ them. Do you think they are effective analogies? Should we be worried about the implications? Why or why not?

5. Callie and Jeremy suggest we do not have many "third places" for young people to congregate, hence the popularity of online spaces such as Facebook. Do you agree with their assessment? Can you think of examples of "third places" that offer an alternative to the Internet?

10

Tourism and Environmental Justice

Freya Higgins-Desbiolles
University of South Australia

Kyle Powys Whyte
Michigan State University

Deirdre Tedmanson
University of South Australia

"Tourism is not just about escaping work and drizzle; it is about power, increasingly internationalized power. That tourism is not discussed as seriously by conventional political commentators as oil or weaponry may tell us more about the ideological construction of 'seriousness' than about the politics of tourism."

—Cynthia Enloe[1]

Tourism is frequently touted as one of the world's largest industries. International tourist arrivals grew by 4.4% in 2011 to a total of 980 million and are predicted to rise to 1 billion in 2012.[2] The Secretary-General of the United Nations World Tourism Organization (UNWTO), Taleb Rifai, stated:

> For a sector directly responsible for 5% of the world's GDP, 6% of total exports and employing one out of every 12 people in advanced and emerging economies alike these results are encouraging, coming as they do at a time in which we urgently need levers to stimulate growth and job creation.[3]

This commercial perspective portrays tourism as an unalloyed blessing to populations worldwide. Discourses on tourism in public and academic spheres follow suit by characterizing it as an industry delivering foreign exchange and jobs to communities around the globe[4] by providing fun and/or fulfillment for clients.[5] Yet beyond this discourse, one finds an abundance of strident criticisms coming from communities and nongovernment organizations (NGOs) at the grassroots. The criticisms testify to negative impacts that ravage people and places daily, which reveal tourism to be no different than other industries that produce injustices.

Tourism has not owned up to justice issues, despite limited gains in certification schemes for sustainable tourism and ecotourism. Tourism scholars hardly discuss justice, with rare exceptions being Scheyvens,[6] Smith and Duffy,[7] Fennell,[8] Hultsman,[9] and Higgins-Desbiolles.[10]

We believe tourism is an area rife with justice issues, especially regarding environmental (in) justice. If tourism is to take environmental justice seriously, there needs to be criteria supporting direct participation to guide the pro-environmental justice activism of NGOs. We offer two examples of NGOs whose activities appear to be progressive on environmental justice issues. We conclude by calling for further work in this area.

Tourism and Injustice

NGOs and a small set of academics have documented injustices brought about by tourism; examples include the Ecumenical Coalition on Tourism, the Tourism Investigation and Monitoring Team, Tourism Concern, and scholars and analysts such as Krippendorf,[11] McLaren,[12] and Turner and Ash.[13] There are two ways of understanding injustice that are relevant to tourism, both of which may be found operating together in various cases. The first involves forms of tourism that are indisputably exploitative (e.g., sex tourism and child sex tourism, organ transplant medical tourism, poverty tourism,[14] and cultural tourism that profanes sacred rituals). The second involves forms of tourism that destroy the places where people live, work, and play (i.e., environmental justice), which is the focus of our chapter. One alarming environmental justice issue is the dispossession of local peoples in places of touristic development. Mowforth and Munt, for example, noted:

> Of all the problems experienced by local communities facing tourism development schemes, the most harrowing involve accounts of people being displaced. Such events normally reflect the distribution of power around the activity of tourism and highlight the powerlessness of many local communities. And it seems rare that displacement and subsequent resettlement of displaced people result in more even and equal development.[15]

Although NGOs such as Tourism Concern have brought attention to dispossession in parts of Africa and Southeast Asia, tourism dispossession is now a global phenomenon. In 2009, for example, the Center of Concern advocated Gullah people's rights against tourism dispossession in the southern United States.[16] However, although widespread, well known, and global, tourism dispossession is hard to accurately measure; increasing pressures for tourism development make it every bit as avaricious as other land use activities—whether development occurs in coastal areas, pristine environments, wild places, challenging environments (e.g., adventure tourism), or unique cultural places that stand out in a rapidly globalizing world.

Another related environmental justice issue is environmental racism. Native Hawaiian academic Trask discussed how tourists drawn to her land for "escape" on their holidays are "participating in the destruction of a host people in a Native place."[17] At that time, Hawaii's visitation statistics showed a tourist ratio of 35 tourists for every native Hawaiian resident.[18] That ratio is now approximately 50 to 1. The resultant crowding, pollution, pressure on Hawaiian resources, and edging out of other endeavors such as fishing, agriculture, and cultural pursuits have resulted in record indigenous Hawaiians being forced to migrate from their homelands or struggling to eke out survival on the margins of a tourism industry where low wages leave many in vulnerable situations as the working poor. In another powerful article, Trask described how significant public and private sector structures promote tourism growth:

> In Hawaii, the destruction of our land and the prostitution of our culture is planned and executed by multi-national corporations, by huge landowners, and by collaborationist state and county governments. The ideological gloss that claims tourism to be

our economic saviour and the "natural" result of Hawaiian culture is manufactured by ad agencies, tour companies, and the state of Hawaii which allocates some $60 million dollars a year to the tourism advertising budget.[19]

Like Trask, de Chavez described tourism as a "deadly force" that opens up lands of indigenous peoples that may have otherwise been left undisturbed for ecotourism. He explained:

> Indigenous peoples are paying a high price for tourism. In their desire to cash in on the billion-dollar profits from this industry, governments, specifically in the Third World, and transnational corporations have disregarded the interests of indigenous peoples. The effects have been devastating. Indigenous peoples have been evicted from their traditional lands, their control and access to their natural resources compromised. They have suffered social degradation brought about by foreign influences and the commercialization of their culture. Even the rich biodiversity of their natural resources has suffered from pollution and environmental damage, unable to support the growing number of tourist arrivals. What few benefits indigenous peoples derive from tourism are far outweighed by the damage it has caused them. They have been made to bear the brunt of an industry over which they have neither say nor control.[20]

These cases of environmental racism suggest an extremely serious environmental justice issue affecting the Global South in particular: the forceful incorporation of people into the global trading system on an unfair basis. Many of the world's poorest peoples are pressured to engage with tourism in the hope of harnessing tourism as a means for development. Lanfant and Graburn contended:

> [Tourism] is a "transmission belt" connecting the developed and the underdeveloped worlds. Tourism policy has become part of a global project which lumps together seemingly contradictory economic interests: the organization of vacations (an idea originating in rich countries) and the aspirations for development of economically weak societies. Thus "free time" resulting from the exploitation of the surplus value of capital is put back into the calculation of economic productivity. Societies inexperienced with industrialization are re-oriented toward "touristification"; tourism comes to be judged by economic and political criteria within the international framework, a vector for global integration.[21]

This "touristification" occurs in the context of the global "free" trade regime being established by powerful countries of the North, international trade and financial institutions such as the World Trade Organization (WTO) and the International Monetary Fund (IMF), and powerful globally networked transnational corporations (TNCs). These actors are forcing a global integration, which includes tourism through the free trade agreement for the service sector. The General Agreement on Trade in Services (GATS) is predicted to lead to greater concentration in the tourism sector as big tourism TNCs continue the trend toward vertical integration. GATS limits the capacity of developing countries to control tourism for their own benefit.[22]

Moreover, the UNWTO, founded as a specialized agency of the United Nations in 2003, and purportedly responsible for tourism, does nothing to address justice. It is the key body in tourism at the international level, having 155 countries as members as well as over 400 affiliate members from industry and the NGO sector. Most important, industry interests are well articulated in the UNWTO's Business Council, which contains some of the most powerful TNCs operating in the tourism industry. UNWTO promotes tourism as a driver of economic growth, inclusive development, and environmental sustainability and offers leadership and support to the sector in advancing knowledge and tourism policies worldwide. Bianchi described this:

> The UNWTO is one of the few UN agencies that essentially represents an industry in contrast to other such UN agencies as UNEP, UNDP, and UNESCO, whose mandate covers a broader scope of human activity from culture and the environment, to science and education. This therefore predisposes the UNWTO to promote the expansion of tourism and the private sector interests behind it.[23]

Tourism not only is rife with environmental injustices, but also is an insufficient international infrastructure for addressing such injustices.

The Demands of Environmental Justice on Tourism

Tourism must be an active force promoting environmental justice. But how can tourism accomplish this? When we say environmental justice, we are not referring only to the particular narrative from the United States beginning with the protests of the PCB landfill in Warren County, North Carolina, the United Church of Christ study on situating hazardous waste facilities, and President Clinton's Executive Order 12898, which mandated federal agencies to incorporate environmental justice into their policies.[24] We are referring more broadly to the idea that actions that affect places where people live, work, and play are important sources of justice or injustice, closely tied to people's health, psychological well-being, social lives, physical health, and education. Environmental justice is important to tourism because of tourism's relation to place. Prior to its commercial or social value, tourism concerns the meaning of place. If space refers to the (socially constructed) abstract dimensions of some area, such as borders and jurisdictions, then place refers to the ways in which human history, culture, and circumstances (e.g., oppression and war) infuse the physical features and systems of an area with meaning.[25]

Places are particularly important because they affect community self-determination. By self-determination, we mean the ability of a community to control its own destiny in ways that draw on the potential of its own historical and cultural capital and resources. Self-determination is a particularly important concept essential to the realization of the human rights of indigenous peoples. Article 3 of the United Nations Declaration on the Rights of Indigenous Peoples states, "Indigenous peoples have the right to self-determination. By virtue of that right they freely determine their political status and freely pursue their economic, social and cultural development."[26] Article 4 continues by clarifying that "indigenous people, in exercising their right to self-determination, have the right to autonomy or self-government in matters relating to their internal and local affairs, as well as ways and means for financing their autonomous functions."[27] Communities' ability to cultivate the places where they live, work, and play is vital to their having opportunities to achieve self-determination. Self-determination is not discussed here in the fuller sense of sovereignty, but rather as a fundamental ethical principle that is key to a community's capacity to encourage and realize its own aspirations.

Tourism is oriented toward place in several important respects. Tourists are attracted to traveling to other areas because of how they imagine them as destinations that are related to or contrasted with their own conceptions of the places where they live. Tourism involves some social imagination about the destination. The places that tourists see as destinations are also places where communities live, work, and play—integral to those communities' self-determination. As an activity that intervenes on several scales, from regional economics to local ecosystem impacts, tourism creates conditions of justice and injustice among the tourists, tourism operators, and residents. Relations of power operate between those who seek to purchase an imagined experience of some place or places and those whose lives are firmly rooted in the place or places that tourists seek to consume. Injustices against residents of particular places are driven by tourism practices that are structured by the motivations of tourists' imaginings about the destinations they seek to experience and/or by tourism operators framing destinations for touristic consumption. Appropriating the experience of an exoticized "other" in their imagined place may be appealing to tourists and lucrative for tourism operators, but at the same time this may be deeply damaging to the people whose lives have been reduced to an entertainment or spectacle for rich outsiders.

There are two important links to environmental justice here. First, as a place-based endeavor, tourism can be an immediate source of harm (as imposition from outside) against communities who already are actively trying to protect the environments where they live, work, and play. Many indigenous peoples, already enduring the long-term and ongoing effects of colonial invasion and its inevitable accompanying trauma, face these circumstances on a daily basis. Second, the environmental justice movement has criticized mainstream environmentalism for having a narrow conception of what, why, and how the environment should be protected, hence excluding the perspectives of indigenous peoples and communities of color.[28]

Mainstream environmentalists have proposed imagined environments worthy of preservation or restoration in ways that reproduce the marginalization and ongoing racism experienced by indigenous peoples and people of color. The relations of power that have sought to "otherize" and silence indigenous voices in mainstream discourses about resource exploitation have also been used by many mainstream environmentalists supposedly offering a different perspective on environmental issues. Bullard and Taylor[29] suggested the mainstream environmental movement has largely attracted a middle-class, White following and hence often privileges their concerns over those of indigenous peoples and communities of color.

This history of environmental justice suggests the importance of the role of NGOs in transforming tourism. Although social movements and associated NGOs have been widely hailed for fostering progressive reform agendas, not all NGOs are equally committed to such agendas. Numerous international NGOs have undertaken cooperation and secured funding from governments, industry, and International Finance Institutions; hence, their commitment to meaningful reforms for sustainability, equity, and justice can be questioned. Morris-Suzuki noted, "The key question is not whether social organizations are 'non-governmental' but whether they encourage critical reflection by members on their own position within national and transnational power structures."[30]

So it is crucial to consider whether tourism NGOs will advance what we call "direct participation" by the affected communities or otherwise advance a shift in power relations that promotes community self-determination. Whyte, for example, suggested, "Even when the intentions behind the practices are caring, love, and concern for humanity," exploitation may result in the absence of direct and "meaningful participation and expression of difference" by the local community in the tourism planning process.[31, 32] Thus a commitment to environmental justice does not necessarily translate into practices that shift the power relations in ways that communities can better seek self-determination via tourism on their own terms. This includes communities' capacity to refuse tourism based on their self-determination needs. To combat this tendency, we believe NGOs should promote the following practices:

1. the meaningful expression of a community's social circumstances and cultural terms in how compensation schemes, consent processes, choices, and trade-offs are determined;

2. the creation and use of open forums to express community differences on how the tourism practices are conducted, especially in relation to communities' unique needs regarding self-determination;

3. discourses used to discuss tourism in the public sphere (advertising, public relations, journalism, etc.) that express direct participation;

4. free, prior, and informed consent and the community right to refusal; and

5. nonexploitative circumstances amenable to communities having real choices and trade-offs regarding whether to engage in tourism or in certain kinds of tourism as opposed to others.

Practices 1 and 2 are particularly important because they are essential for 4 and 5. For example, tourism operators often boast about local community members being able to serve as tourism guides. Is the option of being a tourism guide consistent with 5? Part of determining this would be whether the tourism operators actually fulfilled 1, which would mean they would have had to have actively explored with community members whether giving them the option of no jobs at all or jobs as tourism guides was fair. Is that the optimal pathway to community self-determination?

These practices can also apply to NGOs themselves. Do NGOs facilitate these practices on behalf of the communities they seek to protect? We offer two NGO case studies to illustrate the potential for transforming tourism into a more environmentally just profession.

Equitable Tourism Options (EQUATIONS)

Few NGOs work internationally on the issue of tourism exclusively. Many of the northern NGOs, such as Tourism Concern and Tourism Watch, focus on changing the consumer choices of tourists and to a lesser extent the industry, but Equitable Tourism Options, or EQUATIONS as it is commonly known, adopts a different focus that stems from a grassroots integrity. Advocating local community concerns and working with local communities, EQUATIONS aims to influence government and policy makers as well as the industry to ensure tourism is nonexploitative, equitable, and sustainable.[33]

EQUATIONS was founded in 1985 in response to the pressures that the opening up of the national economy to globalized free trade regimes brought to bear on local, grassroots communities throughout India. India is well known for strong, activist communities; local government structures known as the gram panchayat system; and a strong social justice vision that gives firm foundations to resist imposed development models that hurt the interests of local communities. EQUATIONS is a campaigning NGO that has effectively organized to articulate the rights of local communities and particularly the more disadvantaged including adivasis (indigenous peoples), dalits, women, coastal communities, and the poor. EQUATIONS' vision indicates a strong orientation toward justice and equity:

EQUATIONS envisions a just and equitable world, where all people have the freedom and the right to determine their lives and future. We envision forms of tourism which are non-exploitative, where decision making is democratized, and access to and benefits of tourism are equitably distributed. EQUATIONS believes in the capacity of individuals and communities to actualize their potential for the well-being of society. Towards this, we endorse justice, equity, people centered and movement centered activism, democratization and dialogue as our core values.[34]

EQUATIONS has a strong focus on supporting the struggle of local communities against tourism injustices. The key to this is their campaign and advocacy focus:

> We initiate campaigns and support people's struggles, against unjust, undemocratic and unsustainable forms of tourism. We advocate people's concerns with local, regional and national government and lobby for change. Our advocacy aims for decentralized democracy and we believe that communities should have a decisive voice in the access, control and ownership over their livelihood, natural resources and common resources. We try to ensure people's experience and aspirations influences tourism policies.[35]

As a key strategy, EQUATIONS has taken a strong network approach in its advocacy, so it is well connected for its work and well informed on the issues. These networks spread all over India and include "grassroots organizations, local communities, activists, researchers, trade unions, legal and policy experts, who are concerned, as we are, with ensuring that tourism planning, policy and implementation is equitable, people-centered and just."[36]

EQUATIONS addresses several issues that are of concern to India, including children and tourism; ecosystems, communities, and tourism; economic impacts of tourism; governance, law, and tourism; tourism education; and women and tourism. In their description of this work, EQUATIONS employs a macro approach as well as a grassroots-engaged approach to achieve its justice goals. For instance, in its work on children's rights, EQUATIONS works with local communities, concerned groups, and other stakeholders to ensure that tourism is not allowed to violate children's rights, a particular problem with the growing trend in child sex tourism.

In political terms, EQUATIONS works with local self-governing authorities "...to exercise their rights and to develop guidelines and mechanisms to strengthen local regulation of tourism and to ensure that they play an active and decisive role in tourism development."[36] At the macro level, EQUATIONS "...provide[s] a developing-country perspective at the national and international level on the impacts of trade and economic policies on tourism development and community benefit."[37] Its overall strength lies in

> ...linking grassroots struggles with macro-level policy spaces—both national and international. It also implies that we are constantly speaking on issues of justice and equity from a south perspective which is not very popular. Often we have to resort to fairly confrontative positions and strategies such as campaigns and legal action.[38]

EQUATIONS' work is well respected, and the organization has had notable successes. In Himachal Pradesh, a state in North India, for example, the government, under pressure from the industry lobby, removed a provision in land policy, opening the way for massive private and foreign investment in the tourism sector in Himachal Pradesh, which had previously been restricted. ABF International came to India in 2005 to invest $300 million in a ski village. The proposed project would have granted irrevocable rights to the use of water, power, and land to the company without proper public consultation. The result would have been an assault on the natural resources on which local communities depend for their livelihoods. Him Niti Abhiyan, Jan Jagran Evam Vikas Samiti, and several local NGOs, along with EQUATIONS, conducted a study in 2008 that documented the serious flaws and risks involved in the project. This report, along with a strong campaign of mass protests from local people on the ground, revealed the strong discontent of local communities toward the project. This resistance, combined with the lack of an appropriate environmental impact assessment, resulted in the government of Himachal Pradesh canceling the project.

Alternative Tourism Group and the Code of Responsible Tourism to Palestine

One key issue of injustice currently facing the global community is the ongoing and illegal Israeli occupation of Palestine. This occupation has featured serious injustices such as the erection of the separation barrier, the building of illegal settlements, the restriction of movement through checkpoints and roadblocks, the ongoing violation of human rights, and the continued displacement of people. Serious environmental justice issues arise from these measures, including land confiscations, water and resource deprivations, and stifled economic opportunities.[39] What is little recognized is that tourism has a powerful role to play in the (in)justice issues that are confronted here. Since 1967, when Israel took over Jerusalem and occupied the West Bank and Gaza, Palestinian entry into the tourism market has been quashed by a number of measures that Stein described as "forced underdevelopment"[40] and that we believe constitute an environmental justice issue.

Israel has pursued a two-track course in its use of tourism as a political tool of occupation: It has demonized Palestinians to scare off potential tourists and has also occupied much of the tourism sector for its own benefit. In terms of the former, Israel used political propaganda and travel warnings to paint Palestinians as dishonest and as potential terrorists.[41] In terms of the second strategy, Israel, as an occupying power, has multiple capacities to usurp tourism's potential for its own benefit and to deny it as an industry resource for the Palestinian community. Such measures have included a refusal to train and license Palestinian tour guides, the imposition of crippling municipal taxes, and a refusal to license hotel renovations or new developments in Palestinian areas.[42] It has also been noted that Israeli control of access to airports and highways has given it a chokehold on tourism. As a result, "Israel has maintained a virtual monopoly over the tourism industry, exploiting Palestinian resources and heritage while excluding Palestinians from tourism's economic, political, and human benefits."[43] The worst impact is the damage to people's sense of identity and belonging, as tourism is used as an opportunity to tell a Zionist narrative that erases indigenous Palestinian history and renders Palestinian people all but invisible. In sum, as Kassis concluded, "tourism in Israel became a vehicle for historical myth and the continuation of the occupation."[44]

The Alternative Tourism Group (ATG) of Palestine was established in this context with the vision of using an alternative form of tourism for "resistance and understanding."[45] Established in 1995, the ATG is a Palestinian NGO specializing in tours and pilgrimages to Palestine that offer opportunities to engage with the lived experiences of Palestinians, despite the occupation, with the hope of overturning it. The ATG offers "justice tourism" experiences, which it describes as "tourism that holds as its central goals the creation of economic opportunities for the local community, positive cultural exchange between host and guest through one-on-one interaction, the protection of the environment, and political/historical education."[46] The ATG has many specific objectives, including

- to modify the tendencies of mass tourism in "the Holy Land" to establish a more human-oriented tourism;
- to put foreign tourists in direct contact with the Palestinian population to help them develop a better understanding of Arab Palestinian culture and history;
- to break down the negative stereotypes of Palestine and its people that predominate in the West;
- to achieve more balance between the revenues of the Palestinian and Israeli tourism sectors by using Palestinian infrastructure (hotels, restaurants, transportation, guides, etc.);
- to augment the number of tourists visiting Palestine and increase the length of their stay in Palestinian areas;
- to develop among tourists a knowledge of Palestinian culture and the sociopolitical situation in Palestine;

- to encourage instructive and authentic meetings with the Palestinian people to develop among tourists an objective understanding of everyday realities of the Israeli occupation; and
- to offer tourists the opportunity to share unique experiences with Palestinians through volunteer work with NGOs (olive harvesting, tree planting, etc.).[47]

Through these methods, the ATG "seeks to promote a positive image of Palestine and its people and to contribute towards establishing a just peace in the area."[48] Since 1995, the ATG has hosted more than 20,000 visitors to Palestine.[49] Its programs include pilgrimage tours, political tours, cultural and heritage tours, solidarity tours and homestays, which offer a spectrum of opportunities for visitors at all stages of awareness to open up their hearts and minds to the situation experienced by Palestinians. The ATG is pursuing a multipronged strategy to give voice to the Palestinian community, which is suffering in one of the most severe examples of oppression and marginalization found in contemporary times. In addition to these diverse tour itineraries, in 2007 the ATG helped form the Palestinian Initiative for Responsible Tourism, which brought together all stakeholders in Palestinian tourism to create a strong and sustainable tourism sector. It also was instrumental in the development of a "code of conduct for tourism in the Holy Land."

The vision statement, in addition to commitments to sustainability and fair trading practices, expresses an aim to change travel patterns so that tourists visit Palestinian locations "in order to achieve a more equal distribution of tourism revenues to all people in this land."[50] The code of conduct alerts tourists to ways to engage with the Palestinian people and their lived reality and to commit to sharing what they learn from the Palestinians with their home communities upon their return. It also asks the operators in the Palestinian tourism sector to commit to a set of practices that engages with the tourists in a fair and responsible manner and to consider the impacts they might have on visitors' perceptions of Palestine, its people, and their reality.

This case study demonstrates that tourism is intertwined with serious environmental justice issues and suggests ways in which embedded NGOs can use tourism to counter those injustices. We thus can see tourism's potential as a positive force in meeting a daunting task: challenging and proposing alternatives to an occupation that prevents peaceful coexistence in local and global contexts.

Conclusion

Tourism is an endeavor rife with justice issues and acts of injustice, despite efforts to characterize it as a commercial activity free of ethical concerns. As we have demonstrated in this chapter, powerful interests benefit from exploiting, marginalizing, and dispossessing local communities in their effort to profit from tourism. Although efforts to attain sustainability outcomes in tourism mean that some NGOs have made small gains in developing policies and measures to address environmental concerns, we conclude the path to environmental justice must be populated by indigenous peoples, grassroots support, and NGOs with the local host communities' best interests at heart.

The advocacy efforts of the NGOs we have highlighted suggest justice and equity come from a bottom-up approach and not from a top-down imposition of interventions by global players such as the UNWTO. We believe a need exists for a much greater research emphasis on the relationship between environmental justice and tourism. This is especially important for the Global South and for indigenous peoples around the world. We also believe an urgent need exists for more support for NGOs, such as those highlighted in our two case studies, because they represent a hopeful means for reaching a dynamic enactment of environmental justice in the context of tourism development worldwide.

Discussion Questions

1. Freya, Kyle, and Deirdre are concerned about tourism being a source of injustice rather than a force for promoting justice. They are especially worried about local, indigenous peoples being taken advantage of by powerful tourism operators. Do you see the situation similarly or do you have a different perspective? Please elaborate.

2. Employing what you learned from reading about both case studies, what are the fundamental justice issues at stake? What is EQUATIONS fighting for and what is the ATG fighting for?

3. Talk about the potential of tourism as a source of positive change in the world. Do you think it has a big role to play? If yes, why? If no, why not?

4. Does it make sense to you that if tourism is to lead to cross-cultural understanding, it must be "authentic"? In other words, if we are to understand other cultures by experiencing them, must we make an effort to see the world through the host culture's eyes rather through our own "imagined" eyes? If you agree with this, what are practical implications regarding language, food, customs, etiquette, and so forth?

5. Many people would argue that tourism, especially if practiced sustainably, is a preferable form of economic development for less developed countries than other more extractive industries (e.g., mining, timber, agri-business). How do you see this line of thought? Is it merely an argument from a privileged position or is there more to it?

On Hierarchical Marginalization

Zachary Schwing
University of Utah

One gesture offered by some of the delegates at the "1st International Symposium on Speaking Up and Speaking Out: Working for Social and Environmental Justice Through Parks, Recreation, and Tourism" was to thank or recognize the indigenous peoples who preceded Western Europeans in the Salt Lake Valley. I found this problematic for many reasons. First, it seems to me that a firm connection or firm knowledge about a specific indigenous population is necessary to engage in such a thanking activity. In the absence of that connection or knowledge, a gesture of appreciation seems superficial. Second, the desire for such a gesture implies the current inhabitants of the region must be lacking a certain sensitivity when it comes to appreciating their own cultural heritage. Finally, such an appeal appears to me to be rooted in logical fallacies that often are inherent when discussing indigenous peoples, namely, an appeal to the *noble savage*, which is not only factually wrong but also insulting to an indigenous population. In the following paragraphs, I would like to take you deeper into my thinking about these matters.

Before I say much more, I recognize that real injustice was done to the native peoples of North America from 1500 to the present. This is a history we should not forget, and we should appropriately recognize indigenous cultures by including their stories and needs in social science scholarship and social memory. The problem arises in the method and the agenda of those doing the thanking or the recognizing. A blanket thank-you too easily generalizes the history of indigenous peoples and does not adequately reflect the complexity of the individual stories of those whose ancestors became dispossessed. Furthermore, such generalizations could have a harmful effect on the way we actually do environmental and social justice. So, I begin by acknowledging my own feet of clay and my aspiration to rise above them.

My Assumptions

Here are the key assumptions underlying my point of view. First, human history is largely a story of possession and displacement of cultures, peoples, lands, and resources. Recognition of indigenous claims often occurs and is only acceptable when it is of no consequence to a privileged class. The recognizer risks nothing by paying what is essentially lip service to an indigenous culture that has not inhabited a place for over a century and a half. The recognizer simply forces a sense of guilt on an audience—a sense of guilt with which the audience can do nothing because it is simply a bad meme for which no solution short of time travel exists. Guilt is never a healthy emotion to hold onto for too long. It does not go far in contributing to building the type of equitable society this particular symposium sought to address. Such recognition imposes false guilt and does not successfully press the social justice need in a meaningful way.

The term *indigenous* is also problematic. It classes groups of people in a rather cumbersome way. Indigenous here, of course, refers to peoples who lived in this place prior to European colonialization. Depending on the place, we are now two to five centuries beyond this historical upheaval. What, then, shall we call those of European descent who now live in these places? Will they be returning to their supposed homeland anytime soon? Are they not equally indigenous to their country and place? If we seek to emphasize a distinction between indigenous and foreign in terms of people, does it not lead to deep social divisions, which in turn give rise to resentment, control, and force? It is as if we suspend one person's identity for another's in relation to the land they inhabit. We force those who we perceive to have privilege to float above the land and have no connection to it.

I also do not employ the term *native* as it is even more encumbered than indigenous. It too tends to obscure rather than clarify meaning. Native refers to a place of birth, which all humans have; every person was born somewhere, and most humans have a deep-rooted attachment to their place of origin. Yet only in parts of the formerly colonized world (North and South America and perhaps Australia and New Zealand) do we speak of natives as those who lived there prior to colonization. Even in Africa, the site of some of the worst atrocities of European colonialism, we often speak of European inhabitants as native—French Algerians, Dutch Boers, English Zimbabweans or Kenyans—all of these people claim nativity to their land even if they were descendants of colonists. This is partially because their own home culture in Europe has marginalized them. A layering of marginalization, then, creates a rather odd hierarchy. Layered and hierarchical marginalization is a construct that those with and without privilege can use to suit certain political ends.

With Not For

The problem of ethnicity and the indigenous condition is not simply waved away by recognizing a native people before a talk. It leads to another problematic point: the idea of speaking with rather than speaking for a particular group or class of people. In a session concerning the delivery of leisure services to people with disabilities, there was great emphasis on speaking with the group in question rather than for their needs. Speaking for a given identity is rather prevalent throughout social science disciplines, and I think it should be avoided. The real irony here is that the same indigenous advocates felt the need to speak *for* a group that was not actually in the room. Moreover, it was as if those same individuals felt the need to speak *for* indigenous peoples and *for* their hosts' mishandling of the situation. Feelings do not equate to knowledge, and this sort of feeling activism leaves everyone in the room feeling completely powerless because it relies on generalization and conjecture that "with not for" advocates generally seek to alleviate.

Whose History?

A further problem became evident when one delegate from afar lamented that she could not find any information on which Native American nation or band had inhabited the Salt Lake Valley. The reason for this is that although various bands of Shoshones did hunt in the Salt Lake Valley, it was largely uninhabited and infrequently visited by indigenous peoples. Why else did early Mormon pioneers find it easy to settle here prior to the American Civil War and the Indian Wars that followed on the frontier? Stegner[1] highlighted this in several areas of his book *Mormon Country*, a thorough history of early Mormon settlement of the far western United States. Certainly, southern Utah was more densely populated by various Ute, Paiute, Navajo, and Hopi nations. But the Great Basin region of northern Utah and Nevada was never densely populated and did not have the same territorial battles and claimants as land east of the Rocky Mountains or those to the south and the west of the Salt Lake region. The Salt Lake Valley is now home to only a small reservation of the Goshute band of Shoshones at Skull Valley. They certainly are a local example of a peoples who are literally on the margins of Salt Lake City.

An implied prioritization of culture also exists that seems to describe White culture as inferior if even one indigenous person ever hunted on the land. We must recognize the unforunate fact about all human history that the entire planet we inhabit has been historically the subject of possession and dispossession. The recognition and prioritization of one historical culture over another simply because of one's status as dispossessed troubles the effort to find privileged allies if they feel the need to "take on" historical guilt when it is presented to them. This same phenomenon comes into play in discussions of reparations for slavery. It does not help an argument that the dispossessed people themselves have been long absent, but it does make it easier to create histories of injustice. If we do so, if we call attention to the injustice, we had better seek assurance we are correct in our assessment.

There are certainly lost public memories, especially among marginalized and nonprivileged people. These stories remain as twilight shadows swirling in real places in our present society. Stewart presented an excellent analysis of historical memory and psychology in the context of American cowboy art that speaks to this exact theme in Chapter 19. He demonstrated how cowboy art tends to gloss over the actual history of indigenous peoples and presents an extremely romanticized view of the issue, which in turn has become the dominant theme in public memory. How do we take on injustice without creating resentment, and how do we fully recognize a largely unwritten history without lapsing into the same kind of romanticism?

Fallacies Abound

In recognizing the indigenous nomads who sometimes frequented the Salt Lake Valley, we might also be committing several logical fallacies tied with a misunderstanding of history. When it comes to indigenous culture, we often commit the fallacy of the noble savage. The fallacy was perpetuated by European Enlightenment thinkers who saw the indigenous populations of European overseas colonies as better than the civilized European himself. Thinkers such as Rousseau were extremely influential in perpetuating this fallacy through the 19th and 20th centuries. They observed a culture that was capable of living as one with the land they inhabited and who were a perfectly peaceful and gentle peoples. But it is a fallacy. The indigenous nomads were capable of hunting a given territory to extinction and then moving on. Those that engaged in agriculture used slash-and-burn techniques and moved from place to place in search of fertile soil. Likewise, as historians now tell us, they engaged in bitter and violent struggles, used superstition and conjecture when faced with medical problems, and might not have done any better ethically than any other culture the Earth has ever seen.

A few of the symposium delegates who wanted to honor Salt Lake Valley's indigenous peoples engaged in feminist scholarship. An interesting question for their consideration is, "Did the indigenous cultures they wish to honor treat women justly?" Many traditional cultures worldwide currently engage in practices that automatically make women inferior to men. Yet should we revere them merely because of their indigenous or dispossessed status? In fact, an unfortunate history of rape and assault exists on a number of Native American reservations, usually in remote locations and equipped with their own patriarchal tribal laws. A recent *New York Times* article[2] highlighted the problem of rape on reservations in remote parts of the United States where appeals to local leadership go unheeded largely because these groups practice a form of patriarchic repression. We accept the rule of law, yet we make exceptions for indigenous cultures, and we much more easily excuse rape on tribal land because we are afraid of interfering with a traditional culture.

Likewise, most of these cultures engage in superstitious and dubious medical and prescientific practices that any good social scientist should recognize and reject. The use of "alternative narrative" is not up for debate when it comes to caring for the sick. Science-based medicine is our best option when fighting diseases, especially curable ones. Yet much talk at the symposium was about using "alternative science" when investigating indigenous cultures. Unfortunately, alternative science is akin to alternative medicine. It needs an alternative and primitive status because it either has been shown to be ineffective or has been ineffective in producing usable evidence. Do we risk playing into the superstition of an indigenous culture if we invoke alternative science? Or worse yet, do we risk opening up the discipline of social science to any claim simply because it cannot get past a peer review process?

Whose Culture Is This Anyway?

One reason why I and others at the symposium felt uneasy about the recognition of indigenous peoples is that the gesture was not about indigenous culture at all. It was about one privileged Western culture criticizing another. The White internalization of the Australian or Canadian indigenous story is different from the way in which Americans have internalized their indigenous story into their historical memory. The foreign recognition of indigenous culture in the United States appears odd because it is not a part of common cultural practice in this country.

One member of the symposium who avowed indigenous heritage mentioned at the beginning of his talk said he regretted that his people's traditional lands straddle the United States–Canadian border because it creates certain international difficulties and felt that his people should be able to issue their own passports for entry into and exit from this particular region. If we actually took this claim seriously, we might risk engendering ugly forms of nationalism and the fracturing of territory. Americans and Canadians abhor secessionist movements, yet this is what we risk when we imply that indigenous rights somehow trump those of current inhabitants. How far are we willing to go in the name of tradition? Certainly, the indigenous populations of North America were not in the habit of issuing or possessing passports prior to European arrival. Can we ever protect traditional practice over contemporary culture? Is this not the same false divide that keeps nature out of cities and cities out of nature? Appeals to tradition often create these divides and foster a splitting among people. Just as dispossessing and removing people to a reservation was supremely unjust historically, forcing a nationalistic agenda that pits human against human is equally unjust. In the case of Bosnia-Herzegovina, as in other ethno-nationalistic crises, humans became generalized objects of resentment. It is disconcerting that the politics of recognizing indigenous peoples uses this exact story of dispossession and revenge. Fortunately, violent nationalist movements among indigenous peoples in North America are completely unheard of. The reason for this might be that we live in a society that is at least far more just than the Yugoslavia of the 1980s and early 1990s. This should not be an excuse, however, to disregard real injustice that indigenous peoples experience in our homeland. The question becomes, "How is the issue best addressed?" Certainly it is not by taking refuge in a vague historical concept, for these vague and generalized concepts lead to guilt, resentment, and even violence.

Perhaps the lesson here is that dispossession has been a hallmark of human history, and to truly evolve away from this cycle, we must also end the cycle of revenge and ethno-nationalism that follows it. This is perhaps a positive aspect of our increasingly global culture. We have the tools to understand and evolve away from such fractured and territorial thinking.

Parting Thought

There is no going back to a state of nature, and appeals to indigenous cultures usually rely on this to make their claims. We tend to forget that the indigenous condition or classification does not necessarily mean that such a culture was sustainable. Implying that indigenousness has more value than nonindigenousness is too easy. In a global society, the long-term prospects for such a concept are not good. We must begin to think of ourselves as one people indigenous to one planet. This, of course, cannot occur if we classify people according to their roots, ethnicity, and ancestry. The Earth is small, and we must find justice for all its people. This simply cannot be done if we continue to perpetuate feudal ideas about territory and place. As members of the academy we should take long strides away from classifying ourselves and others as either privileged or nonprivileged, as indigenous or foreign, for in so doing we fall into the same traps we criticize. If science is criticized because it too easily generalizes people, then we should avoid doing so when it comes to questions of ancestry and ethnicity. Recognizing a vague historical concept is no substitute for waging the actual battle for a just, human identity.

PART THREE

Teaching Justice

"Our next challenge will be to more explicitly recognize our work as critical to sustainability and initiate strong partnerships within our communities, among our student populations, and across our campuses."

—Adrienne Cachelin

11

Spirituality as a Resource for Social and Environmental Justice Through Parks, Recreation, Tourism, and Leisure

Paul Heintzman
University of Ottawa

In a paper titled "Emancipating Leisure: The Recovery of Freedom in Leisure," Hemingway[1] was critical of the spiritual conceptualization of leisure articulated by Pieper[2] and others as he saw it as a subjective, internal mental experience that does not place leisure against the social structures of modern Western society. In contrast, in *Leisure: A Spiritual Need*, Doohan, who like Pieper holds a spiritual conceptualization of leisure, wrote:

> ...a dedication to spirituality means the hard work of self-development, and working with and for others, while also learning from and being enriched by them. It means building a better world and directing our future.... This is the multi-faceted work of liberation from all the contemporary slaveries: discrimination, sexism, injustice, economic and political oppression, the arms race, consumerism, exploitation and so on.[3]

Pieper claimed that the spiritual conceptualization of leisure is the basis of culture and that in leisure "truly human values are saved and preserved."[4]

Although current discussions of research on leisure and spirituality often focus on the inner self with little discussion of relationships with others or of community, spiritual life includes more than interiority. True spirituality is expressed in social and environmental relationships and also in social and environmental justice. Willard explained, "An authentic spiritual life always pushes one back into the world."[5] In this chapter, I argue that spirituality and the spiritual dimension of leisure are resources that the parks, recreation, tourism, and leisure fields can draw upon to bring about social and environmental justice. In making this argument, I cover the following topics: the justice dimension of spirituality; the justice dimension of spiritual traditions within parks, recreation, tourism, and leisure (PRTL); a historical example of spirituality's influence upon social and environmental justice related to PRTL; current examples of spirituality's influence upon social and environmental justice related to PRTL; and justice within current research on leisure and spirituality.

The Justice Dimension of Spirituality

If we examine comprehensive definitions of spirituality and spiritual health, it is evident that social and environmental justice is integral to these definitions. For example, Elkins, Hedstrom, Hughes, Leaf, and Sanders defined spirituality as "a way of being and experiencing that comes about through awareness of a transcendent dimension that is characterized by certain identifiable values in regard to self, others, nature, life, and whatever one considers to be Ultimate."[6] This definition is applicable to both humanistic and religious spiritual traditions. For the purpose of this chapter, it is important to note that Elkins et al. identified altruism and idealism as two of the nine components of spirituality. Altruism was defined as

> a strong sense of social justice and commitment to altruistic love and action. A belief that we are our neighbour's keeper and that we are all part of common humanity which creates an awareness of the suffering and pain of others.[7]

Idealism suggests "the spiritual person is a visionary committed to the betterment of the world."[8]

Fisher, Francis, and Johnson suggested spiritual health is a dynamic state of being that involves harmonious relationships within four interrelated spiritual domains:

1. personal domain (wherein one intrarelates with oneself with regard to *meaning, purpose,* and *values* in life. The human spirit creates self-awareness, relating to self-esteem and identity),
2. communal domain (as expressed in the quality and *depth of interpersonal relationships,* between self and others, relating to *morality* and *culture.* This includes love, justice, hope, and faith in humanity),
3. environmental domain (*care* and *nurture* for the physical and biological, to a sense of awe and wonder; for some, the notion of unity or *connectedness with the environment*), and
4. transcendental domain (*relationship* of self *with* something or someone beyond the human level, a *Transcendent Other,* that is, ultimate concern, cosmic force, transcendent reality, or God). This involves *faith* toward, adoration of, and worship of the source of mystery of the universe.[9]

Of particular relevance to the theme of this book are the communal and environmental domains that may be seen to be directly related to social and environmental justice. Vader also described the justice dimension of spiritual health:

> ... spiritual health at the individual level includes elements of generosity, charity [love], solidarity, self-abnegation, concern for others, self-sacrifice, self-discipline, and self-restraint. At the societal level, indicators might be manifestations of solidarity, equity, justice, gender equality, unity in diversity, participative decision-making, and power sharing.[10]

I have emphasized the justice dimensions of spirituality and spiritual health, but recognizing that there are internal (e.g., life purpose and ultimate meaning; love, joy, peace, hope, and fulfillment) and external (e.g., trust, honesty, integrity, altruism, compassion, service) characteristics of spiritual health is important.[11] Wolterstorff stated, the cultivation of the inward dimensions of spirituality are necessary as a foundation for the practice of justice; the interior characteristics radiate into the exterior characteristics of spirituality.[12]

The Justice Dimension of Spiritual Traditions Within the PRTL Literature

Previous literature in the PRTL field has documented how the teachings of the world's major religious and spiritual traditions are resources that can be drawn upon in the pursuit of social and environmental justice. For example, in an exploration of eight major religious/spiritual traditions (Judaism, Christianity, Islam, Hinduism, Jainism, Taoism, Confucianism, and Buddhism), Kaza examined principles related to nature's spiritual significance, environmental ethics guidelines, recommended land management practices, and current environmental activism.[13] Her purpose was to stimulate dialogue on appropriate environmental practices for public lands. She observed that each tradition offers ethical principles applicable to public land management. For example, the Jewish tradition offers the Sabbath concept, Christianity love, Confucianism energy flow, and Buddhism interdependence. She concluded the world's religious traditions "have much to offer the discussion on land management values" as they "represent thousands of years of careful thinking, consideration, testing, and winnowing to essentials."[14] Furthermore, religion has been influential in the lives of many people who have worked for environmental justice. For example, in the United States, John Muir who worked for preservation of Yosemite and creation of the Sierra Club; Theodore Roosevelt who as president established numerous national parks, national forests, federal bird reservations, and national monuments; and Rachel Carson who through her book *Silent Spring* put the environment on the North American agenda were all nurtured in the Christian faith, which informed their environmental work.[15, 16]

Another example of a paper within PRTL that draws upon the world's spiritual and religious traditions is "Leisure, Ethics and the Golden Rule" by Heintzman.[17] The Golden Rule, in its positive and negative forms, is a universal expression that benefiting others is good and harming them is evil. It may be found in many of the major world religions (e.g., Judaism, Christianity, Islam, Hinduism, Jainism, Buddhism, Confucianism, Taoism, Zoroastrianism). The Golden Rule is elaborated upon in the moral teachings in each of the major spiritual traditions within particular locations and within given cultural–economic–political situations such as behavior toward neighbors, parents, children, the rich, the poor, slaves, strangers, and enemies:

> In each case it begins on the common ground of fair dealing and respect for others' lives and property and leads on towards the higher ground of positive generosity, forgiveness, kindness, love, compassion, where we find the ethical evidence of the transformation of human existence from self-centeredness to Reality-centeredness.[18]

Hick suggested the Golden Rule promotes love, compassion, and self-sacrificing concern for others.[19] Heintzman previously documented that this interpretation of the Rule has implications for justice issues in PRTL.[20] How might my recreational activity be affecting the marginalized in our society or in developing countries? Am I establishing or preserving dominance over others through leisure? Am I participating in activities or consuming recreational goods that directly or indirectly support oppressive regimes that exploit peoples in developing nations? Does my recreational behavior create barriers that prevent other people from maximizing their leisure? Do I misuse recreation environments, whether natural or human-made, in ways that detract from another person's experience?

The Golden Rule can also be used to support environmental justice. Some versions of the Golden Rule focus on humans, and others include more than humans. For example, the Jain Kritanga Sutra version uses the term *all creatures*, the Buddhist Scriptures refer to *all living things,* and the Zoroastrian Dadistani-i-dinik mentions *nature*. Therefore, there is no reason that the practice of the rule should not also be extended to all others including all living things and the land. Thus recreation activities can to be judged in terms of their impact on the whole earth community.

A Historical Example of Spirituality's Influence Upon Social and Environmental Justice as Related to PRTL

To exemplify how a spiritual tradition has influenced social and environmental justice in relation to parks, recreation, tourism, and leisure, Baigent documented how the Christian spiritual tradition had a pervasive influence on the Victorian open space movement.[21] Christianity was a significant motivation for some who campaigned for open space to provide mass recreation opportunities for the urban poor. Baigent suggested, "Many Christians saw the problem, their response to it, and the solution as religious."[22] The spiritual basis for this open space advocacy is seen in the writings of Octavia Hill, a Commons Preservation Society supporter whose work for the poor and for open space was founded upon the incarnation, which sanctified all of creation, and also on biblical teaching. The biblical verse "love your neighbor as yourself" (Mark 12:31, NLT) taught the Christian's responsibility to one's neighbor and one's society, and the verse "people do not live by bread alone" (Matt. 4:4) extended their responsibility to bringing beauty, including the beauty of nature, into everyone's life, especially the lives of the poor. Hill's 1877 essay "Open Spaces" described the poor living conditions in inner London and argued that because "every one of those living beings...is a child of God,"[23] wealthier Christians must attend to the physical and nonphysical needs of the inner-city residents, with open space being an important part of nonphysical needs. Hill's interpretation of Christian responsibility involved social justice and a revering of nature: "If you try to accept the duty [to your neighbors] as our Lord showed it ... all God's children will be dear to you, and His earth sacred."[24] Hill viewed open space as a gift of God to be shared by rich and poor, for all are children of God. A similar theology of nature led to a similar social and environmental vision in other Christians involved in the open space movement.

This view that natural areas were to be of equal benefit to rich and poor was in contrast to the secular nature mystic view that the aesthetic beauty of nature was for a certain group of people, that is, the enlightened middle class, and needed to be preserved for them as a sanctuary from the wrong type of people, that is, the uncivilized poor.[25] The contrast between these two views was seen in the debate over recreation use of Epping Forest in southeast England. Many preservationists, in particular those of the middle and upper class, opposed the visits of excursionists and trippers to the forest.[26] Mass tourism threatened the introspective, escapist, individualistic, and exclusive characteristics of transcendentalism, and thus some preservationist societies advocated preservation with limited access. Access was for a landscaped citizenry who did the right sort of things rather than for the cockneys, or the East Enders, who were viewed as the archetypical bad tourists. Christians led the movement to open the forest as much as possible to excursionists and trippers even if this limited their own enjoyment of the forest. For example, Sir Anthony Brady, a devoted Christian, set up the Forest Fund to promote the open forest and organized the largest public protest against enclosure. He wrote, "It was a great thing to enable [working men] on a summer's evening to enjoy the fresh air of heaven, and, if it so pleased them, to look up from Nature to Nature's God."[27] Another Christian, Edward North Buxton, wrote,

> Much as one sympathizes with the pursuits of the contemplative persons seeking solitude, it was not intended to be kept for their exclusive benefit. Our chief care must be for the single annual holiday of the artisan, his tired wife and smoke-filled children.[28]

According to Baigent, for the Christian open space preservationist, God was the ultimate reference, and although God might be imminent in nature, all people including poor people were made in God's image and were not to be deprived of recreation for nature's benefit.[29] Open space was for recreation as well as preservation. In contrast, for the secular nature mystic, nature, described as the "eternal comforter" in the words of secularist Edward Aveling, was the ultimate point of reference, which for some was a justification for limiting access to the masses. Baigent concluded that although there was no one Christian view of nature, of its preservation, and of the recreation associated with it in Victorian England, many open space preservationists were motivated by a Christian understanding of responsibility to others and by a theological view of land and nature that led to open space advocacy characterized by the coexistence of social justice and natural beauty. "A right relationship with God entailed a right relationship with all of creation, that is, with all people and with the natural world...,"[30] so that the action of Christians, churches, and church-related charities influenced why nature was valued, why open space was preserved, how it was managed, "and how it was to be experienced."[31]

Current Examples of Spirituality's Influence Upon Social and Environmental Justice as Related to PRTL

The above historical example is over 100 years old, and more recently Haluza-Delay noted that within a spiritual tradition such as Christianity, churches are concerned with eco-justice alongside social concerns.[32] For example, the National Council of Churches USA Eco-Justice Programs, with its motto of "Justice for God's Planet and God's People," bring together social and environmental justice in their opposition to mountaintop removal mining in Appalachia that destroys God's creation and contaminates communities.[33] In addition to devastation to the landscape, coal-fired power plants have added negative health impacts and economic decline as an extra burden to those communities of color and low-income communities already dealing with historical and societal injustice. Another example of where social and environmental justice overlap in these eco-justice programs is the land and wilderness campaigns such as the campaign in Wyoming where "faith communities are working to protect rare ecosystems in Wyoming while supporting low impact energy development in certain areas" for the benefit of the local communities.[34]

On a more individual level, and more directly related to the PRTL field, DeGraaf described individuals who are inspired by their spirituality to work for social and/or environmental justice.[35] Through an internship in Chicago as part of her recreation degree program, one woman discovered that recreation could play a role in improving people's quality of life and in building community. After graduating, in 2005 this woman cofounded the Green Bean Coffeehouse in Seattle that creates a space and provides programming for homeless people, students, artists, and activists, to connect, develop, and feel part of something larger than themselves. Through human development and tips distributed to a variety of local and international causes, an organization has been built that addresses a number of social concerns in Seattle and around the world.

Another example provided by DeGraaf[36] is a young man who has operated a church camp in upstate New York since 1986:

You sense things are different the moment you arrive at Camp Fowler. Whether it's the sign by the parking area that reads "Future world and local leaders in training here," the bicycles used by the maintenance workers to haul their gear around camp, or the wooden buildings that properly fit their northwood settings—you sense that this camp has been carefully thought through.... [W]hat is striking at Camp Fowler is that all of it is suffused with a spirit of shalom. Among the camp's core values are simplicity, hospitality, and community. In recent years its summer-long themes have been peace and justice. And woven through everything is the theme of earthkeeping.[37]

DeGraaf pointed out that both of these individuals embody a justice inspired by their spirituality.

At the international level, the Arabuko-Sokoke Schools and Ecotourism Scheme (ASSETS) in Kenya is another example of a combined social and environmental justice project inspired by spirituality.[38, 39] Some of Africa's rarest wildlife is found in the Arabuko-Sokoke Forest and Mida Creek region; however, the wildlife and the surrounding human communities are struggling for survival. The ASSETS project, established by the A Rocha (Christians in Conservation) organization in 2001, alleviates poverty through the support of child education and promotes community participation in nature conservation. The program uses funds from tourism, donors (including tourists), and ecotourism facilities, such as boardwalks and suspended walkways established by A Rocha and its partners, to supply eco-bursaries for secondary school children living adjacent to the forest and creek who are not able to afford school fees. By December 2010, bursaries from the ASSETS program had made it possible for 378 local children to attend secondary school. In addition, the student beneficiaries are involved in a variety of conservation activities such as tree planting and environmental education. The program also encourages local people to value the creek and forest by distributing funds from ecotourism to the local communities. Within the local communities, sustainable forms of income generation are developed through activities such as the training of local guides and construction of ecotourism facilities including nature trails and tree platforms. It is hoped that as local communities benefit from the adjacent habitats, they will increasingly value and protect them.

The examples provided illustrate how spirituality may be a resource and inspiration for social and environmental justice. Although these examples are from the spiritual tradition with which I am most familiar, those of other spiritual traditions may find similar examples of social and environmental justice within their own tradition.

Social and Environmental Justice in Current Research on Leisure and Spirituality

In recent years, empirical[40, 41] and nonempirical[42, 43] literature on the relationships between spirituality and the PRTL field has grown. This body of research has tended to focus on how leisure influences spirituality with little attention paid to how spirituality might influence leisure. Unfortunately, much of the empirical research has also focused on the immediate spiritual experience of the participant. Studies such as those by Stringer and McAvoy[44] and Fredrickson and Anderson[45] have been criticized by Haluza-Delay for focusing on wilderness spiritual experiences that "primarily consisted of pleasant emotional states," that "say little about the consequences of such experiences," and that do not assist "in an understanding of spirituality in the service of environmental awareness."[46] Likewise, in the context of outdoor education, Lasenby gave the term *hangover* to "the short-term, immediate effects, which are all highly positive, but do not deal with the long-term transformational effects that spiritual experience might have."[47] Similarly, I noted that research has focused on the internal spiritual benefits of leisure with little attention to the social relationship and social justice dimensions of spirituality, and I recommended more research in this area.[48] These criticisms reflect Unsoeld's statement that "the final test is whether your experience of the sacred in nature enables you to cope more effectively with the problems of man"[49] and also Lane's fear

...that much of what we call 'spirituality' today is overly sanitized and sterile, far removed from the anguish of pain, the anchoredness of place ... [S]pirituality loses its bite, its capacity to speak prophetically to its culture, its demand for justice. Avoiding pain and confrontation, it makes no demands, assumes no risks.[50]

Yet, as we have seen earlier in the chapter, spirituality is very much concerned with social and environmental justice.

Although little research has explored the linkages between spirituality, recreation, and social and/or environmental justice, a recent study by Moore investigated the relationship between spiritual experiences and environmentalism in recreational users of the marine environment.[51] The sample for this study was 74 surfers and 83 scuba divers in New Zealand. Moore found that most surfers and scuba divers had a spiritual experience while engaged in surfing and diving; however, surfers had a higher score (97.02) on the Spiritual Experience Assessment (SEA) scale than did the divers (74.57). An explanation for this difference was that surfers had higher levels than divers on a variety of spiritual tradition items such as intrinsic spirituality, religious practice, and belief in God. Furthermore, divers had much lower scores on an item that measured dependence on a Higher Power. When it came to motivation to engage in the activity, 29.7% of surfers compared to 4.8% of divers were motivated to engage in surfing or diving, respectively, for spiritual reasons.

Using Heintzman's framework for understanding the relationship between nature-based recreation and spirituality,[52] Moore investigated whether antecedent conditions (personal history, current circumstances, attitude, motivation, sociodemographic characteristics, spiritual tradition), setting components (being in nature, being in a different environment, place processes), and recreation components (activity, free time, solitude, group experiences, and facilitation) were the most influential in SEA scores.[53] Perhaps not surprisingly, spiritual tradition that included intrinsic spirituality scores, current religious practice, and belief in God was identified as the most dominant factor in spiritual experience during one's surfing or scuba diving.

Moore also explored whether a link existed between SEA scores and environmental advocacy, which is pertinent to this book's theme.[54] Using the New Ecological Paradigm (NEP),[55] Moore discovered that surfers and divers held pro-ecological scores in the high to medium range, and for both activities, a higher NEP score was associated with a higher correlation with environmental advocacy. However, participants in both activities were not overwhelmingly active in environmental advocacy, were engaged more in environmental stewardship than advocacy, and did not know the difference between the two.

Although Moore[56] did not discover a direct link between the surfers' and divers' SEA scores and advocacy, a link between spirituality and advocacy was created when the NEP scores were analyzed through the framework of the theory of planned behavior.[57] When the NEP (normative) beliefs were combined with behavioral beliefs (that the surf/dive led to positive personality changes with more participation leading to greater change) and control beliefs (participation in the activity led to advocacy), these three beliefs together led to an intention to advocate. However, as noted, although there were strong intentions to advocate, few engaged in environmental advocacy and activities identified as advocacy tended to be stewardship activities. What is significant about Moore's study is that she went beyond simply investigating the spiritual experience associated with these recreation activities to exploring the connection among spirituality, recreation, and environmental advocacy.

Conclusion

In this chapter, we have seen that social and environmental justice are integral to spirituality and spiritual health, that the leisure studies literature has provided examples of how major spiritual traditions provide teachings that may form a foundation for social and environmental justice, and that spiritual traditions have historically and currently been the motivation and foundation for social and environmental justice activities that are related to PRTL issues. However, we have also seen that most of the contemporary literature and empirical research on leisure and spirituality has tended to focus on internal spiritual benefits of leisure and have failed to examine how leisure is influenced by spirituality as well as how leisure may be related to the justice dimensions of spirituality.

PRTL students and practitioners would benefit from becoming familiar with the social and environmental justice dimensions of various spiritual traditions. Within the therapeutic recreation field, for example, Shank noted the profession has a code of ethics, but lacks a moral philosophical foundation for these standards of behavior.[58] Kaza pointed out that familiarity and discussion of values from various spiritual traditions can clarify an individual's own values and how they impact one's professional decisions. [59] Finally, with regard to empirical research, investigations that move beyond the relationship of leisure and internal spiritual benefits to the complex relationships among spirituality, leisure, and social and environmental justice activities should be encouraged.

Discussion Questions

1. Paul suggests that religious traditions may have an important role to play in framing our thinking about social and environmental justice in the context of parks, recreation, tourism, and leisure? Do you agree with him? Why or why not?

2. Please offer examples of ways in which religious traditions have both helped and hindered the attainment of social and environmental justice in leisure contexts?

3. How might spirituality be connected to a particular religious tradition? Put differently, can you be spiritual without being religious?

4. What problems do you see in touting spirituality and/or religious tradition in advocating for social and environmental justice?

5. How would you describe your own spirituality or religious tradition as a force for social and environmental justice?

12

Experiential Education, Social and Environmental Justice Pedagogies, and Globalization
From Theory to Praxis

Mary Breunig
Samantha Dear
Brock University

In this chapter, we invite you to accompany us on a 3-year pedagogical journey as we recount a service leadership course we cotaught at Brock University. The chapter parallels the journey itself, which is framed within Freire's levels of social consciousness.[1,2] We hope this written voyage provides you with insights into and new learning about your own pedagogical praxis.

Mary: Sam and I first met in 2002. Sam was an undergraduate outdoor recreation student at Lakehead University in Thunder Bay, Ontario, Canada. I was a lecturer in the School of Outdoor Recreation, Parks, and Tourism. Our lives came together in a second-year service leadership course. Sam was already a seasoned traveler, and I recall her preparing to travel to China on a fourth-year international field experience with a geography professor. Each student was required to complete a project on a topic of choice. Sam's initial proposal was to complete an analysis of trekking in the Province of Yunann, which turned into an analysis of the power dynamics between trekkers and members of the host committee with whom they traveled. This was Sam's first foray into developing a critical, international consciousness.

Sam: As Mary said, we first met in a second-year leadership course at Lakehead University. What impacted me most was the day when Mary introduced us to the concept of White privilege. The idea that one could be considered a racist simply due to the privileged position she or he was born into left me walking out of class confused and feeling culpable. A desire to further understand the concept and how I was feeling about it led me to knock on Mary's office door to discuss the topic in greater detail, thus igniting my journey of self in relationship to society and social change.

We met again at Brock University in 2009 where Mary was teaching a leadership course similar to the Lakehead course and Sam was pursuing her Master of Arts degree. Sam became a teaching assistant in that course, and together we discussed how best to integrate social and environmental justice pedagogies as one component of the second-year leisure services leadership course. We wanted the course to serve as a platform for students to consider their own positionality and privilege and how they informed their leadership praxes.

What we report here is what we learned through this collaborative teaching experience, including the effectiveness of experiential education as social justice pedagogy, the impact of globalization on the teaching–learning process, and the contributions of Freire's three levels of social consciousness as stepping stones to conscientization.

Experiential Education

Experiential learning and experiential education are buzzwords in the media, in popular literature, in boardrooms, and across university campuses. When people ask what experiential education is, they often talk about Outward Bound or Project Adventure or outdoor activities. Some respond with a bit more sophistication and mention John Dewey or the Experiential Learning Cycle.[3] Meanwhile, the Association for Experiential Education asserts that its vision "is to contribute to making a more just and compassionate world by transforming education." How, then, does experiential education factor into bringing about a more just and compassionate world in light of the above anecdotal evidence of its emphasis on activity?

Experiential education's early roots are in the progressive education movement (1930s), and John Dewey is often cited as its founding father. The idea that experiential education is a philosophy is important and distinguishes it from mere methodology (or a way of teaching). Experiential learning, on the other hand, emphasizes methodology, and Kolb's Experiential Learning Cycle (see Figure 1) exemplifies this method of teaching and learning.

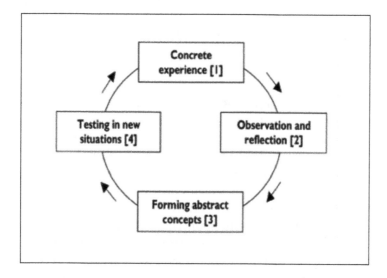

Figure 1. Experiential Learning Cycle. Adapted from *Experiential learning: Experience as the source of learning and development,* by D. Kolb, 1984, Englewood Cliffs, NJ: Prentice-Hall.

Experiential learning holds its own importance as a methodology, but distinguishing it from experiential education is important. Experiential education as a philosophy is focused on purposeful practice, and in the case of contemporary experiential education theory, its purpose is social and environmental justice oriented.[4] Experiential education as a justice-oriented purposeful praxis is relatively new. Indeed, it has yet to find its way into mainstream school environments. It is interesting to note how the philosophical roots of experiential education share the common educational ideal of social change. Herbart, Froebel, James, Parker, Dewey, and Kilpatrick were all dedicated to using education as a means for social change. Hahn developed a number of modern day experiential schools based on this same ideal. Montessori, Steiner, and the early K–12 school initiatives that employed experiential education shared this common goal as well. Experiential education has widespread applications and transformative potential as an educational philosophy and as a vehicle for social change.

It was based on the thinking of these early educational visionaries and in light of this definition of experiential education that we began to think about the application of experiential education philosophy to the second-year leadership course for our leisure studies students at Brock University. To link issues of social and environmental justice with experiential education, we first examined current issues facing the global community.

Globalization

Chomsky defined globalization in its neutral state as "international integration."[5] Globalization thus conceived emphasizes the increased ease of information flow and collaboration throughout the international community. However, defining globalization as a process of cross-cultural exchange is rather naïve in light of more prevalent definitions that define it as a hasty scramble for wealth and power.[6] Viewed this way, globalization has "brought problems of lack of tolerance and respect for others who are culturally and racially different, uneven distribution of resources, ethnic conflict, and struggles of power."[7]

Globalization is thus often viewed in one of two ways: (a) the rich potential of imagining the world as community and (b) an outgrowth of capitalist culture. Rittzer and Ryan employed the term *grobalization* to describe the latter more capitalist-oriented extreme and defined it as "the imperialistic ambitions of nations, corporations, organizations, and the like and their desire, indeed need, to impose themselves on various geographic areas."[8] That said, these two extreme views of globalization are neither discrete nor easily separated from one another. Proceeding from the assumption that this issue is complex, and wishing to explore globalization's potential to effect positive social and environmental change, we began our journey cautiously.

The conversation surrounding how to best equip our students with the knowledge and skills to serve as leaders in a globalized society intensified. In Canada, two education paradigms have emerged: (a) global economic competitiveness and (b) global interdependence.[9] The first paradigm emerged as a reaction to the world becoming increasingly competitive economically. O'Sullivan suggested, "Educational reforms were justified as essential to maintaining Canada's position as a front-rank defender of the free world."[10] The second paradigm represents "interdependent global problems and responsibilities."[11] Given that the majority of Canadians favor the global economic competitiveness paradigm,[12] we understand that global educators who favor the global interdependence paradigm are in the minority. Indeed, Schweifurth avowed that those educators who integrate this perspective into the curriculum are on the periphery of the teaching profession.[13] Nevertheless, advocates of the global interdependence paradigm are firm in their belief that teaching with a global perspective will not only create a learning environment where students see the connection of a subject to real life, but also foster a learning environment that encourages students to become active citizens and agents of social and environmental change.[14] This latter view energized our commitment.

Freire's Levels of Social Consciousness

As we began to develop the curriculum for our service leadership course, it occurred to us that what we wanted to accomplish Freire's three levels of social consciousness:[15, 16] naïve, superstitious, and critical. Naïve individuals lack the understanding that world institutions and societal norms are human designed. Instead, they view these phenomena as universal facts. They also are not inclined to investigate or reflect upon issues of justice or to trouble supposed facts. Finlay and Faith concluded, "The chief characteristic of naive consciousness is an unreflecting acceptance of the solidity and inevitability of the world and one's own views."[17]

Superstitious individuals exhibit heightened critical thinking skills. In this second stage, people are more cognizant of the injustices created by societal institutions and as a result recognize that options for change and transformation exist. However, as Connolly indicated, superstitious individuals have "a concomitant sense of powerlessness to do anything about those options."[18] For example, people at this stage may identify with a particular justice-oriented issue (e.g., food security) because they are passionate about it, but they do not know how to engage in action-oriented behavior, resulting in action paralysis. The final stage of consciousness is critical. At this level of conscientization, individuals understand that "cultural institutions can be analyzed, understood, and therefore—in principle—shaped, modified, and controlled by members of the community."[19] At this stage, individuals have the ability to create pathways forward to engage in action-oriented behavior and are empowered to do so.

The Journey

Our 3-year journey transported us through all three levels of social consciousness as we attempted to teach for and about social justice.

Naïve

One early attempt at integrating social justice pedagogy into the curriculum involved our naïvely merging a lecture on experiential education theory into a newly titled lecture, "social justice and globalization." We tried to create a safe space using activities from Levin's *Experiential Activities for a Better World*,[20] including saying "ouch" to indicate strong feelings about a topic, dropping the ego at the door, attending to language, and not making assumptions about other learners in this large (130+) leadership course. We wanted to teach the important distinction between experiential learning and experiential education. We wanted to tap into students' lived experiences in schools. We discussed Gardner's multiple intelligence theories and ways in which the experiential learning cycle could appeal to various intelligences and learning styles (auditory, visual, kinesthetic) of the learners in the classroom.[21] Some discussion ensued about the ways in which certain learning styles are privileged over others, and with so many kinesthetic learners in the classroom, this resonated with some students even though they could not see it as an issue of justice.

To introduce issues of justice on a global scale, we asked students to look at various pictures including child soldiers and toxic waste dumps. Furthermore, we showed a series of maps that provided illustrations that were distorted by population on a world map. For example, we showed the greatest population base of people living with HIV/AIDS in relation to gross national product.[22] Although these visual representations seemed to effectively capture the students' attention through their shock value, the exercise was not effective at helping students connect this to real global issues. We naïvely assumed they would just understand.

Another activity had students identify items in their "knapsack of privilege" (e.g., Band-Aids that matched their skin color and foods at the university cafeteria that fit their cultural upbringing).[23] At the end of the activity, one student tersely reminded us that she was not an outdoor recreation major. She was a community recreation major and a leisure generalist and thus did not own a knapsack but rather carried a book bag. That comment led to other students weighing in: "I am not privileged, I am poor," "We already talked about all this in the diversity class," and "What does this have to do with leisure?"

In sum, we became aware that (a) our efforts were not connecting to students lived experiences in the manner we thought they would; (b) impassioned teaching did not necessarily lead to impassioned learning; (c) our assumption that students would naturally and organically connect these theories to their leadership praxis was presumptive and not automatic; and (d) "going too deep, too dark, too fast" seemed impactful in the short term, but it neither proved to be effective for long-term retention of ideas nor led to pro-social action.

Superstitious

We realized we needed to backtrack; for students to become aware of their connectedness to these issues, they had to understand how the theories fit with their lived experiences. Our guiding question in this phase was, "How can experiential pedagogues educate in such a way that they connect people's values and beliefs about the world with social and environmental action?"

The second year, we further considered how to expand students' social and environmental justice knowledge through an increased emphasis on experiential education theory and praxis. We asked ourselves, "How can we teach these theories in a manner that connects to a leisure generalist engaging in a leadership practice across a variety of settings? How can we assist students in understanding the justice-oriented importance of this work?" We proceeded in a manner familiar to so many of us in the teaching profession. We consulted with colleagues, friends, and the literature. In the process, we recalled an exercise from a graduate course that identified one's ontology (way of being) and epistemology (way of knowing and seeing the world) through an epistemological lens activity. We brought this to the leadership class the next year as a precursor to the social justice and globalization lecture, asking students to draw an illustration of the lens through which they see the world (see Figure 2 for the starting point). We asked students to imagine this as the lens through which they view the world. We asked them to place concentrically, starting from the inner circle and working their way to the outer circle, from earliest experiences (inner) to most recent experiences (outer), the influences on their lives and their lived experiences that have shaped their view of the world. We then had student volunteers talk about what comprised their lenses and used that as a springboard to talk about opposing epistemological views.

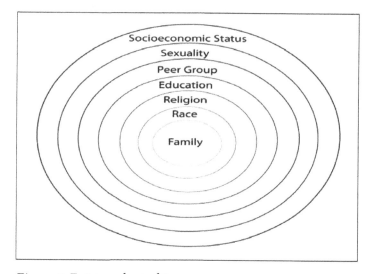

Figure 2. Epistemological Lens

This provided an opportunity for students to actively imagine and situate themselves within society. It also provided them with an experience-based understanding of differences based on lived experiences and upbringing, influences that helped expand their view of the world and their positionality in that world. This helped with our next attempt at "unpacking the knapsack of privilege" exercise that had students identifying privileges (unearned benefits) in their packs. This, alongside the Power Flower activity, seemed to engage students.[24] Power Flower is a tool developed by Canadian social change educators in working with groups to "identify who we are (and who we aren't) as individuals and as a group in relation to those who wield power in our society."[25] This activity, which we introduced to students in a large gymnasium rather than the classroom, helped students more deeply situate themselves both individually and within society. We experienced this deepening ourselves, and student reports articulated it as well: "I had never thought of the unearned birthright stuff as privilege. I get that now"; "For me, when I read about band aids being the colour of my skin and the societal assumptions therein, I was really amazed that I hadn't thought about that kind of thing before"; "I can better understand my own privilege, but I don't know what I can do about it"; and "Most of the people I hang out with at the summer camp I work at look like me and have a similar background, so I don't really need to worry about this stuff in my life or work."

To bring globalization to life within the classroom, we asked students to take 5 minutes to look around the room and examine their clothing labels and consider the furniture and other objects in the room. We then asked them to engage in paired conversation, sharing the names of countries from where the items and objects came, based on the labels and tags. We next asked them to consider the backgrounds and cultures of the people from those countries and asked them to consider the working conditions of those people and in those countries. Some of the queries we posed included the following:

- Who is in this space?
- What are the physical attributes of this space?
- What objects make up the space?
- Where do the objects come from?

We made progress with some of these lessons. At the beginning of the third and final year of our journey, it was heartening to hear experiences students had had at their summer jobs as they attempted to integrate their newly acquired theories and activities. One student in particular discussed her attempts to share her newfound learning with a high school group, saying that the students acted with resistance and would not engage with her in that teachable moment. We were proud to hear of her efforts despite repeated disappointments and encouraged her to keep playing around with when best and how best to teach such a challenging and personal topic. We too had thought more about this.

Critical Consciousness

The guiding question that informed the third and final phase of our 3-year journey was, "How can experiential pedagogues educate for conscientization (critical consciousness and social change/action)?" Once again we turned to colleagues' work about how to continue to expand upon teaching for and about social justice and globalization and how to engage in relevant activities that would connect these theories with students' lived experiences and leadership praxes. We recalled a paper written by Fawcett, Bell, and Russell that contained a hegemony treasure hunt.[26] Students were directed to leave the classroom, view their surroundings with new eyes, and hunt for hegemonic artifacts.

We posed questions such as the following:

- Who or what is privileged by the university system?
- Is this space universally accessible (e.g., elevators, bathrooms)?
- Travel to the senate chambers. Can you identify physical characteristics of the university's leaders?
- Check out the advertisements. Who are the halls named after? Corporation names?
- Go to the library. Who is writing the books? What does that communicate about knowledge and power?
- Travel down a corridor. Are professors in their offices? What are the characteristics of their office spaces, and how are they physically situated within that space?

This activity seemed to resonate with students because it allowed them to view an everyday experience through a different lens. It led them experientially to consider issues of justice within a university setting. From here, we began to believe that we were finally delving into some of the more critical aspects of what we wanted of the students. For example, students reported that they had not previously considered why a book's author would matter. Students had never considered the sociocultural backgrounds or genders of the authors or the year a book was written and how these factors might impact a book's content. They had no idea that every past university president had been a White male. This led them to question their belief that we are living in a gender equitable society.

We were becoming increasingly aware that students were beginning to get it, and alongside this awakening came an array of emotions. Some students exhibited signs of anger, stating with conviction, "Well, let's do something about it!" Others expressed feelings of being overwhelmed or sad. As we reflected on our own personal journeys of conscientization, these emotions resonated with us. Remembering our earlier lessons of going too deep, too dark, too fast, we brainstormed how we could teach these concepts differently so students were not consistently leaving class feeling stuck, overwhelmed, confused, or angry.

One way we addressed this was through Sam's Emotional Graph of Learning About the World (see Figure 3). On this graph, Sam plotted emotional highs and lows associated with her personal journey with conscientization. She began by being intrigued and excited about learning more about the world around her. She then became aware of the injustices in the world. From there, her journey ranged from low emotional points of feeling helpless and angry to being extremely passionate about specific justice-related causes. By explaining the emotional side of her intellectual journey to students, Sam described ways in which her actions were not always as effective as she had hoped.

Sam spoke to students about the importance of looking at action-oriented behavior through a critical lens and told students that when engaging in action, she always asks herself three questions: Is it Western paternalism? Is it exploitive? Is it effective? Her graph ends at the present day where she feels, for now at least, she has found a pathway forward for engaging in purposeful and effective engagement.

After sharing the graph and talking students through that journey, we asked them to create a graph of their own. Our intention behind this activity was grounded in our belief that if students are aware of the stages, they will likely go through when engaged in the conscientization process, be better prepared, and be more resilient through challenging times. We felt that being transparent with our journey helped students become more comfortable with uncertainty and further understand that constant growth is associated with this complex subject. We are still growing through and from all this today.

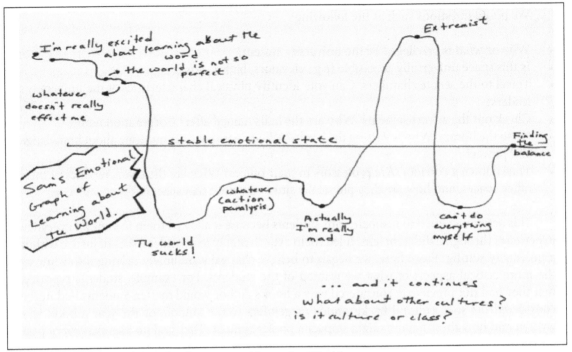

Figure 3. Emotional Graph of Learning About the World

Concluding Remarks

What we have more recently realized from students and from our own learning is that the social consciousness framework[27, 28] is not linear and does not result in arriving and staying at any given level for long. Rather, the process involves a cycling in and cycling out and in praxis may mean that even though a particular critical moment may be revelatory, it may also expose us to a new level of naïveté. What we do know is that Freire's levels of social consciousness have served us and our students well as a guiding framework for exploring social and environmental justice issues.

We leave you with what we believe are some of the most significant pedagogical lessons learned through our 3-year intellectual journey:

- To engage in conscientization, students must first situate themselves within the context of society. They must be guided through their journeys with the use of activity, lectures, readings, dialogue, and self-reflection. Students should be encouraged to recognize their own privilege and how that privilege impacts their ways of knowing and being in the world. Students should also be encouraged to expand their knowledge about the ways in which hegemony governs the world and directly (and silently) influences many aspects of their personal worldviews and lives. Students should critically examine this aspect of their existence.

- Doing social justice pedagogy requires patience and time. It is slow pedagogy. Action comes in many forms. When engaging with justice-oriented thinking and action-oriented work, students should continuously and critically reflect upon their individual motivations and ask themselves three questions: Is it Western paternalism? Is it exploitative? Is it effective?

They should be challenged to answer these questions for themselves and to acknowledge their epistemology as a factor in their thought processes.

- Students should be optimistic. Pedagogues can help with this by not going too deep, too dark, too fast. Shock value pedagogy was effective for gaining student attention. However, it did not contribute to sustainable pathways for students' conscientization journeys. Some of these shock-based teachings were met by resistance, and others resulted in feelings of despair. These were likely setbacks in the students' conscientization journeys.

- Freire's levels of social consciousness should be presented as cyclical rather than hierarchal and linear. We have also learned, similar to so much teaching and learning, that each level can be interpreted differently. There is always collateral learning. We should work in our pedagogical praxes to create spaces for students to learn what they need to learn at any given moment in time and to make opportunities for that learning to be possible and available to them.

- Similar to the stages of human development, we all start off at a level of naïveté. We now believe that individuals cycle between levels of social consciousness—at one moment in time engaging in transformative action and at another moment experiencing a period of action paralysis as new pathways are (re)configured to more fully engage in action-oriented behavior. This is a good thing. We should always hold engagement in action-oriented work and justice-oriented behaviors as our ultimate goals.

Discussion Questions

1. Discuss Freire's three levels of social consciousness. Do you see them as a pathway to a more critical consciousness?

2. Give examples of Freire's three levels of social consciousness (naïve, superstitious, and critical) from your own life. Where do you see yourself along this pathway toward conscientization? Are you there yet?

3. Mary and Samantha think experiential education is a useful method for engaging students in learning about social and environmental justice. Describe your understanding of experiential education and comment on its usefulness for exploring issues related to social and environmental justice.

4. Do you see a more critical consciousness as desirable for you personally? Please elaborate.

5. Do you see learning as a journey? If so, toward what end? What use do you think we are obliged (or not) to make of our learning?

13

Canada's First College of Sustainability

*Teaching About Social and Environmental
Justice and Sustainability*

Susan Tirone
Claire Campbell
Karen Gallant
Dalhousie University

In this, the United Nations Decade of Education for Sustainable Development (2005–2014), universities face the challenge and responsibility of building students' skills and knowledge so they may contribute to the creation of more sustainable societies. Traditional teaching and learning methods prioritizing linear thinking and discrete disciplinary approaches contributed to the social and environmental problems we face today because they prepared university students for a growth-oriented world. Continual growth is no longer possible, and new ways of teaching and learning are now required to prepare leaders, researchers, teachers, and citizens to transition to a sustainable world.[1]

In 2008, Dalhousie University created Canada's first College of Sustainability, which hosts an interdisciplinary undergraduate program: Environment, Sustainability, and Society (ESS). The ESS program promotes dialogue and action as tools for preparing students, academics, and community partners to address challenges related to social and environmental sustainability. ESS is designed to enable students from across campus to combine studies in sustainability with most other degrees on campus. Students enroll in the ESS program as a second major paired with another degree program, or they may take a first year sustainability course as an interest course. Our program draws on the expertise of professors who are cross appointed to the College of Sustainability and whose main appointments are in departments such as history, German, theater, recreation and leisure studies, planning and architecture, law, science, sociology, resource and environmental studies, and international development studies. Faculty members teach as teams, which promotes cross-disciplinary discussions in all classes. Many ESS courses also require students to work in interdisciplinary teams. For example, students in their first year may find themselves working in a group that includes students from international development studies, theater studies, economics, political science, and biology so that they might learn alongside students whose interests are different from their own.

We teach in the College of Sustainability and remain connected to our home departments as cross-appointed faculty members. In this chapter, we draw on our experiences of designing and teaching courses to students in first- and second-year courses in the College of Sustainability. We explain the innovative teaching and learning approaches used in the ESS program, how these approaches develop the critical thinking skills students need to conceptualize social and environmental justice issues, and how discussions about Canada's national park system and leisure experiences serve as a critical platform for the advancement of social and environmental justice ideas.

Shifting From Traditional to Nontraditional Teaching Approaches

Most postsecondary education is delivered by faculty members who are situated in programs where they teach and study with other academics whose research interests are in the same discipline. Students also tend to be grouped with peers who are interested in courses or degrees in the same discipline and their courses of study may provide limited access to courses outside the discipline they are studying. For example, a biology student may have limited opportunities to study a language or to take a social science course. When students in traditional degree programs learn material unrelated to their major area, as is the case with many elective courses, the student is often left to explore the meaningfulness of those courses.

ESS courses emphasize the sharing of information among professors and students whose interests and academic studies are not the same. Our nontraditional approach to sustainability education provides a forum for sharing ideas and developing approaches to action that address how society can fulfill the needs and desires of people today in ways that will ensure the ability of future generations to meet their own needs and desires.[2] In the ESS program, we use a variety of learning and teaching methods such as Problem Based Learning (PBL) and other interdisciplinary, multivoiced approaches designed to introduce students to the complexities of social and environmental justice as well as processes of critical thinking and group problem solving.

Benefiting from this shift in teaching approaches, we highlight what we have learned from teaching social and environmental justice in two ESS courses. We focus on one of the first-year courses: *SUST 1000: Introduction to Environment, Sustainability, and Society*, which is currently cotaught by Claire Campbell, a historian, Canadian Studies scholar, and member of the Faculty of Arts and Social Sciences. Claire coteaches this course with Steven Mannell, who is a member of the Faculty of Architecture and Planning. Their course uses the example of Canada's national parks to problematize our perceptions about these icons of Canadian identity. We then focus on a second-year course: *SUST 2000: Humanity in the Natural World: An Introduction to Problem Based Learning*, which is cotaught by Susan Tirone, a leisure scholar whose home department is the School of Health and Human Performance, and Meinhard Doelle from the Faculty of Law, with the assistance of postdoctoral fellow Karen Gallant. In SUST 2000, leisure behavior serves as an example of how difficult it is to promote behavior change toward sustainability.

SUST 1000: Introduction to Environment, Sustainability, and Society

Since 1885, Canada has presented its national parks to the world as symbols of the country's remarkable diversity of natural environments, a rather singular national affinity for the outdoors. The governing agency of the national park system, Parks Canada, acquired certain landscapes to showcase the country's natural wealth and then made these landscapes accessible to cultivate a sense of national entitlement to and ownership of these places as a common natural heritage. Canada was the first country in the world to create an agency dedicated to managing its national parks in 1911, and that gives Canadians a century's worth of insights into these decisions and their implications.[3] National parks are among the most successful of national icons; images of parks such as Banff and Jasper in the Rocky Mountains are immediately familiar to our Canadian and international students. But the public identity of national parks, promoted by Parks Canada as places of ecological protection, wilderness sanctuaries, and natural treasures, means that students see parks as purely preservationist endeavors and have no sense of the parks' human history. This is the perception we seek to destabilize in the first-year class in the ESS program, *An Introduction to Environment, Sustainability, and Society.*

In SUST 1000, we present national parks as historical artifacts: sites of social conflict, evidence of compromises between competing demands and political strategies, and the manifestation of changing ideas of environmental management over the course of Canada's existence. Specifically, we highlight four episodes that speak to two sets of contradictions inherent in the national park idea. First, the notion of a family of parks as a common national heritage is contrasted against the localized meaning or value of these spaces between an assumed (and imagined) national audience and a regional community, and second, the longstanding paradox of parks as conceived for human use is contrasted alongside parks as responsible for ecological sustainability. In so doing, we want our students to (a) understand that parks, like all landscapes, are made through the dynamic interaction between human societies and the natural world; (b) appreciate the cumulative effects of those societies on that world even in ostensibly protected places; (c) recognize the complex nature of environmental decision making, the so-called wicked problem, where the solution is never readily apparent; and (d) consider the relationship between environmental justice and national identity.[4]

Our students' affection for national parks, as destinations for recreation for many and as a symbol of the Canadian natural environment generally, is in many ways the legacy of decades-long efforts to promote a sense of identification between the national citizenry and the land. In 1887, when it created Rocky Mountain Park (now Banff), the Conservative government in Ottawa borrowed language from the United States in designating "a public park and pleasure ground for the benefit, advantage and enjoyment of the people of Canada."[5] In other words, national parks were not imagined as a way of preserving nature from people, but as a way of reserving nature for the people's use. Which people? The earliest national parks (now known collectively as the Rocky Mountain Parks) were framed by upscale tourist facilities hosted by the transcontinental railways, themselves also a symbol of national achievement over space. But the exclusive quality of these Victorian châteaux was quickly overshadowed by the remaking of the North American landscape for the automobile and the decision by the new Dominion Parks Branch to promote national parks as tourist destinations. The emergent desires of the new urban middle class to get back to nature for spiritual and physical renewal after World War I led to extensive road construction to allow new access to national parks. Within this notion of wild nature as a destination held in reserve for enjoyment and redemption, we try to locate the cultural traditions of Western civilization. Classical and Renaissance ideals of an Arcadia were then transferred to the little-known New World by the imagination of European empires and, subsequently, to the wilderness interior by the Canadian nation-state.

In 1930, the National Parks Act entrenched a dualistic philosophy that has haunted Parks Canada ever since: The mandate of parks to provide for the benefit, education, and enjoyment of the people was paired with a mandate for people to maintain the parks so as to leave them unimpaired for future generations.[6, 7] The dual mandate allows us in SUST 1000 to discuss the significant, nuanced, little understood distinction between concepts of conservation and preservation. We contrast the priorities and principles of scientific forestry as articulated by Gifford Pinchot of the U.S. Forest Service with John Muir's more literary and emotive ideas about protecting the California interior, with Grey Owl's (Archey Belaney's) widely popular advocacy of beaver habitat as an invited resident of Prince Albert National Park in Saskatchewan, and with the second-wave environmentalist groups such as the Canadian Parks and Wilderness Society that decried the development of parks for tourist use.[8, 9] In one key teachable moment, we draw a direct genealogical line between 19th century conservation as wise use of current resources to ensure availability for future generations and today's prevailing language of sustainability and environmental management.[10]

By the 1960s, national parks were sites of active social conflict over not only management decisions but also their very borders. In SUST 1000, we discuss how national park creation often entailed displacement of local communities to make suitably unpeopled scenery for Canada's citizenry. In particular, we examine the story of Métis families who were moved twice out of Jasper and, even more dramatically, the strong protest by francophone Acadians over the proposed expropriation of their land for Kouchibouguac National Park.[11, 12] Here we discuss concepts of national territory, environmental terrorism, and the above-mentioned view of national parks as engines of tourism, which had long convinced provincial governments in the depressed Atlantic region to support localized expropriation in hopes of buoying up their revenues. Opposition to Kouchibouguac and other proposed parks in the Atlantic region over the course of the 1970s helped convince Parks Canada to abandon its longstanding policy of expropriation, showing students again that far from "timeless nature," parks are generational, are susceptible to political circumstances, and can be shaped by public action and attitudes.

At the same time, mainstreaming environmentalist thought and growing awareness of the longstanding wear and tear on the most popular parks drew new attention to the notion of parks as requisitely unimpaired for future generations, ostensibly legislated since 1930. Through the 1980s and 1990s, the concept of ecological integrity was increasingly positioned as paramount in park management.[13, 14] This provides SUST 1000 with another discussion point: using national parks in the Atlantic region to explore the meaning and implications of ecological integrity and the challenges of managing dynamic natural systems when our image of unspoiled nature is often static. Students see that the parks under stress in the region are precisely those designed according to older ideas of what a park should look like, complete with golf courses, resorts, and other amenities, and accordingly are difficult to imagine as wilderness. They also see the extent to which Parks Canada actively manages the ecosystems within park borders, whether restoring aquatic connectivity in the highway-crossed landscape[15] or mitigating the effects of a manicured golf course in Fundy National Park. At the same time, the rhetorical emphasis on ecology and the corresponding visual depictions of parks as natural places provide a disingenuous green cast to these historic landscapes, even as it portrays the critical notion of sustainability. This, coupled with interpretative programs and participatory "citizen science" projects, furthers that original and profound political project of identification between Canadians and territory. This achieves another objective of SUST 1000: encouraging students to consider the historical and political contexts of scientific research, to read across disciplines as much as possible.

Thus, in their first exposure to discussions of sustainability in the college, students are asked to revisit and question what are often long-held views of Canada's iconic landscapes. Our objective as teachers is not to undermine the emotional value of these places for our students, but to ask them to learn to question what human presence or impact may exist in national parks and what effect this has had on our ideas of the health of the Canadian natural environment and on society.

SUST 2000: Humanity in the Natural World: An Introduction to Problem Based Learning

The second example of how the ESS program promotes social and environmental sustainability is from our second-year course, *SUST 2000: Humanity in the Natural World: An Introduction to Problem Based Learning*. PBL is a learning method that uses real-world cases or problems and self-directed learning to develop students' ability to think critically, analyze, and formulate new ways of addressing the problem. This is a team-based approach in which the instructors facilitate learning and are members of the learning team. PBL promotes the development of teamwork and project management skills, as well as students' ability to discover new knowledge.[16] Students work in teams of six to eight, guided by teaching assistants, as they explore a real sustainability problem. In our most recent class in the fall of 2011, problems were drawn from the Halifax Regional Municipality where Dalhousie University is situated. The course, which runs from the beginning of September until early December each year, is composed of two simultaneous activities: a twice weekly lecture and a weekly tutorial meeting. The lectures are designed to provide students with information about various actors such as government officials, regulatory bodies, corporations, NGOs, citizens groups, and individuals as consumers and activists and how their actions either promote or hinder sustainability. Lectures focus on understanding the roles these actors and their actions play and on understanding the complexity of the changes, both individual and societal, that will have to occur as we create a sustainable society.

Included in the series of lectures is one section designed to introduce students to how we understand leisure experience and leisure behavior. Students in the class are mostly unfamiliar with the study of leisure and at times have been reluctant to recognize its significance. We frame leisure in a way that emphasizes its complexity and potential role as an activity and experience that can either facilitate sustainability or contribute to resource depletion, exploitation of vulnerable populations, and pollution. The lecture about leisure experience focuses on developing an appreciation for how difficult it will be for us to change our leisure behavior because we often consider leisure to be compensation for time and energy spent at work. Leisure behavior is also influenced by desires that are fulfilled through consumption and not by other aspects of our lives such as work[17] and desires are difficult to change. We engage students in discussions and reflections about how leisure experience and society's reluctance to change leisure patterns contribute to the sustainability problems of the world today.

In SUST 2000, leisure is presented in the section on understanding consumers' actions. The lectures include an overview of how leisure changed in relation to work through the industrialization, modernization, and urbanization eras and how various attempts at streamlining the workforce such as Fordist and scientific management approaches served to regulate workers' leisure. We explain how work changed in the latter years of the 20th century to a less structured, full-time workforce in many parts of North America, leaving people with more free time, less structure, and less rigidity in their work.[18] The result is that some full-time workers enjoy tremendous work satisfaction from professional careers, but often these careers demand an extraordinary investment of time, leaving little time for leisure. Others enjoy the freedom of less structure in their work, of the ability to change jobs often or work part time, and to have extended periods of time away from work, as is the case for shift workers such as some firefighters and construction workers. However, those who are unable to adapt to unstructured work careers or who lack skills and perseverance to shift into different work roles will not fit into the flexible workforce and consequently will have fewer resources for leisure. We discuss how leisure prioritizes consumption of goods and services and how consumption is affected by these changes in work. We also draw connections between leisure consumption and the inherent issues of resource depletion related to consumer goods such as electronics, unfair exploitation of resources and people from the Global South, and pollution and environmental degradation caused by leisure pursuits.

After each lecture topic, we ask students to write a reflection based on lecture material. Their responses are submitted to our course website and replace the traditional midterm exam. The reflection questions given for the leisure lectures were as follows: What sustainability challenges do you encounter in your leisure? How do you expect that to change once you enter the workforce? The written reflections from the fall 2011 class were enlightening, and this topic elicited the most responses of all reflection questions we posed for the class.

Through the students' reflections, we learned of the array of leisure experiences of class members and of students' expectations that their degrees will result in jobs that pay them well.

They expect their futures to be characterized by more frequent participation in leisure activities and that leisure will occur in more extreme and exotic places. For example, students wrote about how they love to ski, scuba dive, and travel within Canada and to places around the world. Many were golfers who reflected that they had never considered how golf courses consume water resources, and if located in places where water is scarce, golf courses may contribute to severe water insecurity for vulnerable people living nearby. Other students were active volunteers in their leisure and saw that activity as something they will continue after they complete their degree. Some students recognized the importance of leisure for solidifying family ties, and clearly, some students' families invested heavily in vacations and in leisure that the students enjoyed but would not likely be able to afford had they not had parental support.

We also learned of the class privilege of many of our students as they reflected on their leisure experiences, such as travel, skiing, snowboarding, scuba diving, competitive kayaking, and participation in a variety of sports that require individual and team travel, often to places outside of Canada for major competitions. Students reflected that they had not previously considered leisure in the context of unsustainable behavior until now. Examples of the reflections we received follow:

One area that will be difficult to consume less is clothing. I really enjoy clothing and fashion, but I realize that these are social constructs with no bearing on my worth or value as a person. I want to place more emphasis on my non-physical traits, and nurture that aspect of myself, but I still turn my head when I pass a beautiful outfit in a store window (like a beautiful piece of artwork). I hope that as I mature and enter the working world that I remain conscious of this, and that I remember quality over quantity. I know that I will have to buy clothing in my life, but I never want to purchase another item that I don't truly like, and that won't last (no more buying in to trends!). I want the "things" in my life to be useful and practical.

Sustainable leisure time is a subject that has almost never occurred to me during my lifetime. However now that it has occurred to me, it is an apparent problem due to the fact that the human population participates in leisure activities on a regular basis. Not to reference the lecture directly, but I am an avid golfer who every summer spends time in Florida playing golf every day. It is a recreational sport that most of my family participates in and is a bonding time every year. Never has it occurred to me that the lot was probably constructed on exotic habitat that spreads for kilometers … As students currently we do not have the income to spend on elaborate vacations but as we grow older that will change. Even when you produce a family, you might not take as many vacations but every time you do, you will be taking along two to three extra members. Leisure time in my opinion will get more unsustainable as you join the workforce.

My car is a big part of my life as a student, whether it be driving to work or around with my friends, but there are some drawbacks to this. I will admit, I drive around a lot and the fuel economy pertaining to my car is pretty sub-par (15–20 mpg). I work as a mechanic for my father's company, as well as a part time car detailer, and have put a significant amount of my leisure time into the esthetics and performance of this car. The more I study sustainability, the more I realize the impact of my vehicle on the environment.

This assignment provided students with the opportunity to learn about leisure and its importance in their lives. It also involved nonleisure studies students in an exercise that involves thinking about leisure and how it contributes to or hinders social and environmental sustain-ability. In these and in other responses, there is evidence that students gained a strong under-standing of the importance of leisure in their lives. They also demonstrated their understanding of how their leisure choices and leisure consumption may either facilitate sustainability or con-tribute to social and environmental justice. They also realized the difficulty and complexity of individual and social behavior changes necessary to promote sustainable leisure. We think this realization is an important first step for our undergraduate students.

Along with the lecture component of the course, students participated in tutorial sessions where they worked with a small team of students and with a teaching assistant to learn about PBL and to experience this approach to dealing with a sustainability issue. The first phase of the PBL assignment involved an exploration by each group of the array of sustainability problems they knew to exist or those they expected to be evident in the Halifax Regional Municipal-ity (HRM). Students who did not live in HRM were asked to draw upon their experiences of sustainability problems in the places they knew. As groups were composed of students from a variety of disciplines, they were asked to explore what each person knew about sustainability and what skills and knowledge he or she could contribute to the group process.

In the second phase of the PBL assignment, each of the 12 groups was assigned a separate problem to explore over the course of 1 month. Problem topics included ensuring a sustainable food supply, ensuring sustainable public transportation, creating socially and culturally diverse neighborhoods, making suburbia sustainable, and engaging citizens in sustainability. Through-out this second phase, students explored the academic and policy literature to find out how each topic was being analyzed, conceptualized, and theorized and considered the perspectives of various disciplines regarding each problem. Groups were also asked to explore what is being done to address the issue in other jurisdictions. Phase 3 of the PBL assignment then involved developing a recommendation for how the HRM could address each problem. These recom-mendations were presented in poster format to the class and to a public forum at the end of the semester.

Leisure did not feature prominently in the recommendations and poster presentations of all groups, but it was evident in several projects. For example, one group explored the problem of creating socially and culturally diverse neighborhoods. They proposed a plan for a part of the city that contains an area of abandoned military housing. The group proposed this area be developed as mixed residential housing, with an extensive public transit system that would eliminate the need for anyone to own a car. Within their planned neighborhood were several recreation areas, green spaces, wheelchair accessible paths, restaurants, bars, an athletic center, and a community center. Other groups, however, made recommendations that park areas be converted to vegetable gardens without suggesting alternative places for recreation.

Outcomes of Our Learning Methods, Topic, and Approach

The complex and nonlinear nature of issues related to social and environmental sustain-ability align well with PBL and other approaches we use to foster cooperative, interdisciplin-ary, holistic learning. The discussions of Canada's national parks and of leisure are just a few examples of the topics we use in the ESS program. The content and our approaches to learning aim to develop our students' ability to think critically about their world and about people and the behaviors that contribute to sustainability problems.

Within the national parks are stories of displacement, community mobilization, and politi-cal negotiation that are often camouflaged by powerful images of wilderness. In SUST 1000, we want to demonstrate that protected places are consequences of human action, that these places were made according to changing priorities and with substantial consequences for local and regional communities. Moreover, we hope that students identify themselves as participants in the nation-building project of which parks form a part; that these parks form part of their sense of citizenship, whether through physical visitation or imaginative consumption; and that, as a result, they are in some way tied to or beneficiaries of the decisions made about these places.

Among other measures of our success are the responses to reflection questions about leisure in the SUST 2000 course. In reviewing submissions, we were struck by those who reflected on their privilege as White, middle-class young adults who had tremendous opportunities to travel, play sports, and purchase consumer goods whenever they pleased. Many students acknowledged that they expected to increase their leisure after graduation, and they reflected on the impact that would have on the environment and on vulnerable people. Those reflections indicate the students' ability to consider the consequences of their actions. We hope our courses will prepare them to contribute to society as consumers, employees, family members, and involved citizens, in meaningful and sustainable ways.

Another theme that was evident in students' reflections on their leisure is the challenge associated with the radical change necessary to achieve a sustainable and socially just society. Students reflected on how difficult it is to change, and implicit in some of their reflections is resistance to change even as they recognize change is needed. As the course progressed, there was evidence that some students transitioned from thinking of the change needed to achieve a sustainable and just society as something that would be championed by a generalized "other," such as a special interest group or nonprofit organization, to thinking of themselves as agents of change. For example, one PBL group's suggested solution to the problem of ensuring a sustainable food supply included an education program that would be created and led by fourth-year sustainability students. Thus students came to see themselves as capable of not only suggesting solutions that would address sustainability issues, but also enacting them as well.

In the ESS program, our lectures, reflection exercises, and PBL approach create opportunities for students to explore and critique the underlying assumptions of students, their peers, instructors, and popular culture as related to sustainability and lifestyle choices. Students' reflections on leisure suggest that leisure consumption is natural. Many students noted their consumption related to leisure will naturally increase as they launch their professional career and as their income increases. This tendency to view commodification and consumption of leisure as indivisible from leisure itself was also evident in students' group projects, where one group, pursuing the topic of achieving quality of life in a sustainable way, was perplexed by how quality of life could be ensured without increasing consumption. Our approaches to learning, including the multivoice teaching team in SUST 1000 and the PBL approach in SUST 2000, provide a forum for students to explore and question their own preconceptions and biases about what it means to live a socially and environmentally just and sustainable life.

Discussion Questions

1. Susan, Claire, and Karen describe a new College of Sustainability that purposefully puts students and faculty from different disciplines and departments together into one learning community. What might be strengths and weaknesses of this educational arrangement?

2. In SUST 1000, students learn about the Canadian national park system. Did you hear anything in that description that troubled you? If so, what was it and why?

3. What do Susan, Claire, and Karen mean when they say the Canadian national parks were made (their emphasis)?

4. In SUST 2000, students learn about leisure's problematic side. What are some of these problems? Can you relate to them? What can be done about them?

5. What is your interpretation of the word *sustainability*? Do you think it is an effective word for describing the challenge facing our society in the long term? Is it a banner to be rallied around or does it leave something to be desired as a rallying call?

14

Eco-Justice Education

Learning to Speak Up and Out

Adrienne Cachelin
University of Utah

Can ecotourism exist as anything other than an oppressive arm of globalization and actually serve people and conservation in indigenous communities? Is the Slow Food movement a critical recreation effort for environmental justice or is it another weak attempt of the upper middle class that serves to ameliorate guilt and undermine real action? Can the queering of various leisure spaces ensure social justice in a community? These are some of the interesting questions that arise when looking at recreation and leisure through the lenses of social and environmental justice. In this chapter, I suggest that social and environmental justice have a complex and contested relationship that can be brought together effectively under the umbrella of sustainability. An exploration of these ideas and the use of eco-justice education to think these ideas through may help recreation and leisure scholars set directions for the field that position us to make a difference through strong interdisciplinary partnerships in our communities and on our campuses.

Sustainability as Embodiment of Environmental and Social Justice

Most sustainability scholars and sustainability-based organizations include either the "three Es," ecology, equity, and economy, or the "three Ps," planets, people, and profit, as critical elements of sustainability. Recognition of these elements brings us beyond the foundational definition of sustainability "to ensure meeting the needs of the present without compromising the ability of future generations to meet their needs"[1] to a more holistic perspective that encompasses social and environmental justice. This holistic conception is central to the idea that sustainability is a powerful platform for uniting environmental and social justice. We need only consider the lessons of ecological footprinting to gain insight into the inherently linked nature of these ideas.

Ecological footprinting, a technique developed by two scholars at the University of British Columbia to understand how much nature we consume versus how much nature there is to consume, provides a great illustration. These researchers calculated that, to live by our current rates of consumption, we need 1.5 earths.[2] Each year we get further into ecological debt because we use more than the regenerative capacity of ecosystems and we generate synthetic products that cannot be easily absorbed into the ecosystem. This perspective illustrates the ecology or planet piece of sustainability well and also leads us to understand both the equity piece and the economy piece of the sustainability equation. If every person lived like the average North

American, we would need five planets to sustain our consumption.[3] Currently, North Americans live on the temporary surpluses of others who, intentionally or not, use less. Equity issues have far-reaching consequences that prevent us from moving toward ecological health, and therefore human health, at the largest scale. For example, international climate treaties have stalled given the tension between industrialized and nonindustrialized countries that suggest all should have the opportunity to industrialize in the same consumptive way characteristic of North America.[4] Here the inexorable linkages between social justice and the environment become clear. Ultimately, the pursuit of economic prosperity needs to be tempered by an understanding of ecological limits and equity issues. This is why so many ecologically literate citizens call for measures of success that are not wholly economic in nature.[5]

Environmental justice scholars might point out that thus far we are only talking about one element of justice—distribution of resources—when we must also consider the impacts of resource extraction and the degradation that results (e.g., the placement of refineries, manufacturing plants, and toxin-emitting incinerators). Other critical ideas in environmental justice include the importance of inclusive participation in and access to legal and civil procedures, with recognition that all populations and communities are needed for carrying out just processes. Finally, these elements must all be explored in light of the political and economic systems that allow, if not enforce, injustice at every scale.

One example of environmental injustice inherent in the field of parks and recreation is the distribution of parks and green spaces. We know that access to safe and healthy parks is not distributed equitably among all segments of the population[6] just as access to clean water, clean air, and healthy food is not distributed equitably.[7] This is particularly important in the field of environmental justice where environments are conceived of as the places we work, live, play, and learn as opposed to some faraway wilderness that can distract policy makers from important everyday issues. Indeed, also commonplace is that people of color and people who are socioeconomically disadvantaged do not have access to civil and legal procedures that populations with economic means enjoy. For example, park conservation objectives are often achieved at the expense of indigenous peoples who have little or no voice in decision-making processes.[8] This notion of procedural injustice is necessarily linked to "recognition injustice" defined as "unjustified privilege in how social circumstances and cultural terms are represented and considered within social institutions and transactions."[9]

Finally, environmental justice scholars contend that it is incumbent on all of us to ask what economic and political structures allow for or promote injustice and what role citizens and consumers can play. From trade agreements to international differences in environmental, health, and safety regulations, we see the institutionalization of economic and social practices that promote injustice. For example, we might suggest that slavery never actually ended for the United States, but rather was moved overseas because it is both cheaper and less visible that way, less visible in terms not only of our being less connected to the sources of our sustenance, but also of the invisible (from U.S. shores) impacts of extraction and production that underlie serious health issues from asthma to diabetes to cancer.[10] These examples highlight the idea that working toward environmental and social justice is part and parcel of working toward sustainability.

Recreation and Leisure as Essential to Sustainability Education

With the acknowledgement that sustainability encompasses social and environmental justice, education for sustainability becomes a central tenet in the field of recreation and leisure, one we have recognized as important and one in which I suggest we have a critical role. Within sustainability education, an intellectual home for constructivist outdoor and experiential education and an applied social science field, recreation and leisure practitioners can effectively target the affective and behavioral outcomes identified, such as compassion, empathy, communication and collaboration, solidarity, generosity, and conflict resolution.[11] Constructivist, outdoor, and experiential approaches to learning call on us to engage students as participants and collaborative learners rather than empty vessels for the memorization of facts and ideas. Additionally, universal recreation program outcomes, such as leadership, team building, empowerment, and sportspersonship, actively and intentionally build the skills needed for citizenship in a sustainable world. Thus we inherently work toward ends that are critical to education for sustainability (read the promotion of environmental and social justice). Perhaps more important, as an applied social science field, we recognize that deeper understanding and consequent conceptual and behavioral change come from not only ecological knowledge but also our attitudes,[12] which frequently result from outdoor experiences that are educational and recreational in nature.[13] Although these outcomes are critical for sustainability, and although the role for recreation and leisure in educating for sustainability is clear, eco-justice educators would argue that we can do more, both implicitly and explicitly.

Eco-Justice Education as a Tool for Sustainability

In *Speaking Up and Speaking Out: Working for Social and Environmental Justice Through Parks, Recreation, and Tourism* Cachelin suggested the most effective path for affecting social and environmental justice is embracing an ecological narrative in which we adopt Aldo Leopold's Land Ethic: "In short, a land ethic changes the role of Homo sapiens from conqueror of the land-community to plain member and citizen of it. It implies respect for his fellow-members, and also respect for the community as such."[14] Support for this notion from an educational perspective is found in the work of eco-justice education scholars who implore us to look at the cultural roots of our social and ecological crisis.[15] They suggest that an examination of discourses of modernity and its root metaphors, which drive exploitation, is necessary, as is an interruption of this discourse.[16] But what does this discourse actually look like? The following is an examination of a commonly used textbook in terms of both metaphor and driving exploitation: "We try to conserve biodiversity to maintain ecosystem 'services'...," and "our ability to control and exploit ecosystems cannot fail to be improved by an ability to explain and understand them."[17] This widespread conception of conservation is not based in a land ethic and does not imply any concern for the justice elements of sustainability. Rather, it reinforces a hyper-separation of humans and nature.[18]

Research on the manipulation of language in teaching ecology suggests that language framing may be a powerful strategy for sustainability educators.[19] In fact, students responding to paragraphs of text that portrayed humans as a part of an ecosystem were more likely to relate the text to themselves and society, to express sentiments such as "we're all in it together," and to problem solve by making suggestions as to what they themselves could do.[20] Students who read passages suggesting humans are apart from nature more commonly suggested management solutions and/or expressed sentiments involving human dominion over the earth.[21] These response patterns suggest important gains in education for sustainability, effectively targeting issues related to empowerment and compassion.

Yet shedding light on the linked nature of our ecological and social crisis by looking at the root assumptions embedded in our educational language is but one technique eco-justice educators propose[22] for working toward sustainability. Although I find it hopeful and fascinating, it might not be the most effective strategy for all recreation and leisure professionals. Other ideas, many of which I argue are implicit in much of our recreation programming, include

- making sure students understand fair decision making depends on participation,
- connecting students to community,

- recognizing place-based understandings as valuable,
- discussing privilege, and
- looking at sustainability in terms of what does and does not contribute at the local and global levels.

These practices are a perfect fit with the more affective and behavioral goals of education for sustainability. In fact, one description of transformative education for sustainability uses a framework of "head, hands, and heart,"[23] a phrase that resonates deeply with recreation and leisure scholars and practitioners.

Eco-Justice Education for Sustainability in a Recreation and Leisure Context

The utility of eco-justice education in light of the initial questions posed in this chapter should be considered: Can ecotourism exist as anything other than an oppressive arm of globalization and actually serve people and conservation in indigenous communities? Is the Slow Food movement a critical recreation effort for environmental justice or is it another weak attempt of the upper middle class that serves to ameliorate guilt and undermine real action? Can the queering of various leisure spaces ensure social justice in a community? The ideas of eco-justice education might lead us to consider, for example, whether the goals of ecotourism need to include recognition and/or discussion of industrialized countries' privilege in working with indigenous communities to conserve lands and resources. We might ask ourselves whether engagement with Slow Food can connect students to communities and enhance understanding of place, or we may study the queering of leisure spaces with respect to fair decision making and democracy. It seems to me that the critical tools for eco-justice education and sustainability consist of useful insights through which we can more deeply consider our initial questions. We can also celebrate that many of these techniques are inherent in the intentional programming already happening in recreation, in outdoor education, and in considerations of ecotourism. Our next challenge will be to more explicitly recognize our work as critical to sustainability and initiate strong partnerships within our communities, among our student populations, and across our campuses. This integration can only help us in our efforts to be heard when we speak up and out.

Discussion Questions

1. Adrienne asks us to frame social and environmental justice within a larger context of sustainability. Can you do this? Please elaborate.

2. Employing Adrienne's thinking, how would you respond to her questions?

   a. Can ecotourism exist as anything other than an oppressive arm of globalization and actually serve people and conservation in indigenous communities?
   b. Is the Slow Food movement a critical recreation effort for environmental justice or is it another weak attempt of the upper middle class that serves to ameliorate guilt and undermine real action?
   c. Can the queering of various leisure spaces ensure social justice in a community?

3. Adrienne seems to think the field of parks, recreation, tourism, and leisure is particularly well suited to be a leader in sustainability education and, therefore, in promoting social and environmental justice. What do you think?

SYNTHESIS

On Interconnectedness and Interdependence

Anita Ledford
University of Utah

*"When one tugs at a single thing in nature,
he finds it attached to the rest of the world."*

— John Muir

On the first day of the First International Symposium on Speaking Up and Speaking Out: Working for Social and Environmental Justice Through Parks, Recreation, and Tourism, attendees were asked to reflect on themes and topics they wanted to keep on the collective agenda to discuss throughout the remaining sessions. As I looked through my notes, two words kept popping out: *interconnectedness* and *interdependence*. When I brought these words up as potential themes, I was not sure I could explain why I thought these concepts were important and relevant to social and environmental justice. Later that evening, I began to ask myself if the terms were worth further investigation. I was particularly curious about how we define these terms in our field, in what contexts they are used, and how they might apply to social and environmental justice.

Sharon Washington first brought up interconnectedness in her keynote address, "Eating, Breathing, and Living Social and Environmental Justice." She discussed interconnectedness and identity and how people are unable to separate out any one part of their identity. Individuals filter every bit of information they receive through varying aspects of their identity: gender, race, ethnicity, sexual orientation, family history, religious beliefs, and so forth. I will always be a female of European descent. I have connections to Ireland, England, and Germany, traditions that have been passed down through my family for generations. My parents have been married for almost 40 years, and I am the youngest of three children. This history has shaped my individual development in ways that are so ingrained in me there is no way for me to determine how my identity would be changed if I were raised differently. I am an independent individual with the ability to act of my own free will, but I do not exist in a void, closed off from the world around me. Because I cannot separate myself, I must embrace every aspect of me to understand and interact with the world around me. I think Daniel Theriault said it best in his introduction to his talk: "When you are all parts of yourself, you feel free." I would add that when you feel free to be yourself and accept those parts of yourself that you cannot change, you feel more connected to the world around you.

The more I think about interconnectivity, the more I think it occurs primarily at two levels: the individual and the community. By community level, I do not mean one's local community. As the world around us has developed and the information age has taken over, the distances between people and places around the world have shrunk. In such a world, a local homogenized society is neither feasible nor desirable. That does not mean local communities cannot retain some of their unique features and culture. It does mean those features and cultures are now shared with a worldwide community through social media, international trade, and tourism. In the store where I work in Salt Lake City, Utah, I have seen some of the most amazing products: rings made of goat horns from Africa, Nativities carved out of Tagua nuts from Columbia, intricate leatherwork from India, olive wood pieces from the West Bank, debris from the earthquake in Haiti turned into beautiful and intricate metalwork, and recycled newspapers or magazines from Asia turned into a number of things from jewelry to vases. Even though these communities are half a world away, they are now connected to the end buyer because the store makes it a priority to share as much knowledge as possible about the products and the artists who made the products with the customers.

For this synthesis, I was asked to explain what I felt the difference was between interconnectedness and interdependence. The main difference, I think, between the terms is that everything is connected, whether we realize it or not. Interdependence, however, implies a conscious appreciation of a fundamental reliance between and among peoples and the environment that sustains them. What if there really are only six degrees of separation between any one person and any other person in the world? How would that knowledge change the way we treat others or think about people living and working across the street or around the world from us? Would recognizing those potential connections incline us to shed our individualistic selves and honor our interconnectedness to and interdependence on every aspect of the environment around us?

Adrienne Cachelin helped me take my thinking further regarding interconnectedness and interdependence when she challenged us to see ourselves as part of nature rather than apart from nature. In this day and age, forgetting this fundamental insight is easy when so many of us are born into, grow up in, and make our lives in urban environments. We forget where we came from and what we are about as a species. Though I grew up in the mountains of North Carolina surrounded by woods, it was not until I made my first trip across the Mississippi and ended up in the Badlands of South Dakota that I got to see the Milky Way for the first time. The next time I saw that many stars, I was on a trip with my sustainable tourism class. We stepped out of the vans at 11 p.m. in Wyoming's Grand Tetons in total darkness and gazed up in awe of the heavens above us. When you experience the night sky in all its glory, it is hard not to feel a part of the larger living world.

If everything is connected and we are all part of a larger living system, then our individual and collective attempts to honor and respect one another are clearly indispensable to the continued health and well-being of our planet. We can be independent individuals and still be interconnected; we can live in an interdependent society and still be interconnected on a global scale. What we can no longer be is ignorant of our own interconnectedness to the larger community of life. If we are able to acknowledge and understand this fundamental reality, perhaps we can truly move forward with an agenda of social and environmental justice for all.

PART FOUR

Doing Justice

"The greatest achievement of our flight to the moon is a picture of the earth, a living blue-green planet whirling in the dark endless void of space, and the realization that this is home."

—Sigurd Olson

15

Virtue Ethics

An Emerging Discourse in Social and Environmental Justice Inquiry

Donald McLean
Western Illinois University-Quad Cities

Virtue ethics, the ancient tradition of ethical inquiry that focuses on the character and dispositions of moral agents, has been overshadowed by modernist deontological and consequentialist ethical theories. However, since the publication of seminal works such as Anscombe's "Modern Moral Philosophy"[1] and MacIntyre's *After Virtue*[2], there has been a renewed interest in the ethics of character. This revived interest in virtue ethics has generated new scholarship in intellectual fields that, until recently, has relied primarily on deontological and consequentialist ethical theories to advance moral, social, and political analyses on both theoretical and practical levels. For example, in both feminist[3] and environmental ethics[4] literature, there is evidence of a new interest in applying virtue ethics to issues of social and environmental justice because of a growing recognition of the limitations of moral discourses that are restricted to ethical analyses grounded in rights (deontological) and utilitarian (consequentialist) ethical theories. Given that ancient Greeks used virtue ethics to justify a repressive and hierarchical social order, it may seem odd that contemporary liberatory and environmental justice movements could find much intellectual kinship with the elitist/perfectionist ethical and political theories of antiquity. Although the virtue theories of the ancient Greeks were decidedly anthropocentric (human-centered) and androcentric (male-centered), it should not be inferred that virtue ethics theories must support moral prescriptions that are unjust and inequitable. And although deontological and consequentialist ethical reasoning has made tremendous contributions to the advancement of environmental and social justice, it is not surprising that the lack of utilization of the third great school of ethical reasoning, virtue ethics, has led to an overreliance on analyses grounded in rights–based or consequence-based arguments.

Virtue ethics analysis offers new avenues of discourse for social and environmental justice inquiry, some of the most prominent being (a) it focuses on dispositions and traits that promote flourishing (both human and nonhuman); (b) it gives emphasis to affective understanding of ethical and social issues rather than focusing primarily on cognitive understanding as do deontological and consequentialist approaches; (c) it focuses on the self rather than social structures and organizations to understand issues of moral agency. As such, virtue ethics offers an important alternative worldview for understanding ethical issues connected to social and environmental justice.

In this chapter, I explain how the growing character-based discourse of virtue ethics forms a linkage between environmental and social justice literature. I will argue as well that the revived interest in virtue ethics theory presents a promising new approach for the field of recreation and leisure studies from both a research and a teaching perspective. There is a close historical connection between virtue ethics and origins of the Western conception of leisure.[5, 6, 7, 8] The thought of the ancient Greeks, as typified by the writings of Aristotle, maintained that eudaemonia (happiness) was dependent on one being in a state of leisure where one had respite from work and could engage in virtuous activity.[9] However, despite the historical connection between leisure and virtue, relatively little attention has been paid to virtue ethics in the leisure research literature, which at the theoretical and applied levels has been dominated by deontological and consequentialist approaches.

Development of virtue ethics research via the examination of issues of social and environmental justice in a recreation and leisure context would help address this imbalance. Applying a virtue ethics framework to issues of environmental and social justice not only articulates the connection between these two movements in a recreation and leisure services context, but also contributes to the expansion of a virtue ethics approach to professional preparation of future leisure services practitioners.

Two Ways of Doing Ethics

Of the three basic approaches to normative ethics (i.e., deontological, consequentialist, and virtue theories), virtue ethics is the traditional way the ancient Greeks conducted moral inquiry. From the writings of Plato, Aristotle, and the Hellenistic philosophers, it is clear that their way of thinking and talking about ethics was different from the approach most academicians use today. The ancient way of doing ethics centered on how to best live one's life. Our way is to focus on the duties and obligations we have to others. Their way was to examine habits and dispositions in terms of whether these character traits led to happiness. Our modern way of doing ethics is to rationally justify moral rules and principles. The ancients prized individual excellence; our modern approach to ethics tends to favor egalitarianism. Clearly, there are many significant differences between the ancient and modern ways of thinking and talking about ethics and morality. Why is this so?

Taylor argued the split between the ancient and modern ethical reasoning and discourse reflects the fundamentally different worldviews of ancient Greek and early Christian societies. Taylor believed the ancient Greeks based their ethical ideals on the rational, systematic study of human nature.[10] Their approach to ethics, he said, was humanistic. In contrast, Christianity addressed ethical inquiry primarily via faith rather than reason. The religious approach to ethics emphasized obedience to Divine command (such as the Decalogue), with human needs, wants, and aspirations being secondary. With the decline of ancient Greece and the rise of Christianity, a fundamental shift occurred in how ethical inquiry was conceived. One coherent and complex ethical tradition that was based on reason, human nature, and virtue was replaced by another that emphasized faith, divinity, and obligation.

According to Taylor, this transition from one form of moral discourse to another went swimmingly until the rise of modern philosophy. The decline in the belief in a Divine lawgiver (at least among the intelligentsia) has resulted in undermining the religious-based system of ethics. Taylor argued that, as the modern academy lost faith in religious foundations of moral reasoning, it turned to reason to secure a new foundation for an ethics system based on obligations and duties. However, in Taylor's view, the replacing of faith with reason as the epistemological foundation for obligation-based ethical theories has been an abysmal failure:

...One can try to find some source of law other than God and yet higher and more authoritative than human will. And philosophers have tried this—have tried, in other words, to find some law or principle of ethics that would give meaning to this higher sense of right and wrong, without resorting to the idea of any law of God. But it has never succeeded. This should be apparent to anyone who has read any modern philosophical moralists. One finds the discourse larded with such words as "right," "dutiful," "just," and so on. The impression given is that such ethical terms are not to be understood in their merely conventional sense, as expressing only customary permissions and prohibitions more or less idiosyncratic to the philosopher's own culture. And yet, failing to cite any source of them higher than custom, they are left with no clear meaning at all. The reader has a kind of illusion of understanding but no real understanding at all; and philosophers, because they are able to discourse in such terms with consistency and often with much subtlety, are caught up in precisely the same illusion, which in their case is almost impossible to expose.[11]

Essentially, Taylor argued that modern ethical inquiry has tried unsuccessfully to maintain the language and conceptual structure of a system of ethics in which people no longer believe. He pointed to ethical theorizing of Immanuel Kant and John Stuart Mill as two prominent examples of the futility of trying to justify obligation-based ethical theories based on reason rather than faith. Kant is the intellectual grandfather of deontological ethics; Mill serves that role for utilitarian thought. Taylor stated Kant's allegiance to reason rather than faith forces him to find the intellectual foundation for moral obligations in reason itself. However, reason is not up to the task of justifying universal moral principles (what Kant refers to as categorical imperatives):

Reason, accordingly, is invoked to fill what had hitherto been the role of God with respect to moral right and wrong; to command, and thereby create a law and a concept of duty, transcending the laws and duties that, however important, are of merely human fabrication. But of course the difficulty is that reason discovers no such command, nor would even the most sagacious of philosophers have ever suspected the existence of such a law had Kant never lived to invent it.[12]

Kant's followers, it should be noted, have not given up the quest to ground ethics of obligation in the authority of reason. In the *Theory of Justice*,[13] for example, Rawls based what he believes are the two basic principles of social justice to what rational individuals would inevitably agree if they were subject to a veil of ignorance that prevented them from knowing their future prospects in life. If Taylor's critique of meaninglessness of modern obligation-based ethics is correct, then Rawls' project to derive universal principles of social justice is illusory as well.

Utilitarianism, the other great tradition of modern normative ethics, fares no better under Taylor's critique. Taylor argued that Mill attempts to base moral duty not upon reason itself, but rather on the experience of pleasure. Mill, he said, equates pleasure with happiness and posits that pleasure is "uniquely and universally good" and its opposite, pain, is universally and uniquely bad. Taylor thought it was simplistic of Mill to equate the experience of pleasure with happiness, but what he really objected to was the inference Mill then makes that it is one's moral duty to follow the fundamental principle of utilitarianism to "increase the amount of pleasure in the world and minimize the amount of pain."[14] According to Taylor, even if pleasure is unequivocally good and pain is likewise bad, these facts about pain and pleasure do not provide grounds for believing that our duty is to follow the fundamental principle of utilitarianism that we should pursue the greatest good for the greatest number. This non sequitur argument that attempts to link the properties of pleasure and pain to what we are obligated can lead to morally unacceptable conclusions. For example, following the utilitarian principle of maximizing overall pleasure and minimizing pain can require us to do actions that are morally repugnant (e.g., torturing a small number of animals, children, elderly, etc. if that produces a net amount of pleasure for the many). Of course, since the time of Mill, advocates of utilitarianism have attempted various defenses and reformulations of the theory to address its apparent weaknesses. However, if Taylor's analysis is correct, these efforts are pointless because there is no logical connection between pleasure and our moral obligations.

It would appear that modern ethical inquiry is now in a miserable spot. The two mainstay theories of modern ethics, deontology and utilitarianism, use the language and concepts inherited from the Judeo-Christian moral tradition. With modernism and loss of faith in the existence of a divine moral authority, the foundation for obligation-based ethics has dissolved, despite efforts to substitute reason or the experience of pleasure to support the notion that ethical inquiry centers on our duties to others. The result has been a discourse about ethical reasoning and principles that Taylor saw as largely meaningless.

A Solution to Our Problem?

How do we get out of this unfortunate situation? Given that there are three basic approaches to normative ethics (deontological, consequentialist, and virtue ethics), there would seem to be two possibilities: (a) continue to use an obligation-based conception of morality, but once again have faith in a divine lawgiver, or (b) return to using virtue ethics to conduct ethical inquiry. The first solution is unlikely to be accepted, as it would require the adoption of some form of fideism where reason would be subordinate to faith when engaging in ethical inquiry. The second solution might seem unlikely as well, as it would appear to require the reviving of the largely forgotten ethical traditions of antiquity. Yet a growing body of literature is advocating for such a move. Also, the second solution emphasizes reason over faith; though, it must be pointed out that the type of reason employed in virtue ethics is not the theoretical reason of Kant or Mill, but the practical reason of Plato or Aristotle. As well, a return to virtue ethics should be particularly attractive to the discipline of leisure and recreation because, as mentioned previously, the Western conception of leisure is intimately linked to the virtue ethics theories of the ancient Greeks.

The reorientation of ethical inquiry away from an obligation-based discourse to a virtue ethical discourse does not entail the wholesale abandonment of talk of duties, rights, and obligations. From a practical standpoint it is implausible to believe that duty-based ethical reasoning has been a waste of time and effort. For example, social movements such as civil, animal, and environmental rights have been inspired and justified on the basis of modern deontological ethics. Similarly, utilitarianism's influence on public policy has immensely improved the general welfare of the average person. The point of reviving virtue ethics is to broaden rather than restrict our understanding of ethical issues and our ways of doing ethical analysis. Part of the problem of obligation-based ethics is that it has dominated modern ethical inquiry. The reemergence of virtue ethics offers an alternative discourse that can complement our ethical reasoning based on an obligation perspective.

The turn to a virtue ethical discourse therefore does not prescribe a purging of the notions of duty, obligation, rights, and such. Rather, approaching ethical analysis from a standpoint of virtue theory means reframing such concepts in terms of a virtue ethical perspective as well as reintroducing other concepts—such as happiness, prudence, and virtue—to moral discourse. Also, resurrecting virtue ethics does not entail that one must adopt the more objectionable aspects of Aristotelian virtue ethics, such as condoning slavery or the exclusion of women from politics. These sorts of injustices are peculiar to an instantiation of virtue ethical theory rather than a necessary outcome of it. It can equally be pointed out that all sorts of unjust and immoral actions, rules, laws, principles, and policies have been grounded in particular applications of obligation-based ethics.

What do modern incarnations of virtue ethics look like? Ironically, a virtue ethical discourse is arising in feminist/liberatory and environmentalist literature, which is an interesting development as an old, almost forgotten practice of ethical inquiry is now being adopted by two of the youngest of academic disciplines. What is the attraction of virtue ethics? As will be explained next, virtue ethics analysis has a number of distinct advantages over modern obligation-based ethics.

Virtue Ethics and Environmentalism

The connection between environmentalism and modern obligation-based ethics is not difficult to see. Environmental ethics has a strong grounding in rights-based ethical reasoning. Stone argued that trees (and other natural objects) should have legal standing.[15] Leopold's land ethic called for humans to acknowledge certain obligations to the natural world.[16] Nash stated in his aptly named book, *The Rights of Nature*, the essential project of environmental ethics is for humanity to recognize and respect its duties to the natural environment:

Human beings are the moral agents who have the responsibility to articulate and defend the rights of other occupants of the planet. Such a conception of rights means that humans have duties or obligations toward nature. Environmental ethics involves people extending ethics to the environment by the exercise of self-restraint.[17]

Nash saw environmental ethics as the outcome of a historical process in Western society where moral reasoning has gradually extended the concept of rights to more classes of people such as women, laborers, and African Americans. However, he noted it is revolutionary that some people are willing to attribute moral standing to "nonhuman life and nonliving matter."[18] Thus the extension of rights to nature is not so much a change in degree as it is kind.

According to Nash, this extension of rights to nonhuman entities and substances is predicated on an evolution in moral reasoning that began with "the development of an intelligence capable of conceptualizing right and wrong" (i.e., obligation-based ethics) that replaced the preethical morality of self-interest (virtue ethics).[19] This shift from a self-regarding to an evermore other-regarding ethics gradually expanded the "circle of ethical relevancy"[20] to include not only one's family and tribe but also one's nation and species and eventually animals, plants, ecosystems, the planet, and even the universe.

Although the extension of rights to that which is nonhuman is a reasonable explanation for the growth and development of environmental ethics, such a strategy is not without drawbacks. From an obligation-based ethics standpoint, it can be questioned whether ascribing moral standing and rights to animals and substances is reasonable.[21] The questioning of whether extending rights to the nonhuman world is a meaningful proposal appears to illustrate Taylor's point that modern obligation-based ethical discussions can draw us into complex but ultimately futile debates. Nash noted the notion of extending rights to the nonhuman is a radical idea from philosophical and practical standpoints. However, he believed it was simply a matter of time before people accepted the notion of acknowledging our obligations to nature, as has been the case with our eventual acceptance of other socially controversial ideas. But contrary to Nash's optimism, it is not outside the realm of possibility that history will judge the idea of extending rights to nonhuman entities and substances as implausible and misguided. Furthermore, even if it is accepted that rights should be extended to the nonhuman world, there is controversy as to whether rights should be ascribed to individuals or collectives. Should, for example, individual animals have rights, or species, or the ecosystems they inhabit?

An alternative to obligation-based environmental ethics is virtue ethics. However, virtue ethics, with its focus on self-interest can be an anathema to many environmentalists. Nash, as noted above, regarded it as a part of our preethical past, but that may be because he equated self-interest with selfishness. However, it is true that virtue ethics is agent centered, but that does not mean a moral agent who practices virtue ethics must further his or her interests to the disregard and/or detriment of others. On the contrary, Aristotle—virtue ethicist par excellence—devoted Books VIII and IX of the *Nicomachean Ethics* to a careful and insightful examination of the subject of friendship. It would be an impoverished notion of friendship indeed if Aristotle advocated that one should have friends simply for one's own benefit. In fact, he said the opposite: that perfect friendship consists of wishing well to one's friends for their sakes.[22] Therefore, although virtue ethics is an agent-centered moral theory, characterizing it as unconcerned with the interests of others would be incorrect.

Sandler argued a virtue-oriented approach to environmental ethics is preferable to other ethical theories precisely because it is agent centered. Sandler noted, "One of the central preoccupations of environmental ethics is determining the extent to which we ought to enlarge the scope of our moral community."[23] This philosophic issue of to whom or to what we extend moral consideration, he said, often does not reflect our actual lived experiences and is not helpful in guiding our individual actions with respect to the natural environment. Instead, he advocated a virtue ethical approach in which individual moral agents practice environmentally responsive, justified, and productive virtues. He conceived of these environmental virtues in the form of a typology that divides environmental virtues into six categories: Land Virtues, Virtues of Sustainability, Virtues of Communion With Nature, Virtues of Respect for Nature, Virtues of Environmental Activism, and Virtues of Environmental Stewardship. Within each category, Sandler identified associated character traits that are environmentally virtuous. For example, desirable character traits under the category of Virtues of Communion With Nature include wonder, openness, aesthetic sensibility, attentiveness, and love.

Rather than drawing us into philosophical debates as to what rights should be extended to which entities and substances, a virtue ethical discourse directs us to ask not "What are my obligations and duties to the natural environment?" but instead "What type of person am I with respect to the natural environment?" As well, apart from being a more practical way for individuals to resolve moral issues relating to the natural environment, a virtue ethical approach, Sandler argued, is good for the individual:

Good environmental character is not only valuable insofar as it leads to proper action. It is also beneficial to those who possess it. Dispositions to appreciate, respect, wonder, and love nature enable people to find reward, satisfaction, and comfort from their relationship with nature.[24]

Essentially, Sandler suggested that when we flourish, so does the natural environment, and vice versa. Rather than being detrimental to environmental ethics, the agent-centeredness of virtue ethics can help us be more environmentally conscientious in a natural way.

Virtue Ethics and Feminist and Liberatory Movements

Liberatory social and philosophic movements such as feminism are also turning toward virtue ethics and, in doing so, are changing discourse concerning social justice. A focus of modern liberatory movements has been on how to resist systemic oppression. As Tessman noted,[25] some feminists opposed virtue ethics because it is agent centered and it might encourage the belief that the disadvantaged positions of the oppressed are a result of their character flaws. The possibility of a "blame and/or pity the victim" mentality by conservatives and liberals alike therefore serves as an incentive for liberatory movements to be wary of ethical theories and analyses that focus on the self.

However, Tessman argued a virtue ethical discourse is liberating because virtue ethics focuses on the character of the individual rather than on the structural sources of oppression. Tessman believed "that feminist and other liberatory theory and practice can be enriched" by the focus that virtue ethics places on the self because it can "reveal some of the less-obvious harms of oppression."[26] In particular, Tessman was concerned with the moral damage individuals must deal with because of the conditions of oppression they have experienced. Moral damage wrought by oppression can prevent individuals from flourishing in insidious ways. A person subjected to systemic oppression may have difficultly casting off feelings and self-images of inferiority, affecting not only one's well-being but also one's ability to resist further oppression, and may even "act oppressively towards others."[27]

As well, the lack of a critical examination of "traditional" virtues associated with both the oppressors and the oppressed can serve to reinforce structural barriers to flourishing. A virtue ethical analysis has the potential to reveal character traits and dispositions that are liberatory and encourage flourishing and those that are oppressive and inhibit well-being.

However, Tessman did not believe that all liberatory virtues cause their bearers to flourish. She termed some virtues as "burdened" as they can be a mixed blessing as a character trait that is efficacious for resisting oppression. They can also have a corrosive effect on the bearer's well-being. For example, anger can be an effective and appropriate emotion in response to oppression. It can mobilize subordinated people to resist those who dominate. Yet it is difficult to conceive a righteously angry person as happy, particularly if she or he is required to persist in her or his resistance, which is often the case:

> The political resister may certainly be deserving of moral praise, precisely because she/he displays the traits needed for pursuing an end to oppression, which is, one assumes, what someday could enable—for all—a version of flourishing endorsed by the resister: human lives that are free from domination, exploitation, abuse, war, great deprivation. But these goals are likely to remain unattained, and the resister will be in a position of perpetual struggle, with a constant demand for the virtues of resistance. The struggle itself requires character traits that may strain if not wreck psychological health, and presumably such health is part of the good life imagined to follow an end to oppression.[28]

Tessman's position that some liberatory virtues diminish the well-being of their bearers runs counter to the traditional assumption that virtue ethics is essentially eudaemonistic; that is, the possession of certain character traits and dispositions increases the happiness and well-being of the virtuous individual. Nonetheless, Tessman pointed out that many liberatory virtues fit the traditional model in that they are beneficial to their possessors. For example, the cultivation of a disposition to avoid overconsumption is good for the flourishing of the individual and also resistive to the wasteful lifestyles promoted by capitalism. Similarly, she mentioned that "integrity, sociality, sustained focus, creativity, visionary imagination and perseverance may all be suggestive of dispositions that make resistance possible and are also directly tied to flourishing."[29] Although situations exist in which virtues are burdened (i.e., they diminish rather than enhance the bearer's well-being), a virtue ethical approach to environmental and social justice issues also can reveal and encourage character traits and dispositions that not only are helpful to nature and society but also make the lives of virtuous individuals happier.

Virtue and Leisure Services

A virtue ethics approach to environmental and social justice thus enlarges the scope and enhances the richness of ethical inquiry, which, to the present time, has been primarily driven by a bias in modern ethics toward obligation-based discourse. This movement toward virtue ethical analysis of environmental and social justice issues is of particular importance to the field of leisure and recreation. As previously noted, the eudaemonistic, agent-centered nature of virtue ethics is intimately linked to the traditional Western conception of leisure. However, modern leisure service provision has also been influenced by obligation-based principles of modern ethics. For example, public recreation services have mandates to maximize the general welfare of the community and are legally obligated to provide access to those who face various barriers to participation.

Deontological and utilitarian ethical principles undeniably have had a positive influence on leisure services. But there also have been less desirable trends in leisure service provision driven by obligation-based values, such as the uncritical adoption of commercial marketing philosophies by public sector recreation agencies in response to problems of reduced fiscal resources. Often valued for their potential to generate revenue from user fees, these measures are compatible with deontological- and utilitarian-based arguments that public recreation service providers have an obligation to be consumer oriented (deontology) and that servicing individual consumer needs and wants increases overall satisfaction (utilitarianism). Virtue ethics, however, focuses on the individual, but is not neutral as to the worthiness of various recreation and leisure opportunities. A virtue ethical approach to leisure service provision requires providers to be guided by a positive conception of what a good life should be. However, as philosopher Larmore noted, one of the hallmarks of modern thinking is that it tends to avoid discussion of the nature of a good life:

> A characteristic theme of modern thought is that rational agreement about the nature of the good life is improbable. The more we talk about the meaning of life, the more likely it is we will disagree. This experience is one of the principle reasons Aristotelian ethics has lost so much of its prestige in the first centuries of the modern era. Aristotle assumed that the meaning of life or the nature of self-realization could be the object of rational consensus, and so had explained in these terms the worth of the virtues. But Aristotle's trust in the eventual unanimity of reasonable people has shown itself to be far too sanguine. That is why early modern moral philosophy, beginning with Grotius (the true father of modern ethics) sought to circumscribe a core morality, valid for all, as independent as possible of controversial views of the human good.[30]

The adoption of commercial marketing techniques in public recreation services not only has been a strategy for coping with reduced tax revenues, but also appears to have relieved service providers of the need to evaluate the worthiness of the recreation and leisure opportunities they offer to their "customers." Instead of guiding their service provision choices by some notion of what a good life consists of, the individual consumer determines whether particular recreation and leisure activities are worthy by his or her own needs and desires. Crompton observed marketing-oriented leisure services providers answer to the question, "Why do we do what we do today?" They answered, "Because our clients want these services and regard them as high priorities."[31] According to marketing philosophy, the worthiness of recreation and leisure activities is determined by the aggregate demand of various individual user preferences, and the duty of leisure providers is to satisfy those demands.

A return to a virtue ethics-based philosophy of recreation and leisure services provision would require practitioners to base their decisions, in part, on their understanding of the types of recreation and leisure activities that are not merely pleasant or popular, but instead improve the well-being of participants and help them to live better lives. A turn to virtue ethics therefore requires the leisure services profession to determine what is really good about recreation and leisure. Guiding service provision based on some notion of what a good life might be seems objectionable as it appears to recommend that leisure providers foist their recreation and leisure preferences on those whom they serve. However, the idea that goodness of leisure extends beyond individual preferences is well established. For example, the leisure literature identifies social, community, environmental, and economic benefits of parks and recreation, as well as individual benefits that include the achievement of physical and emotional health, personal growth, and a full and meaningful life. Inferring these benefits point to one ideal lifestyle is incorrect, they clearly justify a range of recreation and leisure activities in terms of their goodness for individuals, society, and the environment that goes beyond the mere satisfaction of personal leisure preferences.

Discussions of the worthiness of various types of recreation and leisure are both de-sirable and ongoing in the leisure literature and in practice. Virtue ethical analysis can enhance and deepen these discourses about the goodness of leisure by directing our attention to the types of recreation- and leisure-related character traits and dispositions that can help individuals, societies, and the natural environment flourish. This discourse will need to be pluralistic, as it is implausible to argue that there is a singular conception of what it is to lead a good life. As well, being the bearer of virtuous leisure dispositions and traits can have positive effects on others and the environment; therefore, virtue ethical discourse needs to range beyond narrow individual well-being and examine how leisure virtues can affect things such as environmental and social justice.

Successful expansion of a virtue ethical approach to leisure research and practice will require leisure researchers and practitioners to place greater emphasis on the character traits and dispositions that contribute to the flourishing of individuals, communities, cultures, societies, and the natural environment. This reorientation toward virtue ethical analysis cannot simply be a return to an Aristotelian model of leisure with a monistic conception of an ideal life (which in the case of Aristotle, was the elitist life of the philosopher). Instead, leisure researchers and practitioners will need to develop and articulate pluralistic conceptions of virtuous leisure that take into account demands for inclusivity and choice as well as give greater emphasis to considerations of the worthiness of various forms of leisure. Although such a shift to a virtue ethical analysis in leisure and recreation studies and practice may present significant intellectual and practical challenges, the prospect of promoting and realizing worthwhile growth and development—flourishing—is ultimately what leisure and recreation should be about.

Discussion Questions

1. Contrast obligation ethics with virtue ethics. How do they each play out in the day-to-day living of our lives?

2. Don makes a case for rethinking the usefulness of virtue ethics in matters of social and environmental justice. Are you persuaded by this thinking? Please elaborate.

3. Don uses environmentalism and feminist/liberatory movements to illustrate the applicability of virtue ethics to contemporary life. Does this work for you? Please explain your thinking.

4. How do virtue ethics manifest themselves in a leisure context?

5. If leisure is about choices freely made, then it seems reasonable to talk about virtuous choices and other kinds of choices. Stated differently, it seems reasonable to talk about good and bad leisure choices. Yet Don suggests the park, recreation, and tourism profession has been reluctant to engage in this kind of conversation. Why do you suppose that is so?

16

Recreating Culture

Slow Food, Scholé, *and*
Critical Pedagogy

Rudy Dunlap
Middle Tennessee State University

Throughout human history, meals have been a foundational aspect of culture as well as a quintessential leisure activity.[1] They have also played a primary role in the literal and metaphorical recreation of individuals and communities. This means food and eating are important contexts for exploring the inequity of social relations because the food on one's plate is intimately tied to identity and social status. Today, humans are physically, economically, and intellectually distanced from their food and its origins.[2, 3, 4, 5] Unlike our predecessors, few members of contemporary American society know with any degree of intimacy where their food comes from or under what conditions it is produced. This alienation has broad implications not only for health and well-being, but also in a more immediate sense for the nature of our meal experiences. Several movements and organizations now exist to address the shortcomings of the modern food system, but none have been as explicit in their attention to the dinner table itself as has Slow Food. Numerous commentators have examined Slow Food's innovative approach to the politics of the dinner table, but few have considered Slow Food as a movement that may contribute to our experience and understanding of leisure in contemporary life.[6] In this chapter, I explicitly examine Slow Food as an organization that is preoccupied with leisure and that pursues a form of critical leisure pedagogy. In the course of doing so, I also touch on recent articulations of *scholé* and their application to a critical pedagogy of leisure.

Slow Food

Having originated in the town of Bra in the Piedmont region of northwestern Italy, Slow Food arose from the convergence of several other organizations and movements, including the communist student movement in Italy, the *Associazone Ricreativa Culturale Italiana* (ARCI; Association for the Recreation of Italian Culture), and a critical mass of journalists in the 1980s who viewed themselves as gastronomic reformers.[7] ARCI's origins are telling because, as the name suggested, it was concerned with recreation and rejuvenation of Italian culture, including its gastronomic heritage. Slow Food has continued this tradition by encouraging individuals and communities to engage with and recreate systems that deliver food to their collective dinner tables, albeit on an international scale. These movements, coupled with a series of sensational food contamination scandals among Italian producers, led to the formation of Slow Food's predecessor, ARCIgola, and finally Slow Food itself.

The organization formalized itself with the ratification of the Slow Food Manifesto by its charter delegates at the 1989 *Opéra Comique* in Paris:

> Our century, which began and has developed under the insignia of industrial civilization, first invented the machine and then took it as its life model. We are enslaved by speed and have all succumbed to the same insidious virus: Fast Life, which disrupts our habits, pervades the privacy of our homes and forces us to eat Fast Foods. To be worthy of the name, *Homo Sapiens* should rid himself [*sic*] of speed before it reduces him [*sic*] to a species in danger of extinction. A firm defense of quiet material pleasure is the only way to oppose the universal folly of the Fast Life. May suitable doses of guaranteed sensual pleasure and slow, long-lasting enjoyment preserve us from the contagion of the multitude who mistake frenzy for efficiency. Our defense should begin at the table with *Slow Food*.[8]

As indicated, this Manifesto invited the pursuit of a far-reaching agenda, an agenda that has been principally concerned with issues related to food. However, in the eyes of Petrini as well as many of its other founders, Slow Food is not exclusively a gastronomic movement, but one that espouses a slow philosophy.[9]

Slow Food is now active in more than 100 countries around the world, including the United States, which boasts 250 *convivia* (chapters) and approximately 25,000 members since its establishment in 2000. Slow Food USA seeks nothing less than to fundamentally reshape the practices of contemporary life, beginning with our relations to food. As stated in its mission, Slow Food USA "seek[s] to inspire a transformation in food policy, production practices and market forces so that they ensure equity, sustainability and pleasure in the food we eat."[10] This mission has far-reaching consequences not only for the cultivation and sale of food, but also for the nature of family life, public education, civic engagement, the stewardship of ecosystems, and the viability of local economies.

Slow Food has often been associated with the emergence of foodie-ism or the fetishization of obscure food items and practices. This characterization has allowed critics to dismiss Slow Food as a social club for epicures who have the time and money to obsess over the relative merits of leaf lard rendered from free-range hogs. Its supporters have responded by asking, "What aspect of human society has greater relevance to daily life and the welfare of all individuals than the food we collectively put in our mouths?"[11] Eating is literally a means by which we restore and recreate ourselves and our communities. Because it is principally concerned with food, Slow Food has been hailed as an important vehicle for addressing not only the global agrifood system, but also our environmental crisis more broadly. These observations seem important and obvious, but my purpose here is to contend that Slow Food is also implicitly concerned with the revival of a critical form of leisure pedagogy in contemporary society.

Meals as Leisure

Surprisingly, few leisure scholars have explored issues related to eating. A small amount of literature has addressed the dynamics of food production in the form of community gardening.[12, 13, 14, 15] To date, Mair, Sumner, and Rotteau[16] have undertaken the only concerted examination of consumption-oriented food movements, including Slow Food, from the vantage point of leisure. Mair et al. astutely observed eating is at once a biological necessity and an important site of political struggle. Individuals' choices related to their food purchases and meal experiences are shaped by and have influence on far-reaching economic and political processes. Slow Food exemplifies this dialectic due to its explicit efforts to bolster the agency and autonomy of local food communities in the face of a globalized agrifood industry. In this way, the practice of eating is understood as a venue for critically reflexive leisure practice.[17] I agree with this assessment and would contend that Slow Food encourages devotees to think critically about not only the dinner table but also the function and meaning of leisure in contemporary life.

A Resurgence of *Scholé*

After decades of thought and research, it seems implausible that the leisure studies field should still be exploring the nature of *scholé,* its foundational concept. Even so, as a tool for understanding culture and society, our understanding of leisure must change as human life changes. Two recent volumes, Blackshaw's *Leisure*[18] and Rojek's *The Labour of Leisure,*[19] addressed the state of leisure in contemporary societies in the post-9/11 era, and both do so by reaching back to this classical concept. *Scholé's* resurgence comes in the wake of modernist leisure theory that held sway throughout most of the 20th century.[20] Also known as the derivative theory of leisure, modernist leisure was functional in that it clearly demarcated work and leisure and espoused their inextricable connection. Where work was typically understood as drudgery, leisure was enjoyment. Work encouraged conformity and self-sacrifice; leisure encouraged self-expression, creativity, and indulgence. Work was portrayed as being compulsory, whereas leisure was a domain of freedom and choice. Most important, work was the means by which individuals contributed to society, and leisure was the reward for having done so.[21, 22, 23]

This modernist theory of leisure is a shallow resemblance of its classical predecessor. As presented by Aristotle in both *The Politics* and *Nicomachean Ethics, scholé* describes an existential state of being free from the necessity to labor.[24, 25, 26] Contemporary usage of the term *leisure* tends to focus on an immediate sense of being free from labor, as in having finished with the workday, one is free to go to the movies. However, the classical concept described a person's station in society (i.e., having sufficient wealth so that one could avoid labor altogether).[27] In contrast to its contemporary usage, leisure was not synonymous with idleness. Aristotle assessed work and leisure's relation to one another: "Nature requires that we should be able, not only to work well, but to use leisure well; for as I must repeat once again, the first principle of all action is leisure. Both are required, but leisure is better than occupation and is its end."[28] Richardson-Lear explained, "Leisure in Aristotle's sense is not a time of relaxation; it is the condition of being free from the demands posed by our natural desire for the necessities of life. A leisurely life is one that is not driven by the need to satisfy necessary desires."[29] Thus, *scholé* was a state of repose in which one could survey the status quo and, having done so, conceive of future possibilities. As shall be discussed, this conceptualization is particularly relevant to Slow Food's mission and methodology.

Scholé, then, did not describe a particular activity, but rather a precondition for the exercise of choice and the pursuit of numerous activities. This aspect of choice and decision making is therefore a context for the exercise of virtue. As with all domains of public life, Aristotle contended that one of the principal functions of the state was to educate its citizens in the virtuous uses of leisure.[30] Consistent with his ethical philosophy, Aristotle endorsed a moderate course in the use of leisure, one which charted a middle path between a life of pure contemplation and a life of pure amusement.[31] In his references to these topics in *Politics,* Aristotle recommended that in keeping with humanity's character and to promote human flourishing (eudaemonia), leisure ought to be used for pursuits of an intellectual and social nature. Thus, politics and engagement in the affairs of the state generally were considered virtuous uses of *scholé.*[32, 33, 34] When interpreted this way, *scholé* can be understood as a forum in which citizens convene to engage in a literal form of social and political recreation.

Despite its archaic origins, *scholé* clearly offers modern scholars a means for considering issues of equity and justice as they relate to leisure. It ought not be surprising then that in attempting to chart a path forward, several contemporary scholars have looked backwards to the concept of *scholé*.

Drawing on Bauman's work,[35] Blackshaw described contemporary societies as characterized by a type of liquid leisure that corresponds to the fundamental contingency of everyday life.[36] Old social categories and institutions have been overturned, including the treatment of leisure as simply being the derivative of labor. As opposed to creating an overwhelming sense of anxiety or dread, Blackshaw portrayed this state of contingency as holding the promise of liberation from the constraints of older social categories:

> The emergence of liquid modernity has also been a shift from a structured and structuring society in which our identities were largely predetermined by our social class, gender and "race" to one in which individualization dominates more than anything else, and where our identities always remain a work in progress. Class, gender and ethnicity may still exert some degree of influence on our leisure opportunities, but they certainly do not dictate them. Today we inhabit what is an unstructured sociality (rather than a structured society) in which life is lived noch nicht surrounded by possibilities that have not yet been realized.[37]

This sounds delightful, but seems only to describe the possibility of leisure for those relatively few individuals who benefit from the inequitable arrangements of the global economic order. It is hard to believe this notion of leisure would describe the experiences of the hundreds of millions of people at the bottom of the economic order who subsist on less than $2 a day. Perhaps unwittingly, Blackshaw's use of scholé echoed the inequitable social structure of ancient Athens. Explicitly though, he attempted to align his concept with scholé by contending that leisure ought to serve as a social space in which individuals can engage in a robust process of recreating themselves.

The overly glib nature of Blackshaw's portrayal can be remedied by turning to Rojek's *Labour of Leisure*.[38] He too embraced the fundamental contingency of contemporary life, but diverted from Blackshaw by abandoning the strong notion of freedom in leisure. For Rojek, leisure was a set of situated practices in which individuals could exercise a highly constrained form of agency, the constraining factor being economic scarcity. He explained:

> [Leisure] is a question of how form and practice [are] represented in relation to power. Individuals, groups and the leisure choices they make are located in a context of power. The defining feature of this context is the unequal divisions between individuals and groups in relation to scarcity. This is somewhat disguised in everyday life, because leisure cultures typically focus on surplus, that is, leisure forms and practice are organized around surplus time, surplus wealth and conspicuous consumption. However, surplus is a relative concept. No matter how abundant their access to surplus time and wealth, every individual and group is located in a context of scarcity.[39]

Throughout, Rojek carefully emphasized that the exercise of agency and choice in leisure is always dependent on one's relation to economic scarcity. Rojek invoked the concept of *scholé* to argue that leisure is literally the "school for life" that individuals must use to gain a critical distance on their participation in the global economic system.

Despite their differences, both scholars agreed that if leisure is to remain a vital force in society, it must be through its ability to cultivate a critical faculty within individuals and groups.

True to the critical tradition, a critical leisure must allow individuals to recognize the machinations of oppressive power and to imagine alternative social arrangements. Captured in his concept of the critical hermeneutics of leisure, Blackshaw singled out the powerful metaphor of the individual as consumer as being in need of transformation. He explained, "What we need to do in our lives is get away from the reusable language found in the consumer world to generate new cultural discourses that are able to speak for the first time."[40] The possibility of generating new cultural discourses from "whole cloth" sounds a bit fantastic, but the notion that we ought to distance our leisure from the interests of global capital is relevant to the Slow Food mission. To borrow Ritzer's terminology,[41] leisure ought to function as a space in which individuals transition from being consumers of *nothing* to producers of *something*.

Slow Food: A Movement Preoccupied With Leisure

I contend that Slow Food, which is often treated as a gastronomic and/or agricultural movement, is principally a leisure education movement. In keeping with the concept of *scholé*, Slow Food's approach to gastronomy is one of critical reflection in which we as eaters are encouraged to recognize our potential to recreate the global agriculture infrastructure. Gastronomy, agriculture, and globalization are the topics of conversation, so to speak, but Slow Food's methodological locus is the dinner table and the experience of eating. Rightly so, because if we understand the degradation of our agriculture and gastronomy as resulting from the logic of unchecked capitalism, the remedy is not to be found in the marketplace, but rather in a set of spaces and practices that abandon the reductionist logic of the market altogether.

The Slow Food Manifesto emphasized the celebration of "material pleasures" as the antidote to the Fast Life. Its founders understood that the dinner table must be the scene of action and that it must be constructed in such a way so as to resist commodification. In doing so, it has deliberately promoted the ideal meal experience as being (a) convivial, (b) mindful, and (c) ethical.

Despite being mentioned often in its early literature,[42] the concept of conviviality has fallen by the wayside in Slow Food's efforts. Reflecting its intellectual roots, conviviality does not appear to be part of the global vernacular and was likely disregarded as being too esoteric. Nonetheless, conviviality captures the essence of the Slow Food methodology. It is defined as "1) of or belonging to a feast or banquet; characterized by feasting or jovial companionship; such as befits a feast, festive; 2) fond of feasting and good company, disposed to enjoy festive society; festive, jovial."[43] These are precisely the qualities of a meal experience that are resistant though not immune to easy commodification. The convivial meal is one in which participants are as engaged with one another as they are with the food. As with all feasts, time is taken for the preparation, but especially for the consumption of the meal. Additionally, the ritualized nature of such meals, such as the use of time-honored family recipes, has functioned to cement the bonds between family and friends. Obviously, such festive meals are created using the products of global agribusiness, and commercial interests construct many of our images of the feast. However, to a greater degree than most other meal experiences, the indulgent nature of a home-cooked feast runs counter to the logic of Fast Food's emphasis on efficiency, standardization, control, and profit.[44, 45]

As an antidote to Fast Life, the *slow* in Slow Food makes its case intuitively. However, considered in the light of the dinner table, the slow concept is better understood as *mindfulness*. If individuals intend to celebrate the sensual pleasures of eating, attention must be given to the act itself. They must be attentive to the smells, appearance, texture, and tastes of foods. Ideally, these sensual pleasures have been enhanced through the movement's various efforts to "educate for taste," in which participants are taught to detect the subtleties of fragrance, texture, and appearance. This emphasis on the finer points of pleasure is precisely that which leads to accusations of pedantry and elitism. However, similar to conviviality, this attention to the act of eating also runs counter to Fast Food logic.[46] In educating for taste, Slow Food has endeavored to connect the subtleties of sensation to the act of cultivation. The homegrown tomato, for example, is superior in taste, texture, and appearance because it is intentionally cultivated with such sensations in mind as opposed to industrial cultivation that favors characteristics such as durability, uniformity, and blandness. Thus, mindfulness would seem to be Slow Food's most effective tactic in the face of global agribusiness. In fact, it is actually the aspect of its meal experience that is most susceptible to incorporation. The subtleties of taste are notoriously fickle and susceptible to sustained marketing campaigns. For example, global agribusiness enterprises are quickly bringing to bear their research and development efforts to cultivate items such as the homegrown tomato on an industrial scale.[47] In light of such developments, Slow Food's dinner table experiences must be ethical in addition to pleasurable.

To this end, the food on one's table ought to have arrived there having caused as little environmental, social, and economic harm as possible. This third aspect of the meal experience almost mandates that the eating public engages with the producers of its food. "Know Thy Producer" is the argument which lies at the heart of the Locavore Movement and its exponents.[48, 49, 50] The shorter the connection between producer and consumer, the more accountable the producer will be to the consumer, and accurate or not, this simple notion is largely responsible for the resurgence of local agriculture in the United States (e.g., farmers markets, community gardens, direct marketing production). Individuals exercise their agency as consumers to protect their communities by patronizing local producers who respect the integrity of the local ecosystems and the health of the eating public. To acknowledge the importance of this choice, Petrini has cast the individual eater not merely as a consumer, but as a coproducer with the farmer.[51] Accordingly, the dinner table ought to be understood as a site of coproduction through which participants eat their way to a better world. The entire argument is neatly summed up in Berry's observation that "eating is an agricultural act."[52]

By exalting a meal experience that is convivial, mindful, and ethical, Slow Food has constructed an adversarial movement under the banner of pleasure. This emphasis on pleasure is particularly susceptible to accusations of elitism,[53] as well as to discussions related to the seemingly subjective nature of pleasure as it relates to eating. To paraphrase a former student, "Can Slow Food convincingly claim that the experience of eating a locally grown, ripe peach is inherently more pleasurable than that of eating a fruit roll-up?" This observation is especially relevant given the inequitable access to fresh produce in American society. Petrini and his activist allies have countered with the observation that only in a world that has so thoroughly succumbed to the market-based values of Fast Life and its ethical vacuity is it possible to embrace the sort of relativism that places these two experiences on par with one another. Indeed, Petrini has contended that such an argument is itself elitist to the extent that it redirects attention from influential corporate and political entities that have a stake in making sure that people consume highly processed foods that are detrimental to their health.[54]

Slow Food as Critical Pedagogy

In its efforts to reignite a literal and metaphorical dialogue around the dinner table, Slow Food is engaged in a form of pedagogy that aims to foster critical reflection and action, also known as critical pedagogy. In the tradition of Freire and his successors,[55] critical pedagogy seeks to help individuals identify and gain autonomy from hegemonic discourses and practices. In so doing, Freire's critical pedagogy engages the complementary processes of *conscientization* and *praxis*. Quite simply, conscientization describes the facilitation of a critical thinking process around a particular issue. For Freire, conscientization addressed the way in which systemic illiteracy functioned to benefit the aristocratic class in Brazilian society. Praxis, then, is action informed by the development of critical consciousness, which in Freire's case manifested as a political protest to demand equitable access to the Brazilian public education system.

Slow Food enacts the process of conscientization by exploring the ways in which the industrial food system has intentionally divorced cultivation and consumption from culture and community.[56, 57] Within *convivia*, Slow Food participants encounter food items and practices that are rooted in the culture and history of their region. Similarly, participants engage in praxis by consuming mindfully. In addition to reacquainting oneself with the pleasures of the table, these dual processes of conscientization and praxis aim to recreate the system from which the meal is derived, a realization that leads, perhaps most important for scholars, to a renewed sense of agency within individuals. By pausing to consider Slow Food's manifesto and mission, the individual may self-consciously realize that she or he has the power to not only make different food choices, but also rethink the nature of participation in the food system as a whole.

Slow Food thus exemplifies critical pedagogy in two ways that are closely related. First, it initiates a process of critical thought and action around food and eating. Individual eaters engage with one another to examine the origins of their food and possible alternatives to the status quo. Second, and perhaps more important for scholars of leisure, participation in Slow Food may initiate a larger process of conscientization related to leisure and its function in life more generally. When asked about Slow Food's relation to leisure, Petrini was emphatic that the organization's focus on food ought to be understood in light of a more holistic approach to life.[58] If a collective pause at the dinner table allows people to assess the state of the food system, then this critical orientation should be applied to the nature of society more generally, a suggestion that clearly resonates with the ideals of *scholé*.

Discussion Questions

1. We do not often think about food the way Rudy does. How has his chapter influenced your thinking about food and food systems?

2. What does Rudy mean by Slow Food? How does the Slow Food movement expand your thinking about the significance of food production as a mirror of larger social, cultural, and environmental concerns?

3. Discuss the Slow Food movement as a force for social and environmental justice. Is it elitist? Please explain.

4. How does Slow Food relate to leisure?

5. Having read Rudy's chapter, are you inclined to change what you eat, the way you eat, or how and where you buy what you eat?

17

Ecotourism as a Venue for Environmental and Social Justice

Case Study of a Fijian Vanua

Kelly Bricker
University of Utah

In thinking about the work I do in ecotourism, I am drawn to principles that support environmental justice.[1] Yet we seldom use the term *environmental justice* when we address social, economic, and environmental problems through sustainable tourism. It is high time we did. In this chapter, I first outline the connections between ecotourism and environmental justice. I then illustrate those connections via a case study of environmental justice in the context of an ecotourism project in Fiji. Finally, I conclude with ideas about how to promote environmental justice within the context of sustainable tourism. In so doing, I proceed from the assumption that everyone has a right to clean water and clean air and that no one has a right to degrade or destroy the environment upon which life depends. Dustin, Bricker, and Schwab have expressed in previous writings[2] that we need to create healthy communities where we can live, feed ourselves, raise our families, and send our kids out to play knowing that we are protecting the fundamental resources upon which all life depends.

Establishing Connections

What is the connection between ecotourism and environmental justice? Ecotourism in its truest form is a destination-based idea that adheres to certain principles. The International Ecotourism Society (TIES) defined ecotourism as "responsible travel to natural areas that conserves the environment and improves the well-being of local people."[3] The goals of ecotourism are further explained through a set of principles that has evolved over the years, including the following:[4]

- minimize impact;
- build environmental and cultural awareness and respect;
- provide positive experiences for both visitors and hosts;
- provide direct financial benefits for conservation;
- provide financial benefits and empowerment for local people; and
- raise sensitivity to host countries' political, environmental, and social climate.

Complementing the TIES definition of ecotourism, the Environmental Protection Agency's (EPA) widely adopted definition of environmental justice reads as follows: "Environmental Justice [EJ] is the fair treatment and meaningful involvement of all people regardless of race, color, national origin, or income with respect to the development, implementation, and enforcement of environmental laws, regulations, and policies."[5] The EPA went on to explain: "It [EJ] will be achieved when everyone enjoys the same degree of protection from environmental and health hazards and equal access to the decision-making process to have a healthy environment in which to live, learn, and work."[6]

In principle, this definition applies to governmental actions at all levels (local, state, and federal) as well as private industry. In amplifying the principles supporting EJ, Bullard[7] suggested there are actually three categories of environmental equity issues that frame the larger concept of EJ: procedural inequity, geographical inequity, and social inequity. Procedural inequity addresses questions of fair treatment: the extent that governing rules, regulations, and evaluation criteria are applied uniformly. Examples of procedural inequity are stacking boards and commissions with pro-business interests, holding hearings in remote locations to minimize public participation, and using English-only material to communicate to non-English speaking communities.[8] In the context of ecotourism, for example, EJ conceivably means empowering local people within communities to make decisions about their own destiny when it comes to tourism development as well as ownership and the desired level of tourism development.

Geographical inequity refers to spatial injustices.[9] For example, some neighborhoods, communities, and regions receive direct benefits, such as jobs and tax revenues, from various industries and production; the costs, such as the burdens of waste disposal, are sent elsewhere. Communities hosting waste-disposal facilities receive fewer economic benefits than communities generating the waste. With regard to ecotourism, touristic activities should directly benefit local conservation and the communities where activities take place. So how can ecotourism enhance the community benefits and quality of life, rather than degrade or destroy them? Paraphrasing Hawken, governments that support ecotourism would require these enterprises to

- replace national and international ecotourism products with products created locally and regionally, which would also include the supply chain;
- take responsibility for the effects ecotourism has on the natural world and mitigate the negative effects;
- not rely on exotic sources of capital to develop and grow;
- engage in production processes that are human, worthy, dignified, and intrinsically satisfying;
- create objects of durability and long-term utility whose ultimate use or disposition will not be harmful to future generations; and
- change consumers to customers of a sustainable world through education.[10]

The third category, social inequity, generally refers to the power structure within a society. According to Bullard, "Environmental decisions often mirror the power arrangements of larger society and reflect the still-existing racial bias in the United States and elsewhere."[11] With respect to ecotourism, decision-making structures in countries often do not allow local communities to take charge of tourism development, leaving outside investors, government, or powerful developers with the decision-making power. When ecotourism principles are adhered to, residents who live and work in the community hold decision-making authority and planning power, for the extent and type of tourism development.

A Fijian Case Study

Each element of sustainable tourism (social, economic, environmental) is closely linked to how Fijians conceptualize the social, cultural, and physical dimensions of their lives, or what they call their *vanua*.[12] This important cultural concept relates directly to social and environmental justice and ultimately influences how decisions are made within village communities.

In Fiji, there is concern that rural to urban migration is increasing. This ultimately affects the traditional authoritative structure and organization of labor in rural communities.[13] Although perceived changes from tourism, such as increased commercialization of culture, have been noted, these changes have not extended to lifestyle changes.[14] For example, there is generally a lack of opportunity to earn income in rural Fiji. As a result, the Fijian government has tried to increase the number and variety of jobs.[15] However, the options for jobs in rural Fiji are limited. Formal education levels are low, farming and fishing techniques are simple, and limited opportunities exist for women due to "inherent prejudices of the structure of society and rural social organization."[16]

Tourism in the Rural Highlands of Fiji and Partnerships

Traditionally, tourism has not been a part of the economic development of Fiji's rural highlands. People living in these areas have relied primarily on subsistence farming and/or selling timber to logging companies. Recently, however, a white-water rafting and kayaking company, Rivers Fiji,[17] developed two white-water rafting/kayaking programs in two river canyons serving the villages of Nakavika and Nabukelevu, along with several others along the Wainikoroiluva River and Upper Navua River corridors. Rivers Fiji has enjoyed considerable success and local approval by following the EJ principles outlined.

A key aspect of sustainable tourism development is securing the input of all stakeholders in planning and development phases. Rivers Fiji embraced this principle. The local residents' perceptions of and interest in a white-water rafting company were taken to heart. This process of stakeholder empowerment set the stage for future dialogue and meetings and resulted in hiring practices, educational outreach programs, and training programs included as part of the ongoing operations.

The land along the Upper Navua River is native land, and before anyone outside the landowning group could use it (commercially or otherwise), permission had to be obtained from the *mataqali* (village chiefs) or other kinship groups.[18] In addition, the landowning groups asked a logging company from overseas to release 200 meters on each side of the river so it could be included in a conservation lease. Rivers Fiji was an important partner and provided a means for continuous funding of the conservation area. In so doing, Rivers Fiji introduced a new type of ecotourism development into the rural highlands of Fiji—white-water rafting—with the permission of the Fijian government and the *mataqali*.

Rivers Fiji has now been in operation for 15 years. Since the company began, partnerships have been critical to securing a lease for conservation as well as securing the protection of the river corridor. Unique among typical government leases in Fiji (which are usually for development or extractive use), the lease for conservation on the Upper Navua River was critical to the success of the ecotourism operation. It provided the local communities and Rivers Fiji with the natural capital (i.e., a pristine protected natural corridor) to ensure positive visitor experiences in perpetuity.

The Upper Navua Conservation Area's (UNCA) remoteness and protection from logging and other extractive industries resulted in a form of economic development that allowed it to retain its unique biodiversity. Additionally, the UNCA attracted biologists, botanists, and local nongovernmental organizations (NGOs) dedicated to conservation, resulting in the discovery of two new endemic species of freshwater fish, sightings of the globally endangered pink-billed parrot finch, and sightings of banded iguanas, which are extremely rare in Fiji's forests. The corridor has also been noted as botanically rich, with healthy populations of sago palm, a tree that has been significantly reduced or eliminated entirely in Fiji's freshwater river drainages. These discoveries elevated the river corridor to a unique status among freshwater rivers nationally. Partnerships among the local communities, government, and Rivers Fiji to establish the UNCA also led to the designation of Fiji's first and only Ramsar Site, or International Wetland of Importance. Established April 11, 2006, the UNCA is now one of more than 1,280 wetlands around the world designated as critical to the health and well-being of wetland habitat and human populations.

Community Impact and Collaboration

Rivers Fiji has had a range of social and environmental impacts on the communities along the two river corridors. Research into both the community quality of life and the transitions made by some community members (e.g., from farmer to professional guide) has indicated an overall positive impact.[19, 20] Paraphrasing one community member, tourism development has brought with it the potential to achieve greater things, such as establishing new businesses and giving Fijian children a better education.[21] Rivers Fiji has encouraged decision-making processes that include the *mataqali* in discussions about the river-running schedule, the hiring of guides and other employment practices, the establishment of the UNCA as a Ramsar Site, and the introduction of various management strategies to enhance conservation efforts (e.g., education programs for youth and families). Feedback from the Fijian guides, in particular, suggests they benefit greatly from employment as river guides, enjoy opportunities for promotion and personal growth, and value positive feedback received from guests.[22]

Access

From the beginning, local villagers insisted that infrastructure and access were critical if ecotourism was to prosper in the rural highlands. Bricker wrote, "When the physical situation of the villages is understood, such concerns clearly have validity."[23] Bricker also found that "villagers in Nabukelevu and Nakavika felt that if tourism was to succeed, government assistance was essential, especially with roads, water, and schools and clinics."[24]

As part of the community of partners within the UNCA, Rivers Fiji continues to work to maintain access to the river corridor. Tourism dollars have contributed to the development of access and maintenance of access via infrastructure. These access roads not only help transport tourists to the river, but also are used by communities throughout the rural highlands. These are expensive undertakings, and if Rivers Fiji was to ever close its doors, it would likely impact the residents of the area negatively by reducing access to towns for farming and other business.

Community Benefits

Another issue that matters greatly to local residents is furthering educational opportunities for their children and increased health care in the highlands. Rivers Fiji has worked diligently with partners to increase these services. Specifically, Rivers Fiji took advantage of tourism groups visiting the rural highlands who expressed interest in helping communities obtain greater access to health care. Through a partnership with West Virginia University's Medical School, the Namosi Province Healthcare providers, and logistical support from Rivers Fiji, a health care team now visits the rural highlands annually. The health care team and Rivers Fiji also have collaborated with engineers to assist local communities in developing a potable water system, yet another need identified early in the development of ecotourism in the area.

As part of the effort to protect and conserve the UNCA and secure long-term conservation success against illegal logging activities within the river corridor, Rivers Fiji has worked with several partners to implement the UNCA Environmental Education Outreach Program. This program was developed with the cooperation of NatureFiji-MareqetiViti, entities within the Fijian government, and the nine UNCA *mataqali*, as well as two additional villages that mark the boundaries of the river corridor. Together they decided a place-based, experiential approach, featuring white-water rafting trips, would be the most effective method of delivering the program and of highlighting the unique attributes and importance of the river ecosystem. The program has been highly successful as echoed by the children of the highlands:[25]

> I was brought up on this river to fetch for food with my dad when I was a young girl. We used to walk through small creeks and follow tracks then, but coming on this trip makes me realize that there is more to what it has to offer. Its beauty and what I have seen living within the Upper Navua Conservation area today is a gift from God. I personally need to be grateful and appreciative of what lies within our land.
>
> This is my first time on the trip and I have learned so much about the wild life, the endangered birds, fish and trees, and especially the Sago Palm.

The chaperones, mostly parents of children engaged in the program, also felt the programs had an impact on their lives:

> I will help conserve and protect the Upper Navua because it is so beautiful. Even though I knew the river existed, I took it for granted. I did not realize how important it was to me.
>
> I am grateful this opportunity was given to our children to have a firsthand experience about this adventure trip and also learn the importance of wildlife and how we, the landowners, should make the right decision in conserving this place in the future.

Considering the future of the UNCA and the downstream watershed, we need to remember that the activities that take place upstream affect the health of ecosystems downstream. The once healthy and thriving Beqa Lagoon, where the Navua River meets the Pacific Ocean, has been negatively impacted. Activities such as illegal logging increase the amount of sediment and pollution in the runoff and have far-reaching effects on the entire watershed; hence, the importance of ecologically healthy river systems extends well beyond the communities of the highlands to the coastal regions.

Conclusion

Research has demonstrated that tourism that develops slowly and leaves control with local people is less likely to have negative impacts.[26] This case study of a Fijian *vanua* supports that conclusion. It indicates that working with local communities to plan for conservation of natural resources, starting slowly, paying attention to education and training, maximizing local benefits, and receiving continual evaluation and feedback from local host communities are crucial for ecotourism to be introduced successfully into a rural area with no previous tourism experience.[27, 28]

This case study has also shown it is possible for ecotourism to serve as a means for advancing social and environmental justice. To achieve that noble end, however, the ecotourism and environmental justice principles discussed at the beginning of this chapter must be followed. When carried out properly, sustainable tourism development should ensure the following:

1. Resident control of tourism development. In Fiji generally, native landowners control their resources, and it is crucial to keep it that way. Under the leadership of their *mataqali*, residents in the rural highlands set protocol for employment, influence program development, influence types of product development, establish rules and protocol to be followed when tourists visit, and assist in making sure tourism does not disrupt the routine of village life in negative ways.[29]

2. Cooperation and collaboration. In addition to Rivers Fiji, there should be useful and productive collaboration with health care providers, scientists, government, and local conservation organizations to assist with increased exposure to conservation education, health care, and unique lease arrangements.

3. Ecotourism development in rural areas requires a supportive infrastructure, for example, ease of access, quality water supplies, adequate health care facilities, and educational opportunities for villages. Residents recognized these needs early on, and through cooperative agreements with Rivers Fiji and the support of tourism dollars, some of these needs have been and will continue to be addressed.

Finally, several key issues center on the role of Rivers Fiji and, by extension, the general role of commercial ecotourism operators in conservation and environmental justice with respect to communities. In creating a new ecotourism enterprise, Rivers Fiji knew it was critical to develop a long-term plan to protect the river resources and thus preserve the experience for those who raft or kayak the remote river canyons. There were many threats to the pristine river corridor, including illegal logging, gravel and other mining operations, and new types of tourism experiences populating other river corridors, such as jet boating. To plan for ecotourism in these areas, it was critical to engage local landowners and to understand their wishes and apprehensions with regard to the introduction of tourism. It was equally important to address issues the local landowners felt were critical to the long-term success of the ecotourism project, such as access, health care, and education. To this end, Rivers Fiji embraced a network of partners to address these issues, as well as reinvested tourism dollars to continue to provide direct economic benefits to the communities touched by the river experience.

For Rivers Fiji and for the residents of Fiji's rural highlands, future commercial success depends on protecting the environment and the natural capital. Cultivating and maintaining good relationships with community members, who are partners in the project and who are part of the tourist "product," are also crucial to overall success. Bricker noted in 2001:

> Whereas guides sometimes had to adjust their lifestyle to meet family and community obligations, Rivers Fiji had to be prepared to monitor relationships with residents, learn about operating in an unfamiliar cultural environment, and allow villagers a role in organizing the way work commitments were honored.[30]

In the end, adhering to the principles of eco- and sustainable tourism, touristic enterprises can be a force for social and environmental justice by cultivating partnerships that provide resilience, economic diversity, and biodiversity conservation.

Discussion Questions

1. Kelly connects the definitions of eco- and sustainable tourism to the Environmental Protection Agency's definition of environmental justice. Do you see that connection in the same way Kelly does? Explain why or why not.

2. Based on your understanding of Kelly's chapter, what are the essential ingredients for tourism development to satisfy social and environmental justice concerns?

3. Do you believe ecotourism is a good way for developing countries to prosper economically and simultaneously protect their natural capital? Please explain your thinking.

4. What do you see as potential downsides to ecotourism development? How would you recommend that tourism professionals go about minimizing them?

5. Tourism has been touted by some as a way to promote cross-cultural understanding and peace among widely disparate countries and peoples. Do you think tourism can measure up to this kind of role in the world? What would the industry have to do for this to occur?

18

Healthy Parks and Communities
Green Access and Equity for Los Angeles

Robert García
Seth Strongin
The City Project, Los Angeles, California

The environmental justice movement is evolving to address issues beyond stopping the use of toxins and other harmful activities in low-income or minority communities. The expanded scope of environmental justice, for example, includes an urban park movement that advocates for the creation of public goods, such as parks and school fields that are accessible to community members during nonschool hours.

Los Angeles County, California, is renowned for its diverse geography. From iconic beaches to towering mountains to deserts, the region boasts a variety of opportunities for recreation and enjoying the natural environment. At the same time, it is one of the most racially and ethnically diverse counties in the United States. It would be easy to assume that under these conditions all people, regardless of race, color, national origin, or socioeconomic status, have equal access to the region's green space. Unfortunately, this is not the reality.

The presence of green space alone is not enough. Despite a wealth of green space in the region as a whole, many neighborhoods and communities in Los Angeles are actually park poor. There are unfair park, school, and health disparities based on race, ethnicity, income, poverty, youth, and access to cars. Children of color disproportionately live in communities of concentrated poverty without enough places to play in parks and schools and without access to cars or an adequate transit system to reach parks and school fields in other neighborhoods. The health implications of the lack of physical activity are profound, including obesity, diabetes, and heart disease. If present trends continue, this will be the first generation in the history of this country in which children will have a lower life expectancy than their parents.[1]

Why do parks matter? Parks and other green space provide important benefits to people and the environment. The values at stake include the simple joys of playing in a park or school field; physical, psychological, and social health; improved academic performance; positive alternatives to gangs, crime, drugs, and violence; and economic vitality for all. Parks also offer conservation benefits: land conservation; habitat protection for animals and plants; and a reduction in air, water, and ground pollution. Additionally, parks play an important role in mitigating climate change and promoting climate justice. Parks promote spiritual values such as the protection of the Earth and its people and the preservation of Native American values and sacred sites. Parks provide places to celebrate cultural, historic, and public art resources. Fundamental values of equal justice and democracy underlie each of these other values.

To enjoy these benefits, however, it is essential that people enjoy equal access to parks and green space. Many factors affect green access and equity, including the distance between green space and where people live, natural geographic features, transportation or the lack of it, real and perceived levels of park safety, and sustainable community planning.

Maximizing access to public lands and ensuring the fair treatment of people of all colors, cultures, and incomes will transform Los Angeles into a more livable, democratic, and just place for all. This can serve as a replicable advocacy model for community development in regions throughout the nation.

Why Parks Matter: The Values at Stake

Parks are vital components of a community. They provide opportunities for physical activity; offer a place for children and adults to play and for families and people to gather; serve as venues where culture, history, and art can be celebrated; and function as economic catalysts. Additionally, parks offer important environmental services such as filtering air and water pollution, conserving land, protecting habitat for plants and animals, and helping to mitigate climate change. There is empirical evidence to support the value of parks. Courts recognize that persuasive evidence includes statistical as well as anecdotal evidence. Anecdotal evidence includes stories of individual experiences and the reality of people's lives.

Physical and Psychological Health

Being physically active in parks, and even simply visiting a park, can provide health benefits to all people, from young children to senior citizens. These health benefits include not only physical health but also the joy of having fun, stress reduction, quality of life improvements, and alternatives to risky behavior such as crime, drugs, violence, and gangs.

1. Simple joys. Fun is not frivolous. Children have the right to the simple joys of playing in safe parks and school fields. The United Nations has recognized the child's right to play as a fundamental human right.[2] The United States was founded, in part, for the pursuit of happiness.

2. Physical activity, obesity, and health. Parks and physical activity are an integral part of a comprehensive approach to health care and the built environment. As the costs of medical care continue to increase, improving the built environment, including parks, green space, and walkable green streets, is an effective form of preventive care. Indeed, many experts consider providing safe parks and other recreation spaces as a primary form of preventive medicine.[3]

This is the first generation in the history of the United States for which children are predicted to have a lower life expectancy than their parents. This is largely attributed to increasingly sedentary lifestyles and rising rates of overweight and obesity.[4] Regular physical activity, along with a healthy diet, plays a vital role in preventing obesity and the many chronic health conditions associated with it, such as type 2 diabetes, heart disease, hypertension, and some cancers.[5]

Obesity is also associated with greatly increased costs for medical care and lost productivity. The combined cost to California of overweight, obesity, and physical inactivity is estimated to be $41.2 billion annually.[6] The cost of obesity alone in the United States is $117 billion annually, including health care costs and lost productivity.[7]

Childhood obesity rates are increasing, and at the same time, physical activity levels among children are decreasing. The precipitous decline in children's physical activity levels and escalating rates of childhood obesity and diabetes are alarming.[8] More than one of four adolescents in California (29%)—nearly 1 million teenagers—get less than the recommended level of physical activity.[9]

Children and adults who live in communities with parks, athletic fields, nature centers, and other recreational facilities tend to be more physically active.[10] Research shows that park proximity is associated with higher levels of park use and physical activity among a variety of populations, particularly youth. Having more parks and more park acreage within a community is associated with higher physical activity levels.[11] This is particularly true for low-income communities. One study found that people in low-income areas in Los Angeles who lived within 1 mile of a park visited that park 4 times as frequently and exercised 38% more than people who lived over a mile away.[12] Unfortunately, low-income areas often lack places for physical activity, including parks and school fields. This is one reason why children and teens in low-income areas and children of color are especially vulnerable to obesity.[13]

3. **Psychological well-being.** In modern urban environments, parks and open spaces provide needed reprieves from everyday stressors that lead to mental fatigue. This improves the health of adults and children by reducing stress and depression and improving focus, attention span, productivity, and rates of recovery from illness.[14] Spending time in parks can reduce irritability and impulsivity and promote intellectual and physical development in children and teenagers by providing a safe and engaging environment to interact and develop social skills, language, and reasoning abilities, as well as muscle strength and coordination. Parks also provide a place for social support and an opportunity for self-determination, important factors in reducing stress, lowering anxiety, and improving a person's overall mood. This is true for children and adults.[15]

Researchers have found associations between contact with natural environments and improvements in the functioning of children with Attention Deficit Hyperactivity Disorder.[16] Contact with natural environments, such as trees, has also been associated with increases in the psychological resources of individuals living in public housing to make changes that will improve their lives and decrease their likelihood of finding problems insurmountable.[17]

4. **Recovery from illness and trauma.** Parks and green space have direct healing effects. A classic study demonstrated that views of trees enhanced the recovery of surgical patients and shortened the duration of hospitalizations.[18] Another study found that, for people who had recently experienced a stressful life event, the simple act of driving by parks and green spaces improved their recovery rate.[19] Other research has demonstrated that living in environments with more green space reduces the number of overall health complaints.[20]

Social Development and Community Cohesion

Parks and recreation programs can play an important role in reducing crime and violence. As an antigang initiative, the City of Los Angeles' Summer Night Lights program keeps select parks open from 7 p.m. until midnight throughout the summer, offering recreational activities, mentoring and counseling programs, meals, and other services. In neighborhoods where the program has operated since it began in 2008, there has been a 40.4% overall reduction in gang-related crime, including a 57% reduction in gang-related homicide.[21]

Active recreation and team sports in parks can promote positive choices and help reduce youth violence, crime, drug abuse, and teen pregnancy. Sports and recreation can provide lifelong lessons in teamwork, build character, and improve academic results.[22] Research has shown that children involved in sports and extracurricular activities tend to score higher on standardized tests and are less likely to engage in antisocial behavior.[23] Additionally, interscholastic sports have led to decreased dropout rates for both boys and girls.[24]

Park and recreation programs that serve diverse needs of diverse users bring people together in the public commons for the public good. Numerous studies document that people attach different values to green space and use green space differently, both in urban and nonurban contexts.[25]

Parks and green spaces provide a place for community members to interact socially with other community members. Parks become a source of community pride and inspiration. Social interaction and neighborhood spaces have been identified as key facets of healthy communities, supporting social networks, social support, and social integration.[26] Sociability may contribute to a sense of belonging and community. In a study conducted at a large public housing development in Chicago, Illinois, significantly more people used vegetated areas than similar areas without vegetation, and those individuals were more likely to be engaged in social activities.[27]

Culture, History, and Art

Parks provide important places in which to celebrate diverse culture, heritage, and art, and park monuments should reflect the diversity of a place and its people. For example, The Great Wall of Los Angeles, by University of California at Los Angeles (UCLA) Professor Judy Baca and the Social and Public Art Resource Center (SPARC), is one of the greatest monuments to interracial harmony in the United States. The recently restored half-mile Wall, the longest mural in the world, is in the Los Angeles River channel and is a best practice example of public art in a public park.[28] Another example is the struggle to stop a proposed toll road through Panhe. This area is a 9,000-year-old sacred site of the Native American Acjachemen people and is located in the present-day San Onofre State Beach. This effort illustrates the profound values of religious freedom, democracy, and equal justice for Native Americans that can be celebrated in parks.[29]

Social justice and stewardship of the Earth motivate spiritual leaders to support parks, green space, and equal justice. The United Church of Christ published environmental justice studies on toxins in 1987 and 2007.[30] For example, Cardinal Roger Mahony and the Justice and Peace Commission of the Catholic Archdiocese of Los Angeles actively support equal access to parks and natural space.[31] Protecting the Earth and its people is integral to the values of indigenous peoples around the world.[32] Nobel Peace Prize Laureate Rigoberta Menchú, a Mayan woman from Guatemala, has praised work to promote equal access to parks and recreation as a way of giving children hope and saying no to violence.[33]

Economic Vitality

When cities create urban parks, property values increase, local businesses benefit, and jobs are created, contributing to the local, state, and national economies. Important lessons can be drawn from the New Deal on the importance of including parks and recreation in economic stimulus activities.[34] New Deal projects included 8,000 parks and 40,000 schools. The Civilian Conservation Corps expanded open space and created jobs that kept young people out of regular markets.[35]

A recent study of the San Diego region in Southern California found that being located near open space adds between 5% and 10% to the value of a home, in high- and low-income communities.[36]

Other places across the United States have seen economic benefits as well. In Chattanooga, Tennessee, warehouses were replaced with an 8-mile greenway and property values increased by 127%, and the number of businesses and full-time jobs in the city more than doubled. San Antonio, Texas, revitalized the San Antonio River, and the river park became the most popular attraction in the city's $3.5 billion-dollar tourist industry. After expansion and restoration of the Martin Luther King Jr. National Historic Site in Atlanta, Georgia, the African American neighborhood of Sweet Auburn was revitalized, with dozens of new homes; 500,000 annual visitors boosting local business; and a decrease in crime.[37]

Beyond real estate values, parks and recreation help strengthen and stimulate the economy through sports and recreation-related sales of clothing, equipment, fees, services, and revenues generated from the tourism and hospitality industries. A study by researchers at Sacramento State University found that visitors to state parks in California spend $4.32 billion in park-related expenditures per year statewide. The study also found that each visitor spends an average of $57.63 per visit, including $24.63 within the park and $33 outside the park.[38] Researchers found that the New York state park system generates more than $5 in benefits for every $1 in costs. The annual economic impact of that park system is close to $2 billion in output and sales for private businesses, in addition to providing 20,000 jobs.[39]

Environmental Services and Climate Justice

Parks also play an important role in combating climate change and global warming, as well as in improving the quality of the local environment. Climate change is fundamentally an issue of human rights and environmental justice that connects the local to the global. With rising temperatures, human lives are affected by compromised health, financial burdens, and social and cultural disruptions. People of color, low-income individuals, and indigenous communities are often disproportionately affected by these disruptions because of where they live and because they may lack the financial resources to overcome these challenges.

Parks provide other important environmental services. One service provided by green space is the absorption and natural filtration of storm water. This can help reduce flooding and also improve water quality.[40] Green spaces also promote conservation values, including the protection of habitat for plants and animals and clean air, water, and land.

Parks and open spaces allow people to interact with nature and take value from being in a natural setting. These interactions take on additional importance as more people live in urban settings. For many individuals, particularly in low-income, urban areas, parks represent their only opportunity to escape the built environment, play on grass, and experience diversity of wildlife.[41]

Equal Justice and Democracy

Fundamental principles of equal justice and democracy underlie each of the other values described in this chapter. Those who lack adequate access to these resources are disproportionately at risk of health problems and face more challenges to enjoying quality of life improvements associated with parks and open spaces.

A Collective Vision of Green Access and Equity

Many organizations are working to green the Southern California region, driven by a collective vision for a comprehensive and coherent web of parks, schools, rivers, beaches, mountains, forests, and "Transit to Trails" that promotes human health, a cleaner environment, and economic vitality for all and reflects the growing cultural diversity of Southern California and the nation.

The Olmsted Report of 1930 has provided the inspiration for much of this vision. The firm, started by the sons of Frederick Law Olmsted with Bartholomew & Associates, proposed a vision for a green, prosperous, and culturally rich Los Angeles that has yet to be realized. Olmsted, the designer of Central Park, created the field of landscape architecture and was passionately committed to equal justice through the abolition of slavery. The lessons from the Olmsted Report can be applied not only in Los Angeles but also throughout Southern California and beyond. According to the Olmsted Report:

> Continued prosperity will depend on providing needed parks, because, with the growth of a great metropolis here, the absence of parks will make living conditions less and less attractive, less and less wholesome. . . . In so far, therefore, as the people fail to show the understanding, courage, and organizing ability necessary at this crisis, the growth of the Region will tend to strangle itself.[42]

The Olmsted Report proposed the shared use of parks and schools to make optimal use of land and public resources. The Report recommended the greening of the Los Angeles and San

Gabriel Rivers,[43] doubling public beaches and integrating forests and mountains within the park system.[44] It advocated multibenefit projects for park and flood control purposes[45] and envisioned a transportation system for people to reach parks, school fields, rivers, beaches, mountains, and forests.[46] The Report recognized low-income people often live in less desirable areas, have fewer leisure opportunities, and should receive first consideration in parks and recreation.[47] The Report emphasized that a balanced parks and recreation system serves diverse needs, including active and passive recreation. The Report recommended the creation of a regional park authority with power to raise dedicated funds to acquire and develop parks and other natural public places.[48] Each of these recommendations remains valid today—but unfulfilled.

Implementing the Olmsted vision would have made Los Angeles one of the most beautiful and livable places in the world. Powerful private interests and civic leaders demonstrated a tragic lack of vision and judgment when they killed the Olmsted Report. Politics, bureaucracy, and greed overwhelmed the Olmstedian vision in a triumph of private power over public space and social democracy.[49]

A diverse alliance of civil rights, environmental justice, environmental quality, public health, community, civic, business, and political leaders is coming together to restore and conserve the beauty of Southern California using the principles of the Olmsted vision as a guiding philosophy.

The People and Geography of Los Angeles

The Los Angeles region is densely populated and racially, ethnically, and socioeconomically diverse. The region offers a wealth of green space and parks as a whole, but the green space is spread across a large land area and recreation opportunities are not distributed evenly.[50]

The People of Los Angeles

Los Angeles County is home to more than 9.8 million people.[51] The City of Los Angeles alone has approximately 3.8 million residents, making it the second largest city in the United States by population.[52] The remaining 60% of the county's population is dispersed throughout the other 87 incorporated cities and numerous unincorporated communities. There is significant racial and ethnic diversity among the county's residents, as shown in Table 1.

Table 1

Racial and Ethnic Profile of Los Angeles County[53]

Race or Ethnicity	Population	Percentage of Population
Non-Hispanic White	2,728,321	27.8
Hispanic/Latino	4,687,889	47.7
Black	815,086	8.3
Asian and Pacific Islander	1,348,135	13.7
Native American	18,886	0.2
Total	**9,818,605**	

The population of Los Angeles is not distributed evenly based on race, ethnicity, color, or national origin. Racial or ethnic groups are often concentrated in certain communities throughout the county. For example, the percentage of African Americans living in the cities and neighborhoods of South and Central Los Angeles is far higher than the county average,[54] and the proportion of African Americans in the San Fernando Valley is far lower.[55] Extreme disparities can be seen among neighborhoods within the same city. Neighborhoods in the eastern portion of Los Angeles, such as Boyle Heights and El Sereno, are more than 80% Latino,[56] and fewer than 10% of the residents of some neighborhoods in western Los Angeles are Latino, including Pacific Palisades and Brentwood.[57]

There are also extreme differences in socioeconomic status within Los Angeles. Despite having many affluent neighborhoods, an overwhelming percentage of residents in some parts of the county do not earn a living wage. The annual income needed for a family of four to provide for its basic needs in Los Angeles County was slightly more than $63,000 in 2005, more than 3 times the federal poverty level.[58] Ninety-three percent of households with children in Central Los Angeles and 85% in South Los Angeles fall below this income level. Income disparities are most notable for Latino families, with 89% earning less than 300% of the federal poverty level, compared to only 34% of non-Hispanic White families.[59]

The Geography of Los Angeles

Los Angeles County is spread out over more than 4,000 square miles. The region includes 70 miles of coastline along the Pacific Ocean and mountains reaching elevations of over 10,000 feet.[60] Los Angeles contains rugged forests, winding rivers, deep valleys, and desolate deserts, as well as numerous urban parks. The region's many different geographical features provide a variety of recreational opportunities. In fact, it is possible to go alpine skiing and surfing in the Pacific Ocean in the same day without leaving the county.

Park Access in Los Angeles

Despite an overall wealth of parks and recreational opportunities, not all residents share equal access to the region's green space. Where one lives within Los Angeles factors into how much park access one has, and a closer analysis demonstrates that race, ethnicity, and socioeconomic status impact these disparities as well.

Park Poor, Income Poor, and Communities of Color

California state law defines *park poor* and *income poor* communities to prioritize investment of park bond funds in underserved communities. Park poor is defined as 3 acres or less of parks per thousand residents. Income poor is a median household income of $47,331 or less.[61] Though these criteria apply specifically to the investment of park funds under a specific statewide ballot measure (Proposition 84), they are a best practice example to establish standards to measure progress and equity and hold public officials accountable.

The City Project has used GIS and demographic tools to map the entire state of California at the census tract level to illustrate park and income poor communities that are disproportionately populated by people of color. The City Project advocates that park funding be prioritized in these combined "hot spots."[62]

Measuring Park Access

There are numerous ways to measure park access aside from acres of parks per thousand residents. The ultimate question is whether the parks meet the needs of the community as defined by the community. There is no single rule of thumb that works. A more useful method is a combination of measures, such as park and income poor communities of color. The National Recreation and Park Association, for example, at one time recommended 10 acres of park space per thousand residents but recently has supported a more flexible approach.[63] Most urban areas in California fall short of 10 acres of parks per thousand residents. The total amount of park space within a certain area is important, but this does not take into account who can reach the parks. Another method is distance to the park, measured in miles or walking distance. This does not address whether nearby parks meet the needs of the community, for example, if a nearby park is a pocket park and youth or adults want to play soccer.

Park Acres per Thousand Residents in Los Angeles

In total, there are 874,367 acres of green space in Los Angeles, approximately one third of the total land area,[64] and 9,818,605 residents. On average, there are 89.1 acres of parks per thousand residents. Though the total ratio of acres of parks per thousand residents is high for the county as a whole, the distribution of parks throughout the county is not even. The countywide average masks the vast park, school, and health disparities based on race, ethnicity, income, poverty, and access to cars.

Many neighborhoods in the urban core of Los Angeles are densely populated but offer small amounts of park space. These park poor neighborhoods tend to have disproportionately high percentages of people of color and low-income people. For example, in Los Angeles, Latino neighborhoods have an average of 1.6 acres of green space per thousand residents, African American neighborhoods average only 0.8 acres per thousand residents, and Asian/Pacific Islander neighborhoods provide 1.2 acres per thousand residents. By comparison, non-Hispanic White neighborhoods have 17.4 acres per thousand residents.[65]

There are 26 state assembly districts (AD) fully or partially within Los Angeles County, with park acres per thousand residents ranging from a low of 0.52 in AD 46 in Central Los Angeles, to 3,279 acres per thousand residents in AD 37 in the northwestern county.[66] Figure 1 documents park acres per thousand residents for each district.

As with neighborhoods within the City of Los Angeles, the most park poor and income poor ADs in the County of Los Angeles have disproportionately high percentages of people of color and low-income people. Conversely, most of the park rich districts have disproportionately high percentages of non-Hispanic White and middle- or high-income residents (see Figure 2).

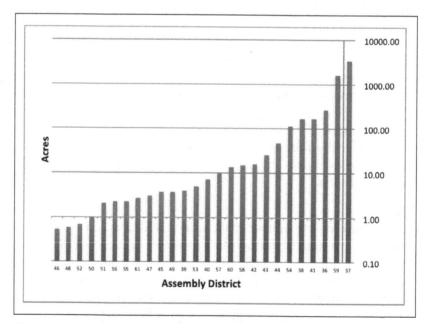

Figure 1. Park Acres per Thousand Residents for Assembly Districts in Los Angeles County (Note: chart has a logarithmic scale)

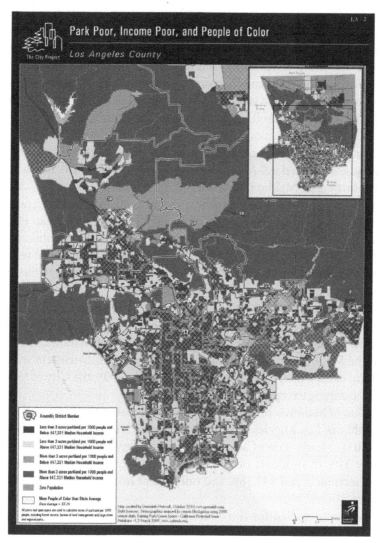

Figure 2. Park Poor, Income Poor, and People of Color in Los Angeles

Disparities in Access to Beaches, Mountains, and Forests

Beaches

Beaches are among California's most valuable public assets. California has the largest ocean economy in the nation, a large portion of which revolves around the state's beaches. In 2000, ocean-related activities in California produced a gross state product of $42.9 billion and provided almost 700,000 jobs and more than $11.4 billion in wages and salaries.[67]

Los Angeles County is world famous for its beaches. The sad reality, however, is that not everyone in Los Angeles has equal access to a beach. Not all beaches in Los Angeles have public access, accurate data on public beach visitation is not always available, and private property owners are trying to cut off public access to public beaches.[68]

Malibu residents have been particularly aggressive in restricting access to beaches alongside multimillion-dollar mansions. In 2005, private property owners on Broad Beach in Malibu took the astounding action of bulldozing away the public beach. The beach bulldozing reduced public access, caused significant environmental and habitat destruction, and destroyed the beauty of the beach.[69] The California Attorney General successfully sued the Broad Beach homeowners group Trancas Property Owners Association for violation of the Coastal Act, interference with public access to the beach, and theft (conversion) of beach minerals.[70]

Media mogul David Geffen, along with the City of Malibu, filed suit to cut off public access to the public beach alongside his beachfront mansion. His suit was dismissed six times before he finally gave up and opened a 9-foot path from the highway to the beach in 2005.[71] Several private property owners in Malibu had erected nonpermitted "Private Beach/No Trespassing" and "No Camping" signs and dispatched private security guards on all-terrain vehicles, which are not permitted on public beaches, or called in the county sheriff in an effort to intimidate the public from using these beaches. After a hearing on improving public access to Malibu's Lechuza Beach, at which a nonprofit representative spoke eloquently about teaching children of color life skills through outdoor activities, a local property owner complained to a state official that she opposes inner-city youth coming to Lechuza Beach.[72]

In 2005, the California Coastal Commission acted in response to The City Project's "Free the Beach!" campaign by ordering the removal of nonpermitted signs and illegal vehicles.[73] The California Coastal Commission also suggested that the City of Malibu remove "No Camping" signs posted at the Malibu city limits because the signs were "inconsistent with the City's ordinances, LCP [local coastal plan], and the Coastal Act."[74] In 2008, the City of Malibu changed the signs to prohibit camping except in designated areas.[75]

The population of Malibu is disproportionately non-Hispanic White and wealthy compared to the general public of Los Angeles County. Malibu is 89% non-Hispanic White, with a median income of $102,031. Nearly 25% of Malibu households have an annual income over $200,000. In contrast, only 31% of residents of Los Angeles County are non-Hispanic White, the median household income is just $42,189, and only 4% of households have an annual income of $200,000 or more.[76]

The Olmsted Report called for the doubling of public beach frontage in the Los Angeles region. According to the Report:

> Public control of the ocean shore, especially where there are broad and satisfactory beaches, is one of the prime needs of the Region, chiefly for the use of throngs of people coming from inlands. . . . [T]he public holdings should be very materially increased.[78]

People who live along the beach in Los Angeles County are generally disproportionately non-Hispanic White and wealthy. The non-Hispanic White population ranges from 89% to 58% in beachfront communities. In all coastal communities, the Black population was too small to be significant. Table 2 shows the demographic distribution in beachside communities in Los Angeles County.

Long Beach is the only exception to the rule. There, the non-Hispanic White population of 47% is less than the state and county average, and the median household income is lower. This may be because Long Beach, unlike other coastal communities in Los Angeles, extends far inland, and a good portion of the coastline is dedicated to the Port of Long Beach. Moreover, as is true for many port towns, Long Beach has historically been a working-class town.[79]

Table 2

Demographics of Coastal Communities in Los Angeles County[77]

Community	Total Population	Non-Hispanic White (%)	Latino (%)	Asian (%)	Median Household Income
Malibu	18,528	85	6	3	$102,052
Pacific Palisades	17,143	89	4	5	$125,711
Santa Monica	54,341	74	12	6	$50,435
Venice (Ocean Park)	24,639	61	24	3	$48,101
Marina del Rey	14,837	80	6	7	$74,444
Playa del Rey	16,830	70	11	8	$67,651
El Segundo	15,970	78	10	7	$61,385
Manhattan Beach	29,017	86	5	5	$102,739
Hermosa Beach	18,442	85	7	4	$81,883
Redondo Beach	27,107	77	10	8	$61,142
Torrance	11,026	80	7	10	$72,920
Palos Verdes Estates	13,340	76	3	17	$123,996
Rancho Palos Verdes	21,525	64	4	25	$104,552
Rolling Hills	1,871	77	5	14	$200,001
L.A. Harbor	34,878	58	28	4	$51,482
Long Beach	100,920	47	31	9	$41,587
L.A. County	9,519,338	31	45	12	$42,289
California	33,871,648	60	32	11	$47,493

Forests and Mountains

Diversifying access to and support for the forests of Los Angeles is an important part of achieving equal access to natural public places. The U.S. Forest Service reported over 90% of visitors to all national forests are non-Hispanic White and less than 5% are Latino, less than 2% are Asian, and only 1% are African American.[80] These tragically low visitation rates are consistent with the rates for the Angeles National Forest discussed later in this chapter and other public green space, including national parks and state parks. One difficulty in providing access to the forests and mountains in and around Los Angeles is the lack of public transit, as noted in the Southern California Association of Governments' environmental justice study[81] and a study by University of Southern California students.[82] One remedy is a Transit to Trails program to provide fun, educational, and healthy trips to mountains, forests, and beaches.

The Angeles National Forest provides by far the most natural public space in Los Angeles County. Twenty-five percent of all land and 78% of all park space in the county is in the Angeles National Forest. Recreation is the predominant use of the forests in Southern California.[83] As a result of its proximity to metropolitan Los Angeles, millions of people visit this forest every year. The Olmsted Report recommended integrating forests and mountains into the regional park system.[84]

Unfortunately, visitors to the Angeles National Forest do not reflect the racial and ethnic diversity of the region, as shown in Table 3. Despite that the majority of Los Angeles residents are people of color, few go to the Angeles National Forest. For example, nearly 45% of the county's population is Latino, but only 11% of visitors to Angeles National Forest are Latinos. Nearly 10% of the residents of Los Angeles County are Black, yet only 1% of visitors to the forest and none of the visitors to the forest's wilderness areas are Black.

Table 3

Angeles National Forest Visitors[85]

Race or Ethnicity	Proportion of Visitors to Angeles National Forest (%)	Proportion of Visitors to Wilderness Areas in Angeles National Forest (%)
Non-Hispanic White	79.2	78.7
Latino	10.8	14.8
Asian/Pacific Islander	4.5	4.0
Black	1.1	0.0
Native American	1.1	0.6
Other	1.4	0.8

The San Gabriel Valley, a subregion of Los Angeles County that lies adjacent to the Angeles National Forest, has among the highest concentrations of residents of Asian descent in the United States. Asians account for an estimated 25% of the total population of the San Gabriel Valley, and eight of the 10 cities in the United States with the highest concentration of Chinese Americans are in the San Gabriel Valley. Yet only 4.5% of visitors to the Angeles were Asian. Reasons for low visitation rates by people of color include a history and pattern of employment discrimination based on race, ethnicity, and gender by the Forest Service in the region, cultural differences in recreation, lack of transit, the privatization of public space, and a history of discriminatory land use and housing policies.[86]

Health Disparities in Los Angeles: Childhood Obesity

As reflected in Figure 3,[87] childhood obesity rates range from 23.1% to 39.1%. The results further demonstrate a relationship between park access and childhood obesity rates, with the ADs with the worst park access also having the highest rates of childhood obesity. Eleven of the 12 ADs with 3 acres of parks per thousand residents or fewer have childhood obesity rates that exceed 30%, and seven of the 10 ADs with 5 or more acres of parks per thousand residents have childhood obesity rates under 30%. There is also substantial clustering of populations along racial, ethnic, and socioeconomic lines. The ADs with the worst park access and highest rates of childhood obesity are disproportionately populated by people of color and low-income residents, and the ADs with best park access are disproportionately populated by non-Hispanic Whites and high-income residents.

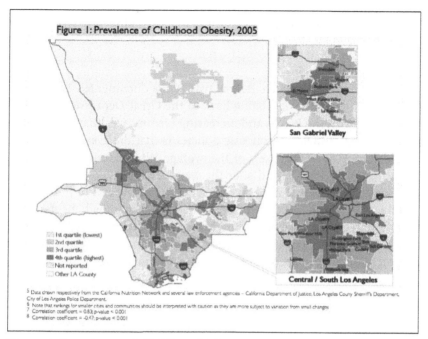

Figure 3. Prevalence of Childhood Obesity in Los Angeles County

The levels of child obesity are intolerably high even for children in the best neighborhoods—over 31% of children in Los Angeles County are overweight[88]—but children of color suffer first and worst. In Los Angeles, children of color disproportionately live in the areas with the highest levels of child obesity and the worst access to parks and school fields. Of the 80 ADs within California, the five districts with the highest rates of overweight children are all within Los Angeles County, with most of those districts clustered in Central and South Los Angeles.[89] On the state level, Latino and Black children are disproportionately overweight compared to non-Hispanic White and Asian children.

A study by the Los Angeles County Department of Public Health mapped the prevalence of childhood obesity for 128 cities and communities in the county, with rates varying widely from a low of 4% in Manhattan Beach to a high of 37% in Maywood (Figure 3). The percentage of overweight and obese children tended to be higher in communities that provide fewer acres of parks, recreational areas, or wilderness areas. The study also found a correlation between weight status and economic hardship. Cities or communities with a high economic burden (higher poverty, unemployment, median income, lower educational attainment, more dependents, crowded housing) also had higher percentages of overweight and obese children.[90] Although this study did not consider disparities based on race, color, or national origin, The City Project and GreenInfo Network have reanalyzed the county data to include race, color, and national origin.

History of Discriminatory Access to Parks and Recreation

The fact that low-income people of color disproportionately lack equal access to parks, school fields, beaches, trails, and forests is not an accident of unplanned growth, and not the result of an efficient free market distribution of land, housing, transit, and jobs, and not a re-flection of individual preferences by people to avoid green space. It is the result of a continuing history and pattern of discriminatory land use, housing, education, and economic policies and practices. The history of discrimination is relevant to understanding how the region came to be the way it is and how it could be better.

Discriminatory Economic Policies

Katznelson's book *When Affirmative Action Was White* documented how racial inequities were aggravated by economic policies dating back to the Great Depression and the New Deal that had the impact of excluding Blacks and increasing income, wealth, and class disparities. A continuing legacy of discriminatory economic policies is that the average Black family in the United States holds just 10% of the assets of the average White family.[91] More than a million Black men fought in World War II, and after the war they fought to make the United States better for themselves. World War II marked the beginning of the end of Jim Crow[92]; however, under the G.I. Bill many veterans of color were excluded from veterans' benefits such as housing and education subsidies. In the past, when beachfront prices were lower, people of color were forbidden from buying, renting, or even using beachfront property. Today, when beachfront property has skyrocketed in value, people of color often cannot afford to buy or rent beachfront property.

Discrimination and the Courts

The California Supreme Court sanctioned racially restrictive housing covenants in 1919, and California courts continued to uphold them as late as 1947. The Federal Housing Authority not only sanctioned restrictive covenants but also developed a recommended formula for their inclusion in subdivision contracts. Restrictive city ordinances, housing covenants, and other racially discriminatory measures dramatically limited access by Black people to housing, jobs, schools, playgrounds, parks, beaches, restaurants, transportation, and other public accommodations.[93]

The landmark U.S. Supreme Court decisions in *Shelley v. Kraemer*[94] in 1948 and *Barrows v. Jackson*[95] in 1951 made racially restrictive housing covenants illegal and unenforceable. Even after those decisions, however, Blacks and other people of color were excluded from White neighborhoods. Sides wrote in his book *L.A. City Limits: African American Los Angeles From the Great Depression to the Present*, "In the postwar era many individual white homeowners, and virtually all the public and private institutions in the housing market, did everything possible to prevent African Americans from living outside areas that were already predominantly black."[96] A U.S. Supreme Court case banned housing discrimination under state law in *Reitman v. Mulkey*.[97]

The City of Los Angeles

Los Angeles pioneered the use of racially restrictive housing covenants. As a result, Blacks increasingly became concentrated in South Central Los Angeles, Chinese in Chinatown, Mexican Americans in East Los Angeles, and Japanese in Little Tokyo. The area surrounding the Los Angeles State Historic Park illustrates this history, and advocates relied on this historical evidence extensively to support the park's creation.[98] El Pueblo de Los Angeles was founded in 1781 near the Native American Tongva village of Yangna, near or at the present site of the Park. The first settlers, the Pobladores, were Spaniards, Catholic missionaries, Native Americans, and Blacks. Mexicans and Californios further established the city before statehood. Chinese began arriving in 1850 in search of gold but were restricted to working on the railroad and in domestic jobs. They were forced to live on the wrong side of the tracks in Old Chinatown, across "Calle de los Negros" ("Nigger Alley") from the Plaza.

The Chinatown massacre of 1871 first brought Los Angeles to national and international attention. In the 1930s, the city forcibly evicted the residents and razed Old Chinatown to build

Union Station. New Chinatown was created at the site of the old Mexican American barrio of Sonoratown, near what is now the state park. Mexican Americans, including U.S. citizens, were deported during the Great Depression as a result of discrimination and competition for jobs.

Japanese arrived because of the labor shortage caused by the Chinese Exclusion Act and settled in Little Tokyo. They were forced into concentration camps at Manzanar and other places during World War II. Little Tokyo became known as Bronzetown when Blacks, arriving from the South to work in the war industry, filled the Japanese vacancies.

The city destroyed the bucolic Latino community in nearby Chavez Ravine with promises of affordable housing, then sold the land to the Dodgers baseball team, which buried the site with 16,000 places for cars to park and no place for children to play.

Despite the prominent role of Blacks in early Los Angeles, Black residential and business patterns were restricted in response to discriminatory housing and land use patterns. "Whites only" deed restrictions, housing covenants, mortgage policies subsidized by the federal government, and other racially discriminatory measures dramatically limited access by people of color to housing, parks, schools, playgrounds, swimming pools, beaches, transportation, and other public accommodations. Property owners continued employing tactics to restrict fair housing through the 1960s and beyond, as discussed previously.

Parks and Pools

Though not codified in law, parks and other public spaces in Los Angeles were "tacitly racialized."[99] For example, Blacks were not allowed in the pool in many municipal parks. At other pools, African Americans, Latinos, and Asians were permitted to swim only on Wednesdays between the hours of 2 p.m. and 5 p.m. This was called "International Day." The pool was then drained, cleaned, and refilled. Pool segregation continued through the 1940s.

There were some places of refuge, however. Central Playgrounds on Central Avenue in Los Angeles allowed African Americans to swim and play sports. Lincoln Park in East Los Angeles was a popular destination for Black youth from South Central and Latino youth from East Los Angeles, who could take the Pacific Electric railroad to reach one of the few parks where they were not feared, despised, and excluded.[100]

Beaches

When Manhattan Beach was incorporated in 1912, the city set aside a two-block area on the ocean for African Americans. Charles and Willa Bruce, a Black couple, bought the land and built the only beach resort in the Los Angeles area that allowed Blacks. Bruce's Beach offered bathhouses, outdoor sports, dining, and dancing to African Americans who craved a share of Southern California's good life. As the area's Black population increased, so did non-Hispanic White opposition to the Black beach. Manhattan Beach, with the help of the Ku Klux Klan, drove out the Black community and closed down Bruce's Beach in the 1930s. City officials forced Black property owners to sell at prices below fair market value through condemnation proceedings. The nearby Peck's Pier—the only pier that allowed Blacks—and the surrounding Black neighborhood were destroyed. Black Angelenos were then relegated to the Blacks-only section of Santa Monica Beach at Pico Boulevard known as the Inkwell. In 2006, Manhattan Beach commemorated the struggle of the Bruce family and the African American community by renaming the park at the historical site as Bruce's Beach Park.[101]

At the turn of the century, Malibu consisted of a 13,316-acre ranch along a 25-mile stretch of beaches, mountains, and canyons, owned by Frederick H. Rindge and later by his widow May. To pay taxes after her husband's death, May Rindge began leasing and selling parcels to movie celebrities and others. Parcels carried racially restrictive covenants that prevented people who were not White from using or occupying beach premises except as domestic servants. Even domestic workers who were not White were prohibited from using the public beach for bathing, fishing, or recreational purposes. The demographics of Malibu today reflect its discriminatory history, with the population overwhelmingly wealthy and White compared to the rest of the county.[102]

Legal Justifications for Equal Access to Parks and Recreation

Park advocates in Los Angeles have used social science research on why parks matter, existing health disparities, and park access inequities to support the use of state and federal civil rights and environmental laws to influence the investment of public resources to create new parks.[103] In the United States, federal civil rights laws prohibit intentional discrimination and unjustified discriminatory impacts for which there are less discriminatory alternatives regardless of intent in the provision of public resources, including access to parks and other public lands. States such as California have parallel laws.

Title VI of the Civil Rights Act of 1964 and its implementing regulations prohibit intentional discrimination based on race, color, or national origin of recipients of federal financial assistance.[104] Cases of intentional discrimination are relatively difficult to uncover in contemporary society, although some cases exist. Evidence of intentional discrimination includes (a) the impact of the action and whether it bears more heavily on one group than another, (b) a history of discrimination, (c) departures from substantive norms in reaching a decision, (d) departures from procedural norms, (e) whether the decision maker knows of the harm a decision will cause, and (f) a pattern or practice of discrimination.[105]

Title VI also prohibits actions that have a discriminatory impact, regardless of whether the impact is intentional or not. The inquiry under the disparate impact standard is (a) whether a practice has a disproportionate impact based on race, color, or national origin; (b) if so, the recipient of public funds bears the burden of proving that such action is justified by business necessity; and (c) even if the action would otherwise be justified, the action is prohibited if there are less discriminatory alternatives to accomplish the same objective.[106]

As a result, recipients of federal financial assistance, such as cities and counties, are prohibited from engaging in practices that have the intent or the effect of discriminating based on race or ethnicity.[107] To receive federal funds, which many municipalities depend on in part, a recipient must certify that its programs and activities comply with Title VI and its regulations.[108] In furtherance of this obligation, recipients of federal financial assistance must collect, maintain, and provide upon request timely, complete, and accurate compliance information.[109]

Stated in positive terms, publicly funded proposals including park projects, plans, and programs call for the preparation of an equity analysis that includes

1. a clear description of what is planned;
2. an analysis of the impact on all populations, including minority and low-income;
3. an analysis of available alternatives;
4. the documented inclusion of minority and low-income populations in the study and decision-making process; and
5. an implementation plan to address any concerns identified in the equity analysis.[110]

The U.S. Office of Management and Budget has circulated guidance specifying that recipients of federal funds are to comply with Title VI of the Civil Rights Act of 1964, as well as other equal opportunity laws and principles.[111] The U.S. Department of Justice, during President Barack Obama's first term, reemphasized the need for federal agencies to enforce, and for recipients of federal funds to proactively comply with, equal justice laws and principles, including

Title VI.[112] The U.S. Court of Appeals for the Ninth Circuit has recently condemned the U.S. Environmental Protection Agency (EPA) for its pattern of failing to investigate environmental justice, including Title VI complaints.[113]

State law in California also prohibits intentional discrimination and unjustified discriminatory impacts under Government Code section 11135 and its regulations, which are analogous to Title VI.[114] In addition, California law defines environmental justice as "the fair treatment of people of all races, cultures, and incomes with respect to the development, adoption, implementation, and enforcement of environmental laws, regulations, and policies."[115]

The California EPA has developed an Environmental Justice Action Plan, which addresses development of guidance on precautionary approaches, cumulative impacts analysis, and public participation.[116] The California State Lands Commission (CSLC) has developed and adopted an Environmental Justice Policy to ensure equity and fairness in its own processes and procedures. The CSLC adopted an amended Environmental Justice Policy in 2002 to ensure that "Environmental Justice is an essential consideration in the Commission's processes, decisions and programs and that all people who live in California have a meaningful way to participate in these activities." The policy commits the CSLC to considering environmental justice in its processes, decision making, and regulatory affairs.[117]

In 2002, the California Coastal Commission adopted a local coastal plan requiring Malibu to maximize public access to the beach and ensuring the fair treatment of people of all races, cultures, and incomes. This was the first time an agency had implemented the statutory definition of environmental justice under California law. Commissioner Pedro Nava told the *Los Angeles Times* he hoped to set a precedent for other communities, ensuring that visitors are not excluded from public land because of their income or race.[118] The Commission adopted the provision in response to advocacy by The City Project on behalf of a diverse alliance.

Despite cutbacks in enforcement of civil rights protections in federal courts, it is important to keep in mind that both intentional discrimination and unjustified discriminatory impacts remain unlawful under federal and state law. As a matter of simple justice, it is unfair to use public tax dollars to subsidize discriminatory intent and discriminatory impacts.[119] Recipients of federal and state funds, including many municipalities and their park and recreation agencies, remain obligated to prohibit both.

Solutions That Make Green Access More Equitable

Fortunately, there are opportunities to correct the existing inequities. Projects recommended below can improve future access to green space in the Los Angeles region. Opportunities to improve park access should be prioritized in the most park poor and income poor areas in Los Angeles, such as the central and southern portions of the county that also have disproportionate percentages of people of color.

Transit to Trails

A full Transit to Trails program to take people to parks, beaches, forests, lakes, and other public natural spaces should be developed and implemented in Los Angeles. A Transit to Trails program would serve everyone in the region, but would be particularly useful to the working poor with limited or no access to cars. A disproportionate number of these residents are people of color and low income.[120]

A successful pilot Transit to Trails program was implemented in Los Angeles County through a partnership among Anahuak Youth Sports Association, Mountains and Recreation Conservation Authority, and The City Project. Inner-city youth traveled to the Santa Monica Mountains National Recreation Area, a vast green space resource that most program participants had never visited before.[121]

A Transit to Trails program provides green access for people who otherwise would not have any. The premise of such a program is to take underprivileged children and their families and friends on fun and educational park, beach, mountain, and river trips. Program participants are transported to green spaces via buses. The trips are led by experienced guides and offer participants the chance to not only experience and connect with nature but also learn about physical activity, healthy eating, and cultural and historical resources.

Implementing Transit to Trails requires relatively low levels of oversight and administrative support. Coordinating trips requires little more than willing participants, guides, equipment, supplies, and transportation. Community groups can work with guides to design a series of programs that caters to the local community. Local retailers can provide donations or discounts for Transit to Trails as a public service program. Transportation can be coordinated with park agencies, municipal transit operators, or school districts, with school buses available for trips on weekends or over the summer.

Today, there is virtually no good way to reach the San Gabriel Mountains or the Angeles National Forest using public transportation.[122] Transit to beaches is limited, time consuming, and expensive.[123] Low-cost transit services should link parks such as the Los Angeles State Historic Park and Rio de Los Angeles State Park. The Southern California Association of Governments has called for a multiagency effort to provide Transit to Trails in its Regional Transportation Plan Environmental Justice Report.[124] The Olmsted Report envisioned a transportation system for people to reach natural public places.[125]

San Gabriel Region National Recreation Area

One strategy for improving access to forests and mountains in Los Angeles County is the creation of a San Gabriel Mountains National Recreation Area. The City Project is partnering with a diverse coalition of community-based organizations, Native Americans, and mainstream environmental groups for the San Gabriel Mountains Forever campaign.[126] The goal is to improve healthy recreational opportunities within the San Gabriel Mountains and along the length of the San Gabriel River.[127]

The proposed National Recreation Area (NRA) will extend beyond the mountains themselves and into the surrounding communities to the south. The vision for this NRA includes opportunities for active and passive recreation that meet the needs of the local community, as defined by the community.[128] Additionally, it is critical that a Transit to Trails program is implemented to ensure that those who live nearby but otherwise have no way to access this vital resource are able to enjoy the benefits that a San Gabriel Mountains NRA can provide for all.

Specific recommendations for the proposed NRA include the following:

1. A Transit to Trails program would take urban youth on fun, educational, and healthful trips to mountains, rivers, and other natural green spaces for no or low cost. It should incorporate education about land, water, wildlife, and cultural history, and the importance of physical activity and healthy eating for lifelong health.
2. NRA plans, programs, and funding need to serve the diverse interests of diverse users in a balanced system that provides recreation, places for physical activity to improve health, active recreation, passive recreation, and wilderness places.
3. Culturally and language-appropriate facilities, signage, and programming that serves the diverse interests of diverse users needs developed.
4. Cultural, art, heritage, and Native American sites need to be honored and preserved. The National Park Service should conduct a thorough survey of relevant places within and adjacent to the NRA that celebrate diversity, democracy, and freedom. Interpretive and educa-

tional programming should recognize the vital contributions that people of color, women, and Native Americans have made to the region.

5. Job training and conservation stewardship programs should be created for youth and nearby community members, ensuring that these programs reflect the diversity of the surrounding region.

6. The NRA needs to implement thoroughly proactive compliance with equal justice laws and principles, including the 1994 President's Order 12898 and Title VI of the Civil Rights Act of 1964 and its regulations by ensuring equal access to the proposed San Gabriel NRA through its own actions and the actions of its recipients.

7. Boundaries should include the San Gabriel River and Rio Hondo River corridors and urban communities south of the San Gabriel Mountains range not directly along the river corridors.

8. Boundaries should ensure connectivity between the urban areas along the San Gabriel and Rio Hondo Rivers, Puente-Chino Hills, and Chino Hills State Park.

Revitalizing the Los Angeles and San Gabriel Rivers

The *America's Great Outdoors Fifty-State Report* has identified improvements to the Los Angeles River and San Gabriel River Trails as one of the top conservation and green access priorities in the United States. Revitalizing these river trails is one of two projects in California highlighted by the U.S. Department of Interior and President Obama's America's Great Outdoors Initiative.

The Los Angeles River stretches 52 miles and crosses 13 cities, flowing through diverse communities from Canoga Park in the San Fernando Valley through downtown Los Angeles to the ocean in Long Beach. The City of Los Angeles has launched the Los Angeles River Revitalization Master Plan process to guide river revitalization for the next 20 years, focusing on the 32 miles that flow through the city from Canoga Park to Vernon. The *New York Times* cited the revitalization plan as a best practice example for "more sustainable, livable and socially just cities."[129]

The Los Angeles River Project Office published the report *Los Angeles River Access and Use: Balancing Equitable Actions With Responsible Stewardship* (the *River Report*) in June 2009, in response to a City Council resolution. The Report noted:

> The City's River revitalization efforts must balance human interests in accessing and using the River with improvements that will ensure an environment supportive of healthy, sustainable biodiversity. The River offers one of the nation's and the world's most significant opportunities to introduce meaningful environmental value back into the post-industrial urban landscape.[130]

The *River Report* emphasized and cited the work of The City Project:

> Numerous local organizations have stressed the importance of making sure that the River's revitalization addresses environmental justice issues (See, e.g., the City Project's work at www.cityprojectca.org.). Of key concern in Los Angeles is the growing disparity of access to and use of open space resources, including parks, ball fields, and natural areas by those living in low-income communities of color. Whole generations are growing up in Los Angeles without any meaningful relationship to the natural environment. . . . The River offers an opportunity to redress environmental justice problems by not only providing numerous new green spaces, but also by ensuring free access to them.[131]

The River Report emphasized the need for river revitalization to address compliance with equal justice laws and principles as one of the six major goals for river revitalization,[132] including

- environmental justice;
- human health and childhood obesity, including health impact assessments;
- economic justice and green local jobs;
- Transit to Trails to take inner-city residents on river, mountain, and beach trips;
- shared use of parks and schools; and
- public art along the river. [133]

This commitment to equal justice laws and principles should guide revitalization along the full length of the river. Communities along the lower 20 miles of the Los Angeles River have disproportionately higher percentages of residents of color and low-income people than communities within the city limits.[134] The county, City of Los Angeles, and other municipalities and agencies need to work together on a regional solution to ensure equitable distribution of the benefits and burdens of revitalizing communities along the entire length of the river. The EPA recently classified the Los Angeles River as traditional navigable waters.[135] This designation makes clear that the public trust doctrine applies to ensure equitable revitalization, as well as clean water protections.

The Olmsted Report called for the greening of the Los Angeles and San Gabriel Rivers, and multiuse projects for parks, schools, and flood control. The County of Los Angeles adopted a Master Plan for the Los Angeles River in 1996.[136] The County also published a Master Plan for the San Gabriel River in 2006.[137] Additionally, the Integrated Regional Water Management Plan for Greater Los Angeles County covers the Los Angeles and San Gabriel Rivers. Planning for revitalization of the full length of the Los Angeles River, the San Gabriel River, and other waterways must be coordinated to achieve social justice, as well as compliance with clean water and civil rights laws.[138] In the past, communities of color have relied on access to justice through the courts against the City of Los Angeles to achieve compliance with clean water laws.[139]

Clean water compliance and flood control should be combined with healthy parks, schools, and communities through multipurpose projects. Green spaces in parks and schools can work to clean water through natural filtration and prevent polluted storm water runoff from reaching the rivers and the ocean. Flood control basins can provide green space for parks and playing fields, such as the Sepulveda flood control basin recreation areas along the Los Angeles River. Funding for clean water and flood control projects can also be used for parks and school fields.

Latino support for community revitalization along the river is strong and continues to grow, according to polling by the William C. Velasquez Institute and anecdotal evidence gathered by the Alianza de los Pueblos del Río. When surveyed about what they would like to see on the river and its banks, Latinos showed significant support for parks and recreation, schools, green space, California-style trees and plants, and soccer and baseball fields. Latinos showed little support for gentrification-oriented development, with one quarter supporting affordable housing but only 2% supporting market rate housing, 3% supporting tourism-related development, and 3% in favor of condominiums and penthouses.[140]

Latinos viewed revitalization priorities significantly differently than non-Hispanic Whites. On average, Latinos favor parks, schools, affordable housing, soccer and baseball fields, and businesses that create jobs by 10 percentage points more than non-Hispanic Whites. In contrast, non-Hispanic Whites favored open green space, California-style trees and plants, and community gardens by 12 percentage points more than Latinos, on average. It is important to note, however, that Latinos and non-Hispanic Whites were united in their opposition to gentrification.[141]

In an important victory for the river, the diverse people living along it, and the environmental justice community, the EPA declared the Los Angeles River as "traditional navigable waters" in July 2010.[142] This designation triggered the protections afforded under the Clean Water Act to the river and its 834-square-mile urban watershed. The EPA specifically cited recreational opportunities, public access, and the presence of ongoing restoration and educational projects as factors that contributed to this designation.[143]

Revitalizing the San Gabriel River poses a related set of challenges. The 3-mile radius along the San Gabriel River is more complex demographically than the 3-mile radius along the Los Angeles River.[144] The San Gabriel and Lower Los Angeles Rivers and Mountains Conservancy has jurisdiction over both rivers and can coordinate equitable revitalization for both.

Lessons Learned

Green spaces, including parks, school fields, rivers, beaches, forests, mountains, and trails, are a necessary part of the infrastructure for healthy, livable, and just communities. The following recommendations for equitable development are based on the lessons learned from the urban greening movement over the past 10 years and will ensure that everyone, especially children and youth of color and low-income communities, benefits equally from infrastructure investments:

1. Prioritize green space projects based on need in communities that are both park poor and income poor. The California legislative criteria for investing park funds in park and income poor communities is a best practice example for defining standards to measure progress and equity and holding public officials accountable.
2. Prioritize projects that address physical, psychological, and social health needs, including childhood obesity and diabetes levels. Applying public health criteria to infrastructure investments could improve health and the quality of life in communities.
3. Prioritize projects that involve the joint use of parks, schools, and pools to make optimal use of scarce land, money, and public resources and that expand open space opportunities in densely developed communities.
4. Programs such as Civilian Conservation Corps and youth job programs should be funded to create green jobs and keep young people in school, keep them physically active and healthy, and lead to permanent jobs and careers as stewards of the earth and its people.
5. Infrastructure projects should create green jobs for local workers, small and disadvantaged business enterprises, and youth.
6. Prioritize cultural, historical, and public art projects, such as the Great Wall of Los Angeles, that celebrate diversity, democracy, and freedom in parks and other public places. Native American sites must be celebrated and preserved.
7. Transportation funding should support Transit to Trails programs as alternatives to single occupancy vehicles to provide access for all to parks, mountains, beaches, and rivers.
8. Funding agencies should ensure compliance with civil rights laws, guaranteeing equal access to public resources including parks and recreation programs. Compliance with civil rights laws should be combined with other laws, including environmental and education laws.
9. Projects should implement principles of equitable development: invest in people, invest in stronger communities, invest in the open, and invest in justice.
10. Implement strategic equity plans to improve parks and recreation in every neighborhood.

Conclusion

Green space plays a valuable role in the life of Los Angeles residents. From the positive physical and psychological impacts parks have on people, to environmental services, to economic vitality, the fundamental values of equal justice and democracy underlie all the values that parks provide. Unfortunately, not everyone in Los Angeles has equal access to green spaces. Low-income communities and communities of color suffer first and worst in park access and related human health disparities.

The goal of this chapter has been to engage, educate, and empower stakeholders to achieve equal justice, democracy, and livability for all by promoting equity in access to green space in Southern California. The City Project has relied on a five-part strategy to improve green access and equity in communities throughout California. First, coalition building brings people together to meet the needs of the community as defined by the community. Second, multidisciplinary research and analyses underlie work such as this chapter, including GIS mapping, demographic analyses, and historical research. Third, strategic media campaigns, involving both traditional and new social media, help focus public attention. Fourth, policy and legal advocacy outside the courts can promote equitable infrastructure results through the planning process. Finally, if other alternatives fail, access to justice through the courts can be a profoundly democratic means of ensuring equal access to public resources within a broader campaign.

The road must be found from hope to change. Opportunities exist to create new green spaces and improve access to existing green spaces throughout Los Angeles. But the presence of green space is only part of the equation. It is imperative that everyone is equally able to access this green space. Achieving equitable green access throughout Los Angeles is not only possible but also necessary for realizing equal justice, democracy, and livability for all.

Discussion Questions

1. Robert and Seth draw a parallel between healthy living environments and social and environmental justice. Are you persuaded by their reasoning that these are, in fact, issues of social and environmental justice? Please explain your thinking.

2. Lack of access to parks and open space seems to be at the heart of what bothers the authors about the living conditions for Los Angeles' low-income families and people of color. In your opinion, is this essentially a planning problem or does it run deeper? Please elaborate.

3. The City Project is a hands-on, roll-up-your-sleeves organization dedicated to improving the living conditions for marginalized populations in Los Angeles. Would you consider devoting your life in such a cause? Why or why not?

4. Based on your reading of this chapter, what kind of effort is required to make meaningful and lasting change in a city of this magnitude?

5. We live in a society that is increasingly urbanized. In other words, more of the citizenry resides in environments such as the one described in this chapter. What are the implications for our connection to nature and our understanding of nature's role in contributing to our health and well-being?

19

Public Memory for an Inclusive Society

William Stewart
University of Illinois

Public memory is a key concept to enhance social and environmental justice. Public memory is about creating value for people and their places. Rather than preserving the past, public memory adapts the past in ways that affect the present.[1] Stated differently, understandings of the past will change as perceptions of current conditions change.[2] Sharing knowledge related to social and environmental injustices leads to a public conversation where new meaning acknowledges the injustice, explains the oppression, and holds potential for empowerment. Creating public memory for an inclusive society brings meanings to shared dialogue about people and their place and, in doing so, allows social and cultural contexts that were previously invisible to become public.[3]

Injustices, power differentials, and acts of oppression are driven by social and cultural forces. Oppression is not simply one individual bullying another. Oppression is about social and cultural contexts that systematically encourage one group's dominance over another.[4] Without recognizing the social and cultural contexts, the injustice may be unapparent, lack sharp distinction as being wrong, and appear as the natural order of society. Social and cultural contexts are the backdrop that allows us to render judgment. Because of its foundation in social and cultural contexts, public memory is a powerful tool to build an emancipatory narrative for a group of people who otherwise would remain marginalized by society without hope for social and cultural mobility.

Working to build a more inclusive society requires raising the visibility of those on the margins. Creating public memory allows personal stories and social histories to become known. By providing a layer of meaning to understand life at the margins, public memory allows others to connect social and cultural contexts to understand the oppression. An important step in working toward social justice is to recognize the need for social justice. It is not just about elevating and empowering those individuals who are oppressed. Working for social justice is about imagining changes in social and cultural contexts to preclude oppression today and in the future.

The purpose of this concluding chapter is to overview public memory as a way to build a more inclusive society and to position the creation of public memory as a relevant goal for leisure research. To illustrate social and cultural contexts of social justice, I portray landscape art as a powerful instrument in building public memory.

Public Memory and Social Justice

Public memory makes the past meaningful. The past is selectively remembered in ways that unify and build identity for people of the present.[5] Public memory is not just a dispassionate remembering; it is also a public forgetting, erasure, and silencing.[6] "Public history" implies claims to accuracy and objectivity and suggests history as singular and authentic. "Public memory" is founded on a collective view of the past and recognizes the multiple and fluid ways in which society creates meaning for people and their places.[7] Rather than asserting an absolute truth, public memory is about a narrative that holds layers and accumulates meaning.[8] Public memory is like a palimpsest where meaning accumulates or gets written over, much like a canvas with successive layers of painting in which each potentially influences the next.[9, 10]

Working for social justice often connects people to place. Social injustice is about a group of people in a specific time and place who have been wronged. Working for social justice is about legitimizing a group of people as having a stake in the way a place is defined. The social and cultural meanings of a place have implications for the meanings of the people attached to the place. Addressing social injustice is to be part of a narrative that builds a more inclusive array of places. Public memory, with its capacity to connect people to place, is effective at changing the public meanings of places and consequently creating a more inclusive array of places. To illustrate the power of public memory of places and its capacity to connect people with place, I offer insight from my experiences in viewing landscape paintings in art museums.

Public Memory Embodied in Landscape Art

Landscape art is steeped in social and cultural values. There are so many angles from which to draw inferences. The painter's intentions, if known, are a reliable basis to formulate the social and cultural values embodied in the art. Familiarity with an artist's history and life events assists in such formulations. The time period of the painting reflects a zeitgeist and furnishes historical fodder for understanding social and cultural values. The intended audience of the artwork, when known, is also a good source of information to characterize social and cultural values—and hence, public memory—embodied in it. Through the public memory embodied in landscape art, the need for social justice comes into view, along with counter-narratives to add to the public memory of the place.

Cowboy art is a genre of landscape art that has had a profound impact on public memory of the American West. To be sure, critics have derided cowboy art for more than a century, and art historians no longer find it worthy of comment.[11, 12] However, the social and cultural values embodied in landscape art, and ultimately the impact of these values, are alive and well today regardless of the esoteric critique of intellectuals. Cowboy art portrays a masculinized West that champions the Anglo conquest and the ruggedness of men who were part of it.[13] Its representation of frontier America pushed many people to the margins, including women, children, American Indians, and other people of color whose lives should be part of the history of western expansion.

Visiting art museums is a highlight of many travel experiences in my life. Whether going to a conference or on a pleasure trip, I often allow time to visit a museum and am especially eager if the museum displays a collection of landscape art. My experiences while viewing paintings and interaction with the museum staff provide insight into the public memory embodied by the art. In the following pages, I selectively characterize the art and artist to provide insight into the impact of the art and its relationship to public memory. These illustrations are centered on my lived experiences of viewing the art and are provided in the spirit of a travel journal.

Frederic Remington was one of the first cowboy artists who was active during the 1890s and 1900s. He was born and raised in New York, took several trips out west, struggled with obesity most of his adult life, and died wealthy due to the commercial success of his artwork. With the last of the "Indian wars" occurring in the late 1880s, Remington painted from a postconquest vantage point yet depicted western life as if preconquest in appearance. He painted for commercial markets and private patronage and largely rode a tide of popular culture ripe with anxiety about the death of America's western frontier.

While visiting Fort Worth, Texas, in 1990, I had the pleasure of visiting the Amon Carter Museum of American Art. The museum boasts one of the largest collections of Remington's art; with "their fascinating details and hypnotic aura of romance, these works provide an unparalleled journey into the Old West."[14] At the museum, I was particularly intrigued with Remington's 1889 painting *Dash for Timber*, which was his first commercial success that launched his career (see Figure 1). Like most of his work, it was painted from his sprawling estate and studio in New Rochelle, New York—now an affluent suburb of New York City.

Figure 1. Dash for Timber, 1889, Frederic Remington

The painting depicts cowboys charging toward the viewer with Apaches quick on their tails. Their horses are straining every muscle with their riders furiously trying to outrun their foes to find cover in a nearby stand of timber. The visual image of cowboys and Indians chasing each other became embedded in our cultural psyche as part of the public memory of the American West and has been reproduced countless times by the American television and movie industry. The reaction of a couple next to me in the gallery said it all: "There's the ole west for ya."

Before attending a conference in Stillwater, Oklahoma, in 2003, I arrived a day early to check out the Gilcrease Museum in Tulsa that "houses the world's largest, most comprehensive collection of art and artifacts of the American West."[15] On that particular day, business was slow, and I was fortunate to have a docent walk with me throughout much of the collection of cowboy art on display. When viewing *Breaking Through the Line* by Charles Schreyvogel, I was struck by the lead gunner with pistol aimed directly at the viewer (see Figure 2). Why would someone imagine such a violent scene putting the viewer in the place of an Indian-about-ready-to-take-a-bullet-from-point-blank-range? After some pondering and without finding good reason, I asked the docent for his explanation. He looked at me with his head slightly lurched forward as if mimicking the lead gunner and said, "That's the way it was." In his follow-up comments, it was clear to him that Schreyvogel was able to "capture the action" between the cavalry and plains Indians. When asked why the collection of paintings depicted a West without women, it came back again: "That's the way it was; the frontier was no place for women."

Figure 2. *Breaking Through the Line*, 1900, Charles Schreyvogel

For many visitors to the Gilcrease, the social and cultural values depicted in the paintings were one and the same as the public memory of the American West. Upon returning home, I did research on Schreyvogel's life history and discovered that he was born and raised in New York City and painted from his home in Hoboken, New Jersey. Although he took several trips to the West, Schreyvogel was a loyal fan of Buffalo Bill Cody's Wild West Shows that made frequent runs through New York City. These Wild West shows entertained urban crowds with their depictions of American Indians as war-like aggressors on White settlers. The social and cultural values of Schreyvogel's artwork are a direct lineage from these Wild West shows.

A precursor to cowboy art is early American landscape painting that portrays American Indians within western landscapes. During a visit to Indianapolis, Indiana, in 2002, I made time to visit the Eiteljorg Museum of American Indians and Western Art. The Eiteljorg is "the only museum of its kind in the Midwest, and one of only two museums east of the Mississippi that explore both Native America and the American West."[16] I came with a mission to view firsthand Alfred Jacob Miller's 1845 canvas titled *The Trapper's Bride*, a painting I came to know through a course I teach on nature and American culture (see Figure 3). I knew that Miller was born and raised in Baltimore, Maryland, and spent several years in Paris, Venice, and the United Kingdom. He made one trip out West in the mid-1830s, then to Scotland where he lived for 2 years, and upon returning to Baltimore, he painted *The Trapper's Bride*.

Figure 3. *The Trapper's Bride*, 1845, Alfred Miller

The docent who shared my experience of viewing the painting was most articulate in outlining distinctions between the social value and the cultural value embodied by the painting and the contemporary culture of Miller. She indicated that at the time of the painting, Americans (who largely lived along the east coast) were curious about American Indian women. Framing them as either virgin, albeit savage, princesses or as promiscuous whores, the social and cultural context of popular culture framed American Indian women from polarized and distinctly contradictory perspectives. The docent went on to describe the original sketches of *The Trapper's Bride* as absent the scarlet-clad seductress in the lower right corner with the main focus of the sketches being the distinction between the worlds of Anglos and American Indians. The two sides of the diagonal—the golden sky above the White trapper and the dark clouds above the chaotic Indian encampment—were symbolic of these two worlds. In what must have been a last-minute decision, Miller inserted the prone, naked, and red-robed woman. In the docent's mind, it was a contrasting image with the demure and white-clad virgin princess and reflected the mystique of American Indian women to East Coast culture at the time of the painting.

During the summer after my daughter was born in 1991, we traveled to Montana on a combined business and pleasure trip. It was there that I peeked into the Montana State House chambers and was surprised to see a large (25 x 12 feet) Charlie Russell painting as the permanent backdrop watching over the session of the state legislature. I learned it was *Lewis and Clark Meeting of the Flatheads in Ross's Hole, September 4, 1805* painted in 1912. Russell was born in St. Louis, Missouri, and moved to Montana in the 1880s just in time to witness the final slaughter of the great Buffalo herds and the spread of barbed wire and plows. He was a prolific painter of the "Old West" and had an international following, and his work was a commercial success during his lifetime. Although Russell was dismissed by art critics and historians alike, one need go no further than the Montana State House to witness the impact of his cowboy art as a purveyor of public memory of the American West.

As an additional layer of meaning to the social and cultural values of cowboy art, let's move forward to the Houston Museum of Fine Arts that sponsored the exhibition *Crimes and Splendors: Desert Cantos of Richard Misrach* in 1996. Misrach was well aware that most of the American West was a "man-mauled desert." Rather than recognizing its beauty, Misrach was disturbed that Americans have tried to civilize it and, in doing so, have led to its destruction. Raised in the Jewish tradition in which there is no greater honor than to bear witness, to never forget, and to tell the truth, Misrach took haunting photographs that assume the role of messenger of public memory to ensure that it will never happen again. Although my experience at the museum was what one might expect when having four children in tow (two of my own and two of my sister's) at an art gallery, I purchased the book and was able to view the photographs of Desert Cantos at a later time in the quiet of my own home.

In his 1970 photograph, *Salton Sea, California*, Misrach depicted the irony of a dry residential pool surrounded by a flooded desert landscape (see Figure 4). The Salton Sea is a geologic depression that filled with water when an irrigation project went awry in 1905. For several decades, it was an outdoor recreation paradise. In the past half century, the "sea's" salinity has increased to the point of being toxic to life—aquatic, avian, and all else. The booming residential and touristic developments were abandoned in the late 1960s, a few years prior to Misrach's photographic essay. Misrach was also aware that he followed other western photographers, par-

Figure 4. *Salton Sea, California,* 1970, Richard Misrach
(from Desert Cantos, University of New Mexico Press)

ticularly Ansel Adams whose popular images portrayed the West as a pristine alpine landscape void of humanity as if fresh from God's creation. Misrach disrupted the traditional social and cultural values of the West to create a new and, in his words, honest portrayal. His images affirm the desert as the major landscape of the West, whose beauty needs protection.

Park Development to Create an Inclusive Society

Park development is guided by social and cultural values resulting in parks that reflect a group's or a community's sense of self. Many parks commemorate veterans; battlefields and memorials tie people who died fighting wars overseas to our hometowns. Countless community parks are dedicated to our cultural obsession with baseball and champion our collective field of dreams. Some parks sanctify and restore the local native landscape with intentions to protect that which is truly American. Whether or not park development is conscious about social and cultural contexts, parks inevitably connect people to place and are instrumental in the creation of public memory.

There are times when leisure research works to homogenize social and cultural values and purposely avoids the idiosyncrasies of a given population or community. Social and cultural values—the grist of public memory—are frequently not problematized. Often framed as (or inferred from) benefits, motivations, psychological outcomes, or preferences, social and cultural values may not be treated with sensitivities to local history, community, or place. There are times when public values for parks are assumed and considered universally shared across a community. "Whose values are reflected in this park?" is a question that may be avoided during planning. This is not say to public input is avoided, but to say that the questions posed and information received often work to homogenize and universalize away local histories of place.

Fortunately, there is a growing awareness of park development as both instrumental and reflective of public memory that works for social and environmental justice. As examples, Glover and Bates[17] studied the demise of participation by African American youth in a community baseball league. Among other implications, their study revealed that park planning in the community they studied had inexplicably developed baseball parks a long distance from the African American neighborhoods. As a consequence, a grassroots league emerged, the "first string," that mimicked the rise of the Negro Leagues in the 1930s and brought a sense of belonging back to the community. The "first string" youth league reinvigorated local families to participate in summer baseball and tied them to a unique history of the place. Rather than being initiated by the local park district, "first string" was an organically derived movement from the families of the neighborhood.

Stewart, Barkley, Kerins, Gladdys, and Glover[18] and Johnson, Glover, and Stewart[19] have also framed park planning as community-based meaning-making. They problematized social and cultural values as a starting point for development of their methods and adapted a photo elicitation technique to evoke values that otherwise would not come to the surface. Rather than "finding" such values, their research framed social and cultural values as needing elicitation, prompting, and coproduction within forums of stakeholders. They organized iterative processes in which stakeholders discovered their collective social and cultural values. Via learning circles, the researchers found that stakeholders learned about themselves and their community within the meaning-making process of the research. Their study elicited "several histories that otherwise would not have been voiced, and therefore not have an opportunity to be represented"[20] as part of the planning process.

Each community has built a public memory with its own traditions of social and cultural values. The extent to which this public memory fosters social and environmental justice may not be apparent to residents of the community, particularly to those in dominant positions of power. Rather than acquiescing to the natural order of a community, leisure researchers are in a position to inquire and be part of social movements that provide additional layers of meaning to public memory. Because of a general lack of public discussion of social and cultural values, public memory is often assumed. Leisure professionals are often in roles conducive to organizing public forums with potential to identify social and cultural values to enhance public memory.

Enhancing public memory is about accumulating an additional layer of meaning to a public memory that is already "out there." Doing so may be framed as revising history and changing traditional values. An important objective for building public memory is to move the public dialogue from "my history" to "our history." Such strategies involve roles for leisure researchers that are distinct from traditional ones. Building public memory involves frameworks and research methods beyond standardized questionnaires and interviews. Scholarship that generates public discussion to enhance social justice is part of a value-based framework for leisure research. These new roles and distinct paradigms for science require eliciting public values for social justice, organizing forums to share and act upon these values, and developing strategies to represent these values and actions to build public memory for an inclusive society.

Discussion Questions

1. They say history is written by the winners. Can you relate this statement to the cowboy art Bill describes?

2. Part of what Bill is talking about is the wielding of power by a dominant culture over marginalized and oppressed groups as well as over the environment itself. Can you see how this might happen so subtly that it is easily overlooked? In such cases, who, in your opinion, is obliged to speak up and speak out for the disenfranchised and dispossessed?

3. Bill suggests there is a role for leisure researchers and practitioners to play in jostling the public's memory of the past, in helping to right wrongs and correct injustices. Examples of such efforts include changing the name of the Custer Battlefield in Montana to the Little Bighorn Battlefield, or in telling the story of Japanese Americans imprisoned at Manzanar in California during World War II. If you are familiar with these histories, discuss how they exemplify what Bill is talking about. If not, can you give other examples?

4. Bill talks about "palimpsests" of meaning. What does that word suggest about our interpretation of social and environmental justice over time?

5. What role, if any, should the park, recreation, and tourism profession play in jostling public memory in the interest of creating a more inclusive society?

SYNTHESIS

Philosophy as Leisure of the Most Vital Kind

Ed Barbanell
University of Utah

On the morning of the day that Venus was to pass across the face of the sun, the last such transit that would occur for over 100 years, I went out on my front porch to make sure that the solar viewing glasses I'd gotten from the planetarium the day before really worked and that I would not permanently blind my children by allowing them to watch the actual event when it unfolded later in the day. I put on the glasses and looked straight at the sun with wide-open, un-flinching eyes, encountering the solidity of that seemingly small yellow circle for the first time in my life. I then imagined in my mind's eye a much smaller black circle inexorably crawling across the sun's face. I felt myself being dragged into deeper contemplation about myriad tiny spheres whirling around in the vast emptiness, and about the infinite scale of time and space, and about the improbability of it all, until a self-inflicted vertigo overcame me, and I simply had to look away. As I took off the glasses and was turning back toward the door, vibrating air and buzzing wings and the familiar-yet-still-startling silhouette of a hummingbird snapped into my attention. I watched it dip down under the eaves of the porch and then rise up slightly to hang, suspended for just a second, before it dropped weightlessly onto the exposed inside corner of a column on the far end of the porch. Then the tiny bird settled itself into a small, whiteish, tightly woven circle of packed twigs that I hadn't noticed being before. I beheld—also for the first time in my life—a hummingbird's nest, with a hummingbird actually in it. I stood there, totally transfixed, mindful but unthinking, for what seemed like several moments, until the little bird flew off again to forage, I presume, and I, feeling giddy as a small child, rushed inside to tell everyone.

There is not much discussion of "leisure" in academic philosophy today. Within my own area of concentration—environmental philosophy—what little recent discussion there has been about it has focused primarily on its connotation of "recreation" in the context of the natural environment. As such, "nature" tends to be conceptualized as a playground: a place in which the only legitimate actions of human beings are for relatively benign recreational purposes. Real work, the modern forms of which are seen as always entailing pollution, defacement, and destruction, is not something we are supposed to inflict on nature. However, in terms of developing a broad-based and acceptable form of environmentalism, such an absolutist attitude about work, play, and nature is problematic. White, for instance, convincingly argued that environmentalists "must come to terms with work because its effects are so widespread and because work itself offers both a fundamental way of knowing nature and perhaps our deepest connection with the natural world."[1]

Moreover, outdoor recreationists—from rock climbers, to skiers, to white-water kayakers—have been frequenting evermore elaborate man-made playgrounds, which serve as safe, inexpensive, and convenient substitutes for the real thing. Besides the real damage that the construction of these facilities does, many people now worry that those whose primary contact with "nature" is conducted through blatantly artificial means will be incapable of developing meaningful environmental ethic. Within contemporary environmental philosophy, then, leisure, if it is considered at all, is done primarily in the guise of recreation, which is opposed to work, and the relationship—both conceptual and causal—among recreation, work, and nature in terms of environmental awareness, and activism is somewhat muddled and unsettled.

Although contemporary philosophers have little to say about leisure, this has not always been the case. Indeed, Aristotle in his major work *Politics* offered the view that leisure is the goal of life: It is the ultimate reason for which we otherwise work and live. The leisure with which Aristotle was concerned has nothing to do with recreation as characterized above. Nor, it should be said, was Aristotle talking about the "leisured life"—a material condition resembling what more recent commentators have labeled conspicuous leisure, neatly described as "the nonproductive consumption of time developed from a sense of the unworthiness of productive work and as evidence of pecuniary ability to afford a life of idleness."[2] Think *The Great Gatsby* or *Lifestyles of the Rich and Famous*. No, what Aristotle meant by leisure was contemplation, or the contemplative life, which is precisely the image of what philosophy is and what philosophers do. We work so that we may philosophize, and philosophy, then, is a kind of leisure.

Regardless of the context in which we use concepts such as work and leisure, and however we might differentiate and characterize them, they are supposed to denote two different things. However, with regard to Aristotle's formulation, we encounter a peculiar conundrum, because, in a not unimportant way, contemporary academic philosophers tend to think of their contemplations as requiring considerable time and effort; in other words, philosophizing is, and should be, a kind of intellectual work, which is precisely what leisure, on first blush, is not supposed to be. Standard dictionary definitions tend to reinforce this understanding: *contemplation* is described in terms such as *thoughtful deliberation* or *thorough consideration*, and *leisure* is cashed out in terms of *freedom from the demands of work* or otherwise filling up *unoccupied time*. Surely, I am deeply occupied in thoughtful and, hopefully, productive work when I am philosophizing. (As long as we're at it, leisure of the recreational sort certainly feels like work, especially when I'm lugging a 50-lb pack up a 20-degree slope on my 2-week annual vacation.) The way out of this apparent conundrum will lead us back to the scene with which I began this pondering, because within it, I believe, lies something vital, as opposed to something merely intellectually curious, about the very nature of contemplation itself, the nature of the philosophic act, and our relationship to the natural world.

The definitive modern philosophical treatment of leisure is still, 60 years after its initial publication, Pieper's *Leisure: The Basis of Culture*. It is a sustained critique of what Pieper saw as the primary anthropological and sociological problem of the still-current age: man conceptualized and idealized as a worker. As such, the Aristotelian formula gets turned on its head so that leisure becomes important only insofar as it can be used to bolster the effectiveness of man-the-worker. Pieper's most pointed accusation was aimed at philosophy itself, whose practitioners have, since the intellectual renaissance, come to conceive of themselves as intellectual workers. Analogous to the physical sciences, philosophers' pursuit of knowledge is, so they believe, only realized "in the act of comparing, examining, relating, distinguishing, abstracting, deducing, demonstrating—all of which are forms of active intellectual effort. Knowledge, man's spiritual, intellectual knowledge . . . is activity, exclusively activity."[3] Pieper argued, this is a mistaken view of the manner and mode in which humans go about learning the most important and profound things in their lives. He asked us to examine what transpires, for example, when we look at a rose:

> What do we do when we become aware of colour and form? Our soul is passive and receptive. We are, to be sure, awake and active, but our attention is not strained; we simply "look"—in so far, that is, as we "contemplate" it and are not already "observing" it (for "observing" implies that we are beginning to count, to measure and to weigh up). Observation is a tense activity. . . . To contemplate, on the other hand, to "look" in this sense, means to open one's eyes receptively to whatever offers itself to one's vision, the things seen enter into us, so to speak, without calling for any effort or strain on our part to possess them.[4]

There is a kind of knowledge that comes at a particular point on the path between "seeing" and "observing"; this moment of contemplation is an awareness, a receptivity that happens when we are ready to hear and to allow the world to enter into us, before we analyze and categorize the input, changing it irrevocably from phenomena into data. The ancients, including Aristotle, understood that contemplation of this sort—the leisure to which the rest of our living and doing is ideally aimed—was a particularly vital kind of knowing because through it, as opposed to the kind of active knowing that allows us to manipulate and anticipate and construct objects in the world, we learn important truths about ourselves as enlightened and spiritual beings. Pieper's lament was that modern philosophy has abandoned the kind of knowing that leads to true insight and wisdom, and it has taken, instead, the scientific path to knowledge, where the truths uncovered may well have an instrumental value yet yield nothing in the way of self-awareness.

The kind of looking and listening essential to this way of profound knowledge-of-ourselves-in-the-world requires certain material conditions. Certainly, time is one of those, time considered as freedom from the relentless pursuit of the necessities that we otherwise need to survive in the world. In this sense, conversant with the dictionary definition, time otherwise unoccupied is the first condition of leisure; leisure actually is time. We can also say that quietude and calmness are necessary characteristics of such leisure time, when our receptivity to the world is most likely to be tuned to the right frequencies. In addition to time, leisure requires a certain attitude or state of mind (mindfulness); stillness and meditation come to the fore as quintessential aspects of leisure-as-contemplation. In the context of our busy lives, those not engaged in regular forms of meditation associate such time/silence/mindfulness to special days and places, such as worshipping on holy days. Indeed, Pieper's ultimate charge against modern philosophy was that it has lost its access to true insight and wisdom because it has abandoned theology and theological epiphany as legitimate sources of knowledge, and reconnecting the philosophical with the theological is one way to cure the malady of the total worker in the modern world.

The idea that religious observance can be a corrective palliative to our work-obsessed, technologically driven society has also been echoed by Anderson. In discussing why until recently Catholics took seriously the prohibition against working on Sundays, he wrote:

> Holy days, and that included Sundays, were days where people, freed from their service to the machine, could enjoy leisure. . . . They were days on which humans, like the Creator, could delight in the goodness and beauty of a world charged with the grandeur of God.[5]

Although a mass return to the fold, as it were, is not a likely outcome, we who spend much of our working days talking to students about the various ways we can and should engage with our natural environments have in common with them a church of sorts, though we are loathe to overtly characterize it as such. Among the things we find in the leisure of our time in nature—in the silent times of mindful receptivity—is a world revealed, of beauty and grandeur, infused with a vibrancy and vitality that is otherwise missing in our workaday world. Nature may have an intrinsic value that should be preserved and protected for its own sake, and it certainly has a particular value for us humans, which is to allow us to find, in the delightful giddiness it sometimes offers us as a gift, the essence of our humanness once again.

As it happened, my children never did get to see the transit of Venus that day because clouds obscured the sky when the event actually happened, though we could—and did—see tons of pictures of it on the Internet the next day. As it turned out, my sons were not interested in seeing the transit happen anyway because their teachers at school had explained to them, in excruciating detail how and why it happened, using models and charts, so they understood all that they thought they needed to about it. We sometimes mistake rareness for specialness and look to the stars for our inspiration, when what we desire is so close and commonplace that it often passes by unnoticed.

But every morning now for well over a month, the first thing my children do—that we all do, if the truth be told—is look to see if the baby hummingbirds have hatched. I am pretty sure my children understand how and why that happens too, but still they look, every day, as do I, all of us still and quiet for a moment or two, usually the only waking moments my young children are thus engaged, not because we desire confirmation of the outcome of certain causes and their effects, but simply because doing so makes us feel more alive and connected to our worlds—the one outside as well as the one inside each of us.

This book is the outcome of a first-of-its-kind symposium about working for social and environmental justice through parks, recreation, tourism and leisure. In that vein, certain things seem to follow from the observations I have offered. Often, leisure is thought of as something that happens away from the places where people usually are, such as their homes and neighborhoods, and sometimes in places typically far away, such as wilderness areas and national parks. On top of this, people seem most concerned about the recreational qualities of leisure. Accordingly, the justice aspects of leisure have tended to manifest themselves in discussions about the availability of specialized equipment and admittance to unaccommodating facilities for marginalized groups who have historically not had ready access to such things. But if the leisure to contemplate the serendipity of nature is as conducive to the ennoblement of the human spirit as I've made it out to be, then working for such justice needs happen closer to home and in more pedestrian ways: In neglected urban areas, parks need to be rehabilitated and trees replanted and waterways cleaned up, so that nature may return and present itself to the people who need ennoblement the most.

Recognizing this—and environmental ethicists and activists are equally if not more at fault here than those in leisure studies—we need to stop fetishizing "unspoiled" places as the only loci for an authentic experience of nature. The legacy we acolytes have inherited from the likes of Henry David Thoreau and John Muir tends to make us venerate untrammeled nature and view with disdain any places infested with vestiges of humans and their accoutrements. This is an atavistic and romantic notion that, as Pollan has so aptly put it, "may have taught us how to worship nature, but it didn't tell us how to live with her. It told us more than we needed to know about virginity and rape, and almost nothing about marriage."[6] Any practical path to a broadly acceptable environmentalism means coming to terms with humans' presence in the world, including those places we most densely inhabit.

Making nature accessible to everyone is a form of social justice because the opportunities it affords for self-enlightenment are vital for reaching our maximum potential as thoughtful, caring human beings. This might mean working to protect places where we, who can afford to, can go for our leisure, such as nature parks and wilderness areas, but more important it means working to reenliven and reimagine the places where people actually work and live because that is where most people are most of the time. Only then will we start seeing such places as true and proper homes, where we live with nature on an ongoing, contemplative, and leisurely basis.

Notes

Chapter 1: What Will Become of Our Twenty Grandchildren?

1. The World Conservation Union estimates that of the 40,000 species it tracks, 40% are threatened or endangered. Opinionator, *New York Times*, 2/10/12.

2. On its 2005 Environmental Sustainability Index, Yale and Columbia University researchers ranked all the world's nations on 75 measures: maintaining air and water quality, limiting greenhouse gas emissions, cooperating in international environmental initiatives, etc. The U.S. ranked 45th, just ahead of Belarus, Ghana, Myanmar, and Slovakia. Highest on sustainability scores were Finland, Norway, Uruguay, Sweden, and Iceland. www.yale.edu/esi.

3. Including the Civil Rights acts of 1964 and 1968, and especially the 1965 Voting Right Act; attacking poverty, indirectly with Head Start, the Elementary and Secondary Education Act, and Job Corps and directly, with Medicaid, food stamps (now SNAP), and aid to families with dependent children (now TANF), and benefits delivered through the tax code.

4. OECD, 2012, April, Development Statics Online. Rodman, David, 2004, Center for Global Development, Index of Donor Performance. Also: www.globalissues.org/article/35 and www.fair.org/index.php?page=2676.

5. Mowatt, R., Johnson, C., Roberts, N., & Kivel, D. Embarrassingly White: Changing the 'Color' of Higher Education in Parks, Recreation, Tourism, and Leisure. Presentation delivered at the 1st International Symposium on Speaking Up and Speaking Out: Working for Social and Environmental Justice through Parks, Recreation, Tourism and Leisure," May 18, 2012, Salt Lake City, UT: University of Utah.

6. Though perhaps awkward, this posits the public and the private sectors as institutions, currently at the heart of polemics bringing the government to a standstill. Religious organizations stand in for charities here since, as a practical matter, churches receive 35% of all charitable giving. Very little of that 35% goes directly to help the poor. Only about 12% of all charitable giving aids the poor in any direct sense. See note 24 below.

7. This was historian Tony Judt's view, which I share. The act's promoters assumed a booming economy forever while insulting millions of hard workers who never had a decent chance to get ahead. Peter Edelman, a highly regarded member of the administration's staff and husband of "Children's Defense Fund" director, Marion Wright-Edelman, resigned in protest.

8. Rattner, Steven. (2012 -3/12). The Rich Get Even Richer. Op-Ed, *New York Times*.

9. A good, accessible source for "Gini Index" is Wikipedia, both for a definition and the data noted here, which were derived from the most recent OECD calculations. Check the footnotes for Divided We Stand: Why Inequality keeps Growing – ISBN 978-92-64-11163-9. http://en.wikipedia.org/Wiki/List_of_countries_by_income_equality.

10. Bartels, Larry. 2008. *Unequal Democracy: The Political Economy of the New Guilded Age.* Princeton, NJ. Princeton University Press. Bartels observed that the middle 1/3rd of income earners had some but not much influence, and that the lion's share of influence was exerted by the 1/3rd of households in the top 1/3rd of the population. That does not come as a surprise.

11. These numbers were rounded to the nearest whole number. They are among 2010 census data summarized nicely by the national Poverty Center, University of Michigan. It is revealing that children under 18 are 22% of the population, but 36% of those living in poverty. It is also revealing that the poverty rate was 11.1% in 1973, 11.3% in 2000 and 15.1% in 2010. It is not just the recent/current recession as the rate has been trending upward since 1980. http://www.npc.umich.edu/poverty/#5.

12. Yen, Hope. 2011 (12/16). Census Shows 1 in 2 people are poor or low-income. Associated Press. At Google.com/hostednews/ap/article.

13. This is based on WHO's Human Development Index score of .9 on a scale of zero to 1. Countries with universal health care are listed, among other places, at: http://truecostblog.com/2009/08/09/countries-with-universal-healthcare-by-date

14. Of the eight component criteria (four measures of poverty, the Gini coefficient, pre-primary education, health care, intergenerational transfers), the U.S. was among the bottom five countries on four criteria, bottom 10 on three, and 11th from the bottom on one. Social Justice in the OECD – How Do The Member States Compare? Sustainable Government Indicators, 2011. At: http://www.sgi-network.org/pdf/SGI11_Social_Justice_OECD.pdf

15. Child Well-being in Rich Countries. United Nations, Innocenti Research Center – Report Card #7. The U.S ranked no better than 17th of 21 on five of the 6 criteria, 12th on the remaining one. Http://.unicef-irc.org/publications/pdf/rc7_eng.pdf.

16. The word "more" indicates that countries such as Albania, Ukraine, Serbia and others were included. Besides ranking 25th for mothers, the ranking for women was 19, but for children – 31. A live link to the full report, State of the World's Mothers 2012 is at: hppt://www.savethechildren.org/site/c8rKLIXMGIPI4E/B.6153061/k.AOBD/Publications. Htm. If keying in such strings is frustrating, simply search for State of the World's Children 2012 and any of a number of sites will get you to the full report.

17. Re: maternal mortality, the U.S. rate is 7 times higher than Italy and Ireland, 15 times higher than Greece. Re: under age 5 mortality, the U.S. rate is double that of nine countries, including the five Scandinavian and Northern European countries always at or near the top. Re: Pre-School enrollments, the percent of U.S. 3-5 year olds in pre-school is 57%, the international average is 77%, and in several countries all children that age are enrolled in pre-school. Paid maternity leave is guaranteed in 178 countries and in 50 paternity leave is also paid. California, New Jersey, Washington state and D.C. have paid maternity leave. Re: political status: In the U.S. Congress women occupy 17% of the seats; they occupy 45% in Sweden, 43% in Iceland.

18. Warren Buffet, "The Sage of Omaha," said, "The 20-year class war is over, and my class won."

19. Chesterton, G. K. (1908) *The man who was Thursday: A nightmare.* New York: Dodd, Mead, & Co.

20. Johnston, David Cay. (2003). *Perfectly legal.* New York: The Penguin Group. See also: Johnston, David Cay. 2007. *Free Lunch.* New York: The Penguin Group.

21. This is not hyperbole. See Wieners, Bradford. 2012 (May 7-13) Tuesdays with Clayton. *Bloomberg Businessweek.* Included the description, "Harvard Business School's Clay Christiansen taught corporate executives how to kill before getting killed in business. Then in the Sunday, May 27, 2012, *New York Times* Sunday Business Section, Azam Ahmed's lead article is entitled, "The Hunch, The Pounce And the Kill." It's about the two billion dollar loss J.P. Morgan Chase took in May 2012 and a very, very rich hedge fund manager currently in talks to buy a $24 million co-op on Fifth Avenue.

22. Gorry, Anthony. 2009 (8/31). Empathy in the Virtual World. The Chronicle Review, *The Chronicle of Higher Education.*

23. "… youth who age out of DSS (Department of Social Services) are still at considerable risk, particularly for homelessness, significant mental health needs, early pregnancy, physical violence, and unwanted sexual contact." The Boston Foundation. 2008. *Preparing Our Kids for Education, Work and Life: A Report of the Task Force on Youth Aging Out of DSS Care.*

24. Most of the data is about father absent households. We will probably find that gender is not so much the issue as having two parents able to devote some of their time to child rearing. We all know gay and lesbian couples raising children very successfully.

25. Women's Health USA 2010 reports general household consumption data at: http://mchb.hrsa.gov/whusa10/popchar/pages/103hc.html? To the findings on births to unwed mothers is the additional challenge of racial differences; among White mothers, 29% of births are to unwed mothers, among Hispanic mothers 53%, among Black mothers 73%. Besides data on births to unwed mothers is a plethora of data on premature births, which is obviously related and which is rooted in poverty and in lack of adequate health care. C.f: http://www.nytimes.com/2012/02/18/us/for-women-under-30-most-births-occur-outside-marriage.html Cf. also: http://www.who.int/pmnch/media/news/2012/2012_04_borntoosoon-execsum-eng.pdf.

26. A brief overview of recent charitable giving data is at: http://www.nps.gov/partnerships/fundraising_individuals_statistics.htm. For a general overview of the topic see the chapter by Havens, John, et.al. 2006. Charitable Giving: How Much, by Whom, to What, and How. In: Powell, Walter and Steinberg, Richard. 2006. *The Non-Profit Sector: a Research Handbook.* Yale Press. For greater detail see: Tax Policy Center of the Congressional Budget Office, Giving USA, Center on Philanthropy at Indiana University, Empty Tomb, Inc., Boston College

Center on Wealth and Philanthropy, and Charity Navigator. Examples of church benevolence aspirations and realities see: Your Church's Budget and Why it May Grieve the Lord at: http://ceruleansanctum.com/2011/08/your-churchs-budget-and-why-it-may-grieve-the-lord.html. For a current, moderately well-heeled church's budget, hopefully representative of a data pool, see: 2012 Church Ministry Action Plan at: http://www.fbcrichmond.org/stewardship/budget.htm. For a comment on why charity can't do it (feed the hungry) alone go to: http://notes.bread.org/2012/05/charity-can't-do-it-aloneby-vicki-escarra.html.

27.   Catholic charitiesusa.org/snapshotsurveyq32010. Further, contrary to popular belief, the U.S. is not overly generous with its foreign aid. As a portion of Gross National Income, the U.S. ranks 19th among developed nations.

28.   Giving USA. 2011 The Annual Report on Philanthropy. Available at: www.givingusareports.org

29.   Polarized America. 2012 At: voteview.com. Based on research by Howard Rosenthal and Keith Poole in affiliation with the Department of Political Science, Univ. of Georgia.

30.   C.f. Saez, Immanuel and Piketty, Thomas. 2006 (May). The Evolution of Top Incomes: Measuring and Interpreting Trends in Economic Inequality. *Papers and Proceedings, American Economics Association, 92*:2. Pp. 200-205. Piketty, Thomas and Saez, Emmanuel. 2003. Income Inequality in the United States, 1913 – 1998. *Quarterly Journal of Economics, 118*:1. Pp. 1-39.

31.   The Great Gatsby Curve. 2012 (1/16) *New York Times.*

32.   Wilkinson, R., & Pickett, K. (2009). *The spirit level: Why greater equality makes societies stronger.* NY: Bloomsbury Press.

33.   Acemoglu, D., & Robinson, J. (2012). *Why nations fail: The origins of power, prosperity, and poverty.* NY: Crown Publishers.

34.   Porter, E. 2012 (3/20). Inequality Undermines Democracy. Economic Scene, *New York Times.*

35.   Piff, Stancato, Cote, Mendoza-Denton, & Keltner. (2012). Higher social class predicts increased unethical behavior. *Proceedings of the National Academy of Sciences* (early edition on line). www.pnas.org/cgi/doi/10.1073/pnas.1118373109.

36.   Edelman, P. (1987). The Next Century of Our Constitution: Rethinking Our Duty to the Poor. *The Hastings Law Journal,* Vol. 39, November: pp.1-61.

Chapter 2: At Whose Expense? How Our Commitment to Conservation Has Propagated Social Injustice

1.   Cited in Ruffins, P. (1990). Mixing a Few More Colors into the Green. Originally published in *Sustainability* (IC #25); available online at http://www.context.org/iclib/ic25/about25/

2.   Cronan, W. (1995). The Trouble with Wilderness; or, Getting Back to the Wrong Nature. In William Cronon (Ed.), *Uncommon ground: Rethinking the human place in nature* (pp. 69-90). New York: W. W. Norton & Co.

3.   Cronan, p. 76.

4.   DeLuca, K., & Demo, A. (2001). Imagining Nature and Erasing Class and Race: Carleton Watkins, John Muir, and the Construction of Wilderness. *Environmental History, 6,* p. 541-560.

5.   DeLuca & Demo, p. 544.

6.   Loc cit., p. 546.

7.   Cronan, p. 73.

8.   Cited in DeLuca & Demo, p. 554.

9.   Dussias, A. M. (2000). Cultural Conflicts Regarding Land Use: The Conflict Between Recreational Users at Devil's Tower and Native American Ceremonial Users. *Vermont Journal of Environmental Law,* 2. Downloaded from http://www.vjel.org/journal/VJEL10005.html.

10. Dussias, p. 2.

11. Spence, M. D. (1999). *Dispossessing the wilderness: Indian removal and the making of the national parks* (p. 139). New York: Oxford University Press.

12. Dowie, M. (2009). *Conservation refugees: The hundred-year conflict between global conservation and native peoples.*

13. Samdahl, D. M. (2011). What can American Beach teach us? Complicity in race, class, and power. In K. Paisley, K. & D. Dustin (Eds.), *Speaking up and speaking out: Working for social and environmental justice through parks, recreation, and leisure* (pp. 83-93). Urbana, IL: Sagamore.

14. Glanton, D. (2001). Gullah Culture in Danger of Fading Away. *National Geographic News.* Available online at http://news.nationalgeographic.com/news/pf/42120361.html

15. DeLuca & Demo, p. 542.

Chapter 3: Beyond the Right to Inclusion: The Intersection of Social and Environmental Justice for Inclusion of Individuals with Disabilities in Leisure

1. Alston, R., Harley, D., & Middleton, R. (2006). The role of rehabilitation in achieving social justice for minorities with disabilities. *Journal of Vocational Rehabilitation, 24,* 129-136.

2. Farrington, J., & Farrington, C. (2005). Rural accessibility, social inclusion and social justice: towards conceptualization. *Journal of Transport Geography, 13,* 1-12.

3. Alston et al.

4. Sylvester, C. (1992). Therapeutic recreation and the right to leisure. *Therapeutic Recreation Journal, 26*(2), 9-20.

5. Loc cit., p. 10.

6. Farrington & Farrington.

7. Ibid.

8. Emira & Thompson (2011).

9. Silva, C., & Howe, P. (2012). Difference, adapted physical activity and human development: Potential contribution of capabilities approach. *Adapted Physical Activity Quarterly, 29,* 25-43.

10. Ibid.

11. Robinson, J., & Godbey, G. (1997). *Time for life: The surprising ways Americans use their time.* The Pennsylvania State University Press: State College, PA.

12. Bedini, L., & Henderson, K. (1994). Women with disabilities and he challenges to leisure services providers. *Journal of Park and Recreation Administration, 12*(1), 17-34.

13. Smith, R., Austin, D., & Kennedy, D. (2001). *Inclusive and special recreation: Opportunities for persons with disabilities* (4th ed.). McGraw Hill: Boston.

14. Loewen, G., & Pollard, W. (2010). The social justice perspective. *Journal of Postsecondary Education and Disability, 23,* 5-17.

15. Smart, J. (2001). *Disability, society, and the individual.* Gaithersburg, MD: Aspen.

16. Silva & Rowe.

17. Alston et al.

18. Smart.

19. Alston et al.

20. Nussbaum, M. (2006). *Frontiers of justice: Disability, nationality, species membership*. Cambridge, MA: Belknap Press.

21. Sylvester, C. (2011). Therapeutic recreation, the International Classification of Functioning, Disability, and Health, and the Capability Approach. *Therapeutic Recreation Journal, 45,* 85-104.

22. Oliver, M. (1990). *The politics of disablement: A sociological approach*. New York: St. Martins Press.

23. Emira, M., & Thompson, D. (2011). In the quest for their trust: the perceptions of families on accessing leisure services for disabled children. *Leisure Studies, 30*:1, 33-48.

24. Vehmas, S. (2004). Dimensions of disability. *Cambridge Quarterly of Healthcare Ethics, 13,* 34-40.

25. Van Puymbroek, M., Porter, H., & McCormick, B. (2009). The international classification of functioning, disability, and health in therapeutic recreation practice. In N. Stumbo (Ed.), *Professional issues in therapeutic recreation* (pp. 43-57). Urbana, IL: Sagamore.

26. Emira & Thompson.

27. World Health Organization. (2001). *International classification of functioning, disability, and health*. Geneva, Switzerland: World Health Organization.

28. Nevel, K. (2010). Down syndrome and aging: A leadership and social justice landscape. *Journal of Cultural Diversity, 17*(1), 34-38.

29. Ibid.

30. Tollefsen, C. (2010). Disability and social justice. In C. D. Ralston & J. Ho (Eds.), *Philosophical reflections on disability* (pp. 211-228). New York: Springer.

31. Ibid.

32. Cutter, S. (1993). *Living with risk: The geography of technological hazards*. London: Edward Arnold.

33. Loc cit., p. 111.

34. Abel, T., & Stephan, M. (2008). Tools of environmental justice and meaningful involvement. *Environmental Practice, 10,* 152-163.

35. Ibid.

36. Mohai, P., & Bryant, B. (1992). Environmental racism: Reviewing the evidence. In B. Bryant, B. & P. Mohai (Eds.), *Race and the incidence of environmental hazards: A time for discourse* (pp. 163-176). Boulder, CO: Westview Press.

37. Charles, A., & Thomas, H. (2007). Deafness and disability: Forgotten components of environmental justice: Illustrated by the case of Local Agenda 21 in South Wales. *Local Environment, 12, 3,* 209-221.

38. Lucas, K. (2006). Providing transport for social inclusion within a framework for environmental justice in the UK. *Transportation Research, 40,* 801-809.

39. Ibid.

40. Rose, J. (2011). Are social and environmental justice incompatible ideals? In K. Paisley & D. Dustin (Eds.), *Speaking up and speaking out: Working for social and environmental justice through parks, recreation, and leisure* (pp. 135-142). Urbana, IL: Sagamore.

41. Nussbaum.

42. Berger, P. L., & Luckmann, T. (1966). *The social construction of reality.* University of Chicago Press.

43. Charles, A. (2004). Limits to the 'greening of society': The experience of the Deaf community in the UK. Unpublished dissertation, Cardiff University.

44. Charles & Thomas.

45. Nussbaum.

46. Loewen & Pollard.

47. Nussbaum.

48. Tollefsen.

49. Kivel, B. (2011). What does society need done and how can we do it? In K. Paisley & D. Dustin (Eds.), *Speaking up and speaking out: Working for social and environmental justice through parks, recreation, and leisure* (pp. 9-14). Urbana, IL: Sagamore.

50. Foreman, P., & Arthur-Kelly, M. (2008). Social justice principles, the law, and research as the bases for inclusion. *Australasian Journal of Special Education, 32*(1), 109-124.

51. Devine, M. (2012). A nationwide look at inclusion: Gains and gaps. *Journal of Park and Recreation Administration, 30*, 1-18.

52. Rose.

53. Loewen & Pollard.

54. Tollefsen.

55. Loewen & Pollard.

56. Nussbaum.

57. Tollefsen.

58. Ibid.

59. Nussbaum.

60. Silva & Howe.

61. Ibid.

62. Ibid.

63. Ibid.

64. Sylvester.

65. Nussbaum.

66. Dantley, M., & Tillman, L. (2006). Social justice and moral transformative leadership. In C. Marshall & M. Olivia (Eds.), *Leadership for social justice: Making revolutions in education* (pp. 16-30). Boston: Allyn & Bacon.

67. Devine, M., & Parr, M. (2008). Social capital and inclusive leisure contexts: A good fit or dichotomous? *Leisure Sciences, 30*, 391-408.

68. Disability Funders Network. (2009). Disability statistics and figures. Retrieved on March 31, 2011 from http://www.disabilityfunders.org/disability-stats-and-facts.

69. Nussbaum.

Chapter 4: Meeting at the Crossroads: Progress for Multiracial People or Delicate Balance amidst Old Divides?

1.   Harris, D. R., & Sim, J. J. (2002). Who is Multiracial? Assessing the Complexity of Lived Race. *American Sociological Review, 67*, 614-627.

2.   American Community Survey. (2009). Data release 2009. Retrieved 30 April 2012 from http://www.census.gov/acs/

3.   Pew Research Center. (2010). One in Seven New U.S. Marriages is Interracial or Interethnic. Retrieved June 28, 2012 from http://www.pewsocialtrends.org/files/2010/10/755-marrying-out.pdf

4.   Associated Press. (2010, May 26). "Black-white marriages triple over last three decades." *The Grio.* Retrieved 25 June 2012 from http://thegrio.com/2010/05/26/interracial-marriage-more-likely-between-black-and-white/

5.   Ibid.

6.   Gramann, J. H. (1996). "Ethnicity, race, and outdoor recreation: A review of trends, policy, and research." Vicksburg, MS, U.S. Army Engineer Waterways Experiment Station.

7.   Rodriguez, D. A., & Roberts, N.S. (2000, Fall). *State of the knowledge report: The association of race/ethnicity, gender, and social class in outdoor recreation experiences.* Fort Collins, CO, Colorado State University. Produced for the National Park Service Social Science Division. Available http://www.nature.nps.gov/socialscience/products.cfm

8.   Sasidharan, V. (2002). Special issue introduction: Understanding recreation and the environment within the context of culture. *Leisure Sciences, 24*, 1-11.

9.   Floyd, M. F., & Shinew, K. J. (1999). Convergence and divergence in leisure style among Whites and African Americans: Toward an interracial contact hypothesis. *Journal of Leisure Research, 31*, 359-384.

10.   Shinew, K. J., Glover, T. D., & Parry, D. C. (2004). Leisure spaces as potential sites for interracial interaction: Community gardens in urban areas. *Journal of Leisure Research, 36*, 336-355.

11.   Hibbler, D. K., & Shinew, K. J. (2002a). Interracial couples experience of leisure: A social construction of a racialized other. *Journal of Leisure Research, 34*, 135-156.

12.   Hibbler, D. K., & Shinew, K. J. (2002b). Moving beyond our comfort zone: The role of leisure service providers in enhancing multiracial families leisure experiences. *Parks and Recreation, 37*(2), 26-35.

13.   Roberts, N. S., & Chitewere, T. (2011). Speaking of justice: Exploring ethnic minority perspectives of the Golden Gate National Recreation Area. *Environmental Practice, 13*(4), 1-16.

14.   Roberts, N. S. (2010). "What Are You, Anyway? From Tea at High Noon to Curry and Masala Dosa: How Identity and Experience Interact to Challenge the System." In K. Paisley & D. Dustin (Eds.), *Speaking up/speaking out: Working for social and environmental justice through parks, recreation, and leisure* (pp. 32-40). Urbana, IL: Sagamore.

15.   Root, M. P. P. (1996). (Ed). *The multiracial experience: Racial borders as the new frontier.* Thousand Oaks, CA: SAGE, p. 14.

16.   U.S. Census. (2011, March). *Population distribution and change: 2000 to 2010.* United States Government Printing Office, C2010BR-01. Washington, DC: Census Briefs 2010, p. 4.

17.   Johnson, A. D. (2006). In 2050, half of U.S. will be people of color. Retrieved June 24, 2012 from http://www.diversityinc.com/public/311.cfm

18.   U.S. Census. (2011, March). *Overview of race and Hispanic origin: 2010.* United States Government Printing Office, C2010BR-02 Washington, DC: Census Briefs 2010, p. 22.

19.   Johnson.

20. Ibid.

21. U.S. Census (2011, March). *Overview of Race and Hispanic Origin: 2010.*

22. Ibid.

23. Price, A. (2010). Chart: The Encouraging Rise of Interracial Marriage. Retrieved June 28, 2012 from http://www.good.is/post/chart-the-encouraging-rise-of-interracial-marriage/

24. Ibid.

25. Ibid.

26. Pew Research Center.

27. Ibid, p. 5.

28. Ibid, p. 6.

29. *USA Today.* (2007). Interracial marriages surge across U.S. Retrieved from http://www.usatoday.com/news/health/2007-04-12-interracial-marriage_N.htm

30. Corrin, W. J., & Cook, T. D. (1999). "Spanning Racial Boundaries: Multiracial Adolescents and Their Families, Peers, Schools, and Neighborhoods." Working Paper No. 99-20, Institute for Policy Research, Northwestern University, Evanston, IL.

31. Davis, J. F. (1991). *Who s black? One nation's definition.* University Park, PA: Pennsylvania State University Press.

32. Goldstein, J. R., & Morning, A. J. (2000). "The Multiple-Race Population of the United States: Issues and Estimates." *Proceedings of the National Academy of Sciences, 97,* 6230-35.

33. Harris & Sim.

34. Hirschman, C., Alba, R., & Reynolds, F. (2000). The Meaning and Measurement of Race in the U.S. Census: Glimpses into the Future. *Demography, 37,* 381-93.

35. Kao, G. (1999). Racial Identity and Academic Performance: An Examination of Biracial Asian and African Youth. *Journal of Asian American Studies, 2,* 223-49.

36. Tafoya, S. M. (2000). "Check One or More ... Mixed Race and Ethnicity in California." *California Counts,* pp. 1-11.

37. Twine, F. W. (1996). Heterosexual alliances: The romantic management of racial identity. In M. Root (Ed.), *The multiracial experience: Racial borders as the new frontier* (pp. 291-304). Thousand Oaks: SAGE.

38. Xie, Y., & Goyette, K. (1998). The Racial Identification of Biracial Children with One Asian Parent: Evidence from the 1990 Census. *Social Forces, 76,* 547-70.

39. Harris & Sim.

40. Ibid.

41. Ibid.

42. Nobles, M. (2000). *Shades of citizenship: Race and the census in modern politics.* Stanford, CA: Stanford University Press.

43. Office of Management and Budget (OMB). (1997). "Revision to the Standards for the Classification of Federal Data on Race and Ethnicity." *Federal Register,* October 30, 1997, 62(210).

44. Harris & Sim, p. 617.

45.   Ibid, p. 624.

46.   Ibid.

47.   Eschbach, K. (1995). The Enduring and Vanishing American Indian: American Indian Population Growth and Intermarriage in 1990. *Ethnic and Racial Studies, 18*, 89-108.

48.   Harris, D. R. (1994). The 1990 Census Count of American Indians: What Do the Numbers Really Mean? *Social Science Quarterly, 75*, 580-93.

49.   Harris & Sim.

50.   Snipp, C. M. (1997). Some Observations about Racial Boundaries and the Experiences of American Indians. *Ethnic and Racial Studies, 20*, 667-89.

51.   Associated Press. (2010, May 26).

52.   Ibid.

53.   Harris & Sim.

54.   Demo, D. H. (1992). The Self-Concept Over Time: Research Issues and Directions. *Annual Review of Sociology, 18*, 303-26.

55.   Harris & Sim.

56.   Ibid.

57.   Telles, E. E., & Lim, N. (1998). Does It Matter Who Answers the Race Question? Racial Classification and Income Inequality in Brazil. *Demography, 35*, 465-74.

58.   Hibbler & Shinew, 2002b, p. 29.

59.   Ibid.

60.   Hibbler, D. K. (2000). Interracial couples experience of leisure: A social construction of a racialized other. Unpublished Doctoral Dissertation, University of Illinois, Urbana, Champaign.

61.   Ibid, p. 53.

62.   Hibbler & Shinew, 2002b.

63.   Jackson, E. L. (2000). Will Research on Leisure Constraints Still be Relevant in the Twenty-First Century? *Journal of Leisure Research, 32*(1), 62-68.

64.   Philips, S. F. (1995). Race and leisure constraints. *Leisure Sciences, 17*, 109-120.

65.   Roberts, N. S., & Rodriguez, D. A. (2008). Use of multiple methods: An examination of constraints effecting ethnic minority visitor use of national parks and management implications. *Ethnic Studies Review 31*(2), 35-70.

66.   Shinew, K. J., Floyd, M. F., & Parry, D. (2004). Understanding the Relationship between Race and Leisure Activities and Constraints: Exploring an Alternative Framework. *Leisure Sciences 26*, 181-199.

67.   Washburne, R. F. (1978). Black Under-Participation in Wildland Recreation: Alternative Explanations. *Leisure Sciences, 1*, 175-189.

68.   National Parks Conservation Association. (n.d.) "The National Parks Community Partners Program," Cultural Diversity and the National Parks, Working Together for Change. Washington, DC: NPCA.

69.   Roberts & Chitewere.

70.   Ibid.

71.   Roberts, N. S. (2008, December). "Use of Public Lands and Open Space for Recreation: Connecting with Diverse Communities." In D. Newsom & B. Gentry (Eds.), *Broadening the base through open space: Addressing demographic trends by saving land and serving people.* Yale Conservation Strategies Workshop Proceedings, July 9-11, 2008, Monterey, CA.

72.   Ibid.

73.   Ibid.

74.   USDA Forest Service 2001.

75.   Roberts, 2008.

76.   USDA Forest Service. (1998, March). *Unlocking the barriers: Keys to communicating with underserved customers.* Washington, DC: USDA Forest Service, Office of Communications, Office of Outreach.

77.   Roberts, N. S. (2007). Golden Gate National Recreation Area: Visitor/Non-visitor Use Constraints: Exploring Ethnic Minority Experiences and Perspectives. *Technical Report prepared for the Golden Gate National Recreation Area and the Golden Gate National Parks Conservancy.* San Francisco, 60 pp. Available at http://bit.ly/WvL0v6

78.   Sachatello-Sawyer, B., & Fenyvesi, S. (2004, Winter). Reaching out with respect: Environmental education with underserved communities. *Clearing Magazine, 115,* 1-4.

79.   Hibbler & Shinew, 2002b.

80.   Ibid, p. 32.

81.   Roberts & Chitewere.

82.   Jacobson, S. K., McDuff, M. D., & Monroe, M. (2006). *Conservation education and outreach techniques.* New York: Oxford University Press.

83.   Harris & Sim, p. 625.

84.   Gwaltney, B. (2006). What is cultural competence? Unpublished paper. Denver, CO: U.S. National Park Service, p. 1.

85.   Gorski, P. C. (2010, September). "Beyond Celebrating Diversity: Twenty Things I Can Do to Be a Better Multicultural Educator." *EdChange: Professional development, research, and resources for multiculturalism, & cultural competence.* Retrieved 27 June 2012 from http://www.edchange.org.

86.   California Newsreel. (2003). RACE–The Power of an Illusion: Ten Things Everyone Should Know About Race. Retrieved 26 June 2012 from http://www.newsreel.org/guides/race/10things.htm

87.   Hibbler & Shinew, 2002b.

88.   Roberts, 2008.

89.   Roberts & Chitewere, p. 366.

90.   Johnson, C. Y., Bowker, J. M., Bergstrom, J. C., & Cordell, K. (2004). Wilderness Values in America: Does Immigrant Status or Ethnicity Matter? *Society and Natural Resources, 17,* 611-628.

91.   Roberts & Chitewere.

Chapter 5: Ecofeminism (s) and Just Leisure in the 21st Century

1.   Firestone, S. (1971). *The dialectic of sex.* New York: Bantam Books.

2.   Daly, M. (1978). *Gynecology: The metaethics of radical feminism.* Boston: Beacon Press.

3.   Henderson, K., & Bialeschki, M. (1990-91). Ecofeminism: Recreation as if nature and woman mattered. *Leisure Information Quarterly, 17*(1), p. 1.

4.   Henderson, K., & Bialeschki, M. (1995). Exploring ecofeminism, recreation, and leisure. *World Leisure and Recreation Association Journal, 37*(2), 41-45.

5.   Henderson, K. (1997a). Ecofeminism and experiential education. *Journal of Experiential Education, 20*(3), 130-133.

6.   Henderson, K. (1997b). Just recreation: Ethics, gender, and equity. *Journal of Park and Recreation Administration, 15*(2), 16-31.

7.   Henderson, K. (2000). Just leisure, ethical fitness, and ecophilosophical issues. In M. McNamee, C. Jennings, & M. Reeves (Eds.), *Just leisure: Policy, ethics, and professionalism* (pp. 93-104). Leisure Studies Association Publication No. 17: Eastbourne, UK.

8.   Fox, K. (1994). Negotiating in a world of change: Ecofeminist guideposts for leisure scholarship. *Journal of Leisure Research, 26*(1), 39-56.

9.   Eaton, H. (2006). Pathways to ecofeminism. *Catholic New Times, 30*(2), 10-16.

10.   Henderson & Bialeschki, 1990-91.

11.   Plant, J. (Ed.). (1989). *Healing the wounds: The promise of ecofeminism.* Philadelphia: New Society Publishers.

12.   Warren, K. (1990). The power and promise of ecological feminism. *Environmental Ethics, 12*, 125-146.

13.   Gaard, G. (2002). Vegetarian ecofeminism. *Frontiers: A Journal of Women Studies 23*(3), 117-146.

14.   Buckingham, S. (2004). Ecofeminism in the twenty-first century. *The Geographical Journal, 170*(2), 146-154.

15.   Humberstone, B. (1998). Re-creation and connections in and with nature. *International Review for the Sociology of Sport, 33*(4), 381-392.

16.   Vance, L. (1997). Ecofeminism and wilderness. *National Women's Studies Journal, 9*(3), 60-76.

17.   Buckingham.

18.   Ibid.

19.   The Green Fuse. (2011). Ecofeminism. Retrieved from: http://www.thegreenfuse.org/ecofem.htm

20.   Reuther, R. (2011). Ecofeminism. Retrieved from: http://www.spunk.org/texts/pubs/openeye/sp000943.txt

21.   Vance.

22.   Marris, E. (2011). *Rambunctious garden: Saving nature in a post-wild world.* New York: Bloomsbury.

23.   Eaton.

24.   Henderson, 1997b.

25.   Henderson, K. (1999). Ecofeminism and the human/environment intersection. *Environmental Papers Series, 2*(1), 8-14.

26.   Adams, M., Bell, L., & Griffin (Eds.). (1997). *Teaching for diversity and social justice.* New York: Routledge.

27.   Taylor, W., Floyd, M., Whitt-Glover, M., & Brooks, J. (2007). Environmental justice: A framework for collaboration between the public health and parks and recreation fields to study disparities in physical activity. *Journal of Physical Activity and Health, 4* (Suppl 1), S50-S63.

28.   Henderson, K. (2009). Just research and physical activity: Diversity is more than an independent variable (research reflection). *Leisure Sciences, 31*, 100-105.

29.   Rioux, M. (1993). Rights, justice, power: An agenda for change. In M. Nagler & E. Kemp (Eds.), *Perspectives on disability* (2nd ed.) (pp. 515-523). Palo Alto, CA: Health Markets Research.

30.   Henderson, 2000.

31.   Rhode, D. (Ed). (1990). *Theoretical perspectives on sexual difference.* New Haven: Yale University Press.

32.   Gaard.

33.   Buckingham.

34.   Henderson & Bialeschki, 1990-91.

35.   Henderson, 1997a.

36.   Henderson, 1999.

37.   Henderson, 1997a.

38.   Fox, K., & McAvoy, L. (1989, April). *Environmental ethics: Strengths and dualisms of six dominant themes.* Paper presented to the Leisure and Ethics Conference, Boston, MA.

39.   McGregor, S. (2004). From care to citizenship: Calling ecofeminism back to politics. *Ethics and the Environment, 9*(1), 56-84.

40.   Seager, J. (1993). *Earth follies.* New York: Routledge.

41.   Loc. cit., p. 219.

42.   McGregor.

43.   Seager.

44.   Reuther.

45.   Murphy, J. (1974). *Concepts of leisure: Philosophical implications.* New York: Prentice-Hall.

46.   Henderson, K., Bialeschki, M., Shaw, S., & Freysinger, V. (1989). *A leisure of one's own: A feminist perspective on women's leisure.* State College, PA: Venture.

47.   Henderson, K., Bialeschki, M., Shaw, S., & Freysinger, V. (1996). *Both gains and gaps: Feminist perspectives on women's leisure.* State College, PA: Venture.

48.   Henderson, 2000.

49.   Humberstone.

50.   Henderson & Bialeschki, 1995.

51.   Buckingham.

52.   Vance.

53.   Marris.

54.   Humberstone.

Chapter 6: Our Town's a Drag: Drag Queens and
Queer Space in Athens, Georgia

1.   The "I" in this opening vignette refers to the first author.

2.   At the time of publication, at least four drag troupes were active in Athens, plus a cadre of individual perform-ers both from the community and from the University. One large draw for performers in the area is the lauded Boybutante Ball, an annual drag ball featuring more than 20 performers each year. For more on the Boybu-tante AIDS Foundation, see www.boybutante.org.

3.   We use the word *queer* as an umbrella term to capture the community that identifies as non-heterosexual (lesbian, gay, bisexual) or gender non-conforming (transgender). Although the term queer continues to make some people uncomfortable, our use of the term in consistent with our theoretical framework.

4.   Young, H. (2011, June 16). Georgia Bar hosts monthly gay night, event called 'fabulous'. Retrieved from The Red & Black website: http://redandblack.com/2011/06/16/georgia-bar-hosts-monthly-gay-night-event-called-fabulous/

5.   Ibid.

6.   Browne, K., Lim, J., & Brown, G. (2007) *Geographies of sexualities: Theory, practices, and politics*. Burlington, Vermont: Ashgate Publishing Company.

7.   Johnson, C. (2008). "Don't call him a cowboy": Masculinity, cowboy drag, and a costume change. *Journal of Leisure Research, 40*(3), 385-403.

8.   Johnson, C., & Samdahl, D. (2005). The night they took over: Misogyny in a country-western gay bar. *Leisure Sciences, 29*, 195-208.

9.   Ibid.

10.   Mondimore, F. (1996). *A natural history of homosexuality*. Baltimore Maryland: The Johns Hopkins University Press.

11.   Rushbrook, D. (2002). Cities, queer space, and the cosmopolitan tourist. *GLQ: A Journal of Lesbian and Gay Studies, 8*(1), 183-206.

12.   Whittle, S. (1994). *The margins of the city: Gay men's urban lives*. Brookfield, Vermont: Ashgate Publishing Company.

13.   Duberman, M. (1994). *Stonewall*. New York, New York: A Plume Book.

14.   Zervigon, A. M. (2009). Drag shows: Drag queens and female impersonators. *GLBTQ Arts*, 1-4.

15.   Bennett, J., & West, I. (2009). "United we stand, divided we fall": AIDS, Armorettes, and the tactical reper-toires of drag. *Southern Communication Journal, 74*(3), 300-313.

16.   Hillman, B. L. (2011). "The most profoundly revolutionary act a homosexual can engage in": Drag and the politics of gender presentation in the San Francisco gay liberation movement, 1964-1972. *Journal of the His-tory of Sexuality, 20*(1), 153-181.

17.   Barnett, J., & Johnson, C. (2012, under review). *We are all royalty: Narrative comparison of a drag queen and king*. Qualitative Communication Research.

18.   Fox, R. (2008). Sober drag queens, digital forests, and bloated 'lesbians': Performing gay identities online. *Qualitative Inquiry, 14*(7), 1245-1263.

19.   Johnson.

20.   Lewis, S., & Johnson, C. (2011). "But it's not that easy": Negotiating trans leisure space. *Leisure/Loisir. 35*(2), 115-132.

21. Hindle, P. (1994). Gay communities and gay space in the city. In S. Whittle (Ed.), *The margins of the city: Gay men's urban lives* (pp. 7-25). Brookfield, Vermont: Ashgate Publishing Company.

22. Barnett, J. T. (2010, April). *Same-sex kissing on America's street corners: A visual rhetorical analysis of the Athens Kiss-in.* Paper presented at the annual conference of the Southern States Communication Association, Memphis, Tennessee.

23. Morris, C. E., & Sloop, J. M. (2006). 'What lips these have kissed': Refiguring the politics of queer public kissing. *Critical Studies in Media Communication, 3*(1), 1-26.

24. DeLuca, K. (1999). Unruly arguments: The body rhetoric of Earth First!, ACT UP, and Queer Nation. *Argumentation and Advocacy, 36*, 9-21.

25. We use the term *straight bars* throughout the chapter to note the heteronormative assumption of all space/bars unless they are specifically signified as *other.*

26. Johnson.

27. Ibid.

28. Hindle.

29. Johnson.

30. Loc cit., p. 399.

31. Halferty, J. (2008). Performing the construction of queer spaces. *Canadian Theatre Review, 134*, p. 18.

32. Ibid.

33. Bennett & West.

34. Jones, R. (2007). Drag queens, drama queens, and friends: Drama and performance as a solidarity-building function in a gay male friendship circle. *Kaleidoscope: A Graduate Journal of Qualitative Communication Research, 6*, 61-84.

35. Paris, J., & Anderson, R. (2001). Faith-based queer space in Washington, DC: The Metropolitan Community Church-DC and Mount Vernon Square. *Gender, Place, and Culture, 8*(2), 149-168.

36. Glesne, C. (2006). *Becoming qualitative researchers: An introduction* (3rd ed.). Boston: Pearson Education, Inc.

37. Loc. cit., p. 5.

38. Creswell, J. W. (2007). *Qualitative inquiry and research design: Choosing among five traditions.* Thousand Oaks, CA: Sage.

39. Ibid.

40. Creswell, J. W. (2009). *Research design* (3rd ed.). Thousand Oaks, CA: Sage Publications.

41. Morris, M. (2000). Dante's left foot kicks queer theory into gear. In S. Talburt & S. R. Steinberg (Eds.), *Thinking queer: Sexuality, culture and education* (pp. 15-32). New York: Peter Lang, p. 23.

42. Frye, M. (1983). On being white: Thinking toward a feminist understanding of race and race supremacy. In M. Frye (Ed.), *The politics of reality: Essays in feminist theory* (pp. 110-127). Trumansburg, NY: The Crossing Press.

43. Butler, J. (1993). *Bodies that matter: On the discursive limits of "sex."* New York, NY: Routledge Press.

44. Butler, J. (1997) *Excitable speech: A politics of the performative.* New York, NY: Routledge Press.

45. Aitchison, C. (1999). New cultural geographies: The spatiality of leisure, gender and sexuality. *Leisure Studies, 18*, 19-39.

46.   Johnson & Samdahl.

47.   Johnson.

48.   Lewis & Johnson, 2011.

49.   Vaid, U. (1995). *Virtual equality: The mainstreaming of gay and lesbian liberation* (1st Anchor Books hardcover ed.). New York: Anchor Books.

50.   Johnson & Samdahl.

51.   Johnson.

52.   Henderson, K., & Frelke, C. (2000). Space as a vital dimension of leisure: The creation of place. *World Leisure, 3,* 18-24.

53.   Butler, 1993.

Chapter 7: Contesting Homelessness: Public Nature, Political Ecology, and Socioenvironmental Justice

1.   Escobar, A. (1996). Construction nature: Elements for a post-structuralist political ecology. *Futures, 28*(4), 325-343.

2.   Forsyth, T. (2008). Political ecology and the epistemology of social justice. *Geoforum, 39*(2), 756-764.

3.   Latour, B. (2004). *Politics of nature: How to bring the sciences into democracy.* Cambridge, MA: Harvard University Press.

4.   Robbins, P. (2004). *Political ecology: A critical introduction.* Malden, MA: Blackwell.

5.   Escobar.

6.   Forsyth, 2008.

7.   Sundberg, J. (2011, p. 322). Diabolical caminos in the desert and cat fights on the rio: A posthumanist political ecology of boundary enforcement in the United States-Mexico borderlands. *Annals of the Association of American Geographers, 101*(2), 318-336.

8.   Robbins.

9.   Robbins, P. (2007). *Lawn people: How grasses, weeds, and chemicals make us who we are.* Philadelphia, PA: Temple University Press.

10.   Harvey, D. (1996, p. 174). *Justice, nature, and the geography of difference.* Cambridge, MA: Blackwell.

11.   Escobar.

12.   Swyngedouw, E., & Heynen, N. (2003, p. 899). Urban political ecology, justice and the politics of scale. *Antipode, 35*(5), 898-918.

13.   Latour, B. (1993). *We have never been modern.* London: Harvester Wheatsheaf.

14.   Latour, 2004.

15.   Mitchell, D. (2003). *The right to the city: Social justice and the fight for public space.* New York, NY: The Guilford Press.

16.   Hardt, M., & Negri, A. (2009, p. 154). *Commonwealth.* Cambridge, MA: Harvard University Press.

17.   Davis, M. (1998). *Ecology of fear: Los Angeles and the imagination of disaster.* New York: Metropolitan Books.

18.   Castree, N. (2001). Socializing nature: Theory, practice, and politics. In N. Castree & B. Braun (Eds.), *Social nature: Theory, practice, and politics* (pp. 1-21). Malden, MA: Blackwell.

19.   Latour, 2004.

20.   Harvey, D. (1985). *The urbanization of capital: Studies in the history and theory of capitalist urbanization.* Oxford: Blackwell.

21.   Christophers, B. (2011). Revisiting the urbanization of capital. *Annals of the Association of American Geographers, 101*(6), 1347-1364.

22.   Harvey, D. (2008). The right to the city. *New Left Review, 53,* 23-40.

23.   Harvey, D. (2009). Their crisis, our challenge. Interview with Marco Berlinguer and Hilary Wainwright. *Red Pepper.* Retrieved October 15, 2011 from http://www.redpepper.org.uk/Their-crisis-our-challenge/.

24.   Rose, J., & Paisley, K. (2012). White privilege in experiential education: A critical reflection. *Leisure Sciences, 34*(2), 136-154.

25.   Holifield, R. (2012, p. 592). Environmental justice as recognition and participation in risk assessment: Negotiating and translating health risk at a superfund site in Indian Country. *Annals of the Association of American Geographers, 102*(3), 591-613.

26.   Ibid.

27.   Smith, N. (1993, p. 89). Homeless/global: Scaling places. In J. Bird, B. Curtis, T. Putnam, G. Robertson, & L. Tickner (Eds.), *Mapping the futures: Local cultures, global change* (pp. 87-120). London: Routledge.

28.   Mitchell.

29.   Foucault, M. (1980, pp. 69-70). *Power/knowledge: Selected interviews and other writings, 1972-1977.* New York, NY: Pantheon.

30.   Marx, K. (1858). The grundrisse. In R. Tucker (Ed.). (1978). *The Marx-Engles reader* (2nd ed.) (pp. 221-293). New York, NY: W.W. Norton & Company.

31.   Mitchell, D. (1997). The annihilation of space by law: The roots and implications of anti-homeless laws in the United States. *Antipode, 29*(3): 303-335.

32.   Goheen, P. (1993). Negotiating access to public space in mid-nineteenth century Toronto. *Journal of Historical Geography 30,* 430-449.

33.   Goheen, P. (1998). Public space and the geography of the modern city. *Progress in Human Geography, 22*(4), 479-496.

34.   Mitchell, 2003, p. 135.

35.   Bahr, H. (1973). *Skid row: An introduction to disaffiliation.* New York, NY: Oxford.

36.   Blau, J. (1992). *The visible poor: Homelessness in the United States.* New York, NY: Oxford.

37.   Gibson, T. (2005). NIMBY and the civic good. *City & Community, 4*(4): 381-401.

38.   Goheen, 1993.

39.   Lee, B., & Price-Spratlen, T. (2004). The geography of homelessness in American communities: Concentration or dispersion? *City & Community, 3*(1), 3-27.

40.   Mitchell, 2003.

41.   Ropers, R. (1988). *The invisible homeless: A new urban ecology.* New York, NY: Human Sciences Press.

42.   Timmer, D., Eitzen, D., & Talley, K. (1994). *Paths to homelessness: Extreme poverty and the urban housing crisis.* Boulder, CO: Westview.

43.   Wakin, M. (2008). Using vehicles to challenge anti-sleeping ordinances. *City & Community, 7*(4): 452-468.

44.   Mitchell, 2003.

45.   Ibid.

46.   Wakin.

47.   Mitchell, 2003.

48.   Hardt & Negri, 2009.

49.   Mitchell, D. (1995). The end of public space? People's Park, definitions of the public, and democracy. *Annals of the Association of American Geographers, 85*(1), 108-133.

50.   Mitchell, 2003.

51.   Mitchell, 1997.

52.   Mitchell, 2003, p. 220.

53.   Gibson, T. (2005). NIMBY and the civic good. *City & Community, 4*(4): 381-401.

54.   Wasserman, J. A., & Clair, J. M. (2010). Housing patterns of homeless people: The ecology of the street in the era of urban renewal. *Journal of Contemporary Ethnography, 40*(1), 71-101.

55.   Fitzgerald, S., Shelley, M., & Dail, P. (2001) Research on homelessness: Sources and implications of uncertainty. *American Behavioral Scientist, 45*(1), 121-148.

56.   Loc. cit, p. 121.

57.   Garapich, M. (2011). "It's a jungle out there. You need to stick together": Anti-institutionalism, alcohol and performed masculinities among Polish homeless men in London. *Liminalities: A Journal of Performance Studies, 7*(3), 1-23.

58.   Ropers.

59.   Ellickson, R. (1996). Controlling chronic misconduct in city spaces: Of panhandlers, skid rows, and public space zoning. *Yale Law Journal, 105*, 1165-1248.

60.   Ibid.

61.   Teir, R. (1998). Restoring order in urban public spaces. *Texas Review of Law & Politics, 2*(2), 255-291.

62.   Baron, J. (2004). Homelessness as a property problem. *The Urban Lawyer, 36*(2), 273-288.

63.   Hafetz, J. (2003). Homeless legal advocacy: New challenges and directions for the future. *Fordham Urban Law Journal, 30*, March.

64.   Lyon-Callo, V. (2004). *Inequality, poverty, and neoliberal governance: Activist ethnography in the homeless sheltering industry.* Toronto, ON: Broadview Press.

65.   Ropers.

66.   Amster, R. (2008). *Lost in space: The criminalization, globalization, and urban ecology of homelessness.* New York, NY: LFB Scholarly Publishing LLC.

67.   Garapich.

68.   Feldman, L. (2006). *Citizens without shelter: Homelessness, democracy, and political exclusion.* Ithaca, NY: Cornell University Press.

69. Arnold, K. (2004). *Homelessness, citizenship, and identity: The uncanniness of late modernity.* New York, NY: SUNY Press.

70. Barak, G. (1991). *Gimme shelter: A social history of homelessness in contemporary America.* New York, NY: Praeger.

71. Mitchell, 2003.

72. Liebow, E. (1993). *Tell them who I am: The lives of homeless women.* New York, NY: Penguin.

73. Ruddick, S. (1996, p. 61). *Young and homeless in Hollywood: Mapping social identities.* New York, NY: Routledge.

74. Cachelin, A. (2010). What lies beyond social and environmental justice? An ecological narrative. In K. Paisley and D. Dustin (Eds.), *Speaking up and speaking out: Working for social and environmental justice through parks, recreation, and leisure* (pp. 193-200). Urbana, IL: Sagamore.

75. Di Chiro, G. (1996). Nature as community: The convergence of environment and social justice. In W. Cronon (Ed.), *Uncommon ground: Rethinking the human place in nature* (pp. 298-320). New York: W.W. Norton & Company.

76. Harvey, 1996.

77. Castree, 2001, p. 12.

78. Braun, B., & Wainwright, J. (2001, p. 45). Nature, poststructuralism, and politics. In N. Castree & B. Braun (Eds.), *Social nature: Theory, practice, and politics* (pp. 41-63). Malden, MA: Blackwell.

79. Cronon, W. (1996). The trouble with wilderness. In W. Cronon (Ed.), *Uncommon ground: Rethinking the human place in nature* (pp. 69-96). New York: W.W. Norton.

80. Deluca, K. (1999, p. 240). In the shadow of whiteness: The consequences of construction of nature in environmental politics. In T. Nakayama & J. Martin (Eds.), *Whiteness: The communication of social identity* (pp. 217-245). Thousand Oaks, CA: Sage.

81. DeLuca (1999) articulates the other side to the progressive need to reconceptualize nature. Namely, previous constructions of nature by mainstream environmental groups as "pristine" or "wilderness" often serves the entrenched interests of dominant races, classes, and genders. "Environmental justice groups challenge not only industrialism, but white wilderness and mainstream environmentalism" (DeLuca, 1999, p. 235).

82. Heynen, N., Kaika, M., & Swyngedouw, E. (2006). Urban political ecology: Politicizing the production of urban natures. In Heynen, N., & Kaika, M., Swyngedouw, E. (Eds.), *In the nature of cities: Urban political ecology and the politics of urban metabolism* (pp. 1-20). London: Routledge.

83. Mvondo, S. A. (2006). Decentralized forest resources and access of minorities to environmental justice: An analysis of the case of the Baka in southern Cameroon. *International Journal of Environmental Studies, 63*(5), 681-689.

84. Adeola, F. O. (2009). From colonialism to internal colonialism and crude socioenvironmental injustice. In F. Steady (Ed.), *Environmental justice in the new millennium: Global perspectives on race, ethnicity, and human rights* (pp. 135-163). New York, NY: Palgrave Macmillan.

85. Castree, 2001, p. 12.

86. Harvey, 1996.

87. Forsyth.

88. Hardt, M. & Negri, A. (2004). *Multitude.* New York, NY: Penguin.

89. Foucault, M. (1980). *Power/knowledge: Selected interviews and other writings, 1972-1977.* New York, NY: Pantheon.

90.   Hardt & Negri, 2004.

91.   Hardt & Negri, 2009.

92.   Castree, N., & Braun, B. (Eds.). (2001). *Social nature: Theory, practice, and politics*. Malden, MA: Blackwell.

Chapter 8: John Dewey's Moral Philosophy as a Route to Social and Environmental Justice through Youth Development Theory

1.   Hemingway, J., & Parr, M. (2000). Leisure research and leisure practice: Three perspectives on constructing the research-practice relation. *Leisure Sciences, 22*, 139-162.

2.   Smith, S., & Godbey, G. (1991). Leisure, recreation, and tourism. *Annals of Tourism Research, 18*, 85-100.

3.   Henderson, K. A. (2010). Leisure studies in the 21st century: The sky is falling? *Leisure Sciences, 32*(4), 391-400.

4.   Witt, P. A., & Caldwell, L.L. (2005). *Recreation and youth development*. State College, PA: Venture.

5.   Witt, P. A., & Caldwell, L. L. (2010). *The rationale for recreation services for youth: An evidenced-based approach*. National Recreation and Park Association monograph.

6.   Roth, J. L., & Brooks-Gunn, J. (2003). Youth development programs: Risk, prevention, and policy. *Journal of Adolescent Health, 32*, 170-182.

7.   Pappas, G. F. (2008). *John Dewey's ethics: Democracy as experience*. Bloomington: Indiana University Press.

8.   Mintz, S. (2004). *Huck's raft: A history of American childhood*. Cambridge: Harvard University Press.

9.   Cavallo, D. (1981). *Muscles and morals: Organized playgrounds and urban reform, 1880-1920*. Philadelphia: University of Pennsylvania Press.

10.   Woodhead, M. (2009). Child development and the development of childhood. In J. Qvortup W. A. Corsaro & M.-S. Honig (Eds.), *The Palgrave handbook of childhood studies* (pp. 46-61). New York: Palgrave.

11.   Burman, E. (2008). *Deconstructing developmental psychology* (2nd ed.). New York: Routledge.

12.   Cavallo, D. (1976). Social reform and the movement to organize children's play during the Progressive era. *History of Childhood Quarterly, 3*(4), 509-522.

13.   Addams, J. (1912). Recreation as a public function in urban communities. *American Journal of Sociology, 17*, 615-619.

14.   Takanishi, R. (1978). Childhood as a social issue: Historical roots of contemporary child advocacy movements. *Journal of Social Issues, 34*(2), 8-28.

15.   Catalano, R. F., Hawkins, J. D., Berglund, M. L., Pollard, J. A., & Arthur, M. W. (2002).Prevention science and positive youth development: Competitive or cooperative frameworks? *Journal of Adolescent Health, 31*, 230-239.

16.   Resnick, M. D. (2000). Protective factors, resiliency, and healthy youth development. *Adolescent Medicine: State of the Art Reviews, 11*(1), 157-164.

17.   Roth & Brooks-Gunn.

18.   Valentine, G. (2003). Boundary crossings: Transitions from childhood to adulthood. *Children's Geographies, 1*(1), 37-52.

19.   Wyn, J., & White, R. (1997). *Rethinking youth*. Thousand Oaks: Sage.

20.   Arnett, J. (2003). Conceptions of the transition to adulthood among emerging adults in American ethnic groups. *New Directions for Child and Adolescent Development, 100*, 63-75.

21. Bocarro, J., Greenwood, P. B., & Henderson, K. A. (2008). An integrative review of youth development research in selected United States recreation journals. *Journal of Park and Recreation Administration, 26*(2), 4-27.

22. Scales, P. C., & Leffert, N. (2004). *Developmental assets: A synthesis of the scientific research on adolescent development.* Minneapolis: Search Institute.

23. Leffert, N., Benson, P. L., Scales, P. C., Sharma, A. R., Drake, D. R., & Blyth, D. A. (1998). Developmental assets: Measurement and prediction of risk behaviors among adolescents. *Applied Developmental Science, 2*(4), 209-230.

24. Scales, P. C., Benson, P. L., Leffert, N., & Blyth, D. A. (2000). Contribution of developmental assets to the prediction of thriving among adolescents. *Applied Developmental Science, 4*(1), 27-46.

25. Granger, R. C. (2002). Creating the conditions linked to positive youth development. *New Directions for Positive Youth Development,* (Fall), 149-164.

26. Kessen, W. (1979). The American child and other cultural inventions. *American Psychologist, 34*(10), 815-820.

27. Bocarro, Greenwood, & Henderson.

28. Robinson, L. (2004). Black adolescent identity and the inadequacies of western psychology. In J. Roche, S. Tucker, R. Thomson, & R. Flynn (Eds.), *Youth in society: Contemporary theory, policy, and practice* (pp. 153-159). London: Sage.

29. Ginwright, S., Cammarota, J., & Noguera, P. (2005). Youth, social justice, and communities: Toward a theory of urban youth policy. *Social Justice, 32*(3), 24-45.

30. Burman, E. (2001). Beyond the baby and the bathwater: Postdualistic developmental psychologies for diverse childhoods. *European Early Childhood Education Research Journal, 9*(1), 5-22.

31. Smith, R. (2010). *A universal child?* New York: Palgrave Macmillan.

32. Maira, S., & Soep, E. (2004). United States of adolescence?: Reconsidering U.S. youth culture studies. *Young, 12*(3), 245-269.

33. Rich, A. (1980). Compulsory heterosexuality and lesbian existence. *Signs, 5*(4), 631-660.

34. Johnson, C. W., & Waldron, J. J. (2011). Are you culturally competent?: Understanding the relationship between leisure and the health of lesbian, gay, and bisexual individuals. In K. Paisley & D. Dustin (Eds.), *Speaking up and speaking out: Working for social and environmental justice through parks, recreation, and leisure* (pp. 171–180). Urbana, IL: Sagamore.

35. Anderson, A. L. (1998). Strengths of gay male youth: An untold story. *Child & Adolescent Social Work Journal, 15*(1), 55-71.

36. D'Augelli, A. R., & Patterson, C. J. (2001). *Lesbian, gay, and bisexual identities and youth: Psychological perspectives.* Oxford: Oxford University Press.

37. Johnson, C. W. (1999). Living the game of hide and seek: Leisure in the lives of gay and lesbian young adults. *Leisure/Loisir, 24*(3), 255-278.

38. Kivel, B. D., & Kleiber, D. A. (2000). Leisure in the identity formation of lesbian/gay youth: Personal, but not social. *Leisure Sciences, 22,* 215-232.

39. Russell, S. T. (2002). Queer in America: Citizenship for sexual minority youth. *Applied Developmental Science, 6*(4), 258-263.

40. Arnett, J. J. (2000). Emerging adulthood: A theory of development from the late teens through the early twenties. *American Psychologist, 55*(5), 469-480.

41. Coles, B. (2004). Welfare services for young people: Better connections? In J. Roche, S. Tucker, R. Thomson, & R. Flynn (Eds.), *Youth in society: Contemporary theory, policy, and practice* (pp. 90-101). London: Sage.

42. Schlegel, A., & Barry, H. (1991). *Adolescence: An anthropological inquiry.* Free Press.

43.   Warner, M. (1999). *The trouble with normal: Sex, politics, and the ethics of queer life*. Harvard University Press: Cambridge.

44.   Witt & Caldwell.

45.   Johnson, C. W. (2003). Speaking the unspeakable. *Parks and Recreation, 38*(3), 21-28.

46.   Russell.

47.   Bocarro, Greenwood, & Henderson.

48.   Cobb, M. (2005). Uncivil wrongs: Race, religion, hate, and incest in queer politics. *Social Text, 23*(3&4), 251-274.

49.   D'Augelli, A. R. (1994). Identity development and sexual orientation: Toward a model of lesbian, gay, and bisexual development. In E. J. Trickett, R. J. Watts, & D. Birman (Eds.), *Human diversity: Perspectives on people in context* (pp. 312-333). San Francisco: Josey-Bass.

50.   Valentine, G., & Skelton, T. (2003). Finding oneself, losing oneself: The lesbian and Gay 'scene' as a paradoxical space. *International Journal of Urban and Regional Research, 27*(4), 849-866.

51.   Valentine, G., Skelton, T., & Butler, R. (2003). Coming out and outcomes: negotiating lesbian and gay identities with, and in, the family. *Environment and Planning D: Society and Space, 21*, 479–499.

52.   Eccles, J., & Gootman, J.A. (2002). *Community programs to promote youth development*. Washington DC: National Academy Press.

53.   Quinlivan, K., & Town, S. (1999). Queer pedagogy, educational practice and lesbian and gay youth. *Qualitative Studies in Education, 12*(5), 509 – 524.

54.   Santelli, J., Ott, M. A., Lyon, M., Rogers, J., Summers, D., & Schlieffer, R. (2006). Abstinence and abstinence-only education: A review of U.S. policies and programs. *Journal of Adolescent Health, 38*, 72-81.

55.   Westbrook, R. B. (1993). *John Dewey and American democracy*. Ithaca: Cornell University Press.

56.   Hildebrand, D. (2008). *Dewey: A beginner's guide*. Oxford: OneWorld Publications.

57.   Pappas.

58.   Hildebrand.

59   Pappas.

60.   Dewey, J. (1958). *Experience and nature*. New York: Dover.

61.   Pappas.

62.   Dewey, J. (1905). The postulate of immediate empiricism. *The Journal of Philosophy, Psychology and Scientific Methods, 2*(15), 393-399.

63.   McDermott, J. J., & Anderson, D. R. (2007). *The drama of possibility: Experience as philosophy of culture*. New York: Fordham University Press.

64.   Ibid.

65.   Dewey, J. (1961). Education as growth. In J. J. McDermott (Ed.), *The philosophy of John Dewey* (pp. 483-494). Chicago: University of Chicago Press.

66.   Loc. cit., p. 484.

67.   Wyn & White.

68. Villarruel, F. A., Montero-Sieburth, M., Dunbar, C., & Outley, C. W. (2005). Dorothy, there is no yellow brick road: The paradox of community youth development approaches for Latino and African American urban youth. In J. L. Mahoney, R. W. Larson & J. Eccles (Eds.), *Organized activities as contexts of development: Extra-curricular activities, after-school, and community programs* (pp. 111-130). New York: Lawrence Erlbaum.

69. Wyn, J., & White, R. (1997). *Rethinking youth.* Thousand Oaks: Sage., p. 52.

70. Dewey.

71. Ibid.

72. Dewey, J. (1963). *Philosophy and civilization.* New York: Capricorn Books.

73. Dewey, J. (1934). *Art as experience.* New York: Capricorn Books.

74. Dewey, J. (1943). *The school and society.* Chicago: University of Chicago Press.

75. D'Augelli.

76. Henderson, K. A. (1997). Just recreation: Ethics, gender, and equity. *Journal of Park and Recreation Administration, 15*(2), 16-31.

Chapter 9: Facebook's Status in the Lives of Generation Y: Exploring Power Structures in an Online Leisure Space

1. Zuckerberg, M. (2009). Mark Zuckerberg Facebook Profile Page. Retrieved from www.facebook.com/mark-zuckerberg.

2. Moglen, E. (2010, February 5). Freedom in the Cloud-NYU lecture [Video file]. Retrieved from http://www.youtube.com/watch?v=QOEMv0S8AcA.

3. Holt, N. (2011). Deep involvement in the World of Warcraft: An 'elfnography'. (Doctoral dissertation). Retrieved from: http://dbs.galib.uga.edu.

4. Facebook. (2012, May 2). Facebook Statistics [Facebook Information Profile Page]. Retrieved from http://www.facebook.com/press/info.php?statistics.

5. Giroux, H. (1994). Doing Cultural Studies: Youth and the challenge of pedagogy. *Harvard Educational Review, 64*(3), 278-308, 299.

6. Ingram, D., & Simon-Ingram, J. (1991). *Critical theory: The essential readings.* New York: Paragon House.

7. Rasmussen, D. (1996). *Handbook of critical theory.* Cambridge, MA: Blackwell Publishers.

8. Ibid.

9. Lindlof, T., & Taylor, B. (2002). *Qualitative communication research methods* (2nd ed.). Thousand Oaks, CA: Sage Publications.

10. Prasad, P. (2005). *Crafting qualitative research: Working in the postpositivist traditions.* Armonk, NY: M.E. Sharpe.

11. Kinchloe, J., & McLaren, P. (2000). Rethinking critical theory and qualitative research. In N. Denzin & Y. Lincoln (Eds.), *Handbook of qualitative research* (pp. 279-314).Thousand Oaks, CA: Sage Publications, p. 291.

12. Prasad, P. (2005). *Crafting qualitative research: Working in the postpositivist traditions.* Armonk, NY: M.E. Sharpe, 140.

13. Adorno, T., & Horkheimer, M. (1972). *Dialectic of enlightenment.* New York, NY: Herder and Herder, Inc.

14. How, A. (1995). *Critical theory.* New York, NY: Palgrave Macmillan.

15.   Geertz, C. (1973). *The Interpretation of cultures: Selected essays by Clifford Geertz.* New York: Basic Books, Inc, 12.

16.   Swidler, A. (1986). Culture in Action: Symbols and Strategies. *American Sociological Review, 51*(2), 273-286, 273.

17.   Loc cit., p. 277.

18.   Leard, D., & Lashua, B. (2006). Popular media, critical pedagogy, and inner city youth. *Canadian Journal of Education, 29*(1), 244-264.

19.   Storey, J. (2003). *Inventing popular culture: From folklore to globalization, Blackwell manifestos.* Malden, MA: Blackwell Pub, 29.

20.   Tapscott, D. (2009). *Grown up digital: How the net generation is changing your world.* New York, NY: McGraw Hill, 73.

21.   Ibid.

22.   Ibid.

23.   Bauerlein, M. (2008). *The dumbest generation: How the digital age stupefies young Americans and jeopardizes our future.* New York, NY: Penguin Group, 173.

24.   Oldenburg, R. (1989). *The great good place: Cafes, coffee shops, community centers, beauty parlors, general stores, bars, hangouts and how they get you through the day.* New York, NY: Paragon House.

25.   Oldenburg, R. (2001). Celebrating the third place: Inspiring stories about the "great good places" at the heart of our communities. New York: Marlowe & Company.

26.   Oldenburg, 1989, p. 20.

27.   Oldenburg, 2001.

28.   boyd, S. (2004). Being wired encourages human contact: The Third Space. Retrieved May 4, 2011 from http://www.corante.com/getreal/archives/004843.html.

29.   Soukup, C. (2006). Computer-mediated communication as a virtual third place: Building Oldenburg's great good places on the world wide web. *New Media Society, 8*(3), 421-440.

30.   Steinkuehler, C. A. (2005). The new third place: Massively multiplayer online gaming in American youth culture. *Journal of Research in Teacher Education, 3,* 16-33.

31.   Oldenburg, 1989, p. 42.

32.   Soukup.

33.   Loc cit., pp. 424-425.

34.   Facebook. (2012, May 2). Facebook Statistics [Facebook Information Profile Page]. Retrieved from http://www.facebook.com/press/info.php?statistics.

35.   Oldenburg, 1989, p. 23. (1989).

36.   Loc cit., p. 22.

37.   boyd, d. (2008). Youth, Identity, and Digital Media. In D. Buckingham (Ed.), *Why youth heart social network sites: The role of networked publics in teenage social life* (pp. 119-142). Cambridge, MA: The MIT Press, 136.

38.   Foucault, M. (1994). *Power.* (Faubian, J. & Rabinow, P. Eds.) New York: The New Press.

39.   Foucault, M. (1995). *Discipline and punishment: The birth of a prison.* New York, NY: Vintage Books.

40. Foucault, M. (1974). *Power/knowledge: Selected interviews and other writings, 1972-1977*. New York, NY: Vintage Books.

41. Li, Q. (2006). Cyberbullying in Schools: A research of gender differences. *School Psychology International, 27*, pp.1-14.

42. Mishna, F., McLuckie, A., & Saim, M. (2009). Real-world dangers in an online reality: A qualitative study examining online relationships and cyber abuse. *Social Work Research, 33*(2), 407-418.

43. Wieser, M., Pauli, P. Grosseibi, M., Molzow, I., & Muhlberger, A. (2010). Virtual Social Interactions in Social Anxiety: The Impact of Sex, Gaze, and Interpersonal Distance. *Sociology, Behavior, and Social Networking. 13*(5), pp. 547-553.

44. Sontag, S. (1979). *On photography*. Westminster, London: Penguin Books, Ltd.

45. Loc cit., p. 39.

46. Foucault, 1995.

47. Ibid.

48. Ibid.

49. Ibid.

50. boyd, 2008, p. 134.

51. Loc cit., p. 135.

52. Oldenburg, 1989, p. 22.

53. Facebook. (2011, May 2). Facebook Statement of Rights and Responsibilities [Facebook Information Profile Page]. Retrieved from http://www.facebook.com/press/info.php?statistics#!/terms.php.

54. Albrechtslund, A. (2008). Online social networking as participatory surveillance. *First Monday, 13*(3), 20-34.

55. Ibid.

56. Foucault, 1995, p. 201.

57. Cohen, N. (2008). The valorization of surveillance: Towards a political economy of Facebook. *Democratic Communique, 22*(1), 5-22.

58. Loc cit., p. 10.

59. Ellerbrok, A. (2010). Empowerment: Analysing technologies of multiple variable visibility. *Surveillance and Society, 8*(2), 200-220, 201.

60. Loc cit., pp. 206-207.

61. Facebook. (2011, May 2). Facebook Privacy Policy [Facebook Information Profile Page]. Retrieved from http://www.facebook.com/policy.php.

62. Cohen, p. 8. (2008).

Chapter 10: Tourism and Environmental Justice

1. Enloe, C. (1989). *Bananas, beaches and bases: Making feminist sense of international politics*. Berkeley, CA: University of California Press.

2.   UNWTO (2012). International tourism to reach one billion in 2012. Retrieved 23   January   2012   from http://media.unwto.org/en/press-release/2012-01-16/international tourism-reach-one-billion-2012.

3.   United Nations Declaration on the Rights of Indigenous Peoples. (2007). Retrieved from http://www.un.org/esa/socdev/unpfii

4.   Smith, S. (1988). Defining tourism: A supply-side view. *Annals of Tourism Research, 15,* 179-190.

5.   Butcher, J. (2003). *The moralisation of tourism: Sun, sand ... and saving the world.*   London: Routledge.

6.   Scheyvens, R. (2002). *Tourism for development: Empowering communities.* Harlow, UK: Prentice-Hall.

7.   Smith, M., & Duffy, R. (2003). *The ethics of tourism development.* London: Routledge.

8.   Fennell, D. A. (2006). *Tourism ethics.* Clevedon, UK: Channel View.

9.   Hultsman, J. (1995). Just tourism: An ethical framework. *Annals of Tourism Research, 22*(3), 553-567.

10.   Higgins-Desbiolles, F. (2008). Justice tourism and alternative globalisation. *Journal of Sustainable Tourism, 16*(3), pp. 345-364.

11.   Krippendorf, J. (1987). *The holiday makers: Understanding the impact of leisure and travel.* Oxford: Butterworth-Heinemann Ltd.

12.   McLaren, D. (2003). *Rethinking tourism and ecotravel* (2nd ed.). West Hartford, CT: Kumarian Press.

13.   Turner, L., & Ash, J. (1976). *The golden hordes: International tourism and the pleasure periphery.* London: Constable.

14.   Whyte, K., Selinger, E., & Outterson, K. (2011). Poverty tourism and the problem of consent. *Journal of Global Ethics, 7*(3), 337-348.

15.   Mowforth, M., & Munt, I. (2003). *Tourism and sustainability: Development and new tourism in the Third World* (2nd ed.). London: Routledge.

16.   Davis, A. (2009). Preserving Gullah Land Rights in the Wake of Tourism Expansion. Center for Concern. Retrieved from http://www.coc.org/files/Gullah%20Land%20Righs_Abiosseh_Davis.pdf

17.   Trask, H. K. (1999). *From a native daughter: Colonialism and sovereignty in Hawai'i.* Honolulu: University of Hawai'i Press, p. 137.

18.   Trask, H. K. (1993). Environmental racism in Hawai'i and the Pacific Basin. ZMag, Speech at University of Colorado at Boulder, 29 September. Retrieved from http://www.zmag.org/ZMag/articles/bartrask.htm.

19.   Trask, Haunani-Kay. (2000). Tourism and the Prostitution of Hawaiian Culture. *Cultural Survival Quarterly, 24*(1). Retrieved from http://www.cultural survival.org/publications/csq

20.   de Chavez, R. (1999). Globalisation and tourism: Deadly mix for indigenous peoples. Third World Resurgence, No. 103. Retrieved from http://www.twnside.org.sg/title/chavez-cn.htm

21.   Lanfant, M. F., & Graburn, N. H. H. (1992). International tourism reconsidered: The principle of the alternative. In V. L. Smith & W. R. Eadington (Eds.), *Tourism alternatives* (pp. 88-112). Chichester, UK: John Wiley and Sons.

22.   Kalisch, A. (2001). Tourism as fair trade: NGO perspectives. London: Tourism Concern.Bianchi, R. (2011). Interview with Ecoclub, 20 July. Retrieved from http://ecoclub.com/articles/interviews/702-raoul-bianchi

23.   Mohai, P., Pellow, D., & Roberts, J. T. (2009). Environmental Justice. *Annual Review of Environment and Resources, 34,* 405-430.

24.   Casey, Edward S. (1996). How to Get from Space to Place in a fairly Short Stretch of Time: Phenomenological Prolegomena. In S. Feld & K. Basso (Eds.), *Senses of place* (pp. 13-52). Santa Fe: School of American Research Press.

25. United Nations Declaration on the Rights of Indigenous Peoples. (2007). Retrieved from http://www.un.org/esa/socdev/unpfii/documents/DRIPS_en.pdf.

26. Ibid.

27. Bullard, R. D. (1990). *Dumping in Dixie: Race, class, and environmental quality.* Boulder: Westview Press.

28. Ibid.

29. Morris-Suzuki, T. (2000). For and against NGOs: The politics of the lived world. *New Left Review, 2,* Mar/Apr, pp. 63-84.

30. Whyte, K. P. (2010). An Environmental Justice Framework for Indigenous Tourism. *Environmental Philosophy, 7*(2), 77-78.

31. Figueroa, R. M. (2006). Evaluating Environmental Justice Claims. In J. Bauer (Ed.), *Forging environmentalism: Justice, livelihood, and contested environments* (pp. 360-376). New York: M.E. Sharpe.

32. Equations. (no date). Equitable Tourism Options. Retrieved from http://www.equitabletourism.org/

33. Ibid.

34. Ibid.

35. Ibid.

36. Ibid.

37. Ibid.

38. Alternative Tourism Group and Joint Advocacy Initiative. (2011). *Life under occupation.* Electronic report. Retrieved from http://www.atg.ps/index.php?page=one_day.

39. Stein, R. L. (1995). Remapping Israeli and Palestinian tourism. *Middle East Report,* Sept–Oct, pp. 16–19.

40. Kassis, R. (2006). 'The Palestinians and justice tourism: another tourism is possible', paper prepared for the Masters of Pilgrimage, Tourism and Cultural Heritage, Bethlehem TEMPUS Programme. Retrieved from <http://www.atg.ps/index.php?page=1177263149.1199956205>

41. Stein, p. 17.

42. Kassis

43. Kassis

44. Stein, p. 18.

45. Alternative Tourism Group. (n.d.). About us. Retrieved from http://www.patg.org/index.php?page=1177263078>.

46. Ibid.

47. Ibid.

48. Kassis, personal communication, March 11, 2009.

49. Palestinian Initiative for Responsible Tourism. (2008). A code of conduct for tourism in the Holy Land: a Palestinian initiative. Retrieved from <http://www.atg.ps/index.php?page=1178694470.1227348702>.

50. Taylor, D. E. (2000). The Rise of the Environmental Justice Paradigm: Injustice Framing and the Social Construction of Environmental Discourses. *American Behavioral Scientist, 43*(4), 508-580.

Chapter 11: Spirituality as a Resource for Social and Environmental Justice through Parks, Recreation, Tourism, and Leisure

1. Hemingway, J. L. (1996). Emancipating leisure: The recovery of freedom in leisure. *Journal of Leisure Research, 28*(1), 27-43.

2. Pieper, J. (1963). *Leisure: The basis of culture.* New York: Random House.

3. Doohan, L. (1990). *Leisure: A spiritual need.* Notre Dame, IN: Ave Maria Press, p. 63.

4. Pieper, p. 44.

5. Willard, D. (1995, March 6). Conversations: What makes spirituality Christian? *Christianity Today, 39*, 16-17, p. 17.

6. Elkins, D. N., Hedstrom, L. J., Hughes, L. L., Leaf, J. A., & Saunders, C. (1988). Toward a humanistic-phenomenological spirituality: Definition, description and measurement. *Journal of Humanistic Psychology, 28*(4), 5-18, p. 10.

7. Loc cit., p. 11.

8. Ibid.

9. Fisher, J. W., Francis, L. J., & Johnson, P. (2000). Assessing spiritual health via four domains of spiritual wellbeing: The SH4DI. *Pastoral Psychology, 49*(2), 133-145, p. 135.

10. Vader, J. P. (2006). Spiritual health: The next frontier. *The European Journal of Public Health, 16*(5), 457.

11. Hawks, S. (1994). Spiritual health: Definition and theory. *Wellness Perspectives, 10*, 3-13.

12. Wolterstorff, N. (1983). *Until peace and justice embrace.* Grand Rapids, MI: Eerdmans.

13. Kaza, S. (1996). Comparative perspectives of world religions: Views of nature and implications for land management. In B. L. Driver, D. Dustin, T. Baltic, G. Elsner, & G. Peterson (Eds.), *Nature and the human spirit: Toward an expanded land management ethic* (pp. 41-60). State College, PA: Venture.

14. Loc cit., p. 57.

15. DeWitt, C. B. (2012). *Song of a scientist.* Grand Rapids, MI: Square Inch Books.

16. Williams, D. C. (2002). *God's wilds: John Muir's vision of nature.* College Station, TX: Texas A&M University.

17. Heintzman, P. (1995). Leisure, ethics and the Golden Rule. *Journal of Applied Recreation Research, 20*(3), 203-222.

18. Hick, J. (1992). The universality of the Golden Rule. In J. Runzo (Ed.), *Ethics, religion and the good society: New directions in a pluralistic world* (pp. 155-166). Louisville, KY: Westminster/John Knox, p. 159.

19. Ibid.

20. Heintzman, 1995.

21. Baigent, E. (2011). 'God's earth will be sacred': Religion, theology, and the open space movement in Victorian England. *Rural History, 22*(1), 31-58.

22. Loc cit., p. 34.

23. Octavia Hill as quoted in Baigent, p. 38.

24. Baigent, p. 38.

25. Baigent.

26.   Ibid.

27.   Sir Anthony Brady as quoted in Baigent, p. 41.

28.   Edward North Buxton as quoted in Baigent, p. 43.

29.   Baigent.

30.   Loc cit., p. 47.

31.   Ibid., p. 46.

32.   Haluza-Delay, R. (2000). Green fire and religious spirit. *The Journal of Experiential Education, 23*(3), 143-149.

33.   National Council of Churches of Christ. (2012a). Mountaintop removal coal mining. Retrieved from http://nccecojustice.org/energy/index_newMTR.php.

34.   National Council of Churches of Christ. (2012b). Wyoming wilderness. Retrieved from http://nccecojustice.org/wilderness/wildwyoming.php.

35.   DeGraaf, D. (2010). *Seeking the common good: Challenges and opportunities for recreation programmers.* Paper presented at the Christian Society for Kinesiology and Leisure Studies annual conference. Calvin College, Grand Rapids, MI. June 10-12, 2010.

36.   Ibid.

37.   Bouma-Prediger, S., & Walsh, B. (2008). *Beyond homelessness: Christian faith in a culture of displacement.* Grand Rapids, MI: Eerdmans.

38.   Rocha, A. (2012). The Arabuko-Sokoke Schools and Ecotourism Scheme (ASSETS). Retrieved from http://www.arocha.org/ke-en/work/communityconservation/assets.html.

39.   ASSETS. (2012). The Scheme. Retrieved from http://assets-kenya.org/scheme.htm.

40.   Fox, R. J. (1997). Women, nature and spirituality: A qualitative study exploring women's wilderness experience. In D. Rowe & P. Brown (Eds.), *Proceedings, ANZALS conference 1997* (pp. 59-64). Newcastle, NSW: Australian and New Zealand Association for Leisure Studies, and the Department of Leisure and Tourism Studies, The University of Newcastle.

41.   Schmidt, C., & Little, D. E. (2007). Qualitative insights into leisure as a spiritual experience. *Journal of Leisure Research, 39*(2), 222-247.

42.   Driver, B. L., Dustin, D., Baltic, T., Elsner, G., & Peterson, G. (Eds.). (1996). *Nature and the human spirit.* State College, PA: Venture.

43.   Dustin, D. (1994). Managing public lands for the human spirit. *Parks and Recreation, 29*(9), 92-96.

44.   Stringer, L. A., & McAvoy, L. H. (1992). The need for something different: Spirituality and the wilderness adventure. *The Journal of Experiential Education, 15*(1), 13-21.

45.   Fredrickson, L. M., & Anderson, D. H. (1999). A qualitative exploration of the wilderness experience as a source of spiritual inspiration. *Journal of Environmental Psychology, 19,* 21-39.

46.   Haluza-Delay, p. 146.

47.   Lasenby, J. (2003). Exploring episode-type spiritual experience associated with outdoor education programs. Unpublished master's thesis, University of Edinburgh, Scotland, p. 62.

48.   Heintzman, P. (2009). The spiritual benefits of leisure. *Leisure/Loisir, 33*(1), 419-445.

49.   Unsoeld, W. (1974). Spiritual values in wilderness. Paper presented at the conference on experiential education. Estes Park, CO, p. 20. Retrieved from http://wilderdom.com/pdf/Unsoeld1974SpiritualValuesInWilderness.pdf.

50. Lane, B. C. (1998). *The solace of fierce landscapes: Exploring desert and mountain spirituality.* Oxford, England: Oxford University Press.

51. Moore, C. (2011). Spiritual experiences and environmentalism of recreational users in the marine environment: New Zealand surfers and scuba divers. Unpublished Master's thesis. Lincoln University, Lincoln, New Zealand.

52. Heintzman, P. (2010). Nature-based recreation and spirituality: A complex relationship. *Leisure Sciences, 32*(1), 72-89.

53. Moore.

54. Ibid.

55. Dunlap, R. E., Van Liere, K. D., Mertig, A. G., & Jones, R. E. (2000). Measuring endorsement of the New Ecological Paradigm: A revised NEP Scale. *Journal of Social Issues, 56*(3), 425-442.

56 Moore.

57. Ajzen, I., & Fishbein, M. (2005). The influence of attitudes on behavior. In D. Albarracín, B. Johnson, & M. Zanna (Eds.), *The handbook of attitudes* (pp. 173-221). Mahwah, NJ: Lawrence Erlbaum Associates.

58. Shank, P. A. (1987). Therapeutic recreation philosophy: A state of cacophony. In C. Sylvester, J. Hemingway, R. Howe-Murphy, K. Mobily, & P. Shank (Eds.), *Philosophy of therapeutic recreation: Ideas and issues* (27-40). Alexandria, VA: National Recreation and Park Association.

59. Kaza.

Chapter 12: Experiential Education, Social and Environmental Justice Pedagogies, and Globalization: From Theory to Praxis

1. Freire, P. (1970). *Pedagogy of the oppressed.* New York: Seabury.

2. Freire, P. (1972). *Cultural action for freedom.* Baltimore: Penguin.

3. Kolb, D. A. (1984). *Experiential learning.* Englewood Cliffs, NJ: Prentice Hall.

4. Breunig, M. (2005). Turning experiential education and critical pedagogy theory into praxis. *Journal of Experiential Education, 28*(2), 106-122.

5. Chomsky, N. (2006). Discussions on globalization [Video File]. Available from http://www.youtube.com/watch?v=AHJPSLgHemM

6. Ellwood, W. (2007). *The no-nonsense guide to globalization* (2nd ed.). Toronto, ON: New Internationalist Publication Ltd.

7. Kirkwood, T. (2001). Our global age requires global education: Clarifying definitional ambiguities. *The Social Studies, 92*(1), 10 -15.

8. Ritzer, G., & Ryan, M. (2004). The Globalization of Nothing. In S. Dasgupta (Ed.), *The changing face of globalization* (pp. 298-317). Panchshell Enclave, New Delhi: Sage Publications.

9. O'Sullivan, B. (1999). Global change and educational reform in Ontario and Canada. *Canadian Journal of Education, 24*(3), 311-325.

10. Loc. cit., p. 1.

11. Ibid.

12. Ibid.

13. Schweisfurth, M. (2006). Education for global citizenship: Teacher agency and curricula structure in Ontario schools. *Educational Review, 58*(1), 41-50.

14. MacDonald, B. (2005). *Guide to Infusing Global Education into the Curriculum.* Canadian Teachers Federation. Retrieved from www.global-ed.org/curriculum-guide.pdf.

15. Friere, 1970.

16. Friere, 1972.

17. Finlay, F., & Faith, V. (1987). Illiteracy and alienation in American colleges: Is Paulo Freire's pedagogy relevant? In I. Shor (Ed.), *More Freire for the classroom: A source book for liberatory teaching* (pp. 63-86). Portsmouth, NH: Cook Publishers.

18. Connolly, M. (2008). Freire in the post-modern classroom: A post-colonial tale. In S. Moore & R. Mitchell (Eds.), *Power, pedagogy and praxis: Social justice in the globalized classroom* (pp. 165-178). Rotterdam: Sense Publications.

19. Finlay & Faith, p. 65.

20. Levin, M., & Arellano, L. (2010). *Experiential activities for a better world: A guidebook for facilitators, teachers, trainers, and group leaders.* Createspace Publishing.

21. Garner, H. (1999). *Intelligence reframed: Multiple intelligences for the 21st century.* New York: Basic Books.

22. Newman, M. (2009). Images of the social and economic world. University of Michigan. Retrieved from http://www-personal.umich.edu/~mejn/cartograms/

23. McIntosh, P. (1988). White privilege: Unpacking the invisible knapsack. Retrieved from http://nymbp.org/reference/WhitePrivilege.pdf

24. http://www.unitedchurches.ca/files/minstaff/pastoral/guidelines; traning-tool-for-everyone.pdf.

25. Arnold, B., James, M., & Thomas. (1991). *Educating for a change.* Toronto, CA: Between the Lines and the Doris Marshall Institute for Education and Action.

26. Fawcett, L., Bell, A. C. & Russell, C. L. (2002). Guiding our environmental praxis: Teaching for social and environmental justice. In W. Leal Filho (Ed.), *Teaching sustainability at universities: Towards curriculum greening* (pp. 223-228). New York: Peter Lang.

27. Friere, 1970.

28. Friere, 1972.

Chapter 13: Canada's First College of Sustainability: Teaching about Social and Environmental Justice

1. Buszard, D., & Kolb, J. (2011). Institutional innovation to deliver post-secondary education for sustainability. *Sustainability: The Journal of Record, 4*(2), 80-84.

2. Bruntland Commission. (1987). *Our Common Future: Report of the World Commission on Environment and Development.* United Nations World Commission on Environment and Development. Published as Annex to General Assembly document A/42/427.

3. MacEachern, A. (2008). "Writing the History of Canadian Parks: Past, Present, and Future," Parks for Tomorrow 40th Anniversary Conference. Calgary. Retrieved from http://dspace.ucalgary.ca/bitstream/1880/46876/1/MacEachern.pdf .

4. Brown, V. A., Harris, J. A., & Russell, J. Y. (2010). *Tackling wicked problems: Through the transdisciplinary imagination.* London: Earthscan.

5. Campbell, C. (2011). (Ed.). *A century of Parks Canada, 1911-2011.* Calgary: University of Calgary Press.

6. Taylor, C. (1990). "Legislating Nature: The National Parks Act of 1930," in R. Lorimer (Ed.), *To see ourselves/to save ourselves: Ecology and culture in Canada.* Montreal: Association for Canadian Studies. pp. 125-37.

7.   MacEachern, A. (2001). *Natural selections: National parks in Atlantic Canada, 1935-1970.* Montreal/Kingston: McGill-Queen's University Press.

8.   Waiser, W. (1989). *Saskatchewan's playground: A history of Prince Albert National Park.* Saskatoon: Fifth House.

9.   Kopas, P. (2007). *Taking the air: Ideas and change in Canada's national parks.* Vancouver: University of British Columbia Press.

10.   Bruntland Commision.

11.   MacLaren, I. (2007). (Ed.). *Culturing wilderness in Jasper National Park: Studies in two centuries of human history in the Upper Athabasca River Watershed.* Edmonton: University of Alberta Press.

12.   Campbell.

13.   Sandilands, C. (2009). "The Cultural Politics of Ecological Integrity: Nature and Nation in Canada's National Parks, 1885-2000." *International Journal of Canadian Studies 39/40,* pp. 161-189.

14.   Parks Canada uses this definition of ecological integrity: "'An ecosystem has integrity when it is deemed characteristic for its natural region, including the composition and abundance of native species and biological communities, rates of change and supporting processes.' In plain language, ecosystems have integrity when they have their native components (plants, animals and other organisms) and processes (such as growth and reproduction) intact." Although paramount since 1988, the 2000 Canada National Parks Act provided the most forceful language to date, stating that "maintenance or restoration of ecological integrity, through the protection of natural resources and natural processes, shall be the first priority … when considering all aspects of the management of parks."

15.   Mersey Tobeatic Research Institute and Parks Canada. (2010). *Annual Report of Research and Monitoring in the Greater Kejimkujik Ecosystem.*

16.   Kwan, A. (2009). Problem-Based Learning. In M. Tight, K. H. Mok, J. Huismand, & C. Morphew (Eds.), *The Routledge international handbook of higher education* (pp. 91–108). New York: Routledge.

17.   Best, S. (2010). *Leisure studies: Themes and perspectives.* London: Sage.

18.   Ibid.

Chapter 14: Ecojustice Education: Learning to Speak Up and Out

1.   World Commission on Environment and Development. (1987). Report of the World Commission on Environment and Development (42/187).

2.   Wackernagel, M., & Rees, W. (1996). *Our ecological footprint: Reducing human impact on earth.* Gabriola Island, BC: New Society.

3.   Ibid.

4.   Margalioth, Y. (in press). Assessing Moral Claims in International Climate Change Negotiations. *Journal of Energy, Climate, and the Environment.*

5.   Lawn, P., (2003). A theoretical foundation to support the Index of Sustainable Economic Welfare (ISEW), Genuine Progress Indicator (GPI), and other related indexes. *Ecological economics, 44*(1), 105-118.

6.   Boone, C., Buckley, G., Grove, M., & Sister, C., Parks and People: An Environmental Justice Inquiry in Baltimore, Maryland. *Annals of the Association of American Geographers, 99*(4), 767-787.

7.   Cole, L., & Foster, S. (2001) *From the ground up: Environmental racism and the rise of the environmental justice movement.* New York: New York University Press.

8.   Ghimire, K., & Pimbert, M. (2000). *Social change and conservation.* London: Earthscan.

9.   Whyte, K. (2010). An Environmental Justice Framework for Indigenous Tourism. *Environmental Philosophy*, p. 80.

10.   Cole & Foster.

11.   Wiek, A., Withycombe, L., Redman, C. (2011). Key competencies in sustainability: A reference framework for academic program development. *Sustainability Science, 6*(2), 203-218.

12.   Ajzen, I., & Fishbein, M. (1980). *Understanding attitudes and predicting behavior.* Upper Saddle River, NJ: Prentice Hall.

13.   Chawla, L. (1998). Significant Life Experiences Revisited: A Review of Research on Sources of Environmental Sensitivity. *Journal of Environmental Education, 29*(3), 11-21.

14.   Leopold, A. (1949). *A Sand County almanac and sketches here and there.* New York: Oxford, p. 201.

15.   Martusewicz, R., Edmundson, J., & Lupinacci, J. (2011). *EcoJustice education: Toward diverse, democratic and sustainable communities.* New York: Routledge.

16.   Ibid.

17.   Begon, M., Townsend, C., & Harper, J. (2006). *Ecology: From individuals to ecosystems.* Malden, Massachusetts: Blackwell.

18.   Cachelin, A., Norvell, R., & Darling, A. (2010). Language fouls in teaching ecology: Why traditional metaphors undermine conservation literacy. *Conservation Biology, 24*(3), 669-674.

19.   Cachelin, A., & Ruddell, E. (in review). Framing for sustainability: The impact of language choice on educational outcomes. *Journal of Environmental Studies and Sciences.*

20.   Cachelin, A., & Paisley, K. (in prep).

21   Ibid.

22.   Martusewicz, R., Edmundson, J., & Lupinacci, J.

23.   Sipos, Y., Battisti, B., & Grimm, K. (2008). Achieving transformative sustainability   learning: Engaging head, hands, and heart. *International Journal of Sustainability in Higher Education, 9*(1), 68-86.

Chapter 15: Virtue Ethics: An Emerging Discourse in Social and Environmental Justice Inquiry

1.   Anscombe, G. E. M. (1958) Modern moral philosophy. *Philosophy 33*, No. 124, pp. 1-19.

2.   MacIntyre, A. (1984). *After virtue* (2nd. ed.). Notre Dame, IN: University of Notre Dame Press.

3.   Tessman, L. (2005). *Burdened virtues: Virtue ethics for liberatory struggles.* Oxford: Oxford University Press.

4.   Sandler, R. (2007). *Character and the environment: A virtue-oriented approach to environmental ethics.* New York: Columbia University Press.

5.   McLean, D. J. (2006). *Philosophy and leisure: Introduction to recreation and leisure.* Champaign, IL: Human Kinetics.

6.   McLean, D. J., & D. Yoder (2005). *Issues in recreation and leisure: Ethical decision making.* Champaign, IL: Human Kinetics.

7.   Sylvester, C. (1991). Discovering a good idea for the sake of goodness: An interpretive critique of subjective leisure. In T. Goodale & P. Witt (Eds.), *Recreation and leisure: Issues in an era of change* (3rd ed.). (pp. 441-454). State College, PA: Venture.

8.   Hemingway, J. (1988). Leisure and civility: reflections on a Greek ideal. *Leisure Sciences, 10*: 179-191.

9. McKeon, R. (2001). *The basic works of Aristotle*. New York: Modern Library.

10. Taylor, R. (2002). *Virtue ethics: An introduction*. Amherst, NY: Prometheus Books.

11. Loc cit., pp. 90-91.

12. Loc cit., p. 92.

13. Rawls, J. (1971). *A theory of justice*. Cambridge, MA: Harvard University Press.

14. Taylor, p. 93.

15. Stone, C. (1974). *Should trees have standing? Toward legal rights for natural objects*. Los Altos, CA: W. Kaufmann.

16. Leopold, A. (1989). *A Sand County almanac, and sketches here and there*. New York: Oxford University Press (Original work published 1949).

17. Nash, R. (1989). *The rights of nature: A history of environmental ethics*. Madison, WI: University of Wisconsin Press, p. 10.

18. Loc cit., p. 7.

19. Loc cit., p. 4.

20. Loc cit., p. 5.

21. Feinberg, J. (1974). The Rights of Animals and Unborn Generations. In William Blackstone (Ed.), *Philosophy and environmental crisis*. Athens, Georgia: University of Georgia Press.

22. McKeon.

23. Sandler, pp. 39-40.

24. Loc cit., p. 2.

25. Tessman.

26. Loc cit., p. 11.

27. Loc cit., p. 49.

28. Loc cit., p. 108.

29. Loc cit., p. 115.

30. Lamore, C. (1996). *The morals of modernity*. Cambridge: Cambridge University Press.

31. Crompton, J. (1991). Marketing: neither snake oil nor panacea. In T. Goodale & P. Witt (Eds.), *Recreation and leisure: Issues in an era of change* (3rd ed.). (pp. 213-229). State College, PA: Venture Publications.

Chapter 16: Recreating Culture: Slow Food, *Scholé*, and Critical Pedagogy

1. Douglas, M. (1984). *Food in the social order: Studies of food and festivities in the three American communities*. New York: Russell Sage Foundation.

2. Allen, P. (2004). *Together at the table: Sustainability and sustenance in the American agrifood system*. University Park, PA: Pennsylvania State University Press.

3. Hinrichs, C., & Lyson, T. (2007). *Remaking the North American food system: Strategies for sustainability*. Lincoln, NE: University of Nebraska Press.

4.   Pollan, M. (2006). *The omnivore's dilemma: A natural history of four meals*. New York: Penguin Press.

5.   Schlosser, E. (2001). *Fast food nation: The dark side of the All-American meal*. Boston, MA: Houghton Mifflin.

6.   Mair, H., Sumner, J., & Rotteau, L. (2008). The politics of eating: Food practices as critically reflexive leisure. *Leisure/Loisir, 32*(2), 379-405.

7.   Petrini, C. (2001). *Slow food: The case for taste*. New York: Columbia University Press.

8.   Ibid.

9.   Petrini, C., personal communication, February 21, 2010.

10.   http://www.slowfoodusa.org

11.   Petrini, C. (2009). *Terra Madre: Forging a global network of sustainable food communities*. White River Junction, VT: Chelsea Green Publishing.

12.   Glover, T. (2004). Social capital in the lived experiences of community gardeners. *Leisure Sciences, 26,* 143–162.

13.   Glover, T., Shinew, K., & Parry, D. (2005). Association, sociability, and civic culture: The democratic effect of community gardening. *Leisure Sciences, 27*(1), 75-92.

14.   Parry, D., Glover, T., & Shinew, K. (2005). "Mary, Mary, quite contrary, how does your garden grow?": Examining gender roles and relations in community gardens. *Leisure Studies, 24*(2), 177-192.

15.   Shinew, K., Glover, T., & Parry, D. (2004). Leisure spaces as potential sites for interracial interaction: Community gardens in urban areas. *Journal of Leisure Research, 36*(3), 336-355.

16.   Mair, Sumner, & Rotteau.

17.   Ibid.

18.   Blackshaw, T. (2010). *Leisure*. New York: Routledge.

19.   Rojek, C. (2010). *The labor of leisure: The culture of free time*. Thousand Oaks, CA: Sage.

20.   Blackshaw.

21.   Iso-Ahola, S. (1980). *The social psychology of leisure and recreation*. Dubuque, IA: W. C. Brown Co.

22.   Kleiber, D. (1999). *Leisure experience and human development: A dialectical interpretation*. New York: Basic Books.

23.   Neulinger, J. (1974). *The psychology of leisure: Research approaches to the study of leisure*. Springfield, IL: Thomas.

24.   Broadie, S. (2007). *Aristotle and beyond* (pp. 184-198). New York: Cambridge University Press.

25.   Hemingway, J. (1988). Leisure and civility: Reflections on a Greek ideal. *Leisure Sciences, 10,* 179-191.

26.   Maynard, S. (2010). Reconstructing *schole* in public leisure services. Unpublished doctoral dissertation. The University of Georgia, Athens, Georgia.

27.   Ober, J. (1989). *Mass and elite in democratic Athens*. Princeton, NJ: Princeton University Press.

28.   Aristotle, Pol 1337b, 30-34.

29.   Richardson-Lear, G. (2004). *Happy lives and the highest good: An essay on Aristotle's Nicomachean Ethics*. Princeton University Press.

30.   Aristotle, *Pol* 1269a. 34-36.

31. Maynard.

32. Broadie.

33. Hemingway.

34. Maynard.

35. Bauman, Z. (2000). *Liquid modernity.* Malden, MA: Blackwell.

36. Blackshaw.

37. Loc. cit., p. 120.

38. Rojek.

39. Loc. cit., p. 19.

40. Blackshaw, p. 149.

41. Ritzer, G. (2007). *The globalization of nothing 2.* Thousand Oaks, CA: Pine Forge Press.

42. Petrini, 2001.

43. Oxford English Dictionary. (2010). Entry for the term *convivial.* Retrieved from http: www.oed.com/view/En try/40856?redirectedFrom=convivial#

44. Ritzer, G. (1996). T*he McDonaldization of society: An investigation into the changing character of contemporary life.* Thousand Oaks, CA: Pine Forge Press.

45. Schlosser.

46. Ritzer, 1996.

47. Estabrook, B. (December 2010). The tomato trials. *Saveur, 134,* 46-47.

48. Berry, W. (2002). *The art of the commonplace: The agrarian essays of Wendell Berry.* Washington, D.C.: Counterpoint.

49. Kingsolver, B. (2007). *Animal, vegetable, miracle: A year of food life.* New York: HarperCollins.

50. Pollan.

51. Petrini, 2009.

52. Berry, p. 321.

53. Bourdieu, P. (1984). *Distinction: A social critique of the judgment of taste.* (R. Nice, Trans.). London: Routledge & Kegan Paul.

54. Petrini, 2009.

55. Freire, P. (1970). *Pedagogy of the oppressed.* (M. Ramos, Trans.). New York: Continuum.

56. Petrini, 2001.

57. Petrini, 2009.

58. Petrini, personal communication, February 21, 2010.

Chapter 17: Ecotourism as a Venue for Environmental and Social Justice: Case Study of a Fijian Vanua

1. Personal viewpoint, environmental justice refers to both the social and environmental aspects of justice definitions—as human beings, we are part of the environment in which we live, therefore I apply the concept as inclusive of social factors as well.

2. See Dustin, D., Bricker, K., & Schwab, K. (2010) People and Nature: Toward an Ecological Model of Health Promotion. *Leisure Sciences, 32*(1): 3-14; and Schwab, K., Dustin, D., & Bricker, K. (2009). Parks, Recreation, and Tourism's Contributions to Utah's Health: An Ecologic Perspective. *Utah Leisure Insights, 29*(1):12-14.

3. The International Ecotourism Society. (2012). What is ecotourism? Retrieved from http://www.ecotourism.org/what-is-ecotourism.

4. Ibid.

5. Environmental Protection Agency (EPA). (2012). Environmental Justice Home Page. Retrieved from http://www.epa.gov/environmentaljustice/index.html

6. Ibid.

7. Robert D. Bullard. Waste and Racism: A Stacked Deck? Forum for Applied Research and Public Policy. Spring 1993. Retrieved from http://eelink.net/EJ/equity.html

8. Ibid.

9. Ibid.

10. Hawkin, P. (1993). *The ecology of commerce.* New York: Harper Collins.

11. Bullard, 1993.

12. Ravvuvu Ravuvu, A. (1983). *Vaka i taukei: The Fijian way of life.* Suva, Fiji: Institute of Pacific Studies, University of the South Pacific.

13. Plange, N. (1996). *Employment opportunities in the rural and subsistence sector of Fiji.* Suva: University of the South Pacific.

14. Ibid.

15. Ibid.

16. Ibid.

17. Bricker, K. (2001). Ecotourism development in the rural highlands of Fiji. In D. Harrison (Ed.), *Tourism and the less developed world: Issues and case studies.* Wallingford, UK: CABI, pp. 235-250.

18. Beeftink, K. 2004. *Perceptions of Ecotourism: A case study of whitewater guides in the rural highlands of Fiji.* Master of Science Thesis, West Virginia University, Morgantown WV.

19. Bricker K., Kerstetter, D., & Beeftink, K. (2012). Tradition and Place: Tourism Development from Highlands to Islands in Fiji (Invited). In Dodd, J. & Sharma, V. (Eds.), *Leisure and tourism: Cultural paradigms.* New Delhi, India: Rawat Publishers.

20. Schultz, J., & Bricker N. (2012). A partnership for education and environmental awareness: Outreach in Fiji's Upper Navua Conservation Area. In K. Bricker, R. Black, & S. Cottrell (Eds.), *Sustainable Tourism and the millennium development goals: Effecting positive change* (pp. 107-114). Burlington, MA: Jones & Bartlett Learning.

21. Beeftink, 2004.

22. Bricker, 2001.

23.   Ibid.

24.   Schultz & Bricker, 2012.

25.   Bricker, 2001.

26.   Ibid.

27.   Bricker, Kerstetter, & Beeftink, 2012.

28.   Bricker, 2001.

29.   Ibid.

Chapter 18: Healthy Parks and Communities: Green Access and Equity for Los Angeles

1.   S. Jay Olshansky, et al. (2005). A Potential Decline in Life Expectancy in the United States in the 21st Century, 352 *New England Journal of Medicine, 1138-45.*

2.   Declaration of the Rights of the Child: General Assembly Resolution 1386 (XIV), Principle 7; United Nations' Convention on the Right of the Child (November 1989).

3.   Trust for America's Health, Prevention for a Healthier California: Investments in Disease Prevention Yield Significant Savings, Stronger Communities. (2008) Retrieved from http://healthyamericans.org/assets/files/CaliforniaROIReport1008.pdf

4.   Olshansky, S.J., Passaro, D., Hershow, R., Layden, J., Carnes, B. A., Brody, J., Hayflick, L., Butler, R. N., Allison, D. B., & Ludwig, D. S. A Possible Decline in Life Expectancy in the United States in the 21st Century. *New England Journal of Medicine, 352*(2005), pp. 1103-1110.

5.   U.S. Department of Health and Human Services & U.S. Department of Education, Promoting Better Health for Young People Through Physical Activity and Sports. (2001). Retrieved from http://www.cdc.gov/nccdphp/dash/presphysactrpt

6.   California Center for Public Health Advocacy, The Economic Costs of Overweight, Obesity, and Physical Inactivity Among California Adults. (2006). Retrieved from http://www.publichealthadvocacy.org/costofobesity.html

7.   U.S. Department of Health and Human Services & U.S. Department of Education, Promoting Better Health for Young People Through Physical Activity and Sports. (2001). Retrieved from http://www.cdc.gov/nccdphp/dash/presphysactrpt

8.   UCLA Center to Eliminate Health Disparities & Samuels and Associates, Failing Fitness: Physical Activity and Physical Education in Schools, University of California Los Angeles. (2007). Retrieved from www.calendow.org/uploadedFiles/failing_fitness.pdf

9.   Babey, S. H., Diamant, A. L., Brown, E. R., & Hart, T. *California Adolescents Increasingly Inactive: Policy Brief.* University of California Los Angeles. (2005). Retrieved from http://www.healthpolicy.ucla.edu/pubs/Publication.aspx?pubID=137

10.   Active Living Research. (2007). *Designing for active living among Children.* Princeton, NJ: Robert Wood Johnson Foundation.

11.   Mowen, A. J. (2010). Parks, Playgrounds and Active Living. Robert Wood Johnson Foundation. Retrieved from www.activelivingresearch.org/files/Synthesis_Mowen_Feb2010.pdf

12.   Cohen, D. A., McKenzie, T. L., Sehgal, A., Williamson, S., Golinelli, D., & Lurie, N. (2007). Contribution of Public Parks to Physical Activity. *American Journal of Public Health, 97,* 509-514.

13. Active Living Research. (2007). Designing for active living among children. Princeton, NJ: Robert Wood Johnson Foundation.

14. Maller, C., Townsend, M., Pryor, A., Brown, P., & St. Leger, L. (2006). Healthy Nature Healthy People: 'Contact With Nature' as an Upstream Health Promotion Intervention for Populations. *Health Promotion International, 21,* 5-53.

15. Ho, C. H., Payne, L., Orsega-Smith, E., & Godbey, G. (2003). Parks. Recreation, and Public Health. *Parks and Recreation, 38,* 18-26.

16. Taylor, A. F., Kuo, F. E., & Sullivan, W. C. (2001). Coping with ADD: The Surprising Connection to Green Play Settings. *Environment and Behavior, 33,* 54-77.

17. Kuo, F. E. (2001). Coping with Poverty Impacts of Environment and Attention in the Inner City. *Environment and Behavior, 33,* 5-34.

18. Ulrich, R. S. (1984). View through a Window May Influence Recovery From Surgery. *Science, 224,* p. 421.

19. Parsons, R., Tassinary, L. G., Ulrich, R. S., Hebl, M. R., & Grossman-Alexander, M. (1998). The view from the road: Implications for stress recovery and immunization. *Journal of Environmental Psychology, 18,* pp. 113-140.

20. S. de Vries, Natural Environments - Healthy Environments? An Exploratory Analysis of the Relationship Between Green Space and Health. Environment and Planning, 33, (2003), at 1717-1731.

21. S. Gold, Crime Falls 40% in Neighborhoods with Summer Night Lights Program. Retrieved from *Los Angeles Times* (October 31, 2010), http://www.latimes.com/news/local/la-me-summer-night-20101030,0,4336841. story.

22. Pate, R., Trost, S. G., Levinj, S., & Dowda, M. (2009). Sports Participation and Health-Related Behaviors among U.S. Youth. *Archives of Pediatrics & Adolescent Medicine, 154*(9), pp. 904-911.

23. Mahoney, J. (2000). School Extracurricular Activity Participation as a Moderator in the Development of Antisocial Patterns. *Child Development, 71,* pp. 502-516.

24. Yin, Z., & Moore, J. B. (2004). Re-Examining the Role of Interscholastic Sport Participation in Education. *Psychological Reports, 94,* pp. 1447-1454.

25. Deming, A. H., & Savoy, L. E. (Eds.). (2002). *The colors of nature: Culture, identity, and the natural world.* Milkweed Editions.

26. Berkman,F., Glass, T., Brisette, I., & Seeman, T. E. (2000). From Social Integration to Health: Durkheim in the New Millennium. *Social Science and Medicine, 51,* pp. 843-857.

27. Sullivan, W. C., Kuo, F. E., & de Pooter, S. (2004). The Fruit of Urban Nature: Vital Neighborhood Spaces. *Environment and Behavior, 36,* pp. 678-700.

28. Robert García & Seth Strongin, Healthy Parks, Schools and Communities: Mapping Green Access and Equity for Southern California, The City Project, (2011), http://www.cityprojectca.org/greenjustice

29. Ibid.

30. Bullard, R. D. (Ed.). (2007). Toxics Waste and Race at Twenty 1987-2007: A Report Prepared for the United Church of Christ Justice & Witness Ministries, United Church of Christ, (2007), www.ucc.org/justice/pdfs/toxic20.pdf

31. Ibid at 26.

32. E. Morales. (2010). There Must Be Coherence between What We Do and What We Say, In: World People's Conference on Climate Change and the Rights of Mother Earth, http://wpccc.wordpress.com

33. Ibid at 26.

34. The City Project, Economic Stimulus, Green Space, and Equal Justice. (2009). http://www.cityprojectca.org/blog/wp-content/uploads/2009/04/stimulus-green-space-justice-200904294.pdf

35. Maher, N. (2008). *Nature's new deal: The Civilian Conservation Corps and the roots of the American environmental movement.* Oxford University Press.

36. The 32nd Street Task Force, Canyon Policy Portfolio: Our Financially Rewarding Natural Wildlands, Canyonlands, (2009), http://sites.google.com/a/32ndstreetcanyon.org/www/home2

37. Poole, J., & Ball, T. (2002). *El Pueblo: The Historic Heart of Los Angeles 11,* pp. 30-31.

38. Ibid at 26.

39. Heintz, J. (2009). *The NYS park system: An economic asset to the Empire State.* University of Massachusetts Amherst: Political Economy Research Institute.

40. Sustainable Sites Initiative, Guidelines and Performance Benchmarks. (2008). www.sustainablesites.org/report/SSI_Guidelines_Draft_2008.pdf

41. Ibid.

42. Olmsted Brothers & Bartholomew and Associates, Parks, Playgrounds and Beaches for the Los Angeles Region 1 (1930) [hereinafter Olmsted Report], reprinted in Greg Hise & William Deverell, Eden by Design (2000). The City Project's digital edition of the Olmsted vision is available at http://www.clipi.org/images/g-olmstedlarge.jpg.

43. See, e.g., Olmsted Report at 129.

44. Ibid. at 85-88, 92-93.

45. Ibid. at 14-16.

46. Ibid. at 13-14, 35-43.

47. Ibid. at 22.

48. Ibid. at 16.

49. See Hise & Deverell, supra, at 7-56; Mike Davis, How Eden Lost Its Garden, in *Ecology of Fear* 59-91 (1998).

50. Ibid at 26.

51. U.S. Census Bureau, Profile of General Population and Housing Characteristics for Los Angeles County, California, In 2010 Demographic Profile Data, (2011a), http://factfinder2.census.gov/faces/tableservices/jsf/pages/productview.xhtml?pid=DEC_10_DP_DPDP1&prodType=table

52. U.S. Census Bureau, Profile of General Population and Housing Characteristics for Los Angeles city, California, In: 2010 Demographic Profile Data, (2011b), http://factfinder2.census.gov/faces/tableservices/jsf/pages/productview.xhtml?pid=DEC_10_DP_DPDP1&prodType=table

53. Ibid at 45.

54. R. Browning, S. Ferrell, M. Garvey, K. Gosnell, M. Hafer, T. Suh, D. Lauder, M. Minkoff, M. Moore, S. Poindexter, K. Schwenke, D. Smith & B. Welsh, Mapping LA: South LA, *Los Angeles Times,* (2010a), http://projects.latimes.com/mapping-la/neighborhoods/region/south-la/

55. R. Browning, S. Ferrell, M. Garvey, K. Gosnell, M. Hafer, T. Suh, D. Lauder, M. Minkoff, M. Moore, S. Poindexter, K. Schwenke, D. Smith & B. Welsh, Mapping LA: San Fernando Valley, *Los Angeles Times,* (2010b), http://projects.latimes.com/mapping-la/neighborhoods/region/san-fernando-valley/

56. R. Browning, S. Ferrell, M. Garvey, K. Gosnell, M. Hafer, T. Suh, D. Lauder, M. Minkoff, M. Moore, S. Poindexter, K. Schwenke, D. Smith & B. Welsh; & B. Welsh, Mapping LA: Eastside, In: *Los Angeles Times,* (2010c), http://projects.latimes.com/mapping-la/neighborhoods/region/eastside/

57. R. Browning, S. Ferrell, M. Garvey, K. Gosnell, M. Hafer, T. Suh, D. Lauder, M. Minkoff, M. Moore, S. Poindexter, K. Schwenke, D. Smith & B. Welsh, Mapping LA: Westside, *Los Angeles Times*, (2010d), at http://projects.latimes.com/mapping-la/neighborhoods/region/westside/

58. Los Angeles County Children's Planning Council. (2006). Children's ScoreCard 2006. County of Los Angeles Department of Public Health, http://childrensplanningcouncil.org/resource-files/committees/cpc/cpcscorecard06.pdf

59. Ibid.

60. County of Los Angeles (2011). Overview, http://1.usa.gov/teWdzP

61. Ibid at 26.

62. Ibid.

63. Wolch, J., Wilson, J., & Fehrenbach, J. (2001). Parks and Park Funding in Los Angeles: An Equity Mapping Analysis. University of Southern California, http://bit.ly/shL3Fl

64. Ibid at 26.

65. Loukaitou-Sideris, A. (2006). Southern California Environmental Report Card 2006: Urban Parks, University of California Los Angeles, http://www.ioe.ucla.edu/media/files/Urban-Parks-2006.pdf

66. Ibid at 26.

67. National Ocean Economies Program. (July 2005). *California's Ocean Economy*. Report to the Resources Agency, State of California.

68. See generally Robert García and Erica Flores Baltodano, Free the Beach! Public Access Equal Justice, and the California Coast, 2 *Stanford Journal of Civil Rights and Civil Liberties 142* (2005).

69. The beach bulldozing drew international attention. Kenneth R. Weiss and Amand Covarrubias, Battle over Broad Beach Takes New Turn, With Earthmoving Equipment, *L.A. Times*, June 9, 2005, at B3; Jamie Wilson, Bulldozer Tactics by Malibu's Super-rich, *The Guardian* (London), June 10, 2005, at 17.

70. Cal. Coastal Comm'n v. Trancas Property Owners Association, Case No. SC 086150 (Ca. Superior Court L.A. County July 6, 2005).

71. Kenneth R. Weiss, Mogul Yields Beach Access to Public, *L.A. Times*, April 15, 2005; Kenneth R. Weiss, Geffen to Reimburse $300,000, *L.A. Times*, April 16, 2005. The City of Malibu dropped out of the suit earlier.

72. Telephone conversation with agency official, June 16, 2005.

73. See Letter from Robert García, et al., to California Coastal Commission re: Commission Cease & Desist Order No. CCC-05-CD-9 (Trancas Property Owners Association, Malibu) (Aug. 8, 2005) (on file with The City Project); Sara Lin, Public's Use of Beach Is Affirmed: Malibu homeowners group must forgo signs and security guards, coastal panel says, L.A. Times, Aug. 15, 2005, at B1.

74. The Coastal Commission has published guides for public beaches along Broad Beach and Carbon Beach in Malibu. The Commission should publish a similarly detailed guide to all public beaches in Los Angeles County and the state. The Broad Beach guide is available at www.cityprojectca.org/pdf/broadbeachaccess.pdf and the Carbon Beach guide is available at www.coastal.ca.gov/access/Carbon_Beach_Access.pdf. On beach access, see generally Olena Horcajo, Jennifer McCard, Brian Selogie, & Ryan Terwilliger, University of Southern California Geography Department, Taking Back the Beach: An Evaluation of Beach Access Issues Along the Los Angeles County Coastline (2006), on file with The City Project and forthcoming at www.cityprojectca.org.

75. Letter from California Coastal Commission to City of Malibu re:"No Overnight Camping SignJan. 24, 2008, available at www.cityprojectca.org/blog/archives/614. See Anne Soble, Executive Director Says LCP Amendment on Camping Is 'Waste of Public Resources and Funds,' Malibu Surfside News, Jan.18, 2008, available at www.cityprojectca.org/blog/archives/544; Jonathan Friedman, 'No camping' signs anger public access group, Malibu Times, Jan. 16, 2008, available at www.cityprojectca.org/blog/archives/542; The City Project blog post, Issue Cease and Desist to Malibu to Take Down "No Camping" Signs, www.cityprojectca.org/blogarchives/539.

76. U.S. Census 2000 data available at www.factfinder.census.gov and compiled by Greeninfo Network for The City Project.

77. Scott Anderson & Mike Godfrey, University of Southern California Geography Department, Coastal Demographic: Los Angeles Pilot Project 1-2 (2003) (on file with The City Project). The study analyzed beach communities from Malibu to Long Beach using 2000 census tracts within approximately one mile from the coast. The household income is an average of the median household incomes within one community as defined by the study. The tracts containing Los Angeles International Airport and Long Beach Harbor were omitted because they contained negligible data.

78. Ibid. at 7.

79. Laslett, J. (1996). Historical Perspectives: Immigration and the Rise of a Distinctive Urban Region, 1900-1970. in R. Waldiner & M. Bozorgmehr (Eds.), *Ethnic Los Angeles* (p. 54).

80. U.S. National Forest Service. (2009). National Visitor Use Monitoring Results.

81. Southern California Association of Governments. (2004). Compliance Procedure for Environmental Justice in the Transportation Planning Process, http://scag.ca.gov/environment/ej.htm

82. Ron Frescas, Chris Martin, and Christine Steenken, University of Southern California Geography Department, Public Transportation to Local National Forests, (2004), http://cityprojectca.org/pdf/uscgeogstudy.pdf.

83. United States Department of Agriculture, Forest Service. (May 2004). Draft Environmental Impact Statement for Revised Land Management Plans for the Angeles. Cleveland, Los Padres, and San Bernardino National Forests, at 3-58 ("DEIS"), on file with The City Project.

84. The Olmsted Report recognized the need to incorporate the Angeles National Forest, the San Gabriel and San Bernardino Mountains, and other outlying areas, including Catalina Island, to serve the recreation and open space needs of Los Angeles County. Olmsted Report, supra, at 85-88, 92-93.

85. Race/Ethnicity of Visitors to the Angeles National Forest. (2000 Survey). Source: U.S. Forest Service, www.losangelesalmanac.com/topics/Parks/pa07.htm.

86. See generally Robert García, Notice of Appeal of Final Environmental Impact Statement and Land Management Plans for Four Forests of Southern California (July 20, 2006), on file with The City Project.

87. Los Angeles County Department of Public Health, Office of Health Assessment and Epidemiology. (October 2007). *Preventing Childhood Obesity: The Need to Create Healthy Places.* A Cities and Communities Health Report.

88. California Center for Public Health Advocacy (2005). The Growing Epidemic: Childhood Obesity Rates on the Rise in California Assembly Districts, http://www.publichealthadvocacy.org/research_pdfs/changes.pdf.

89. Ibid.

90. Los Angeles County Department of Public Health, Office of Health Assessment and Epidemiology. (October 2007). *Preventing Childhood Obesity: The Need to Create Healthy Places.* A Cities and Communities Health Report.

91. Katznelson, K. (2005). *When Affirmative Action was white.* W. W. Norton Co.

92. Litwack, L. (2009). *How free is free? The long death of Jim Crow.* Harvard University Press.

93. California Department of Parks and Recreation. (1988). Five Views: An Ethnic Sites Survey for California, pp. 68-69.

94. 334 U.S. 1 (1948).

95. 346 U.S. 249 (1953).

96. Sides, J. (2003). *L.A. city limits: African American Los Angeles from the Great Depression to the present.* University of California Press.

97.   387 U.S. 369 (1967).

98.   Robert García, Erica S. Flores, Julie Ehrlich, Policy Report, The Cornfield and the Flow of History. (2004). available at www.cityprojectca.org/publications/index.html.

99.   Sides, J. (2003). *L.A. city limits: African American Los Angeles from the Great Depression to the present.* University of California Press.

100. Ibid.

101. García, R., & Flores Baltodano, E. (2005). Free the Beach! Public Access Equal Justice, and the California Coast, 2. *Stanford Journal of Civil Rights and Civil Liberties, 142.*

102. Ibid.

103. Robert García & Seth Strongin, Healthy Parks, Schools and Communities: Mapping Green Access and Equity for Southern California, The City Project, (2011), http://www.cityprojectca.org/greenjustice

104. See, e.g., 40 C.F.R. §7.30 (nondiscrimination regulations for recipients of federal funds from the Environmental Protection Agency); 43 C.F.R. §7.30 (Department of Interior).

105. See *Village of Arlington Heights v. Metropolitan Housing Dev. Corp.,* 429 U.S. 252, 265 (1977); Committee Concerning Cmty. Improvement v. City of Modesto, 583 F.3d 690 (9th Cir. 2009) (statistical disparities in providing municipal services evidence of intentional discrimination under Title VI and 11135; U.S. Dep't Justice, Civil Rights Division, Title VI Legal Manual (2001), available at http://www.justice.gov/crt/cor/coord/vimanual.php.

106. See, e.g., *Larry P. v. Riles,* 793 F.2d 969, 981-83 (9th Cir. 1984). Agencies are obligated to comply with the Title VI regulations, even though private individuals and organizations have no standing to enforce the regulations in court. *Alexander v. Sandoval,* 532 U.S. 275, 293 (2001). Private individuals and organizations do have standing to enforce 11135 regulations in court. See *Darensburg v. Metropolitan Transp. Comm'n,* No. C-05-01597 EDL, 2008 U.S. Dist. LEXIS 63991 (N.D. Cal. Aug. 21, 2008).

107. Title VI provides: "No person in the United States shall on the ground of race, color, or national origin, be excluded from participation in, be denied the benefits of, or be subjected to discrimination under any program or activity receiving Federal financial assistance." 42 U.S.C. § 2000d (2004). Cf. 43 C.F.R. 7.30 (Title VI regulations from the Department of Interior, which has jurisdiction over National Parks and other public lands). See also Executive Order 12,898 on Environmental Justice (Feb. 11, 1994). The Equal Protection Clause of the Fourteenth Amendment to the United States Constitution and parallel state law also prohibits intentional discrimination. Cal. Const., Art. I § 7. See also Section 1983 of the Civil Rights Act of 1871.

108. *Guardians Ass'n v. Civil Service Comm'n,* 463 U.S. 582, 629 (1983) (Justice Marshall, concurring in part and dissenting in part).

109. Cf. Executive Order 12,898 on Environmental Justice (Feb. 11, 1994).

110. Robert García, Elise Meerkatz, and Seth Strongin, Keep Baldwin Hills Clean and Green for Generations to Come (Policy Report The City Project 2010) www.cityprojectca.org/blog/wp-content/uploads/2010/05/Baldwin-Hills-Policy-Report-May-2010-print.pdf.

111. Peter R. Orszag, Director, Office of Management and Budget, Memorandum re: Updated Implementing Guidance for the American Recovery and Reinvestment Act of 2009, April 3, 2009, at page 2 and Guidance at page 6, available at http://www.recovery.gov/About/Documents/m09-15_April3.pdf.

112. See July 10, 2009, Memo from Loretta King, Acting Assistant Attorney General for Civil Rights, to Federal Agency Civil Rights Directors and General Counsels, Strengthening of Enforcement of Title VI of the Civil Rights Act of 1964, available at www.justice.gov/crt/lep/titlevi_enforcement_memo.pdf.

113. *Rosemere Neighborhood Ass'n v. United States Envtl. Prot. Agency,* 581 F.3d 1169, 1175 (9th Cir. 2009). As part of the settlement in the Rosemere case, EPA has released a 23-page spreadsheet listing more than 300 Environmental Justice complaints dating back to 1993 that it has not investigated. The spreadsheet is available on The City Project's web site at www.cityprojectca.org/blog/archives/4517. See generally Dawn Reeves, New EPA Data On Civil Rights Backlog May Help Reshape Equity Agenda, Water Policy Report, April 26, 2010, available at insideEPA.com.

114. See Cal. Gov. Code § 11135; 22 CCR § 98101(i) (2007). See *Darensburg v. Metropolitan Transp. Comm'n*, No. C-05-01597 EDL, 2008 U.S. Dist. LEXIS 63991 (N.D. Cal. Aug. 21, 2008) (standing to sue publicly funded agency for discriminatory impacts on quality of life for people of color under 11135 and its regulations).

115. Cal. Gov. Code § 65040.12.

116. California Environmental Protection Agency, Environmental Justice Action Plan. (2004). http://www.calepa. ca.gov/EnvJustice/ActionPlan/

117. California State Lands Commission, Environmental Justice Policy. (2002). http://www.slc.ca.gov/Policy_Statements/Env_Justice/Environmental%20Justice%20Policy%20Final%20Web.pdf.

118. Seema Mehta, Land-Use Plan OK'd for Malibu, *L.A. Times,* Sept. 14, 2002.

119. See, e.g., *Alexander v. Sandoval,* 532 U.S. 275 (2001); *Gonzaga Univ. v. Doe,* 536 U.S. 273 (2002).

120. See generally García, R., & Rubin, T. (2004). Cross road blues: Transportation justice and the MTA consent decree. In K. Lucas (Ed.), *Running on empty: Transport, social exclusion and environmental justice.*

121. Ibid.

122. Ron Frescas, Chris Martin, and Christine Steenken, University of Southern California Geography Department, Public Transportation to Local National Forests, (2004), http://cityprojectca.org/pdf/uscgeogstudy.pdf.

123. Mike Agrimis, et al.. (2003). University of Southern California Geography Department, Equity and Beach Access in Los Angeles (on file with The City Project). The study identified departure points in heavily Latino, African-American, and low-income communities.

124. See www.cityprojectca.org/blog/archives/750.

125. Olmsted Report at 13-14, 35-43.

126. San Gabriel Mountains Forever. (2010). National Recreation Area, http://www.sangabrielmountains.org/national_recreation_area.

127. The City Project. (2010). Diversifying Access to and Support for the San Gabriel Mountains and Recreation Area, http://www.cityprojectca.org/blog/wp-content/uploads/2010/07/AGO-SG-Justice-PB-20100705.pdf.

128. Ibid.

129. Nicolai Ouroussoff, Reinventing America's Cities: The Time Is Now, *N.Y. Times,* March 29, 2009, www.cityprojectca.org/blog/archives/1405.

130. River Report at 11. The Report is available on the web at clkrep.lacity.org/onlinedocs/2007/07-1342-s5_rpt_boe_6-1-09.pdf.

131. Ibid. at 26.

132. River Report at 5, 20-21. See Title VI of the Civil Rights Act of 1964, California Government Code 11135, and applicable regulations, discussed in section IX below.

133. See, e.g., River Report at 5, 20-21, 25-27, 36, 40, 43.

134. See also Maps 1002-1010. For example, within three miles of the river outside the City, 60% of the population is Hispanic, 10% is black, 43% of children live in poverty, and the median household income is $34,751. Within three miles of the river within the City, 49% of the population is Hispanic, 5% is black, 35% of children live in poverty, and the median household income is $41,681. Total acres of parks per thousand residents is higher within than outside the City (8.3 versus 5.6), while net acres are about the same (5.4 versus 5.6) within and outside the City.

135. Louis Sahagun, L.A.'s River Clears Hurdle, *L.A. Times,* July 8, 2010, available at articles.latimes.com/2010/jul/08/local/la-me-Compton-Creek-20100708.

136. The County's Los Angeles River Plan is available at http://ladpw.org/wmd/watershed/LA/LA_River_Plan.cfm.

137. The County's San Gabriel River Plan is available at http://ladpw.org/wmd/watershed/sg/mp.

138. State and federal clean water laws, CEQA, and NEPA provide the framework for environmental restoration, revitalization and development along the Los Angeles and San Gabriel Rivers. See, e.g., Federal Water Pollution Control Act, 33 U.S.C. §1313(a) et seq.; Porter-Cologne Act, Cal. Water Code §13000 et seq.; National Environmental Policy Act (NEPA), 42 U.S.C. § 4321; California Environmental Quality Act (CEQA), Cal. Pub. Resources Code, § 21000 et seq.). Civil rights laws are discussed below.

139. The City Project working with the community in South Central Los Angeles and Baldwin Hills is ensuring compliance with the Clean Water Act, 33 U.S.C. § 1311(a), and a court order to eliminate persistent and offensive sewer odors that have long plagued residents in African-American Los Angeles, and to improve the sewer system city wide. The Los Angeles sewer system is one of the largest in the nation, making this work significant both in southern California and nationally. After years of complaints, community residents sought access to justice through the courts in 2001 by joining a suit by the United States Department of Justice, the United States Environmental Protection Agency, the California Regional Water Quality Control Board and a mainstream environmental organization to require the City of Los Angeles to fix the sewer system citywide. The suit resulted in a $2 billion settlement agreement and court order in 2004. The Clean Water Act was used for the first time to address sewage odors, separate from spills. EPA officials called the historic agreement "one of the largest sewage cases in U.S. history." In 2009, the parties and the court agreed to modify the settlement agreement to enable community groups to continue to work with the Odor Advisory Board, an independent expert, The City Project, and the city to continue the clean up of the sewer odors. This work in and out of court is a best practice example of community groups, civil rights attorneys, government agencies at the federal, state and local level, and mainstream environmentalists working together to improve quality of life, environmental quality, and environmental justice for all. The community plaintiffs were the Baldwin Hills Estates Homeowners' Association, Inc., Baldwin Hills Village Garden Homes Association, United Homeowners Association, Village Green Owners Association, and Concerned Citizens of South Central Los Angeles. See generally The City Project, Enforcing the Clean Water Act in Communities of Color, www.cityprojectca.org/ourwork/cleanwaterjustice.html.

140. Phone survey by the William C. Velazquez Institute, September 2006, available at http://www.wcvi.org/latino_voter_research/polls/ca/2006/lariverpoll_91106.html.

141. Ibid.

142. The City Project Blog, L.A. River Justice, September 14, 2010, http://www.cityprojectca.org/blog/archives/6368

143. Louis Sahagun, L.A.'s River Clears Hurdle, *Los Angeles Times*, July 8, 2010, http://articles.latimes.com/2010/jul/08/local/la-me-Compton-Creek-20100708.

144. See also Maps 1102-1110, Chart 1201C. There is a higher percentage of Hispanics and Asian/Pacific Islanders compared to the county as a whole. A higher percentage of people live in poverty. The percentage of people with a high school education or less is greater. However, the median household income is higher, and a higher percentage have access to a car.

Chapter 19: Public Memory for an Inclusive Society

1. Lowenthal, D. (1985). *The past is a foreign country*. Cambridge, UK: Cambridge University Press.

2. Blair, C., Dickinson, G., & Ott, B. (2010). Introduction: Rhetoric/memory/place. In Dickinson, G., Blair, C., & Ott, B. (Eds.), *Places of public memory: The rhetoric of museums and memorials* (pp. 1-54). Tuscaloosa, AL: University of Alabama Press.

3. Assmann, J. (1995). Collective memory and cultural identity. *New German Critique, 65*:132.

4. Bullard, R. (1993). *Confronting environmental racism: Voices from the grassroots*. Boston, MA: South End Press.

5. Blair, Dickinson, & Ott.

6.   Connerton, P. (2008). Seven types of forgetting. *Memory Studies, 1*: 59-71.

7.   Phillips, K. (2004). *Framing public memory.* Tuscaloosa, AL: University of Alabama Press.

8.   Stewart, W. (2012). Research to create public memory of wilderness. In Cole, D. (Compiler), *Wilderness Visitor Experiences: Progress on Research and Management, RMRS-P-66* (pp. 201-210). Fort Collins, CO: USDA Forest Service.

9.   Blair, Dickinson, & Ott.

10.   Dustin, personal communication, April 6, 2011.

11.   Sandweiss, M. (1992). Views and reviews: Western art and western history. In W. Cronon, G. Miles, & J. Gitlin (Eds.), *Under an open sky: Rethinking America's Western past* (pp. 185-202). New York, NY: Norton.

12.   Prown, J., Anderson, N., Cronon, W., Dippie, B., Schoelwer, S., Sandweiss, M., & Lamar, H. (1992). *Discovered lands, invented pasts: Transforming visions of the American West.* New Haven, CT: Yale University Press.

13.   Turner, F. (1894). *The significance of the frontier in American history.* E-book from HathiTrust.Digital Library, initially published by the Wisconsin State Historical Society.

14.   http://www.cartermuseum.org/collection/remington-and-russell

15.   http://www.gilcrease.utulsa.edu/Visit

16.   http://www.eiteljorg.org

17.   Glover, T., & Bates, N. (2006). Recapturing a sense of neighbourhood since lost: Nostalgia and the formation of first string, a community team, inc. *Leisure Studies, 25*(3), 329-351.

18.   Stewart, W., Barkley, J., Kerins, A. Gladdys, K., & Glover, T. (2007). Park development on the Urban-Agricultural Fringe. *Journal of Park and Recreation Administration, 25*(4), 117-138.

19.   Johnson, A., Glover, T., & Stewart, W. (2009). One person's trash is another person's treasure: The public place-making of "Mt. Trashmore." *Journal of Park and Recreation Administration, 27*(1), 85-103.

20.   Stewart et al., 2007, p. 135.

Synthesis: Philosophy as Leisure of the Most Vital Kind

1.   White, R. (1995). Are You an Environmentalist or Do You Work for a Living? Work and Nature. In *Uncommon ground: Rethinking the human place in nature.* New York: W.W. Norton & Company, p. 174.

2.   From Veblen (1899). The Theory of the Leisure Class, as quoted in W. Sutherland, *A Philosophy of Leisure, in the Annals of the American Academy of Political and Social Science*, Vol. 313 (September 1957), p. 1.

3.   Pieper, J. (1952). *Leisure: The basis of culture.* New York: Pantheon Books, p. 32.

4.   Loc cit., p. 31.

5.   Anderson, T. (1997). Technology and the Decline of Leisure. In the *Proceedings of the American Catholic Philosophical Association*, Vol. 70, pp. 12-13.

6.   Pollan, M. (1991). *Second nature: A gardener's education.* New York: Grove Press, p. 189.

About the Authors

Ed Barbanell is an associate professor/lecturer of philosophy at the University of Utah. His published work includes a book on water in the American West, and his current research and teaching focus on sustainability and bioregionalism.

Joshua Trey Barnett is a graduate student in the Department of Communication and Culture at Indiana University. His research centers on rhetorics of social and environmental justice movements.

Mary Breunig is an associate professor in the Department of Recreation and Leisure Studies and Social Justice and Equity Studies at Brock University. Her main areas of research include outdoor and experiential education and issues of social and environmental justice, critical pedagogy and Freirean praxis, and outdoor experiential education within the Ontario K-12 schools.

Kelly Bricker is an associate professor and associate department chair in the Department of Parks, Recreation, and Tourism at the University of Utah. Her research interests are in sustainable tourism and ecotourism.

Adrienne Cachelin is an assistant professor/lecturer in the Environmental and Sustainability Studies program and the Department of Parks, Recreation, and Tourism at the University of Utah. Her research interests include language framing in the context of sustainability education, environmental literacy education, and environmental justice.

Claire Campbell is an associate professor of history at Dalhousie University, where she teaches in the Canadian Studies Program and the College of Sustainability. Her research focuses on environmental history.

Sam Dear is a graduate student in the Department of Recreation and Leisure Studies at Brock University. Sam's academic interests are focused on outdoor experiential education and play as tools for international collaboration.

Freya Higgins-Desbiolles is a senior lecturer with the School of Management at the University of South Australia. Her research interests include the politics of tourism, indigenous tourism, impacts of tourism, and the rights of "host" communities.

Mary Ann Devine is an associate professor in Recreation, Parks, and Tourism Management at Kent State University. Her research interests focus on inclusion of individuals with disabilities in recreation, sport, and leisure services.

Rudy Dunlap is an assistant professor in the Leisure, Sport, and Tourism Program in the Department of Health and Human Performance at Middle Tennessee State University. His current research examines the effects of citizen participation in urban agriculture on place sentiment, solidarity, and sense of agency.

Daniel Dustin is professor and chair of the Department of Parks, Recreation, and Tourism at the University of Utah. His academic interests center on environmental stewardship and the moral and ethical bases for leisure and recreation activity preferences and behaviors.

Karen Gallant is a postdoctoral fellow in the School of Health and Human Performance at Dalhousie University. Her research is primarily focused on civic engagement and community health, particularly the role of volunteers and the voluntary sector in community building.

Robert García is the executive director and counsel for The City Project, a Los Angeles-based organization that influences the investment of public resources to achieve results that are equitable, enhance human health and the environment, and promote economic vitality for all communities. The City Project works with diverse coalitions in strategic campaigns to shape public policy and law, and to serve the needs of the community as defined by the community.

Tom Goodale is professor emeritus at George Mason University. A past-president of the Academy of Leisure Sciences and of the Society of Park and Recreation Educators, he is a distinguished alumnus of SUNY-Cortland, distinguished colleague of the Society of Park and Recreation Educators, and a recipient of the National Literary Award from the National Recreation and Park Association. Tom has been awarded honorary doctorate degrees from the University of Waterloo (Canada) and the State University of New York.

Paul Heintzman is an associate professor of Leisure Studies and a member of the Institute of the Environment at the University of Ottawa. His research interests include leisure and spirituality, recreation and the environment, and the philosophy and ethics of leisure.

Karla Henderson is a professor in the Department of Parks, Recreation, and Tourism Management at North Carolina State University. Karla has served as president of the Society of Park and Recreation Educators and the Academy of Leisure Sciences, and in 2011 she was awarded an honorary doctor of science degree from the University of Waterloo in Ontario, Canada.

Corey W. Johnson is an associate professor in the Department of Counseling and Human Development Services, Recreation and Leisure Studies Program at The University of Georgia. His research focuses on the relations between dominant and non-dominant populations in the cultural context of leisure.

Jeremy Jostad is a doctoral candidate in the Department of Parks, Recreation, and Tourism at the University of Utah. His main research interests include small group functioning, group development, and leadership practices in outdoor/adventure education.

Anita Ledford is a master's degree student in the Department of Parks, Recreation, and Tourism at the University of Utah. She believes tourism can be a tool for positive change by addressing many of the environmental and social injustices in the world.

Jada Lindblom is the director of membership and public relations for the Utah Association for Justice. She is currently working toward her master's degree in parks, recreation, and tourism at the University of Utah, specializing in sustainable tourism.

Don McClean is a professor and coordinator in the Department of Recreation, Park, and Tourism Administration at Western Illinois University–Quad Cities in Moline, Illinois. He holds advanced degrees in philosophy and recreation and leisure studies and has served as guest editor for the *Journal of Applied Recreation Research*'s special issue on applied ethics.

Jen Piatt is an assistant professor at Indiana University, Bloomington. She has been a practicing recreation therapist for over 16 years working in acute care, rehabilitation, and outpatient services. Her current research is spinal cord injury and community integration (particularly in rural areas).

Nina Roberts is an associate professor at San Francisco State University and director of the Pacific Leadership Institute. Nina's work provides managers in outdoor recreation, natural resource management, and environmental education with ideas and resources needed to respond more effectively to changing demographics, as well as cultural shifts and trends.

Jeff Rose is an assistant professor/lecturer in the Department of Parks, Recreation, and Tourism at the University of Utah. Jeff is interested in human-environment relations, critical theory, political ecology, neoliberalism, and outdoor education.

Diane Samdahl is a professor of recreation and leisure studies at the University of Georgia. She explores leisure in everyday contexts with particular attention to populations that have been marginalized by mainstream culture on the basis of race, gender, or sexual orientation.

Keri Schwab is an assistant professor/lecturer in the Recreation, Parks, and Tourism Administration Department at California Polytechnic State University, San Luis Obispo. Her research and teaching interests include youth development, community engagement, parent-child leisure interactions, and scholarly teaching.

Zachary Schwing is a master's degree student in the Department of Parks, Recreation, and Tourism at the University of Utah. His interests include wilderness, cross-cultural experiences, and eco- and sustainable tourism.

Callie Spencer is a doctoral student in the Department of Parks, Recreation, and Tourism at the University of Utah. Her research interests include looking at leisure and reality television through a feminist lens, social justice and online leisure spaces, leisure and new media, and poststructuralist approaches to leisure research.

Bill Stewart holds a joint appointment at the University of Illinois as a professor in the Department of Recreation, Sport, and Tourism and in the Department of Landscape Architecture. He also serves as the first director of the interdisciplinary undergraduate program in Health and as the associate dean for the College of Applied Health Sciences. He conducts research on park development and community-based conservation.

Seth Strongin is the former assistant director for policy and research for The City Project, a Los Angeles-based organization dedicated to bringing people together to define the kind of community where they want to live and raise children.

Deirdre Tedmanson is a lecturer in the School of Psychology, Social Work and Social Policy at the University of South Australia. Her research interests include social and political theory, critical organizational studies, gender and sociocultural factors in entrepreneurship, post-colonialism, indigenous enterprise development, social justice, and participatory action research methodologies.

Daniel Theriault is a doctoral candidate at Texas A&M University. His research interests include youth development and the philosophy of leisure.

Susan Tirone is the associate director of the College of Sustainability at Dalhousie University. In her teaching she employs case studies from community development and leisure studies to inform discussions about how employers, employees, volunteers, voters, consumers and engaged citizens might address many sustainability problems.

Sharon Washington is the executive director of the National Writing Project in Berkeley, California. She has over two decades of professional experience and scholarly work in social justice education, higher education administration, teacher preparation, outdoor recreation, sports, and the arts.

Kyle Whyte is an assistant professor of philosophy at Michigan State University in the Environmental Science and Policy Program, the Center for Regional Food Systems, and the American Indian Studies and Peace and Justice Studies programs. His work centers on environmental justice, sustainability ethics, the philosophy of technology and American Indian philosophy.

Index